The Conquest of Ainu Lands

The Conquest of Ainu Lands

ECOLOGY AND CULTURE
IN JAPANESE EXPANSION,
1590 – 1800

BRETT L. WALKER

UNIVERSITY OF CALIFORNIA PRESS
Berkeley   Los Angeles   London

For Yuka

The costs of publishing this book have been supported in part by an award from the Hiromi Arisawa Memorial Fund (named in honor of the renowned economist and the first chairman of the board of the University of Tokyo Press) and financed by the generosity of Japanese citizens and Japanese corporations to recognize excellence in scholarship on Japan.

University of California Press
Berkeley and Los Angeles, California

University of California Press, Ltd.
London, England

First paperback printing 2006

Walker, Brett L.
    The conquest of Ainu lands : ecology and culture in Japanese expansion, 1590–1800 / Brett L. Walker.
        p.   cm.
    Includes bibliographical references and index.
        ISBN 978-0-520-24834-2 (pbk : alk. paper)
        1. Ainu—History. 2. Hokkaido (Japan)—History. 3. Human ecology—Japan—Hokkaido. 4. Japan—History—Tokugawa period, 1600–1868.   I. Title.

DS832W35 2001
952'.025—dc21   2001027244

Printed in the United States of America

13   12   11   10
10   9   8   7   6   5   4

Contents

Illustrations

MAPS

TABLES

Acknowledgments

Family, teachers, and colleagues have helped shape this book, and my life, over the past several years, as the two, for better or worse, have been deeply intertwined. I am forever grateful to my parents, Linda Harbers and Nelson Walker, for encouraging me at an early age to explore my interests, which ranged from wheat farming in Montana to traveling in Japan and other parts of the world. It is within this atmosphere of acceptance and curiosity that I trace my early fascination with foreign cultures and human memories and histories, particularly those of the Japanese. My Japanese parents-in-law, Hara Michiko and the late Hara Sadahiko, have also been supportive and caring, as have Aaron Walker, Hara Tetsuo, Peter Harbers, the late Nancy Rudin, and Mona Goode.

College teachers, specifically Howard Berger, Franklin Specht, and Mary Higdem, taught me to think passionately about history and the natural sciences. I treasure fond memories of talking about the ancient world and gazing out over the Snake River and the Owyhee Mountains while at the Albertson College of Idaho. I enjoyed scouring these mountains with Mary and her other geology students, searching for the remains of prehistoric fish and other beasts. These were important formative years in my approach to writing and thinking about history and its relationship to the natural world, as were my master's degree studies with Linda Walton at Portland State University. Traces of these experiences surely permeate the pages of this book, but if not I hope that at least the enthusiasm for history and learning generated by these experiences is evident.

I owe the majority of my intellectual debt, however, to Jeffrey Hanes, Andrew Goble, Ronald Toby, and Conrad Totman. Professor Hanes was my primary advisor at the University of Oregon, and he taught me, above all else, to formulate questions related to Japan in a way that would prove interesting to other historians. He is an unparalleled classroom teacher, stimulating colleague, and dear friend. This book, I hope he knows, would not have been possible without him. Professor Goble, also at the University of Oregon, taught a fascinating seminar on Japanese medical history, which fostered my interest in medical culture and epidemiology. Hanes and Goble, along with Cynthia Brokaw, Bryna Goodman, James Mohr, Alan Kimball, Stuart McElderry, John Van Sant, and many others at Oregon, broadened my perspective on East Asia and history in ways that profoundly influenced this book.

I will never forget the kind treatment I received, and continue to receive, from Professor Toby. He is, without a doubt, among the world's most learned scholars of early-modern Japan, and this book benefited in many ways from his expertise. That Professor Toby took the time to travel from his home in Urbana, Illinois, to Eugene, Oregon, to serve on my dissertation committee still makes me beam with pride.

Other colleagues and friends have shaped this book in more recent years. Professor Totman, whose pioneering work in Japanese environmental history served as an inspiration, gave the manuscript several readings and tried (I hope to some avail) to introduce me to the pleasures, and oftentimes pains, of writing a book. I still remember sitting in the Yorkside pizzeria near Yale University, staring into a half-eaten slice of pizza, my face red with embarrassment, while he dissected my prose with the casual ease of a seasoned surgeon. In this way, Professor David Howell has also been important. He has proved a valuable teacher and, in more recent years, colleague, and I appreciate his insight and support. Professors Ann Bowman Jannetta, whose expertise on Japanese epidemiology is unrivaled, and Tessa Morris-Suzuki, whose knowledge of the Ainu and Sakhalin Island helped me avoid many mistakes, enriched the pages of this book. I also received comments along the way from Anne Walthall, Harold Bolitho, William Johnston, Peter Duus, and James Ketelaar, as well as from my colleagues Valerie Hansen, Robin Winks, Edward Kamens, John Mack Faragher, John Gaddis, and Jonathan Spence at Yale University. In addition, the comments of my colleagues at Montana State University at Bozeman—Billy ("The Historian Hero") Smith, Michelle Maskiell, Lynda Sexson, Alexander Dawson, Robert Rydell, and others—have added to this manuscript in many ways.

Of my colleagues and friends in Japan, I am most indebted to Inoue Katsuo of Hokkaido University; Kuwabara Masato of Sapporo University; and Akizuki Toshiyuki, who, before his retirement, oversaw the Resource Collection for Northern Studies at Hokkaido University (Hoppō shiryō shitsu). These three scholars were not only gracious hosts while I stayed in Japan (Professor Inoue rushed me to the hospital after I broke my shoulder skiing) but also extraordinary resources on Japanese history in general and local Hokkaido history in particular. Professor Inoue first broke the news to me that my original dissertation topic, though ambitious, was too broad. Akizuki's grasp of resources related to scholarship on the North Pacific remains unrivaled, in my opinion. Tsuchiya Tatsuhide was fairly successful at tutoring me on reading handwritten manuscripts but less successful at teaching me calligraphy. His talents, needless to say, added a great deal of texture to this study. Reading sources related to Ezo together opened new doors for me in understanding Japanese history, and I am grateful for his patience as a friend and his skill as a teacher. I also received comments from Kikuchi Isao, Fumoto Shin'ichi, Ishihara Makoto and Itsuko, and others. Fukuda Takeo, my dear friend, as usual saved me routinely while I lived in Japan.

Funding for this research came from a Fulbright grant. Samuel Shepherd and Iwata Mizuho, who oversaw my experience abroad under the Fulbright Program, were extremely generous with their time. Other funding came from the Council on East Asian Studies and the Department of History at Yale University and from the College of Letters and Science and the Department of History and Philosophy at Montana State University. The staffs at the Resource Collection for Northern Studies at Hokkaido University and the Hokkaido Prefectural Library, Ebetsu, not to mention other sites in Hokkaido, showed extreme patience with my many demands.

Finally, I am most grateful to Hara Yuka, my wife and partner, for her patience and help with this book. She did more than simply put up with this research, dutifully listening to dinnertime conversations on the trade in bear gallbladder; she also read through the notes and manuscript trying her best to keep me from making silly mistakes. I remain deeply indebted to her and hope that the final product is deserving of her effort. As tradition dictates, let me state for the record that any mistakes that remain in this book are my responsibility.

Introduction

In the course of Japan's long history, its borders and its ethnic configuration have undergone some surprisingly dramatic changes. Illustrating this point, maps drawn before the mid–nineteenth century identify Mutsu and Dewa provinces, on the main island of Honshu, as the northernmost territories of the Japanese. These maps are missing the island now known as Hokkaido, "Northern Sea Circuit," a resource-rich, spacious piece of land that constitutes about 21 percent of the total land of Japan today.[1] Some seventeenth-century maps, such as the detailed 1644 *Shōhō Nihon sōzu* [Shōhō map of greater Japan], do crudely outline a northern, amoeba-shaped land formation called Ezochi, a term that means something like "barbarian land." However, compared to the rest of the map, the depiction of Ezo is surprisingly off-scale, off-center, and, with some exceptions, geographically inaccurate.

1

Figure 1. A 1700 map of Ezo, or the present-day islands of Hokkaido and Sakhalin and the Kurils. This provincial map (*kuniezu*) was modeled after an earlier version found in the *Shōhō Nihon sōzu* of 1644, and lacked the shogunal-imposed cartographic standards of other official maps of its day. The original 1700 map, once held at the Tokyo Imperial University Library, was destroyed in the Great Kantō Earthquake and subsequent fires. This map is a copy held at the Hokkaido University Library. *Genroku kuniezu* [Genroku provincial map]. Courtesy of the Resource Collection for Northern Studies, Hokkaido University Library.

Akizuki Toshiyuki, a historian of the North Pacific, speculates that the Ezochi map was the product of some early exploration or the circumnavigation of Hokkaido and that the later 1700 *Genroku kuniezu* [Genroku provincial map], absent some detail, is nearly identical to its earlier cousin (see figure 1). On both maps, the order of many of the place names is accurate, explains Akizuki, and some features, such as a giant swamp about midway down the Ishikari River and several large bays, could have been identified only through some exploration. However, in the depiction of Sakhalin Island and the Kuril Islands, most of the place names are out of order and include bizarre references to Eurasian continental locations in the Amur region, but their very presence suggests that the information was obtained through conversations with Ainu.[2] Most of the place names are, after all, major Ainu *kotan*, or villages, making this a map of Ainu lands.

The *Shōhō Nihon sōzu* was the product of a realmwide mapping project mandated by the Edo shogunate, the military government (*bakufu*) founded by Tokugawa Ieyasu in 1603, and was crafted from individual provincial maps (*kuniezu*) submitted to the capital by domainal lords (*daimyō*). As part of the formation of a strong regime run by the Tokugawa shoguns, these provincial maps served important political and military purposes and needed to conform to a rigid cartographic standard, with 6 *sun* (7.2 inches) equaling 1 *ri* (2.44 miles), or a ratio of about 21,500 to 1. Once submitted to the capital, the provincial maps were redrawn by Hōjō Ujinaga at a newly calculated ratio, and the composite became known as the *Shōhō Nihon sōzu*.[3] When the entire map was finished, the greater realm of Japan, with its rugged coastline and twisting rivers, was positioned under the gaze of the shogun, his councillors, and his military advisors in Edo. The final product is an astonishing map for its day, and it accurately portrays district borders, coastal ports, village names, and other political and geographic information; but the portion of the map depicting the northern section of Ezochi, in particular, is basically a patchwork of Ainu villages and exotic islands. These places remained couched in obscurity; they had been heard of but not yet seen by Japanese officialdom. In the seventeenth century, when Hōjō and his colleagues put the final touches on the *Shōhō Nihon sōzu*, this northern land was inhabited by the Ainu, an indigenous people of the northern part of

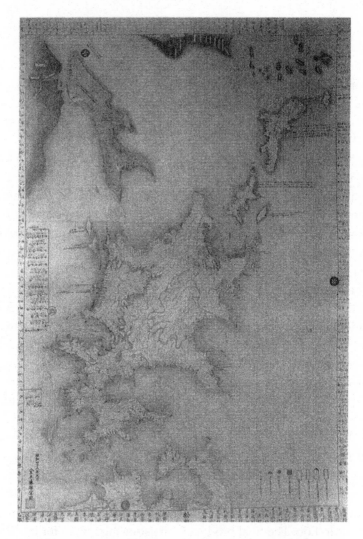

Figure 2. A map of Ezo from the 1830s. Drawn almost a century and a half after the *Genroku kuniezu*, it demonstrates a more sophisticated knowledge of the region documented in the final years of the Edo period (1600–1868). In particular, the Kuril Islands and Sakhalin Island had been explored by this time, and permanent Japanese fishery settlements had been constructed. *Ezochi zenzu* [Complete map of Ezochi]. Courtesy of the Resource Collection for Northern Studies, Hokkaido University Library.

the present-day Japanese Archipelago, and although Ezo's presence on the map may have foreshadowed later Japanese claims to the island, it was still seen as a foreign place beyond the cultural pale.[4]

By the 1830s, however, cartographic portrayals of Ezo had changed considerably. Two centuries of increasing interaction and exploration had led to a more accurate geographic knowledge of this northern territory. No longer an amoeba-shaped landmass, as in the 1644 or 1700 maps, Ezo had a recognizable shape in such maps as the 1830s *Ezochi zenzu* [Complete map of Ezochi], and there were detailed references to village names, coastal inlets and ports, rivers and watersheds, prominent offshore islands, and even specific mountain ranges (see figure 2). In provincial maps from the 1830s, moreover, such as the *Tenpō okuniezu* [1838 provincial map], a product of the last official mapping project of the Edo shogunate, Ezo was basically scaled to fit within the domestic space of the rest of Japan, suggesting that this once foreign place—this place that was once "off the map," so to speak—had been absorbed within the fluid boundaries of Japan.[5]

This cartographic shift in the official portrayal of Ezo coincides with a political shift in Ezo's status in relation to Japan: over a period of nearly two hundred years, the region had been transformed from a foreign place to a northern administrative district of sorts. To trace Japan's absorption of Ezo and its Ainu inhabitants, historians must analyze the layers of this two-century core sample extracted from the terrain of a longer historical process by which Hokkaido became part of the Japanese Archipelago and the Ainu, once a semi-independent people, became ethnic minorities in the Japanese state. That absorption process is the topic of this book, and excavating the roots of Ainu absorption and narrating how it occurred require us to sift through the ecological and cultural strata deposited on the northern landscape of Ezo. In this book, I treat Ezo as a historical site, as a good geologist would, centering it and its inhabitants, whether Ainu or Japanese, in the narrative. I purposefully do not refer to Ezo as the Japanese frontier, as is common practice, because as a conceptual tool, the notion of the frontier peripheralizes Ezo in relation to the process of state formation and economic development in Japan. When Ezo is positioned as a frontier, widespread trade, cultural interaction, economic growth, and state expansion in Ezo are often cast as part of the pageantry of Japanese national progress, rather than as the subjugation of the Ainu homeland, that place Ainu considered to be their hunting and fishing grounds and the core of their sacred order.

My analysis, for this reason, extends laterally to explore diverse facets of Ezo during the early Tokugawa years, rather than linearly to investigate a longer historical trajectory and process in the Japanese conquest and settlement of Hokkaido. In the chapters to come, I highlight the distinct peoples that understood this region and its animal life to be at the core of their respective epistemological universes, because preserved in these universes, like fossilized images of prehistoric monsters embedded in stone, lie early traces of the weakening of Ainu society in the face of Japanese advances. Centering Ezo as a site downplays—but does not entirely dismiss, as chapter 1 illustrates—the role of the state in shaping Japanese national destiny or serving as the vanguard in the eventual settlement of Hokkaido. In this respect, I attempt a balanced approach, one that weaves together a story of human-animal relations, disease, medicine, inter-Ainu conflict, market growth, subsistence practices, shared ritual experiences, and environmental degradation, along with the more conventional tale of expanding Japanese state interests in Ezo. Put succinctly then, as a historical site, the place I investigate is (with necessary exceptions) neither the pre-1590 nor post-1800 world of the Japanese or the Ainu, but rather a temporally and spatially localized ecological and cultural snapshot suspended in a two-century historical moment, a moment that profoundly disadvantaged the Ainu and hastened their eventual conquest by the Japanese. In this approach to borderlands, or even ethnic and cultural contact points, I have found like company among the New Western historians.

FRONTIERS, BORDERLANDS,
AND THE MIDDLE GROUND

It hardly needs to be said that Frederick Jackson Turner's now famous thesis on the role of the frontier in forging American political and cultural life has attracted the intense scrutiny of American historians. Turner positioned the westward migration of European settlers on the North American continent within the broader narrative of U.S. history by arguing that the "existence of an area of free land, its continuous recession, and the advance of American settlement westward, explain American development."[6] Kerwin Lee Klein points out that Turner implied that the process of settling the frontier gave birth to certain "intellectual traits" and to the "growth of democracy" and that these characteristics and trends later became celebrated hallmarks of American life.[7]

Positioning frontier lands within the context of national development is not, of course, unique to Turner or to American history. In fact, Turner's frontier thesis resembles the work of some Japanese historians who viewed the move into Ezo, and later Manchuria, as part of Japanese national development. Takakura Shin'ichirō, for example, a pioneer in the study of the Ainu, wrote in the early 1940s, the high point of Japanese imperialism, that the history of Japan is the history of national development based on continuous expansion. Even in the broadest sense, he continued, the history of Japan is the history of the expansion of the living sphere of the Yamato (ethnic Japanese) people.[8] With this idea Takakura helped lay the groundwork for a Japanese frontier thesis that plotted the steady march of the Yamato people into the northern island of Hokkaido and, ultimately, Manchuria. Takakura defined the field of Ainu studies in Japan and elsewhere for decades, and despite his ethnocentric vantage point, his work remains unrivaled in the field of Ainu-Japanese studies.[9]

A more recent case in point is Yamamoto Hirofumi's study of seventeenth-century Japanese foreign relations. Reacting to historians who argue against the *sakoku* thesis, that is, against the notion that Japan was a closed country in the Tokugawa years, Yamamoto suggests more broadly that many specific examples of early-modern foreign contact pointed out by these historians were not, strictly speaking, foreign relations at all. Rather, he asserts that these regions were subordinate to the early-modern Japanese state or were at least incorporated into an anti-Christian "defensive perimeter"; thus, he basically positions them on the edge as frontiers and thereby deprives them of their status as autonomously foreign places. He argues that in the 1630s, when Japanese policymakers implemented maritime prohibitions (*kaikin*), they sealed up the country from any outside contact and placed these lands within their administrative purview. Specifically, Yamamoto's thesis places the Ryukyu Kingdom and Ezo, as well as Korea to a certain extent, as the administrative frontiers of the early-modern Japanese state.[10]

In the field of U.S. history, dissatisfaction with the frontier thesis has led to the emergence of the New Western history, which posits that viewing the once expanding boundaries of the United States as simply "frontiers" badly distorts historical analysis of Native American homelands and, ultimately, belies the complexity of their conquest. With a few possible exceptions, no single historian has made this point as lucidly as Patricia Nelson Limerick. In *The Legacy of Conquest*, Limerick submits that by rejecting the frontier process as a model of analysis, "we gain the freedom to think of the West as a place—as many complicated environments occupied by natives who considered their homelands to be the center, not the edge." She argues elsewhere that the frontier model is both "nationalist and racist" and that when "cleared of its ethnocentrism, the term [frontier] loses an exact definition." She suggests that the frontier model should be rethought as a process that involves portraying diverse peoples and their "encounters with each other and with the natural environment."[11]

Richard White, another New Western historian, offers a compelling alternative to the view that ethnic and cultural contact points in the American West can be lumped together as "frontiers." He suggests that the frontier be rethought as a "middle ground," a place located "in between cultures, peoples, and in between empires and the nonstate world." He eloquently describes the middle ground as a place where the local context and historical moment shape cultural and political interaction among diverse groups of people. It is, he explains in the context of the Great Lakes region, the "area between the historical foreground of European invasion and occupation and the back-ground of Indian defeat and retreat." White adds, "On the middle ground diverse peoples adjust their differences through what amounts to a process of creative, and often expedient, misunderstandings. . . . They often misinterpret and distort both the values and practices of those they deal with, but from these misunderstandings arise new meanings and through them new practices— the shared meanings and practices of the middle ground."[12]

The New Western history, then, has sought to complicate the centrality of process in frontier studies and, as White points out, to illustrate how the middle ground arose from ethnic and cultural interaction between people and the natural world. In other words, with the focus now on place rather than exclusively on process, borderland history is no longer simply the tale of the conquerors.

In recent historiography related to Ezo, an approach to analyzing trade and other contact between Ainu and Japanese that downplays the ethnocentric vantage point of the Japanese, an approach similar to the New Western history in that it positions Ezo as a place rather than process, has been slow to permeate recent scholarship. To be sure, in the past several decades, a new generation of Japanese historians has shifted attention away from the political and economic process of "developing" (*kaitaku*) the northern frontier, to exploring the cultural and ethnic distinctiveness of this borderland itself. In the new historiography, Ezo is positioned not as a frontier, or not as open lands just waiting to be developed by the Japanese, but as a foreign land that served as the northern border for the early-modern Japanese polity.[13] Kikuchi Isao nicely represents this generation of scholarship. In his fascinating work, he places Japanese contact with the Ainu in the context of the early-modern Japanese system, borrowed from China, of foreign relations and international order (*ka'i chitsujo*), which emphasized a two-tiered structure that viewed foreign relations as ceremonial meetings between a "civilized center" (represented by Japan) and a "barbarian edge" (represented by such groups as the Ainu). Because of this emphasis on an early-modern "system" of foreign relations, Kikuchi's treatment of contact with the Ainu and their homeland needs to be seen as part of a longer historiographical trajectory linked to earlier critiques of *sakoku*.[14] He thus places contact with the Ainu in the same context as relations with other foreign countries, such as Tsushima domain and Korea or Satsuma domain and the Ryukyu Kingdom. He admits that Ezo was, strictly speaking, not a foreign "country" like Korea, but because its inhabitants spoke a foreign language and had distinct cultural traditions, the place where they lived—Ezo—was thus seen by the Japanese of the day as a foreign country.

In this early-modern system of foreign relations and international order, the one employed by the Tokugawa regime, little room remained for anything resembling White's "middle ground," or cultural and ethnic slippage in an ambiguous space—both familiar and foreign, civilized and barbaric—where the lines between the center (*ka*) and edge (*i*) were blurred through the interaction between two peoples. The *ka'i chitsujo* demanded, by its very nature and conception, that cultural, geographic, and even ethnic lines be drawn between people. Of course, as Kikuchi and others demonstrate, placing relations with Ezo in the context of an early-modern system of international order is highly instructive (I explore this point in chapter 8), but by too closely adhering to this system one risks overlooking a historical reality: Ezo's conquest (at least from the perspective of the Ainu). Moreover, the early-modern system of international order resembles in its own way a new kind of frontier thesis. In the context of Ezo, an emphasis on the delineation of "Japanese" borders, and on the construction of "Japanese" identities, places the move into the Ainu homeland as an integral part of "Japanese" history and belies the more complex and troublesome story of increasing Japanese advances into Ezochi, in particular at the ecological and cultural levels. Borders between Ainu and Japanese were erected in Ezo (something I explore in chapter 1), but the Japanese-manufactured goods and foreign pathogens that so altered Ainu society and hastened their conquest failed to recognize these boundaries. In other words, one might say that as part of an earlier frontier thesis, or even the *ka'i chitsujo* of the Tokugawa world, Ezo failed to escape the orbit of the Japanese colonizers.[15]

More recently, David Howell has explored the possibility of a middle ground in Ezo during the early-modern period. In the ambiguous space of Ezo, he points out, along with a heightening of material and technological exchange between Ainu and Japanese, there was interaction at the human level that exemplifies the ways in which the middle ground influenced individual lives. In 1634, for example, records from a Dutch ship made reference to a trader whose father was Japanese and whose mother was Ainu, and who spoke both languages. Howell submits that prior to Shakushain's War in 1669 (after which more-rigid ethnic boundaries between Ainu and Japanese were erected), a middle ground existed where Ainu and Japanese interacted, at the basic human level, to form altogether new relationships. Howell also provides the example of Iwano-

suke, of Kennichi village, who appears to have been thoroughly assimilated to the everyday customs of Japanese life. He had a Japanese name,
explains Howell, lived in a predominantly Japanese village, and wore his
hair in a trendy Japanese fashion. However, on the seventh day of the
new year, Iwanosuke underwent what Howell calls a "curious metamor-
phosis." Like a proper Ainu, he grew his hair long and, "as a representative of the Ainu people," or the country of Ezo, went to Fukuyama Castle
to participate in an audience with the Matsumae lord. Howell argues that
"Iwanosuke assumed what had become for him a false identity for reasons that had little to do with old Ainu customs and everything to do
with the institutions of the Matsumae domain."[16] In different ways, both
of these examples reveal people who stood at the intersection of Ainu and
Japanese life. Howell argues that "contact and interdependence led to
the birth of a new identity" for such people, and even if a middle ground
did not exist at the macro level, everyday Ainu and Japanese worked and
lived together in the fisheries, making ethnic interaction a reality.[17]

   For this book, the notion of the middle ground, as a broader historical
context, is crucial because the contrast between Ainu society before and
after the period investigated, a period that might be seen as a kind of
middle ground in itself, is striking. Like the "area between the historical
foreground of European invasion and occupation and the back-ground of
Indian defeat and retreat" investigated by White, Ezo, when positioned
as a middle ground, demonstrates how early Ainu groups once stood as
militantly independent people, forging inter-island alliances and boldly
repelling Mongol invasions of Sakhalin Island in 1263 and 1284, and frus-
trating Japanese advances in southern Ezo on at least nine different occasions between 1456 and 1536. However, by the end of the eighteenth
century, Ainu communities were dependent on trade with Japan, and the
Ainu were resigned to watching as Japanese exploited once-bountiful
hunting and fishing grounds, reportedly raped their wives, drowned
their prized hunting dogs, and eventually settled their homeland. In the
space of about two centuries, the Ainu degenerated from a relatively autonomous people, willing to spill blood for their land and way of life, to
a miserably dependent people plagued by dislocation and epidemic disease—viewed by later Japanese and foreign observers as in dire need of

benevolent care (*buiku*) or even as a dying race (*horobiyuku minzoku*)—
and hence easily manhandled by the late-Tokugawa and early-Meiji
states. The point is that the Ainu culture that emerged in the seventeenth
and eighteenth centuries was in some respects a product of interaction on
the middle ground, as was much of Japanese behavior in Ezo; and so,
ironically, because this Ainu culture sprouted from the seeds of contact
with Japanese, its very existence spelled its own dependency and, ultimately, its own destruction.

TOWARD A NEW EARLY-MODERN JAPAN

This Ezo-centered approach can be extended beyond the northern frontier, into Japan proper, to cast in a fresh light issues more confined to
early-modern Japanese studies. For example, I address several ongoing
debates about state formation in the late sixteenth and early seventeenth
centuries, suggesting that from the perspective of Ezo, the fledgling
Japanese polity that emerged from the turmoil of the late-medieval era
boasted more central authority, or at least more political influence, than
recent portrayals acknowledge. In particular, when I focus on aspects of
the early-modern symbolic economy and on the alliances forged in the
ceremonial arena of gift giving and audience, the political core emerges
as at least powerful enough to project its hegemony into territories once
outside its range of power, into places such as Ezo with its Ainu inhabitants. Moreover, this projection of state authority into Ezo, and the ensuing consequences, should be viewed as further refuting the already badly
damaged *sakoku* thesis. In the weary eyes of Ainu leaders such as
Shakushain, who died in defense of his sacred land and a vanishing way
of life among his people, neither the Edo shogunate nor domains acting
under its authority appeared to be governments run by isolationists. A
Eurocentric approach, Ronald Toby points out, led to the false impression
that Japan was a closed country; an Ezo-centered approach, however, illustrates that Japan was expanding in the Tokugawa years, a notion that
highlights the importance of the historical site, or ethnic vantage point,
from which the past is rendered as history.[18]

In the chapters ahead, I will also attempt to integrate discussions of ecological change and environmental degradation into debates concerning early-modern commercial growth, and even Japanese expansion in East Asia. Environmental degradation resulting from trade in Ezo cautions against the argument that commercial growth in early-modern Japan was confined to, as some suggest, a "total environment."[19] In the Tokugawa years, the Japanese did not set their collective sights exclusively on resources that lay within the traditional provinces or confine themselves to a "total environment," but rather cast their gaze widely over Hokkaido, the Kuril Islands, and much of Sakhalin Island, searching for new resources to fuel the flames of market growth, to fertilize cash crops, and to feed a stable urban population. In this way, even in early-modern Japan, the environmental context was not fixed but was, as Conrad Totman insists, "shaping and being shaped by human activities." Environmental changes were "crucial variables in the Tokugawa economic experience."[20]

This economic expansion into Ezo, in addition to having implications for Ainu and other groups in the North Pacific, raises intriguing questions concerning whether Japanese colonialism in East Asia should be viewed as an exclusively post-Meiji phenomenon, or in other words, as the imperialist implications of modernization shaped predominantly by Western models. To begin with, in the realm of what Alfred Crosby calls "ecological imperialism," the exchange of contagions in Ezo and the demographic and cultural consequences of massive epidemics introduce the horrible specter of the interactions between semi-insular populations such as the Ainu and endemic-disease carriers such as the Japanese. Of all the many facets of Ainu-Japanese relations discussed in this book, disease cleared the way for the Japanese settlement of Hokkaido possibly more than any other factor and, hence, pushes historians to confront the ecological implications of expansion in Japan's pre-Meiji world. On a political level, moreover, the link between the state, merchants, and foreign conquest in Ezo resembles the later Japanese colonial experience in Korea, where, as Peter Duus argues, the "symbiotic ties" formed between government and business facilitated the national enterprise of the annexation of Korea. The political process of colonizing Korea, writes Duus,

14   INTRODUCTION

was associated with the "penetration of the Korean market by an anony-
mous army of Japanese traders, sojourners, and settlers," resembling,
with important distinctions, the situation in Ezo.[21]

Therefore, this study presents a new vantage point from which to view
the life and death of what Japanese historians call *kinsei*, that is, the early-
modern period in Japan. The Edo shogunate, at least in relation to Ezo,
was a regime that boasted a fairly strong core—a core bolstered by real
political power and, more importantly, by the pervasive symbolic personal relations that solidified, with gifts and audiences, ties between the
shogun and the domainal lords who remained scattered throughout the
country. This regime then projected this complex web of legitimizing
strategies beyond the traditional confines of the polity, even beyond
those people understood to be ethnic Japanese, employing ritual and audience as a means to shore up its influence over Ainu chiefs in distant
lands. This was a fairly far-flung extension of state power: the Ainu were
a people, with their elm-bark clothing, poison arrows, and owl ceremonies, who stood well outside the wildest imaginations of most
Japanese of the day.

Once in these lands, the state allied with merchants to exploit resources, inadvertently introduced deadly contagions to local populations, and sponsored the introduction of a market culture, the hub of
which became the trading post; and the introduction of that culture led to
local environmental degradation, the emergence of new social hierarchies, and pervasive cultural changes among the Ainu. For example, in
the Ainu mind, animals that in the past had been viewed as exclusively
gods (whose killing liberated spirits and cemented sacred ties to the land)
metamorphosed into what Japanese physician Ōuchi Yoan called "hunted commodities" to be exchanged at posts for Japanese-manufactured
items. The Japanese, too, began to view the natural world differently, cataloging and categorizing it, fostering the birth of a natural history and
positioning the environment for its more thorough exploitation in the
context of the commercial growth of the day.[22] The cataloging of Ezo
products and medicines by such scholars as Matsumae Hironaga, in the
eighteenth-century *Matsumaeshi* [Matsumae record], illustrates this point
in the context of trade with the Ainu. However, positioning Ezo for its

more thorough exploitation meant not simply exploring and trading but also waging war against certain Ainu chiefdoms that resisted Japanese designs.[23] Fighting ensued with the Shibuchari Ainu in 1669, and later the Edo shogunate ordered military deployments in southern Sakhalin, as well as in the Kurils, protecting the area from the menace of such "maritime barbarians" as the Russians. In the process, the Edo shogunate demarcated new borders for the realm, only now with the admittedly tentative strokes of swords wielded by domainal and shogunal armies.

To make these points and many others, chapter 1 begins with some historical background leading up to the latter part of the career of Oda Nobunaga, the warlord hailed as the first great unifier of late-sixteenth-century Japan, and his efforts to bring the defiant lords of the northeast under his hegemony. The chapter then explores in more detail the policies of the second and third great unifiers, Toyotomi Hideyoshi and Tokugawa Ieyasu, and focuses on the consolidation of the early-modern state in southern Ezo. It is this state presence in the north, particularly the formation of trade monopolies, that sets the stage for chapter 2, which explores the bloodiest war fought between the Japanese and Ainu: Shakushain's War of 1669. Although chapter 2 investigates the ethnic and political tensions that fanned the flames of this deadly conflagration, it focuses primarily on identifying the roots of the war, which can be traced to transformations in Ainu society and culture that resulted from trade with Japanese. Chapters 3 and 4 explore this trade in more detail, highlighting the kinds of goods exchanged; the relationships between trade, the environment, and economic autonomy; and the integration of goods, now emblems of prestige, into the ritual practices and political hierarchies of both Japanese and Ainu.

Chapters 5 and 6 shift our attention from Ainu relations with Japanese to more far-flung commercial and cultural relations that linked the Ainu to Eurasian continental groups such as the Chinese, the Tungus, the Ul'chi, and even the Russians. In many ways the Ainu were a maritime people, and disruption of their overseas relations by Japanese officials contributed to the ultimate absorption of the Ainu into the borders of Japan by depriving them of alternative trading partners. Chapter 7 turns our attention back toward the northern ecology of Ezo and looks at the role that epidemic disease and the trade in pharmaceuticals played in Japanese conquest. Not surprisingly, disease profoundly weakened Ainu society, but it also led to new medical practices that attracted the attention of Japanese physicians and officials. In an ironic twist, some of the medicines used by Ainu to combat disease were sought by Japanese and then exchanged as gifts in political circles. This practice, I argue, strengthened early-modern political ties already developing between Japan's core and Ainu communities in the north. Finally, chapter 8 investigates ritualized gift giving between the Ainu and the Japanese and describes how it was manipulated to bolster Japanese centrality in the north. Here, some Ainu rituals were even recrafted by Japanese to strengthen their claim to administrative suzerainty over Ainu lands.

NOTE TO THE READER

Following traditional practice, I have written all Japanese names with the surname preceding the given name. Ainu names, however, are written exactly as they appear in the original sources, despite the fact that the Japanese syllabary alters the original pronunciation, which in most cases is lost. Diacritical marks appear on most Japanese words and names, except in common words such as Tokyo and Ryukyu. All Chinese is romanized according to the Pinyin system, and the diacritical marks are excluded. In most cases the Ainu language has been standardized according to Kayano Shigeru's *Ainugo jiten* [A dictionary of the Ainu language].[24] Most geographic locations are written as they appear in the sources and thus sometimes differ from contemporary readings. Locations can be referenced on the maps provided in the text. Finally, months have been left in the lunar calendar, whereas years are estimated according to the modern Western calendar. Equivalents for weights and measures are usually provided in the text.

1 The Consolidation
of the Early-Modern Japanese State
in the North

In the late eighteenth century, when geographer Furukawa Koshōken crossed over from Hirosaki domain and arrived in the Matsumae castle town for the first time, he was struck by how much certain aspects of Fukuyama resembled Kyoto. The nicely kept homes, with beautiful flowers arranged in the front gardens, evoked in Furukawa's mind the ancient capital along the Kamo River.[1] Not only the environment in the Matsumae castle town but also the political culture inside Fukuyama Castle itself was transformed in the late sixteenth century by trends emanating from Kyoto. This chapter traces these trends and the extension of the Japanese state into southern Ezo, which in the seventeenth century became "Japanese land," or Wajinchi (see map 1).[2] By that time, Ainu subsistence practice and cultural life had become enmeshed with Japanese political development, and this political development determined

17

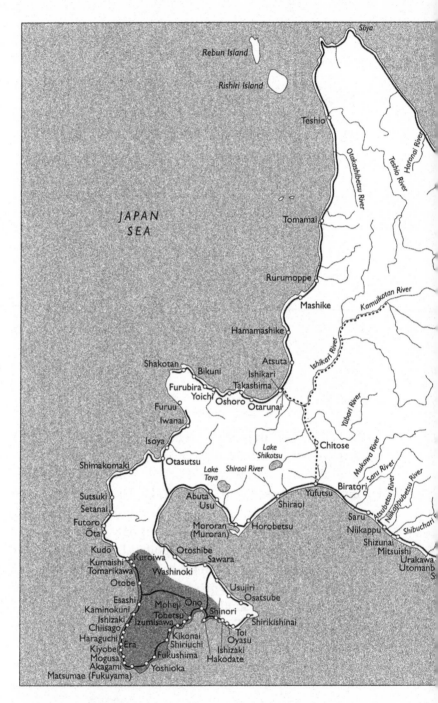

Map 1. Hokkaido during the Edo period (1600–1868).

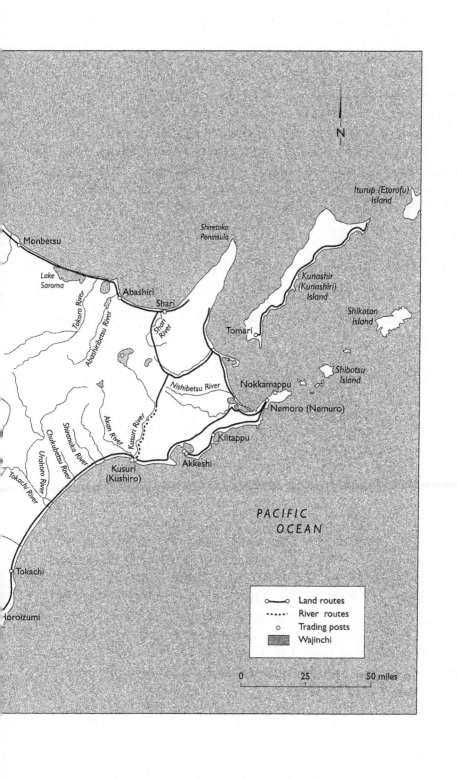

N

Iturup (Etorofu)
Island

Monbetsu

Lake
Saroma

Tokoro River

Abashiri

Shari

Shari River

Abashiribetsu River

Shiretoko
Peninsula

Kunashir
(Kunashiri)
Island

Shikotan
Island

Tomari

Nishibetsu River

Nokkamappu

Shibotsu
Island

Akan River

Kusuri River

Shiranuka River

Chukubetsu River

Urahoro River

Tokachi River

Kusuri
(Kushiro)

Akkeshi

Kiitappu

Nemoro (Nemuro)

PACIFIC
OCEAN

Tokachi

Horoizumi

Land routes

River routes

Trading posts

Wajinchi

0   25   50 miles

the pace of trade in Ezo. How this lucrative trade evolved, and the broader political and financial purposes it served for the Japanese, are important foreground for later chapters in this book. Extending our examination through the birth of the early-modern Japanese state in the north not only provides texture to our understanding of trade in Ezo but also sheds light on the process of political and military consolidation that swept Japan in the late sixteenth and early seventeenth centuries. This process culminated with the emergence of what Japanese historians call *kinsei*, or the early-modern period in Japan.

THE EARLY HISTORY: POLITICS, POWER, AND THE EMISHI

As the number of Japanese traders and explorers in Ezo increased in the seventeenth and eighteenth centuries, they discovered an Ainu society that had probably developed from earlier contact between four main archaeological cultures over different periods of time—the Epi-Jōmon (250 B.C.E.–700 C.E.), the Okhotsk (600–1000 C.E.), the Satsumon (700–1200 C.E.), and the later Japanese—making the society a kind of composite born from multiethnic and multicultural interaction. Until about the twelfth century, Japanese chroniclers included these pre-Ainu groups in a broader category of people called the Emishi or, sometimes, the Ebisu. To be Emishi, however, was not necessarily to be distinct from the Japanese of the emerging political and cultural core in Nara or Heian, the seats of the fledgling imperial government. The three major ethnic groups of the Japanese Archipelago—the Ainu, the Ryukyu Islanders, and the dominant Japanese—all appear to be of Southeast Asian descent, although they developed distinct cultural traditions. Prior to the Heian period, elite Japanese viewed the Emishi more as "crude and unrefined people," or people who rejected the political and cultural practices of the court and its courtiers. It took increased contact, largely in the form of pacification wars and limited trade, to reposition the Emishi in the Japanese mind from mere political outcasts to a culturally and, to some degree, ethnically distinct people.[3]

However, as political and cultural outcasts, the Emishi neatly served

THE CONSOLIDATION OF THE EARLY-MODERN STATE

the purposes of the Japanese elite. Some of the earliest contacts between the Japanese and the Emishi were politically orchestrated by the Great Kings (*daiō*) of the Yamato confederacy (300–710 C.E.), an early polity that existed even before the advent of Nara or Heian, when Japan was still known to continental leaders as the Kingdom of Wa (known to present-day archaeologists as the Kofun period) and was ruled by theurgic and militaristic chiefs. The Great Kings, some of whom were women, gradu-ally found themselves attracted to the potent notion of governing a Chinese-style "middle kingdom," with its pretensions to global centrality. These Great Kings sought to build a similar Japan-centered model, albeit somewhat smaller and more insular, on the Japanese Archipelago. The seventh-century Great Kings began to refashion themselves as Chinese-style universal monarchs, notes Joan Piggott, "presiding over a multiethnic realm and receiving homage from far and wide."[4] This meant encouraging tributary visits from "barbarian countries" on the political and cultural fringe. As typical "barbarians," Emishi chiefs served as kings from quasi-countries in the developing diplomatic order of the Japanese state; they fit nicely within the borrowed Chinese conception of international order that Japan was employing as a model.[5]

In the eighth and ninth centuries, the Heian government (794–1185) undertook lengthy campaigns to pacify the "barbarians" and open new lands in the northeast. At the center of these campaigns was the semi-mythological "barbarian-subduing generalissimo" (*seii taishōgun*) Saka-noue no Tamuramaro.[6] Fighting between Japanese and Emishi stretched from present-day Miyagi Prefecture to Iwate Prefecture, involving villages throughout northeastern Japan and resulting in several new districts being opened in what was once Emishi land. In these newly opened districts, the Emishi that recognized the authority of and paid tribute to the Japanese were designated as *fushū* or *ifu*, "captives." These northern border regions, lumped together as the Six Northern Districts, were placed under a local magistracy. By the tenth century, powerful families such as the Abe, "chief of the eastern barbarians," administered the Six Northern Districts for the Heian government. It was through these official posts that the borders of the burgeoning Japanese polity could be maintained and the "barbarian" fringe pacified.[7]

At about this time, Japanese chroniclers began making passing reference to a new group called the Watarishima Emishi, a people who appear to differ from earlier Emishi groups. In tribute, for example, the Watarishima Emishi brought animal skins rather than horses, and Dewa lords prohibited other groups from trading with the Watarishima Emishi, suggesting that their tribute was exotic enough to warrant trade restrictions. Emori Susumu, a historian of Hokkaido, points out that the Watarishima Emishi share many traits with the people that would later be identified as the Ezo and, ultimately, the Ainu. First, the Watarishima Emishi were more than simply an agricultural people: hunting constituted an important part of their subsistence practice. Second, they carried on a small-scale trade with the Japanese in Dewa, which included the exchange of a variety of animal skins. Third, the Watarishima Emishi were distinct from the Emishi of Mutsu and lived predominately on the northernmost tip of Honshu and on Hokkaido. The name Watarishima Emishi can be roughly translated as "Emishi who cross from the island." Finally, they exhibit elements of what archaeologists refer to as the Satsumon culture. Scholars trace the beginnings of the Satsumon culture in Hokkaido to about the eighth or ninth century and suggest that the culture was characterized by changes in earthenware production, by increasingly square-shaped domiciles with indoor cooking hearths, and by a marked increase in the number and variety of metal items acquired in trade. Archaeologists have unearthed iron goods such as harpoon tips, arrowheads, sickles, hoes, and a variety of personal metal ornaments at sites in northern Honshu and southern Hokkaido. These items are the core material goods of the Satsumon culture.[8]

Satsumon trading was not limited to metal goods, however. Suggesting an exchange in technology, samples of Japanese-style pottery, such as *sueki* (an ashen-color, kiln-fired earthenware) and *suzuyaki* (pottery largely from the northern part of present-day Ishikawa Prefecture), as well as some porcelain, have been unearthed at archaeological sites. The Satsumon people also practiced small-scale agriculture; traces of barley, millet, barnyard grass, buckwheat, and Indian millet plots have been found at many Satsumon sites. Moreover, at sites near Shizuura, on the Tsugaru Peninsula, archaeologists have identified spindles for making fabric, earthenware tools, and slag derived from melting down metal, which was used for making bricks and cement called *noro*. At sites near Satsumae, also on the Tsugaru Peninsula, archaeologists have cataloged similar relics, including large quantities of *suzuyaki*. Although there remains a great deal of diversity at these Satsumon sites, they display elements that resemble the Ainu culture of later centuries. Sites near Matsumae, in southern Hokkaido, show a move toward a society concerned with agriculture as well as with salmon fisheries; and a reliance on fisheries emerged as one of the hallmarks of the later Ainu. Satsumon agriculture, for its part, shares similarities with later Ainu small-scale farming, but it also resembles the agriculture of eighth-century Japan, again suggesting early technological exchange among the major ethnic groups on the Japanese Archipelago. One example frequently cited is the use of elevated grain storehouses to keep out mice. These clever devices also became a standard feature of the Ainu villages of the Tokugawa years (see figure 3). Emori Susumu posits that this increased contact with the Japanese of Dewa sparked many of the changes that marked the transition from the Epi-Jōmon culture to the Satsumon-dominated proto-Ainu culture. The prominent place of foreign metal items acquired in trade and technological exchange in the arena of agriculture and pottery remain the primary cases in point.[9]

In the eleventh century, following the Former Nine Years War and the Latter Three Years War, watershed events in the rise of the warrior elite in Japan, the Hiraizumi Fujiwara emerged as the foremost military power in northeastern Japan. Some speculate that members of the Hiraizumi Fujiwara (such as Kiyohira, Motohira, Hidehira, and Yasuhira) might have been descendants of the Emishi or closely associated with Emishi groups. Mimi Yiengpruksawan has approached the debate about their possible "Emishi-ness" from the perspective of an art historian, suggesting that the Konjikidō, a temple built in Hiraizumi by Fujiwara Kiyohira, may have served as an Emishi-style tomb. She points out that although the temple contains many potent Buddhist icons and resembled Heian architectural style, the fact that Kiyohira and his sons were mummified suggests that they may have been a part of what she calls elsewhere a "northern sphere of transmaritime culture." Or, more provocatively, she suggests that the Hiraizumi Fujiwara may have been a branch of a larg-

Figure 3. Sketch of an Ainu *kotan,* or village, featuring a *heper-set,* a holding cage for bear cubs used in ritual; a *pu,* or elevated storage hut used for grain; a *ci-set,* or house; and a *nusa,* a ritual center with shaven-wood fetishes. The elevated storage hut is similar to huts used by early Japanese groups to store grain. *Ezo fūzokuzu* [Illustrations of Ainu customs]. Courtesy of the Resource Collection for Northern Studies, Hokkaido University Library.

er group that later became known as or somehow associated with the Ainu. She explains that later Japanese explorers noted that Ainu on Sakhalin Island mummified their chiefs after death, and the practice was also widespread among the Tungus and other Eurasian continental peoples living around the Amur Estuary. Much of Ainu ritual and material culture, including, in all probability, the burial style used by the Hiraizumi Fujiwara, can be traced to these continental societies.[10]

Regardless of how they treated their dead, the Hiraizumi Fujiwara managed to greatly expand their administrative sphere in the north. At one point it stretched from Shirakawanoseki, in present-day Fukushima Prefecture, to Sotogahama on the Tsugaru Peninsula. By the twelfth century, moreover, the Hiraizumi Fujiwara had opened several new districts

to cultivation and settlement and had basically eradicated what remained of Emishi villages. All remaining Emishi were confined to the
northernmost tip of Honshu, Hokkaido, southern Sakhalin, and the Kuril
Archipelago. This shift in administrative practice, the confinement of
Emishi to areas in the north, corresponded with a shift in terminology,
and Japanese increasingly referred to Emishi as Ezo, a term that resonated with cultural and ethnic nuances.[11]

Yet, the emergence of Ainu culture was not determined solely by in-
fluences from the south. The Okhotsk culture of northeastern Hokkaido,
which stretched from the Hamamasu region near the Ishikari River
through the Okhotsk Sea coastline and even into the Kurils, also contributed to the development of later Ainu society. To date, archaeologists
have recovered the best examples of Okhotsk culture from the shell-
mounds near Moyoro, and its development appears to coincide approximately with the birth of the Satsumon culture. The Okhotsk culture possessed many continental elements, and its roots can be traced to marine
mammal–hunting peoples, such as the Nivkh of Sakhalin, as well as the
Ul'chi and other peoples of the Amur Estuary. It is popularly held that in
earlier centuries, continental groups likely interacted with the Epi-Jōmon
and that this interaction possibly intensified during the Mongol invasion, forming the Okhotsk culture on Hokkaido.[12]

Scholars also believe, as mentioned, that the Ainu of Japan's early-
modern period represent a composite of the Epi-Jōmon, Satsumon, and
Okhotsk cultural groups. However, despite having developed in close
proximity to each other, the Satsumon and Okhotsk cultures differed in
many respects. Everything from subsistence practice and type of domi-
cile to ceremonial and material culture reveals fundamental variances.
Consider designs on pottery, for example: Okhotsk sites show that marine motifs were popular, with highly stylized depictions of waves or
marine life. That Satsumon pottery is less stylized suggests that the volume of trade with the Japanese in Dewa was larger in the Satsumon culture than in the Okhotsk. Eventually, however, in the first half of the
twelfth century, these two cultures fused, and although the Satsumon
emerged as dominant, many traces of the Okhotsk remained, including
the roots of what became the Ainu bear ceremony. Thus, the Ainu, in

part a product of this fusion, tended to locate their communities near the mouths of rivers, where marine mammals, fisheries, and rich hunting grounds could all be exploited.[13] They drew on the heritages of both the Satsumon and Okhotsk.

With the emergence of the medieval era (1185–1568), the Japanese increasingly referred to the foreign lands north of the Tsugaru Peninsula (Hokkaido, southern Sakhalin, and the Kurils) as Ezogashima, eventually Ezo for short, meaning "barbarian islands." During the early stages of the formation of the medieval polity under Minamoto Yoritomo, Ezogashima served as a border region marking the northern reaches of the realm.[14] Following the subjugation campaigns by Minamoto armies, areas north of Sotogahama on the Tsugaru Peninsula and south of Kikaigashima near southern Kyushu were considered outside the administrative sphere of the Kamakura shogunate (1185–1333), the first warrior government, and thus outside Japan. Legal codes concerning relations with Ezogashima reveal that "pacification of the eastern barbarians" was viewed by the Kamakura shogunate as one of the three great affairs of state. Moreover, Ezogashima emerged as an increasingly attractive place to banish political prisoners: many sources from the twelfth and thirteenth centuries note that prisoners were exiled there.[15]

Furthermore, during their campaigns, Minamoto armies dislodged the Hiraizumi rulers. Ultimately, the Andō family was granted the title of governor of Ezo (*kanrei*) and placed in charge of administering the northern border and pacifying the barbarians for the medieval state. That the Andō frequently adopted titles such as "shogun of Hinomoto" appears on the surface to associate them with the northern cultural sphere, and some suspect that they may have been, like the Hiraizumi Fujiwara, descendants of early Emishi families.[16] Whatever the Andō origins, under their auspices, a lucrative trade eventually developed between Tosaminato, an official port city on the Tsugaru Peninsula established in 1223, and Ezogashima. Special ships exempted from Kamakura tariffs brought goods originating from Ezogashima, such as salmon and animal skins, to ports on the Japan Sea coast. Other ships, such as "barbarian ships" (*ibune*) and "court ships" (*miyakobune*), also brought a fairly steady flow of goods from Ezogashima to Japan throughout the sixteenth century.

These political and commercial developments in northeastern Japan ushered in the full-blown emergence of Ainu culture. With more regularity in trade, Japanese goods became a standard feature of Ainu material life. Historians point out that the increasingly important role of trade led to the emergence of powerful chiefs who oversaw trade with the Japanese. This sparked new social hierarchies, forms of political leadership linked to prestige, ceremonies that incorporated Japanese items, and a material culture reminiscent of that of the Ainu.[17] Moreover, by the early fifteenth century, after their ancestral groups had been continually pushed northward, the Ainu had come to call much of Ezo their homeland. In fact, early efforts by the Andō family to assert more political and commercial influence over southern Ezo ended in bloody rebuffs. One such example is Koshamain's War, a mid-fifteenth-century conflict between Japanese and Ainu loyal to Koshamain, which highlighted the urgency that some chiefs felt to defend claims to their homeland and the animals and fish that lived there, as well as to unrestricted rights to trade. In this short war, which was actually sparked by a minor dispute over a sword, Koshamain and his followers managed to destroy some twelve Japanese forts in southern Ezo before being defeated.[18]

ODA NOBUNAGA AND THE FIRST STEP TOWARD REUNIFICATION

The Kakizaki family—or the Matsumae family, as it was known after 1599—was in vassalage to the later Andō family and was an influential presence in southern Ezo at this time. The Kakizaki fought with distinction in Koshamain's War, particularly in the person of Takeda Nobuhiro, a general of Kakizaki Sueshige. (Later, in fact, by celebrating the military exploits of Nobuhiro, who according to legend killed Koshamain, Matsumae lords glorified him as the progenitor of their family.) Yet, despite the family's exemplary role in Koshamain's War, the Kakizaki rise to power did not really begin until after the political and military turbulence of the Era of the Warring States (Sengoku jidai, 1467–1568). Although the family emerged as a regional player during the sixteenth-century

Minato War (a violent secessionist struggle that erupted between two Andō branch families, the Minato and the Hiyama), it was with the unification efforts of Oda Nobunaga, the first great unifier, that the Kakizaki began to wield independent authority in the north.[19]

By 1575 Nobunaga had greatly expanded his territory, and he made his son, Nobutada, Akita Jōnosuke in an attempt to further extend, at least symbolically, his vision for unification over the northeast, traditionally one of the more defiant regions of medieval Japan. He again manifested his indirect suzerain claims by granting Andō Chikasue, the family patriarch, the status of lower fifth-rank vassal, and in 1580, he changed this status to the upper fifth-rank. Nobunaga sought to strengthen personal ties between himself and such powerful warring-states lords (sengoku daimyō) as Chikasue. The Kakizaki family was integrated into these personal meetings in 1578, when Nanbu Suekata, an Andō family retainer who frequently visited Nobunaga to deliver hawks as gifts, visited the hegemon at Azuchi Castle. Nanbu brought along Kakizaki Masahiro (the fourth son of Kakizaki Suehiro), who apparently received a slip of paper (okirigami) from Nobunaga during the visit. The message on this paper remains a mystery, but Asao Naohiro, a historian of Japan's early-modern period, speculates that it was related to the improving political status of the Kakizaki in Ezo.[20]

These personal ties between the unifying core in Kyoto and the sometimes defiant northeast tightened further when Andō Chikasue died in 1587. A classic warring-states lord in every way, he had ordered the brutal murder of Asari Yoshimasa, an Andō vassal, in 1583 after having invited him to Akita (under the false pretense of celebrating their friendship) and apparently having gotten him thoroughly drunk. (Kakizaki Yoshihiro, the Andō vassal who later met with Toyotomi Hideyoshi and Tokugawa Ieyasu, cut Asari down after another vassal botched the job.)[21] Following the death of Chikasue, thirteen-year-old Andō Sanesue emerged as the Minato Andō heir. However, Sanesue was quickly challenged by the lord of Toshima Castle, Andō Michisue, who launched a surprise attack against Sanesue, forcing him to retreat from Minato to Hiyama Castle. The ensuing conflict, the Minato War, spread like a brushfire and engulfed the northeast. Sanesue recruited military assis-

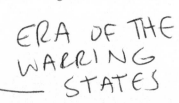

ERA OF THE
WARRING
STATES

tance from the Akaotsu family of Yuri and from Ōura Tamenobu of Tsugaru; Michisue rallied the Tozawa of Nanbu and Senpoku, both in northeastern Japan.

In the late 1580s, much of northeastern Japan lay on the brink of a full-blown war. Regional conflicts that had festered beneath the surface emerged, profoundly threatening the fledgling order forged by Nobunaga. However, it should not be surprising that the center could not intervene in the Minato War even at this juncture: it was faced with turmoil of its own. In events that have come to symbolize the violence and political confusion of the day (*gekokujō*, "low rising against the high"), Nobunaga, after having taken the first step toward the reunification of Japan, had been murdered in 1582 by Akechi Mitsuhide, a disgruntled vassal. Upon Nobunaga's death, several powerful players maneuvered for supremacy in the political void left by the first unifier. Perhaps the most unlikely successor emerged victorious: the flamboyant Toyotomi Hideyoshi, an extremely resourceful man with a modest background. Hideyoshi dealt with the Andō family with a strong hand and in a way that influenced the transformation of the Kakizaki from Andō vassal to lord of Wajinchi.[22]

TOYOTOMI HIDEYOSHI: PEACEMAKER

Under Hideyoshi—who pushed for greater political centering—the rights to control shipping in Ezo shifted completely from local Andō authority to the broader public authority (*kōgi*) that he claimed. This shift illustrates the role of Hideyoshi's Kyoto regime in authenticating the political, diplomatic, and commercial power of domainal lords, a crucial step in the reunification of Japan and the birth of *kinsei*, following the Era of the Warring States. Authorizing foreign trade and other commercial activity was one way that Hideyoshi, in particular, sought to strengthen his mandate to rule the entire realm.[23] Investing the Kakizaki family with privileges to oversee shipping in Ezo was an extension of this self-declared realmwide mandate. The Kakizaki family, moreover, like other domainal households, had much to gain from some semblance of a strong central government. The emerging political core proved a potent source of real legitimacy in the political confusion of the years around 1600. Thus the formation of Wajinchi under Kakizaki and, later, Matsumae rule illustrates a balance between centripetal and centrifugal political interests.[24]

By 1587, Hideyoshi's grip on power had tightened considerably. With the subsequent defeat of the defiant lords of Kyushu in the southwest, and the warm reception of Ieyasu, the second-most powerful man in the land, as a vassal to the Toyotomi side, Hideyoshi became peacemaker and demanded an end to all fighting in the realm by issuing the *Sōbuji* orders, which called for a suspension of hostilities throughout the realm. Hideyoshi directed the *Sōbuji* orders at the warring-states lords of the Kantō, the alluvial plain of present-day Tokyo, and at the northeastern lords, such as the disputing factions of the Andō family and their allies. However, the bitter fighting in the northeast continued, and in 1589, according to a letter from Maeda Toshiie to Nanbu Nobunao, Hideyoshi was making plans to travel to the northern provinces of Dewa and Mutsu to punish the Andō himself. According to this document, he planned to place all Andō lands under Toyotomi hegemony; the Nanbu and Uesugi households would then watch over this new territory.[25] Hideyoshi, in other words, had every intention of dealing with the Andō family severely for ignoring the *Sōbuji* orders. Hideyoshi never made the trip; he did, however, dispatch powerful survey magistrates (*kenchi bugyō*), including Uesugi Kagekatsu and Ōtani Yoshitada (perhaps Yoshitsugu), to the Senpoku region; and Maeda Toshiie and Kimura Hidetsuna (perhaps Shigekore) visited Akita and Hirosaki.[26] By forcing local lords to allow their land to be breeched, measured, and assessed by the emerging center, even with the crude instruments of the day, Hideyoshi's cadastral surveys functioned as a powerful tool with which to tighten his grip over the defiant northeast.[27]

This policy toward the northern lords, particularly the Andō family, reveals the steps taken by Hideyoshi toward ending the late-medieval disorder (in many ways symbolized by the feuding within the Andō family) and constructing what Mary Elizabeth Berry refers to as a federal political order, with Hideyoshi serving as the centerpiece.[28] Berry emphasizes the role of personal relations, strongly reminiscent of the political ties of the medieval era, in strengthening the political channels necessary for unifying the realm. She explains that during the early years of reunification, "the actual functioning of high politics was marked by the elaboration of personal attachment. The unifiers did not renounce medieval forms of political association, they capitalized upon them."[29] Hideyoshi's approach to defusing conflicts in the northeast, the very fact that he decided to meet with Kakizaki Yoshihiro and Andō Sanesue in person in 1590, supports Berry's observations. The authority of the Kakizaki in southern Ezo, and their newly emerging ties to Kyoto, became inseparable from the political reunification orchestrated by Hideyoshi, who sought to settle the Minato War. The ties forged by Hideyoshi were enough to draw the Kakizaki, and other lords on the periphery of the late-medieval polity, into the process of peacemaking that was sweeping late-sixteenth-century Japan. Many warrior families, such as the Kakizaki, drew on their relations to Hideyoshi and on his claim to broader public authority, hoping to gain legitimacy for their own local status and land holdings. This type of security, of course, had been absent just decades earlier.

HIDEYOSHI AND POLICY TOWARD NORTH ASIA

While Hideyoshi's magistrates conducted surveys bringing to a close the Minato war, Yoshihiro, the patriarch of the Kakizaki household, crossed over from Fukuyama, the family's stronghold in southern Ezo, and met with Maeda Toshiie in Hirosaki. Yoshihiro also traveled to Akita and Senpoku, where he met with Kimura Hidetsuna and Ōtani Yoshitada, respectively. At these meetings, it was decided that because Sanesue, the new lord of the Andō family, was only thirteen years old, Yoshihiro should accompany him to Kyoto for an audience with Hideyoshi. In 1590, Yoshihiro and Sanesue departed Tosaminato, the northern port city, and arrived at the capital in the twelfth month. In Kyoto they would have seen a city being reborn thanks to lavish gifts bestowed by Hideyoshi and others, one of the most stunning buildings being Hideyoshi's own Jurakudai Palace. Prior to their arrival at the palace, Toshiie and Hidetsuna had announced to Hideyoshi that Yoshihiro, the "lord of Ezo Island" (*Ezo no shima [no] nushi*), was among those traveling to Kyoto.[30] Despite this lofty sounding title, the status of the Kakizaki family changed little during this first visit, which was aimed more at Andō investiture. Yet, as Kaiho Mineo, a prominent historian of Hokkaido, points out, the fact that Yoshihiro was received as the "lord of Ezo Island" reveals that Hideyoshi had come to believe that Kakizaki Yoshihiro was a leading political player in Ezo.[31]

In 1593, Yoshihiro again traveled southward, this time to meet Hideyoshi at Nagoya in Hizen Province, on the southern island of Kyushu, the headquarters and staging area for the developing invasion of the Korean Peninsula. Hideyoshi, while planning the invasion, remembered his meeting with the "lord of Ezo Island" (this time referred to as *Ezo no chishima no yakata*) and thus summoned him to Nagoya. Hideyoshi, during this second meeting, had more in mind than domestic reunification. For years he had trumpeted his intent to force Ming China and Korea to accept the suzerainty of Japan, which he increasingly referred to as *Shinkoku*, or the "land of the gods." He once wrote in a bombastic letter to the viceroy of the Indies that Japan had a divine right to rule the entire world.[32] In Nagoya, Hideyoshi and Yoshihiro explored the possibility of a northern route through Ezo into Orankai (Tartary, the area of Manchuria and Siberia northeast of Korea) and, ultimately, into Korea and China.[33] Hideyoshi's belief in a northern route to Korea is hardly surprising considering the information available to him. In Hideyoshi's day, Ezo was thought to be part of the Eurasian continent. For example, Hideyoshi had in his possession a folding-fan map, based on an earlier map received from European missionaries, that placed Ezo on the continent near Manchuria. Akizuki Toshiyuki explains that many early European maps, such as those attributed to Matteo Ricci, placed Ezo on the continent and that some of these maps, in one form or another, were known to be in Hideyoshi's possession.[34] Moreover, Hideyoshi might have known that records existed concerning an official envoy dispatched by the king of Ezogachishima to Korea in 1482, although it is possible that this was an imposter envoy.[35]

Luis Frois, a missionary, wrote that while at Nagoya in 1593 he had noticed that Hideyoshi had a large map of the continent spread out before him which illustrated Korea divided into eight color-coded provinces and which showed that Ezo might serve as a route into Manchuria, China, and the Korean Peninsula. Frois suggested that Hideyoshi had several such maps spread out in what appears to have been a war room of sorts. He also explained that it was known that the Korean, Tartar, and Jurchen people frequently intermixed and that they sometimes traded in Ezo. He went on to note, moreover, that in recent years the region had been plagued by unification wars.[36] Later, Katō Kiyomasa, a powerful Kyushu lord and general in the invasion of Korea, fueled speculation when he wrote to Hideyoshi that after the attack on Hamgyŏng-do he had crossed into Orankai and had captured a Japanese fisherman named Gotō Jirō from Matsumae. Gotō had been living in the region for nearly twenty years, was fluent in both Korean and Japanese, and had apparently suggested to Katō that Matsumae was close to Orankai (and therefore Korea).[37]

Katō likely briefed Hideyoshi on Gotō's story. The official biography of Hideyoshi, the *Taikōki* [Record of the retired regent], explains that Hideyoshi was aware that Gotō had been captured during the invasion of Orankai.[38] Moreover, because Hideyoshi understood Ezo to be part of the continent and close enough to Orankai so that frequent trade took place between the two peoples, Matsumae Kagehiro's seventeenth-century domainal history *Shinra no kiroku* [Record of Shinra] portrays Hideyoshi as extremely excited about the second meeting with Yoshihiro and what it meant for his designs in Korea. The very fact that Kagehiro described Ezo as becoming a useful thing for Hideyoshi after the Hizen meeting suggests that Hideyoshi viewed the northern region as valuable for his overseas plans.[39] It seems that among other reasons, Hideyoshi sought not only to recognize the position of the Kakizaki family so as to utilize Ezo as a possible northern route into Korea but also to strengthen the family as a bulwark against Jurchen and Tartar unification wars in Orankai that might spill over in Ezo.[40]

During the short Nagoya meeting, Hideyoshi granted Yoshihiro the courtesy title Shima-no-kami and invited Yoshihiro to travel periodically for attendance (*sankin*) in Kyoto.[41] Hideyoshi even granted Yoshihiro a generous piece of land in Ōmi Province to defray the costs of attendance, but Yoshihiro declined the offer on filial grounds, pointing out that his elderly father, Suehiro, needed his attention. At this point, Kinoshita Yoshimasa, Hideyoshi's advisor close to the negotiations, suggested instead that Yoshihiro be given formal authority to levy shipping duties on all trade in Ezo. To make attendance more convenient, Kinoshita next proposed that the Kakizaki family be given liberal access to post stations located throughout the northeast. Hideyoshi agreed and in the first month of 1593 granted Yoshihiro a vermilion-seal order, the highest form of documentary authority, investing the Kakizaki with the right to levy shipping duties in Ezo. Hideyoshi granted Kakizaki lords local authority over all shipping in Ezo, which in turn obliged the Kakizaki to recognize, to their own immediate political and financial advantage, the broader public authority to do so claimed by Hideyoshi.[42]

In the late sixteenth century, then, Hideyoshi radically transformed the political relationship between the Kakizaki and nearby Ezochi. Now, Kakizaki ports became the center of the region's trade activity. This transformation should be viewed in light of both the process of reunification initiated by Hideyoshi and his overseas designs in Korea and China. It should be noted, moreover, that not all parties involved benefited in this whirlwind of change, and Hideyoshi was not afraid to step on a few toes to get his wishes. Most pertinently, he stripped Andō Sanesue of the right to oversee trade in Ezo. Instead, he looked to the Kakizaki, who had since 1515 managed trade for the Andō from the fort at Fukuyama (there was no castle town yet), to levy shipping duties in Ezo. The vermilion-seal order made the Kakizaki family a vassal of the Toyotomi, rather than the Andō, and invested the family with rights to control commercial shipping in Ezo.[43] Demonstrating what this meant for the Ainu, the *Shinra no kiroku* flamboyantly crows that when Yoshihiro returned to Ezo after his meeting with Hideyoshi, he gathered Ainu "from the east and the west" and read to them, in translation, the vermilion-seal order. He warned that if Ainu failed to observe the directives, Hideyoshi would send a military force of 100,000 warriors to crush the offenders.[44] Hideyoshi had sanctioned Kakizaki claims to trade in lands inhabited by Ainu and had provided the threat of badly needed military muscle and political legitimacy. Moreover, in the arena of personal attachment, Hideyoshi had extended his control beyond the confines of the traditional provinces of the realm, which suggests that not all his overseas ambitions ended in utter disaster.

TOKUGAWA IEYASU: A NEW FOCAL POINT

The late sixteenth century was an era of rapid change and political upheaval in Japan. After the death of Hideyoshi in 1598 and the epic battle of Sekigahara, Ieyasu became the dominant military and political figure. Nonetheless, other domainal lords continued to wield considerable independent authority, and the political relationship between the Kakizaki family and the Edo shogunate fits this model.[45] The Kakizaki family gained politically from the recognition of their position as lords of Ezo Island, even though they had to accommodate occasional inspections and make periodic trips to Edo, called the *sankin kōtai* (the shogunate often partially reimbursed the expenses incurred on these trips). In the eyes of a lord on the political fringe, such accommodations were a small price to pay for realmwide recognition of privileges to monopolize trade in Ezo.

In the eleventh month of 1599, even prior to the Tokugawa victory at Sekigahara, Kakizaki Yoshihiro and his second son, Tsuguhiro, traveled to Osaka Castle to meet with Ieyasu. In a clear demonstration of submission, Yoshihiro offered Ieyasu a genealogical chart of the Kakizaki family and a map of Ezo during this visit. Moreover, in another "token of submission," as Harold Bolitho refers to the "obligation imposed on han [domain] leaders to surrender their own name and acquire new ones," the Kakizaki name was changed to Matsumae.[46] From this point forward, the Matsumae family was considered a vassal of the Tokugawa household, rather than the Toyotomi. No man could honorably serve two masters, so the emergence of a new master required a new man, or a new name.[47]

Surviving in the fluid political landscape of the early seventeenth century required savvy political maneuvering on the part of the Matsumae family. In the sixth month of 1600, prior to the battle of Sekigahara, Yoshihiro had shrewdly abdicated in favor of his son Morihiro. Some assume that Morihiro, although head of the Matsumae family, never became lord of Matsumae domain proper, thus downplaying his role in the rise of the Matsumae under early Tokugawa rule.[48] However, following the Tokugawa victory at Sekigahara, Yoshihiro dispatched Morihiro to Edo. In the spring of 1601, Morihiro met with Honda Masanobu, one of Ieyasu's most trusted advisors, building personal ties between Fukuyama Castle and Edo.

As a former Toyotomi vassal, Yoshihiro had every right to fear for his political life in the post-Sekigahara reorganization, and abdicating to Morihiro proved essential to maintaining a degree of flexibility in the cloud of uncertainty following the Tokugawa victory. Only months after the epic battle, Morihiro wrote from Fushimi Castle, where he was in attendance, that prominent Toyotomi vassals such as Uesugi Kagekatsu, Satake Yoshinobu, and the powerful Shimazu of Satsuma, had lost their domains or come under intense Tokugawa scrutiny. In contrast, Tokugawa vassals such as Ii Naomasa, Honda Tadakatsu, Ikeda Terumasa, Fukushima Masanori, Asano Yukinaga, and Kobayakawa Hideaki were given new roles or larger domains in the new order. Morihiro observed that some Toyotomi vassals had abdicated in favor of their heirs to avoid losing their domains or attracting Tokugawa disfavor.[49] This is precisely the role that Morihiro played. He became a fifth-rank vassal of the Tokugawa household and obtained the courtesy title Wakasa-no-kami in the fifth month of 1601, establishing personal ties to Ieyasu and securing a place for the Matsumae in the emerging Tokugawa order. Several years after the post-Sekigahara reorganization, Yoshihiro too finally became a fifth-rank vassal of the Tokugawa.[50]

In the winter of 1603, Yoshihiro again traveled south for the purpose of attendance. While Yoshihiro was in Edo, Ieyasu granted him a generous rice stipend, partially reimbursing the expense of the lengthy trip. In the first month of 1604, Honda Masanobu spoke with Yoshihiro concerning gold mines in Ezo, remarking that Japanese merchants had expressed a desire to exploit reported "mountains of gold." Ieyasu suggested that Yoshihiro should be placed in charge of managing the gold mines, expanding upon the earlier control over shipping granted by Hideyoshi.[51] The position of the Matsumae family in southern Ezo was formally institutionalized that same month when Masanobu presented a black-seal order to Yoshihiro, stamped with Ieyasu's cipher, granting the Matsumae family exclusive rights to trade with the Ainu. The brief document read,

[1] It shall be unlawful for people from outside provinces to enter or exit Matsumae to trade with the Ainu without the consent of Matsumae Shima-no-kami.
[2] It shall be unlawful for [Japanese] people to cross freely into Ezo for trade, [but] Ainu should be considered free to go where they please.
[3] It is strictly prohibited for [Japanese] people to inflict injustices or crimes upon the Ainu.

If people act contrary [to these edicts], [they] shall be punished rigorously. Carefully observe the above [edicts].[52]

The policy of granting the Matsumae exclusive rights over trade with the Ainu would be reaffirmed by later shoguns until the mid–eighteenth century.[53] Few changes would be made to the black-seal order, moreover, even after maritime prohibitions (kaikin), which prohibited trade with most European countries, were put in place by shogun Tokugawa Iemitsu in the late 1630s, and later in 1686, when the shogunate moved to restrict trade between Satsuma domain and China via the Ryukyu Kingdom to two thousand ryō.[54] Trade in the north was considered foreign trade, but the fact that tobacco, saké, and rice—rather than precious metals—were exported sheltered the Matsumae family from the close scrutiny of the watchful eyes of shogunal advisors such as Arai Hakuseki. The 1604 black-seal order institutionalized the hereditary place of the Matsumae as overseer of trade in Ezo, and that arrangement basically remained in place until 1799.[55] It also meant, however, that the Matsumae family was reliant on this trade to survive in the Tokugawa polity. As David Howell argues, Matsumae "domain's reliance on the Ainu trade and its consequent lack of an agricultural base meant that its institutions were founded upon a set of mutual dependencies: the Ainu's dependence on Japanese commodities; its own dependence on the Ainu trade; and the merchants' dependence on the domain for protection and privileges." The results were simple, writes Howell: "Matsumae institutions were thus not only highly conducive to commercialization, they were predicated upon it."[56] How Matsumae expanded its commercial interests in Ezo is the topic of chapters to come.

In 1603, during Yoshihiro's final visit to Edo Castle, Ieyasu introduced him to Yanagawa Shigeoki, a domainal elder of the Sō family of Tsushima. As Hideyoshi had, Ieyasu explained that because Matsumae was so close to Korea, the Sō and Matsumae lords should strive to better their own relationship as well as their relationships with the continent. They talked at length about the northern section of Korea (Kitakorai), leading one to suspect that Ieyasu probably worried that Manchu armies, which had gained considerable power even at this early date, might spill over into Ezo. (Hideyoshi may have had similar fears during the Jurchen-Tartar unification wars described by Frois.)[57] In short, he probably wanted them to keep a watchful eye on continental affairs, a notion consistent with Ronald Toby's position that even after 1600 "there remained beyond Japan's shores potential sources of danger that the bakufu [shogunate] could not keep directly under control, but only under careful scrutiny."[58] Yoshihiro, Ieyasu, and Shigeoki also talked about the medicinal properties of *takeri*, or dried fur seal penis, and about fur seal migration patterns. Later, Yoshihiro went to Shigeoki's Edo residence and presented him sea otter pelts, probably from Urup, in the Kurils, and the following day Shigeoki presented Yoshihiro some Korean garlic.[59]

In the 1604 black-seal order, Ieyasu did not specify the political or legal rights of the Matsumae family in Ezo. As shogun he simply granted the Matsumae widespread authority over trade there. Nonetheless, he provided the Matsumae with the necessary legitimacy to monopolize such trade. In turn, this trade monopoly allowed Matsumae administration at the local level to determine the form of land distribution, shipping duties, and economic development. But even such local administration, observes Howell, "was predicated upon the domain's participation as an integral part of the bakuhan system," or early-modern state, and hence should not be seen as a sign of weakness in Ieyasu's regime.[60] The authority that expanding regimes assert over the lands they colonize is frequently poorly defined. As William Cronon argues, the Massachusetts Bay Company charter, granted by the English Crown in the seventeenth century, "was so permissive, and gave so little indication as to how land should be allocated within the new colony, the company and its settlers found themselves faced with having to devise their own method for distributing lands." According to Cronon, one reason that the charter granted by the Crown was overly permissive was that "the King's personal claim to the territory was so tenuous."[61] The same might be said of shogunal and Matsumae authority in Ezo.

The Matsumae family was obviously not an English company, nor was Ieyasu interested in territorial claims when he issued the black-seal order to Yoshihiro. He was simply placing foreign trade and realm-related security concerns within a broader framework. However, as Takakura Shin'ichirō has pointed out, the merchants contracted by Matsumae vassals to conduct trade and develop fisheries closely resembled the chartered companies prominent in the history of European imperialism.[62] Moreover, the finances of the Matsumae family were not wholly unlike those of the Massachusetts Bay Company: both were invested with commercial rights to provide commodities extracted from the natural environment of foreign lands. These rights eventually included, in the case of Matsumae, the right to distribute trade fiefs (akinaiba), located throughout Ezochi, to domainal vassals. Finally, the exploitation of foreign lands both by the Matsumae family and by the Massachusetts Bay Company was fueled by market growth in their respective home countries.

THE POSITION OF WAJINCHI AND
THE MATSUMAE FAMILY IN THE TOKUGAWA POLITY

The popular Wakan sansai zue [An illustrated Japanese-Chinese encyclopedia] compiled by Terashima Ryōan in 1713 described Ezochi as a foreign land. However, the work also noted that Fukuyama Castle, situated on the southern tip of Wajinchi, was considered to be within the broader orbit of the Tokugawa polity. The castle stood as a portal to "barbarian land," as Tsushima domain did to Korea and as Satsuma domain did to the Ryukyu Kingdom. These three domains bordered countries that the Wakan sansai zue lists under the heading Peoples of Foreign Countries (ikoku jinbutsu). In contrast, Holland, the Philippines, England—and even

mythical groups ranging from "cyclopean people" to "fish people"—
were placed under the separate heading Outside Barbarian Peoples (*gai'i
jinbutsu*). The status of Ezochi in the early eighteenth century, in other
words, resembled the status of "inner barbarians" in the Chinese diplomatic order; Ezochi was indisputably foreign but nonetheless within the
orbit of Japanese cultural influence and commercial interests. In the case
of the Ainu, the *Wakan sansai zue* traces the incorporation of ancient
Emishi groups into the Japanese cultural orbit back to the glorified pacification campaigns of Yamato Takeru-no-mikoto, the mythical unifier of
Japan.[63]

Even after Kakizaki Yoshihiro's meetings with Hideyoshi, Fukuyama
Castle was considered by many to be outside the cultural boundaries of
Japan. In an episode that often goes unnoticed, before departing Kyoto in
1593 (on his way home from Nagoya), Yoshihiro received from his men-
tor, Satomura Shōha, a piece of calligraphy by the master Fujiwara Teika.
Satomura inscribed a message on the wooden box used to store the art,
explaining that, considering how distant Ezo was, he was moved by
Yoshihiro's desire to cultivate his heart with Japanese refinement (*Wakoku
no fūga ni kokoro o some*).[64] Obviously, these remarks invite the question of
why somebody considered Japanese would need to cultivate Japanese refinement in his heart. The Matsumae lords were Japanese, but they were
clearly on the cultural fringe of late-sixteenth-century Japan.[65]

In a different kind of example of the ambiguous status of the Matsumae family in the Tokugawa polity, early-eighteenth-century scholar and
shogunal advisor Arai Hakuseki listed two hundred domainal families in
his lengthy study of Tokugawa-period domains. This work, which ranks
among the most complete studies of domainal rule, included extensive remarks concerning the Sō of Tsushima and the Shimazu of Satsuma, who,
like the Matsumae, both engaged in foreign trade. But the study mentions
neither the Matsumae family nor Ezo.[66] Hakuseki, who also wrote one of
the earliest ethnographies of the Ainu, knew of the Matsumae family and
their administrative role in Ezo but apparently did not consider them to
be a domain-holding family. Later, in the mid–eighteenth century, the
issue was clarified somewhat by a source which asserted that after Ieyasu
founded the Edo shogunate, the Matsumae lord became the "Great King"
of Ezo. By presenting fishery products as gifts in Edo, it continues, the

Great Kings were gradually integrated into the warrior system of government. Ezochi, however, was still considered to be a foreign land, outside the sphere of Matsumae and Tokugawa control.[67]

Some Matsumae lords chafed at the title "Great King" of Ezo. In another interesting episode, Yamada Sansen wrote in 1841 that while he was visiting Sendai, in the northeast, several prominent lords were also present, including the lord of Satsuma, Shimazu Shigehide, and Matsumae Akihiro. When Shigehide was introduced to Akihiro, the Satsuma lord responded by saying, "So this is the 'Great King' of Ezo," apparently embarrassing Akihiro. No doubt the title "Great King" of Ezo was seen by Akihiro as below his peer domainal lords, who were called *daimyō*.[68] Yet, even Matsumae lords recognized their ambiguous status and that of their domain. In 1618, following his landmark meetings with Hideyoshi and Ieyasu, Matsumae Yoshihiro boasted to Jeronimo de Angelis, a Portuguese missionary, that Matsumae was "not part of Japan."[69] Almost two centuries later, the view of Matsumae lords had changed little. In a conversation with Ōhara Sakingo, Michihiro, the eighth lord of the Matsumae family, explained that Matsumae, or the area of Wajinchi, should not be considered a domain in the traditional sense. Rather his domain had been carved out by the hard work of his ancestors through their pacification of the Ainu and, therefore, should be seen as "similar to foreign lands" (*i'iki ni hitoshiki kuni nari*).[70]

Probably the most provocative remarks were those made in 1856 by Mukoyama Seisai, a shogunal official. He noted that Matsumae became a ten-thousand-*koku* household under Ieyasu, but unlike other domains, Matsumae did not pay yearly rice taxes to the Edo shogunate. He explained that Matsumae lords were basically the "chiefs of Ezo Island" and that Matsumae, or Wajinchi, is "outside our country" (*wagakuni no soto nari*) and so does not practice the same internal administration as other domains. Ezo itself, concluded Seisai, is only "a country under the reins" of Japan (*kibi no kuni nari*).[71] The extension of Matsumae political influence inside Ezochi (largely a product of trade relations and post–Shakushain's War policy reforms, a topic discussed in later chapters) spearheaded this process of placing Ainu lands "under the reins" of the early-modern state.

The trade-fief system (*akinaiba chigyōsei*) lay at the center of this con-

fusion over the status of the Matsumae family within the broader structure of the Tokugawa polity. Although Hideyoshi's magistrates undertook cadastral surveys as far north as Akita and Hirosaki domains, they
never reached Wajinchi or any other part of Ezo.[72] Yet, despite the insti-
tutional connection between Hideyoshi's land surveys and military service under the *gun'yaku* system, a largely fictional form of realmwide
military conscription, the Kakizaki family was obliged—even without a
properly surveyed *kokudaka*, or assessment of arable land within domainal boundaries (1 *koku* was about 5.1 bushels in 1801)—to supply
troops for the subjugation of the defiant Kunohe Masazane in 1591.
Among Kakizaki troops were Ainu armed with bows and poison arrows,
which proved particularly effective, according to northeastern military
documents.[73]

Despite possessing no surveyed *kokudaka* status, Matsumae rulers
were frequently mentioned as having ten thousand *koku*. Matsumae
Hironaga remarked that Matsumae possessed no *kokudaka* status, but by
the time the Matsumae lord traveled for attendance in Edo in 1680, it had
been integrated into the *gun'yaku* system, supplying troops equivalent to
a ten-thousand-*koku* domain.[74] Other documents appear to identify 1719
as the year that the shogunate recognized the patriarch of the Matsumae
family as a ten-thousand-*koku* lord.[75] Many documents identify Matsumae rulers as having ten thousand *koku*, but nothing is mentioned of an
assessed *kokudaka* status for Matsumae as a domain.[76] Even Meiji-era attempts to determine domainal productivity for the purpose of levying
more-modern forms of taxation suggest that Matsumae, although part of
the Tokugawa polity, remained outside the *kokudaka* system. None of the
villages in Wajinchi, not even villages near Fukuyama Castle, were ever
surveyed.[77] The reason is simple really: villagers rarely, if ever, grew any
rice or equivalent yield from arable land.

Matsumae was not alone, however, among domains that depended on
foreign trade and yet were still granted *kokudaka* status. The examples of
Tsushima and Satsuma domains are worth pursuing briefly. In 1609,
Shimazu Iehisa, lord of Satsuma, received authorization from Edo to invade the Ryukyus and force King Shō Nei into submission.[78] Following
the fall of Naha, the Ryukyuan capital, the Shimazu family assigned and

then incorporated the *kokudaka* of the Ryukyu Kingdom into its holdings. This increased Satsuma *kokudaka* to the point that Satsuma bettered its status within the domainal hierarchy.[79] The point is that Satsuma incorporated Ryukyu within this Japanese system, assigning it a *kokudaka*, whereas Ezo always remained alien to Japanese forms of standardization. Later, in the mid–eighteenth century, notes Gregory Smits, Ryukyuan policymakers, such as Sai On, even went so far as to revise these surveys, updating the small kingdom's assessed *kokudaka*. The goal was to better utilize Ryukyuan resources and to make the kingdom more like Japan, which Sai believed to be among the model Confucian countries.[80] Tsushima domain, although never considered a foreign land, was ranked at one hundred thousand *koku*. This rather high ranking came after the establishment of Sō privileges in Pusan, but it nonetheless illustrates that other domains dependent on trade did possess *kokudaka* status. Again, however, Wajinchi and Ezochi remained outside this Tokugawa system of official suzerainty.

THE WAJINCHI-EZOCHI LINE

Cadastral surveys were central in demarcating borders in Japan, and in assigning a *kokudaka*, but even without these, Matsumae officials drew up borders in Ezo. After Shakushain's War, discussed in chapter 2, Matsumae officials divided Ezo into two spheres, Wajinchi and Ezochi. There is some reason to believe that the border between the two was established in 1633, just prior to a shogunal inspection; but the important point is that the border constantly moved northward, and this movement in effect led to the slow absorption of Ainu territory as commercial growth sparked increased Japanese settlement. The border was created to restrict Ainu and Japanese movement in Ezo, and in 1669 the border stretched between Kumaishi and Shinori, in the east near the Ōno Mountains. The border was guarded, and the shogunate reportedly dispatched inspectors to make sure that guard posts were built and properly staffed.

In 1691, Matsumae officials issued edicts directing local guards to uncover all illicit trade near the Kumaishi post. These orders specified that even if Ainu managed to cross over to Wajinchi in attempts to purchase necessities such as rice, they should be quickly turned away.[81] Later, following the establishment of direct rule in Ezo by the Edo shogunate (1799–1821), Habuto Masayasu of the Hakodate magistracy reaffirmed these orders. He wrote in 1807 that the Wajinchi-Ezochi line ran east from Kumaishi to the Ōno Mountains. Beyond these two points, he explained, were Ainu lands.[82] Remarks such as these have led some to infer that trade with Ainu integrated Wajinchi (or Matsumae domain) into the Tokugawa polity by strictly carving out the borders of the realm. Wajinchi, in this model, became part of the Tokugawa order because it was integrated into the *sakoku* system.[83]

In theory, the Wajinchi-Ezochi line might have served to demarcate the political and cultural boundaries of the Tokugawa polity, but in practice it was porous and permitted Japanese to exploit Ezochi easily.[84] Even in Japan, provincial border crossings, regulated through provincial barriers, were not as restricted as once thought. Commercial travelers and religious pilgrims crossed quite freely from region to region. In Ezo, the economic activity of Matsumae vassals, as well as that of many Wajinchi villagers, remained dependent on their ability to cross into Ezochi. Of course, the Matsumae family regulated crossing at guard posts, but only to protect its coveted trade monopoly. A similar situation existed in Japan: Constantine Vaporis argues of Japan that domestic travel "restrictions applied by government officials [during the Tokugawa period] were largely inspired by economic concerns rather than a desire for totalitarian control."[85] In the case of Ezo, moreover, travel to trading posts in Ezochi was done almost exclusively by merchant ships, making customs houses (*okinokuchi bansho*) the most important loci of control.

The economic behavior of the Matsumae family, embodied in its trading posts, further illustrates the permeability of the Wajinchi-Ezochi line. Provincial maps and surveys (*gōchō*), mandated by the Edo shogunate, often expose shifting borders among Japanese domains and thus shifting ranges of production.[86] The Matsumae family also sent provincial maps and surveys to Edo on three occasions: the first two drawn up in 1644 and 1700, the third in 1838. As mentioned in the introduction, the first

Matsumae map, the *Shōhō Nihon sōzu*, on which the second was largely based, contains no visual or written references to domainal or village rice yield, called *muradaka*.[87] The 1700 map is less detailed than the earlier map but is otherwise essentially the same.[88] The 1838 map, however, is far more detailed. The two earliest official maps of Ezo deviate from contemporary maps of Japanese provinces in revealing ways. The former were scaled differently than other maps, deviating from shogunal cartographic standards. Moreover, most details were probably obtained through conversations with Ainu. They were maps of foreign lands rather than of a homogenized geographic space, and the maps' authors betrayed a fundamental interest in trade.

Trading post records from 1739 are even more revealing of the permeability of the Wajinchi-Ezochi line. All the fifty-three trade fiefs held by Matsumae vassals were located in Ezochi.[89] There were none in Wajinchi. In short, Matsumae vassals kept their residences in Wajinchi, but maintaining their political and economic status as warrior elites required trading and exploiting Ainu resources. Beyond these trade privileges, vassals possessed no territorial rights, in the form of actual fiefs, in Ezochi, other than those trading privileges designated locally by Matsumae lords. However, domainal vassals in Japan also possessed ambiguously defined rights to their fiefs. In Kaga domain, observes Philip Brown, many vassals "were very poorly positioned to define their own rights to the land," although they did tax peasants within their fiefs.[90] Records related to trading posts make it clear that the Matsumae family tied its political autonomy and financial survival to exploiting resources in Ezochi, even if defining its rights to those resources proved unnecessary. Furthermore, in an illustration of the widespread economic autonomy of the Matsumae family, privileges to exploit these lands were formulated by domainal officials rather than by the Edo shogunate.[91]

Even Japanese villagers passed through the porous border at Kumaishi. In 1786, the shogun's senior councillor, Tanuma Okitsugu, dispatched several officials to Wajinchi to investigate conditions in Ezo.[92] One of them, Kondō Jūzō, surveyed and drew up detailed maps of the entire western and northern coasts of Ezo. On the Japan Sea coastline, from Fukuyama to Kumaishi, in the area conventionally identified as

Wajinchi, Kondō surveyed the number of Japanese households and the total population in individual Wajinchi villages. In what might be called a modified version of the cadastral survey, rather than assess village production in terms of village rice yield (*muradaka*), Kondō identified the respective industries of each village and hinted at their range of production. In western Wajinchi, he identified thirty-nine villages. The economies of sixteen of these relied on entering Ezochi to harvest abalone, herring, and kelp; to collect firewood; and to exploit other fisheries. This meant that the economic activity of 41 percent of the villages in western Wajinchi, the very heart of the Wajinchi fishery, depended in some way on crossing over into Ezochi and exploiting the natural resources there. Despite the detail of his maps and surveys, Kondō did not record a guard post near Kumaishi; he noted only that the road after Kumaishi became particularly dangerous.[93] Most importantly for our discussion of the position of Ezo in the Tokugawa polity, Kondō considered Ainu lands to be within *Wajin* villagers' range of production and therefore within their range of ecological and cultural influence.

CONCLUSION

The birth of Matsumae authority in southern Ezo sheds light on how politics was conducted in sixteenth- and seventeenth-century Japan. Yet, the rise of Matsumae also exposes the political and geographical limits of Tokugawa rule. For the Matsumae family, political investiture by Hideyoshi and Ieyasu lay at the heart of Matsumae oversight of trade with the Ainu. Philip Brown states that political investiture "remained one of the greatest tools hegemons had for rewarding or punishing daimyo [domain lords]." He argues that by "accepting a new appointment, the source of the rights of possession shifted. They now came from the overlord's investiture, and (barring enemy conquest) their retention was in some measure dependent on his continued goodwill."[94] Similarly, when Hideyoshi and Ieyasu invested the Matsumae family with exclusive rights over trade in Ezo, its authority in Ezo was no longer autonomously generated, no longer a product of earlier medieval alliances.

The "rights of possession," in other words, had shifted to the hegemon of the day. In the case of Ezo, and the Matsumae family, this new investiture meant rights recognized throughout the realm to exploit the northern landscape, rights that severely affected Ainu society and touched off the bloody fighting of 1669 known as Shakushain's War. It is to this violent conflict, born out of the early-seventeenth-century commercial and political developments discussed in this chapter, that we must now turn our attention.

2 Shakushain's War

In 1675, on the North American continent, an extremely bloody conflict broke out between New England settlers and a Wampanoag leader named King Philip. After settlers hanged three men loyal to King Philip, the Wampanoag chief attacked his enemies, sparking what Jill LePore refers to as not only one of "the most fatal wars in all of American history but also one of the most merciless."[1] LePore concludes her study of this conflict by suggesting that the "story of King Philip's War . . . is the story of how the English colonists became Americans." It is a story of how these colonists "positioned themselves in relation to the indigenous people of America and of Europe." She also traces shifts in Native American forms of association, from "tribal alliances to campaigns for political sovereignty to pan-Indianism." LePore submits that both sides solidified conceptions of the ethnic and political "self" through deadly confrontation with the ethnic and political "other." This type of ethnic confrontation took place at about the same time on other parts of the continent. In 1680, for example, Pueblos rebelled against Spanish rule in a violent conflict that also contributed to the formation of ethnic and political identities among the Spanish and the Pueblos.[3] War forces individuals and groups to take sides, to pit "us" against "them," and frequently these lines are drawn ethnically.

A conflict similar to King Philip's War occurred in Ezo at about the same time Shakushain's War of 1669. A multilayered struggle, Shakushain's War eludes categorization; at times it was an ethnic war, pitting Japanese armies against Ainu loyal to Shakushain, but it was also a conflict among Ainu chiefdoms themselves, an example of the violent fighting that erupted as certain Ainu groups maneuvered for better access to the animals traded with the Japanese. The war began when Hae and Shibuchari Ainu, the two main groups involved, engaged in deadly fighting that largely stemmed from disputes over access to fisheries and fur-bearing animals, over contested borders along the Shibuchari River, and over the lofty ambitions of certain chiefs. These border conflicts drew Fukuyama Castle, and eventually the Edo shogunate, into fighting a war on the distant soils of Ezochi, and in the aftermath of the conflict, forced Matsumae officials to play a more direct role in Ainu affairs. Shakushain's War stands as a watershed in the history of the Japanese conquest of Ezo—it was the last attempt by anything resembling a pan-Ainu alliance to expel militarily the Japanese from their homeland.

BORDER CONFLICTS BETWEEN
THE HAE AND SHIBUCHARI AINU

In the sixth month of 1669, over half a century after the Matsumae family had been granted a trade monopoly in Ezo, Shakushain and his band of Ainu loyalists attacked Japanese in Shiraoi, on the eastern coast of Ezo (see map 2). Less than one month later, the Matsumae lord received word that Ainu had carried out similar attacks near Yoichi, in the west. When more reliable reports finally came trickling in, officials learned that Ainu

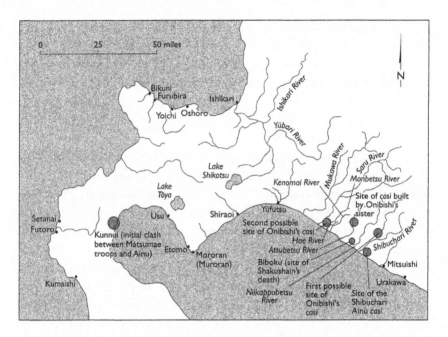

Map 2. Theater of conflict during Shakushain's War, 1669. Adapted from Okuyama Ryō, *Ainu suibōshi* (Sapporo: Miyama Shobō, 1966), 73.

armed with poison arrows and some firearms had managed to kill 273 Japanese in these two quick sorties. Within two weeks of these reports, Matsumae officials received even more unsettling news from Ainu loyal to Matsumae (*mikataezo*). Shakushain had reached Etomo, at the most a ten-day march from the Matsumae stronghold in southern Wajinchi. Ainu warriors, it appeared, lay on the brink of expelling the Japanese from southern Ezo.

The dominant interpreters of Shakushain's War, Emori Susumu and Kaiho Mineo, follow a line of thinking similar to LePore's, focusing on ethnic strife and trade-related grievances. Emori views Shakushain's War as a large-scale ethnic revolt, and upon close inspection, there is compelling evidence to support his interpretation.[4] Many of the threats made by Shakushain and by Japanese military commanders, at least according to the narrative provided in Japanese chronicles, smack of ethnic hatred. Following the death of Utomasa of the Saru region, for example, Shakushain called on Ainu chiefs to "slash their way to the capital of Matsumae" (*Matsumae e kirinobori*) and push the Japanese from southern Ezo. He warned that Japanese planned to systematically poison all Ainu elders. Similarly, before departing for eastern Ezo, Matsumae vassal Kakizaki Hiroshige told Ainu loyal to Fukuyama Castle that Matsumae Yasuhiro, a liege vassal of the Tokugawa family, had come from Edo to lead Matsumae armies because the shogunate sought to "destroy all the Ainu" (*Ezo nokorazu metsubō no jisetsu*). Once Matsumae troops subjugated Ezo, Hiroshige cryptically added, the shogunate would introduce peasants to Wajinchi and encourage the development of agriculture, fisheries, and organized hunting. He asserted that if all the Ainu were murdered, "Matsumae vassals and townspeople would not have to worry about them anymore."[5] In other words, he threatened the Ainu with genocide.

In contrast, Kaiho suggests that the economic policies of Fukuyama Castle forced Ainu to lash out against Matsumae's trade monopoly and increasingly unfair exchange rates. He asserts that Ainu chafed at strict prohibitions that frustrated their growing desire for metal products, rice, and saké, a desire that prompted them to insist on unrestricted access to trade, even if it meant sidestepping customs houses in Wajinchi.[6] In 1669, many Ainu still viewed themselves as a people who could trade where, and with whom, they pleased. The Ainu had long been a people defined by multiethnic and multicultural interaction, enriching their culture through the exchange of goods and technology; and they resented a narrowly focused trade with Japan that was strictly overseen by Fukuyama Castle. Thus, Haukase, chief of the Ishikari region in western Ezo, sought to undermine the trade restrictions by circumventing customs houses and obtaining important metal products and "high quality rice" directly from such locations as Hirosaki and Akita domains, in the northeast. On one occasion, Ishikari Ainu told Maki Tadaemon, a Hirosaki-domain spy, that they were anxious to reopen trade directly with Takaoka, the castle town of Hirosaki until 1628, "as their ancestors had in the past," before Ieyasu had granted the Matsumae family control over trade.[7] Had bold moves such as this succeeded, they would have undermined the foundation of Matsumae legitimacy in Wajinchi.

Emori and Kaiho's interpretations illuminate crucial aspects of the story. However, if they lack anything, it is a thorough exploration of the complex border conflicts that festered prior to Shakushain's War. These earlier conflicts suggest that Shakushain's War was also an ecological conflict, a war fought over the animals and fish that inhabited the natural environment of Ezo. Ethnic hatred may have contributed to the intensity of the violence, but it did not start Shakushain's War. Rather, the war started with territorial disputes between neighboring Ainu chiefdoms, specifically the Hae and Shibuchari. It was a war spawned by a demand for trade, a conflict rooted in the weakening of the bond that the Ainu had shared with the animals that inhabited their lands. As discussed in the next chapter, Ainu demarcated territorial boundaries through hunting, fishing, and plant-gathering, but they articulated these practices metaphysically. The Ainu of the Ishikari region believed that they shared a sacred relationship with the animals that lived there: the animals let themselves be hunted so that Ainu might live, and Ainu played the roles of liberators, freeing the godlike essences (*kamuy*) of animals via the slaughter. As this spiritual relationship with animals and *kamuy* eroded in the face of a market culture, which was epitomized by activity at trading posts, so too did the acceptance of chiefdom borders. The growing Ainu demand for trade goods, which sparked competition among Ainu chiefdoms, lured Ainu into fighting among themselves, which dissolved any hope of a unified front against Japanese advances.

A Hirosaki domainal record, the *Tsugaru ittōshi* [Tsugaru unification record], remains one of the best sources on Shakushain's War. In the early 1670s, when the fires of Shakushain's War had finally cooled, Hirosaki officials conducted a detailed investigation of the 1669 conflict for the Edo shogunate. Hirosaki officials proved a good choice for conducting the investigation because they were eager to expose Matsumae mismanagement of trade. Hirosaki had long chafed at Matsumae's monopoly of the lucrative trade in Ezo and the access to northern fisheries. Unlike Matsumae records, or even those kept by the Tokugawa vassal Matsumae Yasuhiro, Hirosaki records offer a glimpse into the origins of Ainu warring in the east, without being heavily biased in favor of the Matsumae family. Much of the information was acquired through interviews with Ainu chiefs in Ezo, without permission from Fukuyama

Castle. This source, in concert with other documents, allows the historian to recreate a plausible scenario for what sparked the fighting in eastern Ezo that eventually led to full-blown war with the Japanese.

Even in the early seventeenth century, Ainu chiefs from the lower part of the Shibuchari River enjoyed influence that extended well beyond their chiefdom borders. Sentaiin, the father of Kamokutain, leader of the Shibuchari Ainu before Shakushain, was by all accounts an intimidating figure. Sentaiin freely fished and hunted inside the neighboring Hae chiefdom without regard for chiefdom borders. The precise location of the Hae chiefdom, sometimes called Haekuru, remains unknown, but it was either up the Shibuchari River about eight miles from Shakushain, or west of Shibuchari toward the Saru River (see map 2). Onibishi, chief of the Hae Ainu, was furious but could do little about it. With the death of Sentaiin, however, Kamokutain became chief of the Shibuchari, and Onibishi took revenge for Sentaiin's liberal use of Hae resources by boldly murdering Kamokutain. (The murder took place during a six-year war that had erupted when Shakushain murdered one of Onibishi's subordinates during a three-day meeting between the two men in 1648.) Upon the death of Kamokutain, Shakushain became chief of the Shibuchari Ainu. (Using vocabulary familiar to Japanese, the *Tsugaru ittōshi* explains that Shakushain was originally a warrior without a lord, or a *rōnin*, but he eventually served under Kamokutain as village elder.) The Shibuchari territory that Shakushain inherited, sometimes called Menashikuru, was larger than most chiefdoms of its day.[8]

A survey conducted immediately after Shakushain's War placed the area around the Shibuchari River, and parts of the Monbetsu area, as Shakushain's chiefdom. The same survey identified the Saru chiefdom, to the west of Shibuchari, as being under three separate leaders: Rashaukain, Taizō, and Nishinosuke. The Saru territory was also vast, and it included the Saru River and parts of the Monbetsu River.[9] With the exception of the Saru and Shibuchari groups, however, the chiefdoms west of Shakushain were confined to one river system. The Atsubetsu region was under Ramai; while immediately west of Shakushain, the Biboku region was under Hachirōemon. To the east of Shakushain were several smaller chiefdoms: Mitsuishi (under Makanosuke), Urakawa (under Harayakeshahain

Figure 4. Inter-Ainu fighting, sometimes called *topattumi.* Such fighting became a more common feature of Ezochi as Ainu competed for resources for subsistence or for trade with Japanese. These wars often took the form of minor raids on unsuspecting *kotan,* or villages, but they also erupted into larger interchiefdom conflicts, such as the fighting between the Shibuchari and Hae Ainu in the seventeenth century. *Ezotō kikan* [Strange sights from Ezo Islands]. Courtesy of the Resource Collection for Northern Studies, Hokkaido University Library.

and Yayatarikoro), and Mukuchi (under Seutain).[10] Hae, Onibishi's chiefdom, was not listed in this survey, possibly having been absorbed during Shakushain's War.

Upon coming to power, Shakushain attacked Hae Ainu for the murder of Kamokutain, and fighting lasted several years, until 1655 (see figure 4). Matsumae was slow to take action to stop the fighting, but, finally, in 1655 Satō Gonzaemon and Shimonokuni Naiki, two Matsumae officials, persuaded Onibishi and Shakushain to attend an audience at Fukuyama Castle with Lord Takahiro, where a tentative peace was reached between the two Ainu leaders.[11] Matsumae interests, and commerce at trading posts, necessitated that the domain intervene in this conflict.

The peace settlement held until 1666, whereupon familiar disputes over hunting and fishing grounds ignited new fighting. A report compiled by Matsumae Yasuhiro, the Tokugawa vassal who would lead Matsumae armies against Shakushain, sheds some light on what sparked the renewed violence. Yasuhiro noted, for example, that Hae Ainu frequently crossed into Shibuchari territory and pillaged their natural resources (*sūnen kasumerare sōrō o munen ni zonji sōrō*).[12] Moreover, in 1666 tensions ran high when Onibishi asked Shakushain for a bear cub to be used in a ritual killing, explaining, "my land is very unhappy, as we have not been able to capture even one bear." Probably disregarding long-standing chiefly proprieties, Shakushain simply ignored the request, infuriating Onibishi. In the winter of 1666, Shakushain led a deer-hunting party of about ten people up the Shibuchari River. Upon discovering the Shibuchari hunters in Hae territory, Onibishi told them that they were "strictly forbidden" to hunt within his borders.[13] At the center of both these events were disputes over rights to exploit animals. Many of these animals were captured for ceremonies (such as bear) or hunted and trapped for their skins (such as deer), which were then traded with Japanese at trading posts.

In the summer of 1667, a Hae Ainu (Tsukakoposhi's nephew) who shared kinship ties with Onibishi captured a live crane, which he hoped to trade at the local trading post (see figure 5). He caught the crane in the Urakawa region, which Shakushain understood to be within his own sphere of influence. (Urakawa Ainu would later fight on behalf of Shakushain.) The angry chief lured the man to his village under the pretense of an invitation to drink saké together, whereupon Kanrinka, Shakushain's younger brother (or, according to other documents, Kanririka, Shakushain's son), murdered the hapless guest for crossing Shibuchari land and capturing the crane without Shakushain's approval. Shortly afterward, the man's family demanded that Onibishi avenge the murder. At first the Hae chief consented and made preparations to lead a military expedition of ninety Hae Ainu against the Shibuchari; however, on the advice of his Japanese friend Bunshirō, head of the gold-mining camp on

Figure 5. Trapping a crane in Ezo. When Tsukakoposhi's nephew captured a live crane for trade, it prompted his murder by Kanrinka, Shakushain's younger brother, and became one factor in the outbreak of hostilities between Shibuchari and Hae Ainu and, ultimately, Shakushain's War. *Ezotō kikan* [Strange sights from Ezo Islands]. Courtesy of the Resource Collection for Northern Studies, Hokkaido University Library.

the Shibuchari River, he instead demanded compensatory gifts (*tsugunai*) from Shakushain. His demand totaled three hundred pieces of *tsugunai* from Shakushain, but in the end he received only eleven.[14] Needless to say, Onibishi grew increasingly dissatisfied with his chiefdom's relationship with the Shibuchari Ainu.

INTENSIFICATION OF MATSUMAE INVOLVEMENT

In the twelfth month of 1667, even as the conflict between Hae and Shibuchari Ainu was heating up, Bunshirō departed from the Shibuchari area for Fukuyama Castle, where he reportedly met with Matsumae's gold-mining magistrate (*kinzan bugyō*), Kakizaki Sakuzaemon. Bun-shirō's mission was to relay information concerning the Hae-Shibuchari war, as well as to secure badly needed supplies for his mining operations along the Shibuchari River. Norita Yasuemon, an official writing a year after Shakushain's War, suggested that from this point forward, because of Onibishi's close ties to the mining camp, Shakushain had started to view Onibishi as an ally (*gohiiki*) of the Matsumae family. Norita also noted that Shakushain began to feel boxed in along the Shibuchari River, boldly warning that he would crush Onibishi and his ally, the Matsumae family, if they ordered him to be subordinate to Onibishi.[15]

Even in 1667, two years before he attacked Japanese in Shiraoi, Shakushain already felt cornered in the east. He was becoming increasingly alarmed by apparent ties between Onibishi and Japanese miners, ties that became all the more dangerous for Shakushain when Bunshirō traveled to Fukuyama Castle and met with Matsumae officials. The possibility that Onibishi had forged an alliance with the Japanese miners forced Shakushain to assume a more defensive posture. Shakushain had always been hostile to Japanese miners because they disrupted Shibu-chari salmon runs and (according to some folklore that will be discussed later) threatened his villages with starvation. In the face of this alliance, real or imagined, he ordered the construction of a new fortress, or *casi*, along the Shibuchari River and warned that he knelt before nobody.[16] Matsumae lords were not directly involved in the conflict at this juncture, but their interests in the east forced them to move toward defusing the fighting and, more importantly, toward taking sides.

So, Matsumae drew a line in eastern Ezo. When Bunshirō returned to the Shibuchari River in the second month of 1668, he relayed orders from Lord Takahiro that Shakushain was to give Onibishi *tsugunai*. Shaku-shain, however, ignored the order. Indeed, he went one step further, opting to take the offensive. In the fourth month of 1668, while Onibishi was visiting Bunshirō at the mining camp to discuss the issue of *tsugunai*, Shakushain led ten armed men up the Shibuchari River and murdered Onibishi's two younger brothers while they were tending crops in the mountains. When Onibishi returned home the next day, he was informed by two Japanese miners of the killings and was warned that Shakushain might still be in the area. Onibishi quickly fled back to the Japanese mining camp. However, Shakushain learned of Onibishi's flight back to Bunshirō's house, and he promptly led a force of fifty armed Ainu intending to murder Onibishi.[17]

The force surrounded the mining settlement. Bunshirō pleaded with Shakushain that Onibishi be allowed to give *tsugunai*; Shakushain responded by ordering that the house be burned to the ground. Then, in a dramatic scene, Onibishi came running out of Bunshirō's smoke-filled house gasping for air and telling Shakushain that he wanted to hold a *caranke*, a traditional Ainu meeting to discuss differences. Then, however, for reasons not clear in the documents, Onibishi attempted to run away, and he was killed under a hail of Shibuchari arrows.[18] With the attack on the mining camp and Onibishi's death, it became clear to Matsumae officials that Shakushain constituted a serious threat to their interests in the east. Matsumae officials needed trade and access to animals and fisheries in Ezochi, and Onibishi had traditionally cooperated with Japanese in the east; but with the Hae chief out of the picture, Shakushain appeared capable of destroying more than just the mining camp on the Shibuchari. Hence, the political and, potentially, military balance of power had shifted in eastern Ezo, and Matsumae security and commercial concerns surely appeared threatened.

⌐ ecological

THE FALL OF THE HAE AINU

The roots of fighting between Hae and Shibuchari Ainu lay firmly planted in disputes over animals that were captured for ceremony or hunted and trapped for subsistence and trade and that embellished the political ambitions of certain chiefs. Documents such as the *Tsugaru ittōshi* and the *Ezo hōki* [Ainu revolt], neither of which was written by Matsumae officials, consistently describe such Shibuchari chiefs as Sentaiin, Kamokutain, and Shakushain as being both wealthy and politically powerful. For Shakushain, as the *Ezo hōki* explains, regional political influence was contingent upon "good land" and "many utensils," as well as upon charisma and physical strength.[19] Moreover, disputes concerning deer hunting, bear cubs, and in the end, the murder of a Hae Ainu over a live crane brought Ainu relations to an impasse in the east. By 1668, Fukuyama Castle could no longer simply watch from the sidelines as its security and financial interests eroded.

After Onibishi's murder, two Hae elders, Chikunashi and Harou, ordered an assassin to murder Shakushain, but he never had an opportunity to do so. Two months later, however, in the sixth month of 1668, thirty Hae Ainu, including Chikunashi and his mother, raided the newly constructed Shibuchari *casi*, which was built on a mountain overlooking the eastern bank of the Shibuchari River. They set fire to the structure and cut down several Shibuchari Ainu as they fled the flames. Chikunashi and his mother reportedly killed about fifteen Ainu in the surprise attack.[20] That attack proved to be the last Hae triumph, however, and a few months later they made their last stand. Onibishi's sister, who had emerged as a powerful figure in Hae politics, but about whom very little is known, had ordered that a second *casi* be built upstream on the Atsubetsu River, as Onibishi's original *casi* was in disrepair. This move, moreover, might have been part of a Hae retreat westward in the face of Shakushain's growing power. In response to the Chikunashi raid, Shakushain dispatched Ehiteki, an elder from Urakawa, to take the Atsubetsu *casi* by force. But Ehiteki retreated after three of his men were killed by musket fire from the *casi*. The *Tsugaru ittōshi* describes Ehiteki as suspecting that warriors "other than Ainu" were defending the *casi*. "Shisam," or Japanese, he may well have thought as he retreated into the stands of timber.[21]

In the seventh month of 1668, a force of about 120 Urakawa Ainu, this time led by Tsunoushi, again descended on the Atsubetsu *casi*. Their assault was perfectly timed. Most of the Hae Ainu, badly in need of supplies, had left the fortification in search of food, and the attackers took the *casi* without difficulty. The fall of the *casi* turned out to be a decisive victory, and from this point forward Hae Ainu could offer no resistance to Shakushain. So, again, they appealed to Fukuyama Castle. Hae elders, such as Chikunashi and Harou, understood that without outside assistance they would lose their territory to Shakushain. In the twelfth month of 1668, the two Hae elders departed for Fukuyama Castle. They asked

Matsumae officials for military hardware and other supplies, but the officials responded that there was no precedent for supplying weapons to Ainu—who in this context were formally characterized as peasants (*hyakushō*)—and therefore refused the request.[22]

Not ready to give up, Utomasa, a Saru elder who had married Onibishi's sister, departed for Fukuyama Castle in the fourth month of 1669 to request military aid again. Like Chikunashi and Harou, he was denied assistance. However, Matsumae officials recognized that something had to be done, and they agreed to send intermediaries to defuse the conflict. With that partial success, Utomasa headed home, but en route he died of smallpox at Nodaoi, near Oshamanbe. The Matsumae lord nevertheless dispatched the intermediaries, and a temporary peace settlement was reached. In the sixth month of 1669, however, Kakizaki Sakuzaemon, the gold-mining magistrate, reported that trade ships dispatched from Matsumae had been attacked by Ainu, and Japanese had been killed.[23] In this way, Matsumae was dragged into the violent war in eastern Ezo.

In this web of entangled Ainu-Japanese relations, Hae ties to the Matsumae family and the mining camp stand out as key factors in shaping alignments and defining the nature of the conflict. In the early years of the Shibuchari-Hae conflict, Hae Ainu had sought Matsumae intervention in what was a quarrel among Ainu. From at least the early 1660s onward, such Hae Ainu as Onibishi and Harou had worked through the mining camp and the gold-mining magistrate, Kakizaki Sakuzaemon, to resolve their war with the Shibuchari. Gold mining on the Shibuchari River, however, had always been a sore spot in Japanese–Shibuchari Ainu relations; and Onibishi, located upstream from the camp and probably indifferent to downstream damage, remained complacent, and even cooperative, toward Japanese commercial expansion.[24] No documents discussed up to this point specifically refer to the Hae Ainu's receiving military weaponry or supplies from the Japanese settlement, but the Shibuchari attack on Atsubetsu was repelled by some firearms (the smoke from the musket fire was reportedly thick), suggesting that Hae Ainu may have been secretly supplied with Japanese weapons or assisted by Japanese fighters bearing firearms.

Originally, then, the lines of this conflict were not drawn with ethnic distinctions in mind. Rather, competition over animals for ceremony and trade sparked the fighting among Ainu that eventually pitted Shakushain against the Matsumae lord, the ally of the Hae Ainu. Once Fukuyama appeared to side with Onibishi, Shakushain chose *Wajin*, "ethnic Japanese," as his primary targets, rallying other Ainu to his side. Here ethnicity did play an important role: Shakushain pitted himself and other Ainu throughout Hokkaido, Kunashir, and Iturup against the Matsumae family. As the war progressed, ethnicity developed into a powerful ingredient: neither side could lose sight of the fact that it was fighting a foreign people and, in the case of the Ainu, struggling to preserve a vanishing way of life.

THE RESPONSE OF THE EDO SHOGUNATE

Ōi Haruo has argued that Japanese documents related to Shakushain's War are so inconsistent that many specific details should be considered completely unreliable. He chastises historians for relying on existing documentation and suggests that archaeological and ethnographic data complicate the idea that Shakushain's War was an ethnic war between Japanese and Ainu.[25] Of course, Ōi is correct to point out that Japanese documentation distorts some information. However, neither the Ainu nor the Japanese were ever a unified ethnic block. The two documents that Ōi criticizes most diligently—the *Ezo hōki* and the *Tsugaru ittōshi*—were in fact written by authors who had very different perspectives, and, if used carefully, the documents shed a great deal of light on the events of the 1660s.

As his surname suggests, Matsumae Yasuhiro, who compiled the *Ezo hōki*, had patrilineal roots that extended to the Matsumae family. He also volunteered his services to lead Matsumae armies against Shakushain. However, he was a shogunal vassal (*koshōgumi*) dispatched from Edo as a military representative of the shogun. He betrayed his intense familial loyalties on several occasions, particularly when hunting down Hirosaki spies in Ezochi. He threatened to "shoot them on sight," because he thought they might soil the good name of the Matsumae family by spreading rumors that Wajinchi was a place "without order" (*buchōhō*).[26] Nonetheless, his report was probably meant to be an official shogunal record of the events of 1669. Much of it reads like a chronological list of events, mainly focusing on that year.

The editors of the *Tsugaru ittōshi* had a completely different agenda, as mentioned earlier, although their report was also requested by the shogunate, and it traces events back several decades prior to 1669.[27] Hirosaki domain went so far as to dispatch spies to interview Ainu chiefs, probably hoping to build a case of misrule against the Matsumae family. Weakening the position of Fukuyama Castle would have been a positive economic development for the other domains of northeastern Japan. So, just as there was no united front on the Ainu side, neither was there one on the Japanese side. Indeed, Luke Roberts suggests that the Tokugawa polity might best be described as a patchwork of small countries "that were individually strengthening their nature as countries in the realm of economic policy."[28] These small countries, spurred by both merchant and warrior interests, formulated policies to guard their economic interests, including instituting domainal import protections, marketing outside the domain, and fostering import-export economies. To a limited degree, domainal merchants even developed a sense of *kokueki,* "domainal prosperity," that ultimately shaped policy within the domain.[29] Mark Ravina, in his study of Japan's early-modern political economy, argues a similar case: it was with fiscal policy that domains were most concerned and where "shogunal control and oversight were weakest."[30] The domains of northeastern Japan, particularly Hirosaki, were no different (in fact Hirosaki is one of the domains investigated by Ravina), and they may have seen a politically weakened Matsumae family as an opportunity to profit financially and politically in trade.

The *Ezo hōki* explains that following the death of Utomasa in 1669 from smallpox, Shakushain dispatched Chimenha to the west and Uenshirushi to the east to meet with chiefdom elders. Shakushain's message was simple: he claimed that Matsumae had poisoned Utomasa and that next they planned to kill all the Ainu. He even called on Ainu from Sakhalin and the southern Kurils to cross over to Hokkaido and move against Kunnui and plunder provisions there. As the *Ezo hōki* speculates, Shakushain sought to create a united Ainu front (*ichimi*) against the Japanese. In return, he promised his allies "any land they wanted" and, even more importantly, "complete autonomy" (*jiyū*) from the Japanese.[31]

Attacks against Japanese began in the sixth month of 1669. On the fourteenth day of that month, Matsumae officials received reports that Shakushain had attacked Japanese in Shiraoi. Later, on the fifth day of the seventh month, officials received word that similar attacks had killed several Japanese in the west near Yoichi. As we have already seen, about 273 Japanese were reportedly killed in these initial attacks.[32] Late in the seventh month, Matsumae officials received reports that Shakushain had reached Etomo, near Muroran. He was about halfway between Shibuchari territory and Fukuyama Castle. The next day, Matsumae vassal Kakizaki Hiroshige was dispatched with the domainal army to Kunnui, where he made camp. Two days later, Shakushain launched a series of sorties against the Matsumae army at Kunnui, but stormy weather and flooding rivers forced him to retreat. A stalemate then ensued.[33]

Reports that Shakushain had "pillaged Japanese territory" quickly spread throughout Japan.[34] In the sixth month of 1669, the lord of Hirosaki, Tsugaru Nobumasa, received reports of the conflict while in Edo. He quickly made his way back to his domain in the northeast and started making plans to dispatch Hirosaki armies to Ezo from such ports as Ajigasawa, Ikarigaseki, and Tosaminato to intervene in the war if necessary. Edo insisted that Hirosaki armies were to be dispatched only under shogunal order and that, in the meantime, information was to be gathered through such spies as Sudō Sōemon and Yoshimura Jōzaemon.[35]

The Edo shogunate, acting as protector of the realm, then dispatched vassal Matsumae Yasuhiro, who had volunteered for the assignment, to command Matsumae armies against Shakushain. The war was an affair, the shogunate reasoned, best not left in the hands of the eleven-year-old lord of Fukuyama Castle, Norihiro. The *Tokugawa jikki* [True chronicles of the Tokugawa] explains the situation in Ezo as follows:

1669.7.20: On this day, *koshōgumi* Matsumae Hachizaemon Yasuhiro was given liege to proceed to Ezo. This [has to do with the events of the] eighteenth day [and the] Ainu chief named Shakushain. Factions bound together and rebelled. Nineteen merchant ships were plundered. Moreover, 273 Matsumae samurai, merchants and so forth were murdered. In response, we have received information that lord *hyōgo* [Matsumae] Norihiro dispatched a punitive force of about one thousand domain warriors. We intend to assist [this punitive force]. Orders have also been given to the Tsugaru [of Hirosaki domain] to mobilize reinforcements.

1669.9.28: For subduing the barbarians [*Ezo seibatsu no koto*], Matsumae *hyōgo* Norihiro was graciously lent three thousand bales of rice. These are to meet military expenses.

1669.10.11: Again, last month, on both the twenty-third and twenty-fourth days, fifty-five Ainu were arrested and incarcerated. This is information from Matsumae. . . .

1672.2.8: Matsumae Hachizaemon Yasuhiro. [He was] dispatched to Matsumae because the lord of the main house, Norihiro, is just a youth.[36]

Shortly after the fighting started in Ezo, as the *Tokugawa jikki* explains, the Edo shogunate took three critical steps to intervene in the war and assert its authority as protector of the realm. First, it ordered northeastern domains, such as Hirosaki, to prepare to provide military reinforcements under the realmwide regulations for military service, the *gun'yaku* system. Second, it sent provisions, three thousand bales of rice, to Fukuyama Castle to help finance the war effort. Third, it dispatched an eager Matsumae Yasuhiro, somebody who could bridge shogunal and Matsumae interests, to lead Matsumae armies against the defiant Shakushain.[37] Kikuchi Isao has emphasized this point, arguing that as a descendent of the Matsumae family, Yasuhiro had intense loyalties to his northern ancestors, but it should not be forgotten that he departed for Ezo under orders from shogun Tokugawa Ietsuna, as a representative of Edo. Yasuhiro was a Tokugawa vassal charged with "subduing the barbarians."[38] The shogunate, in other words, understood the conflict to be within the purview of its mandate to maintain the security of the realm. Resurrecting the fears of Ieyasu's day, rumors that Ainu might have contacted continental peoples, specifically the Tartar of Orankai, about a possible military alliance against the Matsumae probably brought shogunal concerns to a head. Hayashi Shunsai, an advisor to the shogunate, wrote,

I have heard rumors that merchants from Matsumae went to Ezo to buy falcons, whereupon the Ezo rose en masse and killed thirty people from

Matsumae. Some say that [the Ezo are intent on] attacking Matsumae, and consequently Matsumae is preparing for this. Others say that the Ezo are considering whether to seek the assistance of the Tatars [Orankai], and therefore the senior councillors gave orders to the Tsugaru family that in the case of an untoward turn of events at Matsumae they were to help them out; the Tsugaru will shortly return to their domain, prepare their forces and wait.[39]

As the Hirosaki lord was rushed back to his domain, the minds of shogunal officials might very well have been filled with images of North Asian hoards spilling in through Ezo and defeating the Matsumae, and possibly even the Edo shogunate, as the Manchu had the Ming dynasty only a few decades earlier in China.[40]

The northeastern domains were quickly organized for war. Under shogunal orders, Sugiyama Hachibei, a Tsugaru vassal, arrived in Wajinchi from Hirosaki in the ninth month of 1669 with over seven hundred Hirosaki troops. They made their headquarters at the Sennenji Temple and requested that they be allowed to proceed to Kunnui; but they were denied access to the battlefield and never saw any fighting. Matsumae Yasuhiro did allow an expeditionary force from Hirosaki to move as far as Ōno, near Hakodate, but by this time the conflict was basically over. In the eleventh month, Hirosaki troops departed Matsumae for home, arriving home three days later.[41]

Other domains also prepared to send reinforcements. Although they never made it to Matsumae, Akita officials Ishizuka Ichimasa and Tomura Kuranojō had made preparations for 1,322 Akita troops to depart for Ezo if ordered to do so by the shogunate.[42] Akita domain also dispatched official Ogawa Kyūemon to Fukuyama Castle to gather information for both domainal and shogunal officials.[43] Meanwhile, Okudera Hachizaemon and Nagata Zenzaemon, from neighboring Morioka domain, were ordered to gather information concerning the conflict. Morioka also dispatched Kawashima Kakuemon, Ōura Jiemon, and Tashiro Jingoemon to Noheji in preparation to cross over to Matsumae with domainal troops if ordered to do so by the shogunate. In this same capacity, Morioka dispatched Kurosawa Denbei and Nonomura Uemon to Tanabu.[44] The relative speed and decisiveness with which the shogunate dealt with Shakushain's War illustrates how the shogunate viewed its role on the borders of the realm. Within weeks of the initial reports from Ezo, the local military leadership of the Matsumae family was usurped by a Tokugawa vassal. This must have been a serious blow to the pride of Matsumae vassals such as Kakizaki Hiroshige, who led the first advance against Shakushain. Moreover, another point to consider is Tokugawa perceptions of the Manchu conquest of the Ming dynasty. In the mid–seventeenth century, Tokugawa officials had seriously mulled over the prospect of assisting Ming loyalists against the Manchu intruders, or at least supplying them with badly needed military aid; and Shakushain's War could have been seen in the same context. It is not unimaginable, for example, that Edo officials believed that the northern inhabitants of Ezo, with their Orankai allies, might too establish a conquest dynasty in Japan, only some sixty years after Ieyasu had established peace in the realm. Manchu armies might invade Japan via the northern route that Hideyoshi had considered to reach China. The Manchus, after all, came from this northern region and were familiar with the geography. Seen in this light, then, campaigns to "subdue the barbarians" were urgent prerogatives of the shogunate; after all, it was the imperial duty of the "barbarian-subduing generalissimo" (*seii taishō-gun;* the formal imperial title of the shogun) to defend the realm.

In the eighth month of 1669, Matsumae Yasuhiro arrived at Fukuyama Castle. He immediately assumed control over military operations, landing in Kunnui that same month. Following a meeting between Matsumae Yasuhiro and Kakizaki Hiroshige, about one thousand Matsumae troops departed for the Shibuchari region. Earlier, Satō Gonzaemon had landed in Biboku, just west of Shibuchari, while Kakizaki Sakuzaemon moved into Atsuma (Hamatsuma) in the Ibutsu (Yūfutsu) area. Matsumae Gizaemon and Niida Yoribei, two other domainal commanders, had moved to the Saru River region. They in effect surrounded Shakushain and called on him to submit gifts and end the fighting.[45] By this time both sides had sustained heavy casualties.

By the tenth month of 1669, Ainu in the east, including Shakushain, had surrendered to Matsumae armies after exchanging gifts. On the twenty-second day of the tenth month, however, while celebrating their newly forged peace settlement in Biboku with liberal helpings of saké, Shakushain, Chimenha, Uenshirushi, and other Ainu generals were cut down by Matsumae warriors.[46] Matsumae forces then burned the Shibu-chari *casi* to the ground. Two years later Kakizaki Hiroshige would lead domainal armies to disperse some contentious Ainu who had gathered in Shiraoi and Kunnui, but the conflict was basically over by the time Shakushain was killed at the end of 1669.

The shogunate rewarded Matsumae Yasuhiro with five hundred *koku* of rice and land for his efforts in "subduing the barbarians." In 1671, he attended an audience with the shogun and in 1672 became general inspector of Matsumae, or Matsumae *ometsuke*. That year, he again departed for Ezo with his three sons and more than one hundred attendants, arriving in Matsumae in the third month of 1672 to oversee the final settlement (*shioki*) with the Ainu.[47] Japanese who had collaborated with Shakushain—such as Sakuemon from Shōnai, Ichizaemon from Owari, and Sukenoshin (or Sukenojō) from Mogami—were executed on the spot. Shōdayū (from Sendai or possibly Echigo), a Japanese gold miner who was Shakushain's son-in-law, was burned at the stake in Biboku.[48] Again, the fact that some Japanese had sided with Ainu, and had in the end given their lives, illustrates that Shakushain's War was not only an ethnic conflict. Political, personal, and economic considerations also demarcated the two sides.

ecological

MATSUMAE'S TRADE POLICY AND SHAKUSHAIN'S WAR

Later investigations of Shakushain's War by Hirosaki spies exposed the fact that the origins of this conflict lay in inter-Ainu conflicts over natural resources that were made more inflammatory by Matsumae trade policies. Specifically, Japanese had begun to exploit Ainu with manipulative exchange rates, low-quality goods, and threats of violence, forcing some Ainu, such as groups around Yoichi, into a state of poverty and near starvation. Officials knew that Ainu had long relied on trade with Japanese and others, something that will be explored in more detail in the next chapter, but the domain used Ainu dependency to its own financial advantage. That is to say, what had changed was not the Ainu appetite for trade goods but Matsumae's success in establishing a monopoly role that it exploited with intensifying ruthlessness.

In 1670, the Hirosaki investigation uncovered these ruthless business practices in interviews with Ainu elders. Yoichi Ainu explained to Hirosaki official Maki Tadaemon that one reason Ainu from the west had participated in the conflict was that the Japanese way of doing business was corrupt. Particularly with regard to exchange rates, Ainu felt that they were being "badly ripped off" (*daibu no oshiuri*) by Matsumae vassals. Yoichi Ainu lamented that rice bales that had once contained nearly ten gallons now contained only about four gallons. Similarly, they described problems in the shellfish trade: "If, for example, one string of shellfish is missing from a bundle, the Matsumae make us pay twenty strings of shellfish the next year as interest. If we do not pay, our children are taken instead." Yoichi Ainu explained that Japanese trading practices had made their lives particularly difficult.[49]

A similar report came in 1670 from Kannishikoru of Shirifuka (near Iwanai). He told Maki that "in the old days," under Matsumae Yoshihiro, Ainu had received a large bale of rice for five bundles of dried salmon. But, Kannishikoru lamented, under the current economic policies of Kakizaki Hiroshige (clearly no friend of the Ainu, as he had led the initial military campaign at Kunnui in the seventh month of 1669), Ainu now received only a small bale for the same five bundles of salmon. "Because we are only Ainu it does not matter whether we say yes or no," he explained, and Ainu were forced to trade at these rates. Kannishikoru recalled that Ainu elders had lodged a complaint (*gososho*) with officials but were told that they were selfish to want better exchange rates.[50]

Harkening back to a time before Matsumae received exclusive rights to oversee trade in Ezo, Ishikari Ainu, speaking on behalf of Haukase, lamented that their ancestors had gone directly to Takaoka, the Hirosaki castle town, to trade. They explained that considering the way the Matsumae family did business, they should trade directly with Takaoka behind the back of Fukuyama Castle and its customs houses. They added that if they were allowed to trade directly with Takaoka, they might, for a change, acquire "high-quality rice."[51] In fact, Japanese merchants from

Ōmi may have advised Ainu to sidestep Matsumae middlemen in Ezo, which would have removed restrictions and increased profits for Ainu and merchants alike.[52] Surely, any such business practices may well have backfired, however, by placing increased economic pressure on Fukuyama Castle, making it all the more predatory.

The secret interviews conducted by Maki also shed light on the dire impact that trade was having on Ainu society. In the sixth month of 1670, Bikuni and Furubira Ainu arrived at Horomoi (possibly near Otoshibe) to help build a compound where *tsugunai* could be presented to Matsumae officials. They explained to Maki that during the exchange of *tsugunai* they planned to lodge a complaint to Matsumae officials concerning Japanese business practices. Similarly, chiefs from Sōya and Rishiri Island traveled to Horomoi to oversee the *tsugunai* ceremony. The trade embargo resulting from Shakushain's War had made life particularly difficult for Ainu in the north. Sōya and Rishiri chiefs warned that if the *tsugunai* ceremony failed and trading was not resumed, Ainu in that region would have grave problems.[53]

The Ainu need for trade was apparent nearly everywhere Maki stopped. He wrote that while at Oshoro Bay near Yoichi, sixty or seventy Ainu ventured out to the vessel and presented gifts (*shinmotsu*) every day. Maki told them in vain that trade was prohibited, and he noted in his report that he staunchly refused to accept any gifts. Under increasing Ainu pressure, however, he finally accepted a few items. Then Ainu quickly demanded something in return. It was obvious that they wanted to trade.[54] Maki wrote that it had been over a year since Yoichi Ainu had seen a merchant vessel, and they were facing possible starvation.[55] That Ainu were desperate for trade is revealed by another episode. At some earlier point, a messenger from Fukuyama Castle, following an exchange with Ishikari Ainu, had explained to Maki that when it came to trade, Ainu were extremely selfish. Not only did they take merchandise designated for trade, but, the messenger said, "if you are not careful they often take supplies and luggage not meant to be traded."[56]

Even during Shakushain's War, military commanders had recognized the Ainu dependency on trade and had used it to their strategic advantage. After Shakushain evacuated the Shibuchari region toward Kusuri, he threatened that no matter how many years or lives it took, Ainu would not give up their struggle. Unmoved, military commanders countered that the absence of trade in Ezo would cause serious problems for Ainu; the commanders considered Ainu unable to subsist without goods from Japan. Commanders warned the Ainu that whether by military force or by trade embargo, Matsumae troops would be able to do as they pleased.[57] This is not to say that the Matsumae family was not also dependent on trade; it was, but it was able to fall back on assistance from Edo in the form of rice and military aid. If we discount possible overtures to Orankai, Shakushain had enjoyed no such luxury.

In one final episode, in the fourth month of 1670, Maki reported that Ishikari and Shirifuka Ainu were talking of renewing the struggle against Matsumae armies, as they had heard that Matsumae armies intended to "kill all the Ainu" anyway. However, revealing their desire to trade, spokesmen for the Yoichi Ainu pleaded with Haukase of the Ishikari Ainu that renewing the struggle would mean a delay in the renewal of trade, and possibly starvation. The Yoichi Ainu, badly in need of supplies, asked the Ishikari and Shirifuka Ainu to give up their plans. The Ishikari Ainu, under Haukase, had in fact built a camp at the mouth of the Ishikari River with over three hundred huts, and they were prepared to renew the conflict. But they yielded to pressure from other Ainu chiefdoms.[58]

These examples might seem to belabor the point, but the social upheaval caused by Shakushain's War revealed tears in Ainu autonomy. Shakushain's War was possibly the only occasion between 1590 and 1800 in which Japanese halted most trade with Ainu, and the trade stoppage exposed the degree to which Ainu had come to depend on trade. At almost every juncture, particularly in the west, Maki Tadaemon encountered reminders of the Ainu desire for trade. He described Ainu from Yoichi as "starving" for trade, suggesting that they may have been threatened with famine. Clearly, rice and other goods obtained in trade had long since become elements in the subsistence systems of Ainu in western Ezo, thus intensifying the dire impact of Matsumae's monopoly on trade.

In 1669, Ainu struck out at Japanese for what they considered economic abuses, but those very actions exposed their dependence on their enemy. Matsumae's trade policies, the brainchild of Kakizaki Hiroshige, threatened the Ainu's basic ability to subsist. Ethnicity may have played a role in defining sides in this conflict, but the roots of Shakushain's War lay in social and economic changes affecting Ainu communities. Even while the war was underway, ethnic lines were often blurred. The large contingent of *mikataezo*, that is, Ainu friendly to Fukuyama Castle, and the several Japanese who fought with Shakushain illustrate that ethnicity only partially explains the demarcation of sides in this conflict. That the *mikataezo* were from areas close to Wajinchi suggests that their lives had become altered by constant contact with Japan. When pulled from both sides—to join Lord Norihiro or Shakushain—they moved toward Japan, to which their economic futures were most visibly tied. It is also difficult to overestimate the role that fear of Japanese retribution might have played in these choices.

In the eyes of Matsumae officials, Ainu designs for unrestricted trade cut to the heart of their domain's political and economic role in Ezo and threatened its place in the Tokugawa polity. By attempting to circumvent customs houses, some Ainu sought to completely work around official commercial channels in Wajinchi. Their struggle was geared toward asserting their rights as semi-autonomous maritime people who could trade with whom they wanted, and this posture challenged the very foundation of the Japanese presence in southern Ezo.

CONCLUSION

Shakushain's War stands out as a watershed event in the history of the conquest of Ezo. Shakushain exploded onto the scene as a charismatic leader who proved able to bridge regional differences among Ainu communities, threatening to unite them against the Japanese intrusion from the south. The Edo shogunate reacted by solidifying its own united front of military allies in the northeast, replacing local Matsumae generals with men of its own choosing, thus illustrating its self-appointed role as defender of the realm. Matsumae's exploitative trade policies and other provocations prodded Shakushain to launch the 1669 conflict, but at the same time they assured his defeat. Powerful chiefs were born from trade with the Japanese; they even adorned themselves, and solidified their political power, with goods acquired at trading posts. Chiefs such as Shakushain possessed "many utensils" and "good land" and controlled considerable spheres of influence. They needed these spheres to assure themselves of access to fur-bearing animals that could be killed, processed, and traded for items of prestige and wealth within their chiefdoms. The original border disputes between Hae and Shibuchari Ainu were rooted in conflicts such as these, struggles over animals for subsistence, trade, and ritual. By the mid–seventeenth century, therefore, trade had taken its toll on Ainu society. The trade embargo against Shakushain exposed the fact that Ainu were unable to execute, because of economic dependency, a final military bid to defend their lands from Japanese conquest. So, we must now turn our attention to the roots of this dependency on trade.

3 The Ecology of Ainu
Autonomy and Dependence

We have seen that trade and other forms of contact with Japanese sparked the changes in Ainu society that provided the dangerous kindling for the outbreak of Shakushain's War. Powerful chiefdoms such as the Hae and Shibuchari, who shared a common border along the upper section of the Shibuchari River, fought sporadically over access to animals for subsistence, ritual, and trade. In the midst of the fighting, Matsumae generals understood that their trade embargo in Ezo remained the single most effective means to bring the defiant Shakushain to his knees; and as reported by Maki Tadaemon, the embargo had left groups around Yoichi on the verge of starvation at the conclusion of the conflict. If Shakushain's War exposed the tears in Ainu autonomy that existed even in the late 1660s, the aftermath of the war enlarged the tears, as the rapid construction of trading posts throughout the late seventeenth century made Ainu even more dependent on these posts for their livelihood. Throughout Matsumae's tenure as overseer of the trade with Ainu, threats to halt trade remained the most effect method to wield influence over even the most powerful chiefs. As discussed in chapter 6, when the shogunate dispatched officials to investigate the "secret" Russian trade in the 1780s, Matsumae officials warned Ainu elders that if they spoke openly about the trade with shogunal officials, the elders would be gouged to death with spears; but equally damaging, at least from the perspective of Ainu communities, was the threat that Matsumae would stop dispatching trade ships. It appears that with Japanese goods so readily available, Ainu became reliant on imported grains and fabrics to feed and clothe their families; and other merchandise became tied to Ainu political hierarchies, perceptions of personal wealth, and ritual life. Subsequently, at the same time that Ainu came to depend on and draw personal prestige from trade goods, we will see later that they overexploited animals and fisheries that were critical to their survival and were needed to pay for imports.

AINU SUBSISTENCE PRACTICE AND DEPENDENCY

Any analysis of Ainu dependency must begin with a brief discussion of the term "dependency" as it is used in this study. Richard White applies dependency theory to the history of three North American Indian nations in his signal work, *The Roots of Dependency*. He identifies social changes that occurred in the Choctaw, Pawnee, and Navajo nations as a result of trade with Europeans. He argues that dependency among Native Americans meant that people "who had once been able to feed and clothe themselves with some security became unable to do so. Environments that had once easily sustained Native American populations underwent increasing degradation as familiar resources could not support the peoples who depended on them."[1]

White concludes that the cultural and economic impact of the market economy, more than any other single force, destroyed Native American subsistence systems and undermined their autonomy. The "productive systems" of these peoples, he notes, were "geared toward subsistence rather than the market," and as Native Americans overextended hunting to meet market demands, they became dependent on Europeans for their survival.[2] He cautions, however, that dependency should not be viewed as simply an economic or material condition. Instead, because Native Americans projected their relationship with the environment through their own cultural lens, dependency also meant deep and, ultimately, fatal cultural and political changes among Native American nations.

Ainu subsistence practice and material culture underwent a similar transformation in the seventeenth and eighteenth centuries. Matsumae vassals, under the trade-fief system, built trading posts in the most potentially lucrative parts of Ezochi, strategically choosing watersheds, coastal streams, bays, and other places near Ainu communities. At these sites they gradually commodified local fauna—that is, they identified what White calls the "animals of enterprise," resources upon which Ainu subsistence and social autonomy had depended for centuries, but which would now serve the growing market economy in Japan.[3] Consequently, Ainu productive systems changed, and the purpose of hunting and fishing became the acquisition of the political power and personal prestige that animal skins bought at trading posts. These changes were accompanied by shifts in deeper sentiments about killing animals. In time, deer and salmon, critical to Ainu survival, became overhunted and overfished. Pressure from hunting, combined with other environmental factors such as pestilence and hard weather, drove game from habitual feeding grounds. Ainu became dependent on goods acquired in trade to supplement their weakening subsistence system as the salmon and deer, which had once fed and clothed their communities, were exported to satisfy new Ainu wants, as well as commercial demand in Japan.[4]

Historically, the distribution of animal life on the island known today as Hokkaido was shaped by regional plant and climatic diversity, and so, therefore, was the distribution of Matsumae trading posts in the seventeenth and eighteenth centuries. Generally speaking, the western section of Hokkaido receives heavy snowfall in the winter, whereas the eastern section receives a comparatively moderate blanket. Such animals as deer, brown bear, marten, red fox, and the Steller's sea eagle, all important products in trade, migrated to eastern Ezo every winter in search of food.[5] There, Ainu hunters trapped and shot them for their hides and feathers.

Trade records note that with the exception of posts located at Sōya in the north, and on the lower section of the Ishikari River, where "Ainu brought animal skins down from the headwaters," furs and feathers were not major trade items at the other twenty-six posts in western Ezo. Posts there were almost exclusively for fisheries. Posts east of Lake Shikotsu, however, handled a variety of pelts, feathers, and other goods, as well as fish products.[6] The Steller's sea eagle, for example, which bred on the coasts of the Okhotsk Sea as far north as the Kamchatka Peninsula and then migrated to the inland marshes near Kusuri (present-day Kushiro) to winter, was a valuable trade commodity because Japan's warrior elite used its feathers, called *maba*, as fletching on their arrows.[7] Although there was some trade in eagle feathers on Sakhalin Island, most of them moved through posts at Kusuri, Akkeshi, and Kiitappu, all in eastern Ezo.[8]

The type and distribution of natural resources in Ezo shaped Matsumae's economy in other ways as well. Sakakura Genjirō, an official from a Japanese mining house, pointed out that Matsumae's economy differed radically from that of other early-modern domains. For example, the Matsumae family did not encourage wetland rice cultivation, as other warrior houses did. Sakakura explained that this was not because of poor land quality but because rice cultivation would have interrupted harvesting of the more lucrative fisheries. He remarked that most settlers in Wajinchi devoted the majority of their time to herring and salmon.[9] Matsumae vassals, however, collected their stipends from trading with Ainu, much as vassals from Tsushima domain survived on trade with Korea.

Ainu subsistence, as well, was shaped by the distinctive landscape of Ezo. No two Ainu communities undertook exactly the same subsistence activity, so it is important to explore the political and environmental factors that determined intercommunity variation. Although Ainu today sometimes use the term *Aynu-mosir*, "human land," to harken back to a day when Ezo was the "last free land of the Ainu,"[10] the term, however appealing, belies the linguistic regionalism and political disunity that actually prevailed in Ezo. Kaiho Mineo argues that the Ainu of the early

Tokugawa years can be divided into five broad political spheres united under figures called "greater generals" (sōtaishō) in the Japanese sources: (1) the Shumukuru (Ainu, Sarunkur) group, inhabiting the region roughly between Niikappu and Mukawa; (2) the Menashikuru (Ainu, Menaskur) group, located between Shizunai and Urakawa; (3) the Ishikari group, inhabiting the Ishikari plain; (4) the Uchiura group, inhabiting the region between Shirikishinai and Otoshibe; and (5) the Sōya group of northern Ezo.[11] Kaiho draws almost exclusively on political and social dissimilarities when demarcating these spheres, and his divisions correspond to those identified by Kōno Hiromichi. Kōno, who conducted studies of Ainu burial rituals in the 1930s, divided Hokkaido Ainu into spheres that closely resemble Kaiho's.[12]

However, even more central than abstract political spheres in shaping Ainu identity were patrilineal political alignments called petiwor, or river-based chiefdoms, which were composed of several villages situated along major watersheds or coastal rivers and their tributaries. These Ainu chiefdoms were basically spatial units demarcated by the boundaries of such subsistence practices as hunting, fishing, and plant gathering. Inhabitants of a particular petiwor also linked their identity to a powerful sine itokpa, or a patrilineal household, with a single-male ancestral symbol such as markings on an arrow shaft; and this household served as the political center of the chiefdom.[13] In any given chiefdom, moreover, Ainu had self-declared rights to exploit resources within that productive space. These rights were articulated and sanctioned metaphysically rather than economically or politically, and chiefdom borders were authenticated by a sacred relationship that Ainu groups cultivated with local kamuy, or gods, which largely took animal forms.

Ainu viewed the natural environment of Ezo as a sacred space teeming with kamuy in the form of animals, plants, fish, and even contagions. To kill an animal to feed and clothe one's family was to free the kamuy from its ephemeral temporal guise, a process that involved the active participation of the animal and that was construed by Ainu as a spiritual act which legitimized their place in the natural landscape. Only worthy hunters killed game (see figure 6). Gestures of atonement for animal slaughter, which took the form of sacred acts directed at animals and

Figure 6.   Ainu hunting a bear. Ainu folklore often stressed that only virtuous hunters, those who had high moral character and conducted rituals aimed at the myriad deities, were able to kill game such as brown bear. It was, suggests this folklore, the bear god that willingly made itself available to hunters of such worthy character. Ainu hunted these larger animals with handheld bows, or *caniku*, using poison arrows called *surkuay. Tōkai yawa* [Night talk from eastern Ezo]. Courtesy of the Resource Collection for Northern Studies, Hokkaido University Library.

fish, appeared both in the hunt and later in ceremony. In the most idealistic sense, animals were often seen as willing participants in the kill. Drawing on Ainu folklore, for example, Honda Katsuichi emphasizes this point through a fictional Ainu orator, or *ekashi,* who transports us into the mind of the bear god. "Even the highest-ranked gods must visit the land of the *ainu* [humans] every few years," the bear god explains. "They don't visit just any *ainu,* of course, but they pick one who's skilled at making *inau* [ceremonial fetishes] and is good-natured."[14]

In Honda's story, having found such a worthy Ainu, the bear god describes his encounter with the Ainu hunter, "[I] wandered out purposefully to be seen by him, whereupon he swiftly hid behind a tree and put an arrow to his bow as he waited for me. Pretending not to notice, I passed by him. The twang of the bowstring sounded, and the god of the arrow pierced me. As I heard the bowstring sound two or three times more, I lost consciousness." The hunter then brings the large bear back to his *kotan*, where "songs and dances were performed," and the bear is struck by the dancing of a youth. Exposing Ainu attitudes about the kill, the bear explains, "I again received many gifts and was sent back to the land of the gods, but still remained in the dark about the youth. I went down to Ainu Moshir repeatedly in order to be shot by an arrow and invited to the *kotan* so that I could find out about him and see more of his mesmerizing dances."[15] Ainu hunters killed these animal-gods, in other words, because they chose to be killed. James Serpell, writing of hunting peoples in general, makes this point as well. He explains that the "successful hunter achieves his goal, not primarily through practical knowledge or skill, but rather by virtue of his respectful attitudes and behavior toward the quarry." Only then, Serpell continues, "will the animals consider him worthy of the gift of meat and allow themselves to be killed."[16] These observations, for the most part, hold true for Ainu as well, as highlighted by the above ethnographic account.

The identities of local Ainu groups, furthermore, were taken from these river-based chiefdoms. Ainu from the Saru River were known— and knew themselves—as Sarunkur, "people of the Saru River" (the term *kur* means "people"). The strong ties to the region around the Shibuchari River felt by both the Shibuchari and Hae Ainu prior to Shakushain's War stand out as an example of local identity. Sources such as the *Tsugaru ittōshi* specifically referred to the two groups involved in the war as the Menashikuru (Shibuchari) and the Haekuru (Hae), suggesting that they had forged local identities that they had communicated to Japanese. So does a later instance observed by Matsuura Takeshirō, a shogunal official. He noted that in eastern Ezo, where competition over resources was most acute, chiefdoms even erected boundary poles to demarcate their territorial base.[17] Most of these river-based chiefdoms appear initially to have been self-sustaining, under normal circumstances providing the salmon and deer necessary to feed and clothe their inhabitants.[18]

Figure 7. A spring-bow trap. Ainu hunters used these traps, called *kuari* or *amappo*, to kill the more crafty fur-bearing animals such as the northern fox. The skins of these animals were traded with Japanese at trading posts for rice, tobacco, saké, and other goods. *Ezotō kikan* [Strange sights from Ezo Islands]. Courtesy of the Resource Collection for Northern Studies, Hokkaido University Library.

Hunting was critical to the survival of all Ainu chiefdoms, and they divided deer- and bear-hunting into spring and autumn tasks. The autumn deer hunt, called *yuk iramante*, played a particularly valuable role in Ainu subsistence because dried venison butchered in the autumn sustained them throughout the winter months.[19] Excellent hunters, Ainu used a variety of methods to kill deer, bear, and small game. However, the hand-held bow (*caniku*) and the spring-bow trap (*kuari* or *amappo*) remained the weapons of choice until the Meiji government prohibited their use and modified deer-hunting regulations throughout Hokkaido in the 1870s (see figure 7).[20] Ainu hunters equipped the spring-bow trap with bamboo arrowheads laced with an aconite poison (*surkuay*), using it in coordina-

Figure 8. Ainu fishing for salmon, the "divine fish," with a *marep,* a traditional harpoonlike instrument. *Ezotō kikan* [Strange sights from Ezo Islands]. Courtesy of the Resource Collection for Northern Studies, Hokkaido University Library.

tion with a deer fence built along game trails to steer deer toward the loaded traps.[21]

Also critical to Ainu subsistence were the watersheds and coastal rivers of Ezo. In the summer and autumn months they filled with spawning trout and salmon, providing a variety of fish that were inseparably tied to the survival and ritual life of all river-based Ainu chiefdoms. In the summer, Ainu fished for diadromous trout (*icaniw* or *icanuy*; trout that migrated between salt and fresh waters), undertaking no major hunting trips that might divert their energies. Similarly, salmon—which Ainu believed to be *kamuy-cep,* the "divine fish"—began moving upstream in large numbers in the autumn to spawn. Ainu fished for salmon and trout using nets worked from small boats (*yasya*) and basket traps (*uray*) placed in holding waters. They also hunted from small huts (*oruncise*) using a *marep,* a harpoonlike instrument with a hook at the end (see figure 8).[22]

Of course, these fish and game, which were most important to Ainu survival and ritual, never stayed in one location; and chiefdom boundaries tended to be elastic or overlap to accommodate game migration. When spawning salmon first entered major rivers such as the Tokachi or Saru in eastern Ezo, for example, many Ainu from chiefdoms upstream would travel down to the mouth of the river, seeking permission from local elders to fish salmon fresh from the ocean. Later, as the salmon approached their upstream spawning beds, Ainu from chiefdoms near the mouth of these same rivers might travel upstream to fish salmon there. Chiefdoms negotiated access to these resources. It was also at these fluid and poorly defined boundaries where the rights to resources were sometimes disputed, and chiefdom wars, such as that between the Shibuchari and Hae Ainu, erupted when animals or fish became scarce or when pressure for trade increased. Trading posts further aggravated these border relations by increasing the value of the resources that lay within chiefdom boundaries.

EARLY MINING ACTIVITY
AND ENVIRONMENTAL DEGRADATION IN EZO

Early on, Matsumae economic activity began to disrupt Ainu subsistence practice. Shortly after its investiture with exclusive rights to trade with Ainu, the Matsumae family sought to diversify the kinds of resources it exploited in Ezochi. In 1604, as noted, the shogunal official Honda Masanobu spoke with Matsumae Yoshihiro about the possibility of mining gold in Ezo. By 1617, gold miners, using placer techniques, had begun extracting gold from streams in Sotsuko and Ōsawa on the Oshima Peninsula, and in 1620, the Matsumae lord, Kinhiro, presented one hundred *ryō* in gold, which Japanese had extracted from these sites, as a gift to shogun Tokugawa Hidetada. At that time, the Matsumae lord received approval from shogunal officials Doi Toshikatsu, a senior councillor, and Aoyama Tadatoshi to continue opening new mining sites in Ezo.[23] By then, Matsumae's gold-mining operations and salmon fisheries were starting to disrupt Ainu seasonal fishing in eastern Ezo, placing new pressure on chiefdom boundaries and Ainu-Japanese relations.

Under the direction of domainal officials Kakizaki Hiroshige and Satō

Kaemon, Fukuyama Castle intensified placer mining, moving deeper into Ezochi. By 1628, miners were extracting large amounts of gold from the headwaters of the Shiriuchi River in western Ezo. Only three years later, they were also extracting gold from Shimakomaki, also in western Ezo, and by 1633, they had moved into the Shibuchari and Kenomai Rivers in eastern Ezo. By 1635, miners had taken gold from streams in Tokachi and Unbetsu (near Samani), in the Hidaka region of eastern Ezo, and from Kunnui and the headwaters of the Yūbari River.[24] It was at one of these mining camps that Bunshirō worked, and there he fostered the strong ties to Onibishi that so frustrated and, ultimately, angered Shakushain, helping to spark Shakushain's War.

The seventeenth century also witnessed the expansion of mining in Japan. One reason was that precious metals—gold, silver, and copper— were the major Japanese export commodities in the early Tokugawa years. Facilitating both the expansion of the mining industry and the exploitation of these valuable resources were technological innovations in excavation, drainage, surveying, and smelting.[25] In fact, foreign trade "speeded the pace of innovation by increasing the demand first for silver and later for gold and copper."[26] The Matsumae family used a variety of techniques to extract gold from Wajinchi and, later, Ezochi; and most techniques involved redirecting the river's current to flush out or expose metal deposits.[27]

In Japan, as elsewhere, such placer mining techniques had the potential to devastate rivers and local fisheries. While in Wajinchi, Portuguese missionary Diego Carvalho observed some local mining operations:

> Their way of extracting gold from these mines is as follows. When they have decided on the mountain range in which, according to experts, there ought to be gold, friends and acquaintances get together and united in a body purchase from the *tono* [lord] of Matsumae so many *ells* [one *ell* is about forty-five inches] of one of the rivers which flow through the said range, for so many bars of gold, and they must needs pay these bars whether they find gold or not. And when a great number of such groups come to the river, they divert the flow of water along a different course and then dig into the sand which remains, until they reach the living stone and rock beneath the river bed. And in the sand lodged in the rents and fissures of the rock is found gold as fine as beach gravel.[28]

and lead to Ainu Starvation

Tawara Hiromi, pointing to the impact of this process, argues that altering the flow of streams and depositing large quantities of sediment in the water likely disrupted migrating salmon and destroyed spawning beds.[29] In 1724, for example, merchants reported that more than two hundred Ainu had starved to death in the Ishikari region because of poor salmon runs. That same year, moreover, widespread starvation was reported in the Lake Shikotsu area.[30]

Indeed, one Ainu *yukar*, or epic poem, from the Hidaka region suggests that gold mining—under the auspices of Bunshirō, who, as mentioned, oversaw the Japanese camp established along the Shibuchari River—sparked Shakushain's War.[31] Bunshirō and his miners had badly churned up the Shibuchari River, preventing salmon from ascending the river to spawn. Local Ainu from Peppana, Ichipu, and Rupeshipe, all in the Shibuchari area, found themselves with a dangerously limited supply of fish for the coming winter. Ainu chiefs protested but were treacherously murdered. The *yukar* indicates that when Shakushain heard this, he launched an attack against Japanese, killing hundreds, many of them miners.[32] No doubt this story oversimplifies the origins of the conflict, but it is known that Shakushain's attitude toward Japanese miners, who disrupted his streams and allied themselves with Onibishi, was less than congenial. It is important to remember that he had burned Bunshirō's house to the ground. Matsumae's financial needs had thus already had an impact on Ainu living in the early seventeenth century, weakening their subsistence practice through environmental degradation. Whether the Hidaka poem accurately describes events leading up to Shakushain's War is less important than the fact that poor salmon runs were clearly disastrous for Ainu.

Gold mining, however, was not the only Japanese enterprise that degraded salmon fisheries. In 1670, Maki Tadaemon, the Hirosaki domain spy who, as we have seen, had clandestinely entered Ezochi to gather information, made stops at Horomoi, Oshoro, and Nomanai and spoke with local Ainu elders.[33] He directly solicited reports from elders as far north as Rishiri and Sōya, in northern Ezo, about the causes of Shakushain's War. Kannishikoru, the elder from the Shirifuka region, complained that Japanese merchants in search of salmon had recently entered Ezochi in large numbers. He explained that "they cast huge nets in the rivers and the salmon that they catch are all taken to markets in Kamigata [Kyoto and vicinity] for sale."[34] Kannishikoru also noted that Ainu had approached Matsumae officials, pleading that if they took all the salmon, Ainu would be unable to feed themselves. Officials answered by beating them and accusing them of being greedy. The officials explained to Kannishikoru that these rivers were now trade fiefs (*chigyōsho*), which must have surprised Kannishikoru, who considered himself chief of Shirifuka.[35]

GRAIN IN AINU SUBSISTENCE AND DEPENDENCY

The regional disappearance of resources such as salmon was not the only result of Matsumae's economic activity; trade proved a double-edged sword for most Ainu. At the same time that trade provided Ainu with the impetus to increase their hunting and fishing activity, it also introduced Japanese grain, which began to supplement their diet, further nurturing dependency. With the intensification of trade with Japanese, the importance of Japanese grains in the Ainu diet appears to have increased markedly.[36] Matsumae Norihiro, for example, wrote to Edo senior councillors in 1715 that Ainu predominantly subsisted on bear, herring, whale, fur seal, and a variety of fisheries. He also included rice among common Ainu foods, noting that with the exception of millet and lily grass, Ainu raised few grains but ate a substantial amount of rice acquired in trade. He remarked that they were also extremely fond of tobacco and saké.[37]

Yamamoto Tadashi argues that one reason eighteenth-century Ainu ate so much rice was that Fukuyama Castle prohibited them from raising their own grains. Pointing to archaeological evidence from the Usujiri site in Minamikayabe, he speculates that Ainu had long cultivated simple grains but that the Japanese prohibited them from raising traditional crops, as well as rice.[38] With rice and saké being lucrative export products in domainal trade, Matsumae officials used local prohibitions to nurture Ainu dependency on Japanese cereals and saké, thus bolstering activity at trading posts. In 1786, shogunal official Matsumoto Hidemochi recorded that Matsumae lords prohibited Ainu from raising grain. One of the explanations given was that Matsumae's "financial circumstances" necessitated the prohibition. And around 1790, Mogami Tokunai, another shogunal official, wrote that the local regulations of Fukuyama Castle prohibited Japanese from bringing seeds, for rice or any other grain, into Ezochi. He remarked that because of these prohibitions, "Ainu do not understand the way to cultivate grains, and would not even know a rice field if they saw one." This was why, he concluded, erroneously it appears, "they eat only fish and animal flesh."[39] Maintaining the vitality of Matsumae's trading posts required that trade regulations be aimed at fostering demand for Japanese goods. It was clear to the domain's officials that the demand for Japanese grain was central to their survival in the early-modern polity and to commercial expansion into Ezochi.

During the same 1780s investigation that produced Matsumoto Hidemochi's comments, Satō Genrokurō, a shogunal official, wrote that at one point Ainu from the upper section of the Ishikari River had successfully cultivated a plot of rice, but when Fukuyama Castle caught wind of the enterprise, Matsumae officials were dispatched, and they ripped up the seedlings and forced the Ainu involved to offer amends. On another occasion, Satō was asked by Shonko, a chief from eastern Ezo, for seeds and information on how to cultivate them. He explained that Matsumae regulations prohibited Ainu from learning how to cultivate these important crops.[40] It is unlikely that Shonko received any seeds, but there was no shortage of rice being shipped to Ezo, both for trade and for consumption by Japanese in Wajinchi. A shogunal inspector was informed in 1761 that 40,291 *koku* of rice entered Ezo from Japan.[41] In 1788, only twenty-seven years later, Mogami recorded that the Matsumae family imported 66,700 *koku* of Morioka, Hirosaki, Sendai, Echigo, Sakata, Shirakawa, and Shibata rice. Of this total, Matsumae vassals used 10,000 *koku* for trade (5,000 *koku* in eastern Ezo and 5,000 *koku* in western Ezo).[42]

A second explanation for agriculture's role in the development of Ainu dependency has to do with the gender dynamics of Ainu productive systems. Tessa Morris-Suzuki argues that there were actually two types of farming in Ainu communities: dog farming and small-scale shifting cultivation. Dog farming was largely confined to Sakhalin Ainu, who raised dogs for hunting, sled hauling, companionship, and food.[43] In shifting

cultivation, crops such as sorghum, millet, beans, barley, and some veg-
etables were cared for largely by women in the summer months. Women
collected wild plants as well. The notion that Ainu ate only flesh, Morris-
Suzuki submits, is part of a deeply rooted intellectual misconception. If
Ainu are in fact the descendants of the Epi-Jōmon culture, or even the
slightly later Yayoi and Kofun cultures (200–650 C.E.), that would make
their ancestors participants in the earliest forms of "Japanese" agricultural society. She continues that when Ainu women, the backbone of
Ainu agriculture, left their plots to work in nearby fisheries, their community's subsistence system weakened as a result. Thus, agriculture, although small-scale compared to some Japanese standards, was a crucial
component in the emergence of Ainu dependency.[44]

With declines in game supplies, prohibitions against cultivating grain
or even importing seeds into Ezochi, and changes in the gender dynamics of community agriculture, Ainu became increasingly dependent on
rice acquired in trade. Matsumae's rice and yeast (kōji) were essential in-
gredients in making saké, which in the seventeenth century became an
ever-present feature of Ainu rituals and daily life. These prohibitions
were aimed at preserving, or even creating, Ainu demand for Japanese
products. To what degree Ainu actually became dependent on Japanese
grain is in truth impossible to determine. Most likely, grain never constituted a large enough portion of the Ainu diet to seriously undermine
their ability to subsist. But Japanese prohibitions such as these expose
both the Matsumae reliance on trade and officials' halfhearted attempt to
organize a conscious policy geared toward engendering dependency.
Matsumae officials nurtured Ainu dependency with strict regulations because they believed that their own economic survival, and political autonomy in Ezo, were contingent upon it.

AINU EXPORTS TO JAPAN

Hunted Commodities

Prior to the early 1620s, trade between Ainu and Japanese was conducted only at Fukuyama (see figure 9). Once a year different Ainu groups

Figure 9.   Archaeological remains from the old port at Matsumae (Fukuyama).
The land mass visible in the distance is Honshu Island as seen from southern
Hokkaido.

traveled to Fukuyama Castle in small Ainu crafts called *nawatojibune* in
Japanese to trade with merchants and Matsumae lords. While in Fukuyama, the traders stayed in temporary huts (*marugoya*) built along the
beaches.[45] These huts, which Ainu traders built just outside of Fukuyama,
highlighted the temporary character of this trade, with Ainu traveling
long distances for a limited season of exchange. Although the volume of
this trade was modest, it brought into the castle town many of the goods
that Japanese later exported via trading posts.

   However, after Shakushain's War, Matsumae leaders expanded trade
by distributing trade fiefs, strategically placing them along coastal rivers
in Ezochi. The locus of trade, now the trading post, was thus brought
closer to traditional Ainu hunting and fishing grounds. This change laid
the foundation for the rise of the market culture that surrounded the
trading post and helped engender Ainu dependency. Unlike in the early

in Ezochi ≠ instead
of Fukuyama

Fukuyama exchange, trade schedules now were, of necessity, coordinated with Ainu seasonal hunting and fishing, and commerce was now more closely synchronized with the rhythms of Ainu subsistence practice and ritual life. Many Japanese goods were readily available at these posts and were integrated into Ainu ritual and domestic life. From this point forward, Ainu subsistence practice functioned less and less independently of Japanese economic concerns in Ezo.

Satō Genrokurō recorded that in the northwest, the Matsumae trading post at Sōya was opened up in the 1680s; and in the east, Akkeshi was opened up in the 1640s, Kiitappu in the late seventeenth century, and Kunashir Island in the 1750s. He noted that Matsumae used these posts exclusively for trade with Ainu.[46] By the late eighteenth century such merchants as Hidaya Kyūbei, who contracted out trading posts in the east, had transformed some trading posts from crude shacks to virtual markets, offering traders a variety of services ranging from lodging to transportation.[47]

Satō wrote that Fukuyama Castle had originally regulated trade with Japan proper through the customs houses, or *okinokuchi bugyō*, permitting trade in Ezo only once a year. However, as merchants opened up branch shops (*demise*) in such ports as Esashi and Hakodate, they began bypassing the houses and trading directly in Ezochi. When Satō questioned Matsumae vassals as to why they permitted merchants to bypass the houses, they responded evasively; merchants who did this were in "special ships" (*negaibune*), they argued, regulated by officials in Matsumae, Hakodate, and Esashi.[48] Leveling what became a common attack on the situation in Wajinchi, Satō argued that the Matsumae family was blurring the social distinction between merchants and warriors, one of the hallmarks of the Confucian-inspired authorizing strategy of the early-modern regime. He noted that "in Matsumae, what vassals do and what merchants do is, of course, the same thing." Domain elder Matsumae Kenmotsu, he explained, "does not have his own store, but on his trade fief he does basically the same thing that merchants do." Even the town magistrate, Kudō Heizaemon, collected his income from a nearby trading post.[49] This blurring of the line between warrior and merchant became a major bone of contention for those who wanted the Edo

Why does this matter?

shogunate to take control of Ezo. They argued that domain vassals myopically concerned with buying and selling were hardly in a position to properly govern the northern boundary.

The reliance on trade, as well as the fuzzy distinction between warrior and merchant, existed further south as well, especially in Tsushima domain. In the early seventeenth century, Tsushima had received rights (*kayaku*) to control foreign trade with Korea, and the shogunate encouraged Tsushima-Korea relations thereafter, lest the domain come to Edo looking for financial aid during a trade slump. Profits from trade became a substantial portion of the revenues for Tsushima and its vassals, and even as late as the nineteenth century, the domain imported Korean beans, carrots, cotton, and rice for domain consumption and for vassal stipends.[50] Further south, inhabitants of Satsuma domain improved their lifestyles through profits from trade with China via the Ryukyu Kingdom.[51] Not only rice stipends, then, but also trade was central to supporting the vassals of Tsushima and Satsuma.

In Ezo, cooperation between warriors and merchants seems to have had more complex socioeconomic repercussions than in the far south and to have transformed the fundamental nature of trade. Matsumae vassals became so indebted to merchants, who advanced them on credit the goods and grain that they traded in Ezochi, that their trade fiefs became essentially "pawned lands" to Japanese merchants, according to Satō Genrokurō. He noted that as Matsumae creditors, merchants were given a "free hand" to shape trade and that the trading posts became permanent marketplaces (*akinaigoya*), where merchants freely exploited the Ainu in year-round trade.[52] By the mid–eighteenth century, Matsumae finances relied on vassals' successfully securing credit by contracting out their trade fiefs to merchants from Japan. This trend not only led to an increase in the volume of trade but also fundamentally altered its character. The trading post, where these merchants set up shop, now became a local monopoly, playing a role analogous to that of Fukuyama in the 1620s. By the late eighteenth century, some trade fiefs in eastern Ezo—Akkeshi, for example, which had by that time been contracted out by retainer Ōhara Kamegorō to Hidaya Kyūbei—included not just the trading post itself but also travel inns, storehouses, shrines built for the fox god and other

Buddhist and Shinto deities, guard posts, and even horse stables.[53] In 1799, the trading post at Kiitappu kept forty horses, largely used for personnel transport.[54]

The existence of large, permanent trading posts along the rivers and watersheds allowed Ainu to quickly trade animal skins and fish products (which normally would have been used to feed and clothe their communities) for rice, tobacco, saké, and other Japanese items; and this trade sometimes created new scarcities. Moreover, the hunt, which had once dramatized the spiritual relationship between Ainu chiefdoms and their local environment, and the *kamuy* that lived there, took on more-commercial connotations. Although this transformation in Ainu productive patterns occurred from at least the mid–seventeenth century onward, there are several accounts from the nineteenth century that illustrate the trend particularly well.

In the mid–nineteenth century, Ōuchi Yoan, an Edo physician, observed that Ainu hunted and fished not simply to feed and clothe themselves but to accumulate animal skins and other products for trade with Japanese. He remarked that as a result of this trade, animals had become "hunted commodities" (*shubutsu*)—a notion similar to White's "animals of enterprise"—that is, products valued not for their spiritual presence, immediate usefulness, or worth in small interchiefdom exchange but for the price they brought when traded with Japanese merchants. Ōuchi wrote, "Now, the Ainu, if the winter fishing months end, tour the deep mountain recesses to seize hibernating bears or deer, fox, river otter, marten, eagles, and other animals, as well as seal and sea lion that come out on the beach. This becomes their livelihood. These goods are brought to the trading post and traded for rice, saké, tobacco, cotton, and needles and thread. This is called taking 'hunted commodities.'"[55] In 1838, Kunitomo Zen'an, from Mito domain, noted that when not working in fisheries, Ainu traveled into the mountains to hunt animals for their skins. They then traded these pelts for Japanese goods, including saké and grain. By the 1830s, in fact, Ainu hunted largely for the purpose of killing animals for trade, and had significantly less time for more productive forms of subsistence-related activity.[56]

By the seventeenth and eighteenth centuries, a wide variety of goods

Figure 10.   The inside of an Ainu home. The large amount of Japanese-manufactured clothing, lacquerware, and iron goods inside the home illustrates how Japanese items had become integrated into Ainu domestic and ritual life. *Ezo fūzokuzu* [Illustrations of Ainu customs]. Courtesy of the Resource Collection for Northern Studies, Hokkaido University Library.

were clearly being traded in Ezo, but the types of products gradually changed over time as certain items accrued greater value in Japanese and Ainu societies. In the early trade between Ainu and Japanese, items tended to be those with cultural capital, such as animal skins that could be given as gifts in Edo. Precious metals such as copper remained conspicuously absent from the Ainu-Japanese trade, unlike other foreign trading in Japan.[57] Rice and saké were standard items traded by Japanese, but they also provided tobacco, salt, yeast, iron pots and kettles, thread, large knives (*debabōchō*), needles, used utensils and tools, used clothing, dye, cotton, hemp cloth and other fabrics, lacquerware (*nurimono*), gold and silver lacquer works (*makie*), various iron tools, and small swords (*makiri*).[58] As Kaiho Mineo points out, an investigation of the types of goods traded

at different times throughout the seventeenth and eighteenth centuries reveals the growing place of metal products in Ainu domestic life and ritual. Because the Ainu did not manufacture their own iron products, the increased use of metal items contributed to their growing dependency, even
as it led to decreased production of native earthenware goods. Thus, during the 1611–21 period Ainu received goods such as rice, clothing, yeast,
saké, and some iron eating utensils, whereas between 1621 and 1739 such
iron products as axes, sickles, hatchets, kettles, ceremonial swords, and
pipes dominated their acquisitions (see figure 10).[59]

Security considerations played a modest role in determining the types
of goods exchanged at trading posts. Under Lord Yoshihiro, domainal officials had frequently traded weapons and armor with Ainu, but the
practice petered out with Lord Kinhiro, who ruled between 1617 and
1641.[60] The exact reason for this policy change remains unclear, but
Matsumae leaders likely realized that arming the Ainu threatened their
own military superiority in Ezo. It was also at about this time that affairs
heated up between the Shibuchari and Hae Ainu. Nonetheless, Ainu continued to possess weaponry. These weapons, however, were rarely used
for military purposes. Instead, most Ainu regarded them as treasures
(*ikor*). Furukawa Koshōken, for example, remarked in 1788 that along
with sword hilts and sheaths, Japanese long swords (*tachi,* or *tannep-ikor*
in Ainu) were abundant in Ezo and were considered extremely valuable.[61] However, as a result of the above-mentioned policy change, Ainu
began to look for new ways of obtaining these highly valued goods.
Indeed, trade restrictions had been one complaint of Haukase and the
Ishikari Ainu in the aftermath of Shakushain's War.

In the early seventeenth century, Ainu mostly offered fish products
and animal skins. By 1739, however, over twenty-five kinds of products
were commonly traded, including pharmaceuticals and exotic clothing
from China.[62] The products that Ainu presented for trade changed over
time, but they can be divided into four broadly defined categories: (1) animal and bird products, (2) pharmaceuticals and plant products, including kelp, (3) fisheries yield, and (4) imported goods from the Eurasian
continent or the North Pacific.

The most common animal and bird products traded in Ezo were live hawks, eagle feathers, animal skins, marine mammal products, cranes, and geese, both alive and dead. Pharmaceuticals included such medicines as *takeri*, bear gallbladders, *ikema* (*Cynanchum caudatum*), *eburiko* (*Fomitopsis officinalis*), and *okurikankiri* (the crawfish shell and stomach area, which is enriched with calcium, carbonic acid, and phosphoric acid). Plant products included shiitake mushrooms, lumber, black lichen, a great variety of kelp, *atsushi* (*attus* in Ainu; a fabric made from elm bark), and *shinanawa* (*harkika*; rope made from elm bark). Fisheries yield included everything from large-scale salmon and herring catches to the somewhat smaller, although no less important, sea cucumber and abalone trade. Other common fisheries were salmon, herring, dried shark (*hoshizame*), dried codfish (*hidara*), trout, *kasube* fish, dried abalone (*shiraboshi awabi*), boiled and dried sea cucumber (*iriko*), and skewered shellfish (*kushigai*). Goods imported via Sakhalin Island included a variety of products manufactured by the Chinese and other continental peoples: colored beads (*mushinosudama* and *aodama*), bronze medallions, Ezo silks (*nishiki* and *jittoku*), Chinese cottons, some Russian goods, and various ornaments and other knickknacks.[63]

In essence, the diverse goods that came from the foreign lands of Ezo and beyond found two clienteles. Some goods were prized as gifts by the Japanese ruling elite, and others carried much broader market value in cities like Osaka and Edo. The thirteen tail feathers from the Steller's sea eagle could not be found in Japan, nor could skins from the Ezo brown bear. Even Ezo deer differed from their Japanese relatives. Similarly, textile products obtained in trade on Sakhalin, such as *jittoku* and *nishiki*, were frequently higher in quality than the silks imported through Nagasaki, because they were part of the official Chinese dynastic trade. These goods proved valuable as cultural capital in the form of gifts at official levels.

Baled Goods

The *tawaramono*, or baled-goods, trade, traditionally a state-sponsored activity overseen by the Edo shogunate because of its Nagasaki connection, remains among the best-documented commercial activities in Ezo and serves as a lucid example of how business was conducted at trading posts. As Hezutsu Tōsaku noted in 1784, *tawaramono* comprised items such as dried sea cucumber, dried abalone, and Shinori kelp. They were harvested and assembled in Ezo and then shipped to Nagasaki, where they were used in the official China trade.[64] By the beginning of the eighteenth century, in fact, *tawaramono* and other exports such as copper had almost replaced silver in the Nagasaki trade with China.[65] Later, under senior councillor Tanuma Okitsugu, the shogunate extended licenses to merchants in Osaka and Edo to bring these goods from Ezo to the southern foreign entrepôt, and then took a percentage of the profits for itself.[66]

The scale of Ezo's *tawaramono* exports was substantial. In 1788, merchants Abuya Mohei and Abuya Senpachi remarked in a note sent to their Osaka associates that 100,000 *kin* (about 132,000 pounds) of dried sea cucumber and abalone and 3,000 *kokume* (about 134,400 gallons) of Shinori kelp had been shipped to Nagasaki that year, despite the fact that "these products had become scarce." This same note records that the total licensing fees (*unjōkin*) paid to the Matsumae family for that year were 400 *ryō* in gold. In light of the growing cost of obtaining sea cucumber and abalone from Ainu, added Mohei and Senpachi, they were requesting additional cash.[67] Two other merchants, Hōraiya Chōbei and Ōtsuya Buzaemon, noted in 1788 that their total purchase of dried sea cucumber and abalone came to 8,948 *ryō* for that year.[68]

Ainu were integral in the *tawaramono* trade. Kushihara Seihō wrote in the 1790s that on a "lucky day," one net from an Ainu boat (*ibune*) took 120–30 live sea cucumber and that the total daily catch was about 2,000 per Ainu. The fishermen brought their catch to a fishery hut, where a Japanese manager counted them in the Ainu language. The manager grabbed five sea cucumber, and the Ainu said *shineppu* (one). In handfuls of five the sea cucumber were counted: *toppu* (two), *reppu* (three), *inuppu* (four), and so on to ten handfuls. The manager then made one of the five strokes of the Chinese ideograph *shō* in his notebook. When he completed one *shō*, representing 250 sea cucumber, he brushed a black stripe on the arm of the Ainu trader. For each mark on the arm, a trader received one cup of saké at the trading post, an incentive to gather more dried sea cucumber for the Nagasaki trade. For two *shō*, or 500 sea cucumber, the

Ainu received one *tawara* of rice (about four gallons).[69] (One might speculate that the arm marks served as a visual reminder of Japanese superiority over the Ainu, a dehumanizing sign that placed Ainu in a subordinate position to their merchant counterparts. Indeed, tattooing carried great symbolic value in Ainu society.)

Kushihara noted that near Sōya a total of about 300 boats (400 Ainu traders) worked the northern coasts for sea cucumber. Kushihara, a mathematician by training, estimated that if each boat took 400 sea cucumber, then about 120,000 were taken in one day. Because there were 12,000 sea cucumber in one *tawaramono*, about 300 bales were put together in one month. Kushihara noted that merchants took the dried sea cucumber caught in Sōya to Matsumae, where the Nagasaki *tawaramono gakari*, the shogunal official who oversaw the *tawaramono* trade, standardized purchase rates.[70]

Kushihara observed that Ainu traded according to two basic systems: the seasonal credit system (*kashi tsukeoki*) and direct exchange (*genkin kōeki*). In the seasonal credit system, Ainu purchased items such as fishing gear, sea cucumber nets, saké, rice, and clothing from the trading post on credit. The trading-post manager recorded credit-related information in his notebook, expecting Ainu to repay their debts with dried sea cucumber the following season.[71] Managers recorded the date, the product traded, the amount, and the name of the Ainu trader. They also noted whether the trading post had any outstanding loans to Ainu.[72] Moreover, merchants standardized local exchange rates in terms of bales of rice. Of the seasonal credit system, a shogunal inspector noted in 1717 that sixty-one trading posts permitted Ainu to trade on credit, without bringing actual "harvests." Ainu later brought their eagle feathers, deer pelts, or salmon and traded them directly with Japanese merchants.[73]

In direct exchange, Ainu brought sea cucumber to the trading post and exchanged them directly for Japanese goods. Kushihara observed that all an Ainu had to do was bring 100 dried sea cucumber to the trading post and say that he wanted *aburashake*, and in return he received three cups of saké. If the Ainu wanted tobacco, he asked for *tanbako* and traded 150 dried sea cucumber for one bundle of tobacco. For lacquerware cups, he asked for *yayakan*, and so on.[74] Not surprisingly, trade proved lucrative for Ainu living in areas with abundant resources. At trading posts in the east, for example, a high-quality sea otter pelt or the tail feathers from a sea eagle were traded at an extremely high premium, bringing in several bales of rice and yeast, barrels of saké, and numerous bundles of tobacco.[75] The trading post had become, in this sense, a bustling market, which shaped the seasonal rhythms of Ainu hunting and fishing.

The main difference between the two trading systems was the exchange rate. Kushihara noted that Ainu who traded in small quantities by direct exchange were at a disadvantage, whereas the seasonal credit system was more equitable. For Ainu, the seasonal credit system was clearly the better deal. If the 300 *tawaramono* that could be put together in one month by Sōya Ainu were traded by direct exchange, rather than by the seasonal credit system, Ainu stood to lose twenty-six *koku* of rice.[76] Like some rural money-lending in Japan, which allowed peasant entrepreneurs to gain access to needed capital, the seasonal credit system also allowed Ainu of limited means to get involved in the lucrative sea cucumber trade.[77]

CONCLUSION

With trading posts situated near Ainu communities, the acquisition and use of Japanese goods became integrated into the very fabric of Ainu society. The emergence of a market culture, moreover, symbolized by the "hunted commodities" Ainu hunters and trappers brought to posts, rapidly transformed the productive rhythms of Ainu life: trade became a part of Ainu daily habits and subsistence practice. The trade, as this chapter has shown, grew from a small-scale exchange at Fukuyama to a broader trade system interwoven into a complex web of vassal stipends, the shogunal-sponsored Nagasaki *tawaramono* trade, and merchant interests in Ezo. As we have seen, Matsumae officials even attempted to nurture Ainu demand for rice by prohibiting the importation of seed into Ezochi. As vassal trade fiefs became "pawned lands" for powerful merchant interests to run with a "free hand," trade in Ezo intensified and quickly spread to even remote areas in the north and east.

The increased demand for Japanese goods was not, however, fueled solely by Matsumae policy or market growth in Japan but also by changes that occurred in Ainu society as a result of trade. The ever-present trading post facilitated a shift in the value of familiar natural resources; Ainu appreciated resources not simply for their direct utilitarian value but for the price they brought at the trading post. This trend exposes the changing character of Ainu society and its growing dependency on trade with the Japanese.

4 Symbolism and Environment in Trade

In the late eighteenth century, Kushihara Seihō told the story of a Sōya Ainu named Itakui and a Yūbetsu Ainu named Hakiritsu who were on their way to their temporary hut when Itakui happened to ask about Hakiritsu's parents. As a rule, Kushihara explained, Ainu avoided asking about family, and as it happened, one of Hakiritsu's parents had only recently passed away. In accordance with Ainu custom, Itakui was now obliged to give Hakiritsu a compensatory gift (*tsugunai*) for having intruded on his privacy. Itakui promptly went to the nearest trading post with five hundred dried sea cucumber and traded them directly for one barrel of saké, which he gave to Hakiritsu.[1] This brief story is important because it illustrates how goods acquired in trade with Japanese, rather than sea cucumbers themselves (or Ainu-crafted items for that matter), had come to serve for making amends and smoothing over tension with-

99

in Ainu communities. Items such as saké, or even rice and lacquerware, in other words, had been sown into the very soil of Ainu life.

In addition to smoothing over tension between individual Ainu, with the construction of trading posts in Ezochi, Japanese items also became tied to Ainu notions of personal prestige and political status, and many items were converted into objects of worship and integrated into seasonal rituals. At the same time, to the south, in Tokugawa political circles, objects extracted from the environment of Ezo, such as hawks for falconry, were integrated into Japanese elite culture. This symbolic economy, which proved influential among both Japanese and Ainu, began to place added pressure on certain desirable species such as deer, salmon, and hawks. As the demand for trade in both societies increased, localized overhunting depleted many of these and other animal species whose skins purchased valuable items at trading posts. In short, trade led to the exploitation of resources at a pace that local environments could not sustain. As some animals became scarce, and formerly self-sustaining chiefdoms felt the squeeze of the trading post, they pushed outward in search of new resources, breaching neighboring chiefdom borders, as in the case of Shakushain's War. In the end, unified resistance to the Japanese intrusion into Ezo proved impossible in this volatile atmosphere.

HAWKS AND HEGEMONS: THE POLITICAL SYMBOLISM OF GIFTS

Many of the exported Ainu goods accrued different values in different social contexts. For example, products such as salmon and kelp carried economic value because they could be sold in Osaka and other cities. In contrast, goods such as eagle feathers, some animal skins, pharmaceuticals, and hawks possessed symbolic value as cultural capital in Japanese political circles. With the exchange of these latter goods, the early-modern Japanese elite profited from cultural capital just as their counterparts in other countries did. In the context of Europe, for example, Pierre Bourdieu argues that cultural capital aided the political and cultural elite thereby creating the image of an "autonomous space" that set the elite apart from other sectors of society. Goods that carried symbolic power created the "sense of distinction" that the elite associated with authority over others.[2] Eagle feathers, bear pelts, and hawks resonated with such power among the elite of Japan. These goods, which the Ainu forwarded from distant "barbarian lands," became tied to political status in Japan, and they flowed through the political networks that were so central to the rise of the Matsumae family in the late sixteenth and early seventeenth centuries.

In 1615, for example, Nishirain (or Nishirakeain) of the Menashikuru arrived in Fukuyama carrying ten sea otter pelts. These pelts were from Sea Otter Island (Urup Island in the Kurils) and were considered extremely valuable. One was reportedly the size of a bear skin. In a gesture that exemplifies how these exotic gifts from Ezo helped ingratiate the Matsumae family to the hegemons of early-modern Japan, Matsumae Yoshihiro presented this large pelt to Ieyasu as a gift, congratulating the aging leader on his victory over the pretender Toyotomi Hideyori in the battle for Osaka Castle that year.[3]

Three years later, Jeronimo de Angelis, a Portuguese missionary who traveled to Fukuyama before the crackdown on Christianity, noted that every year about one hundred Ainu vessels came to Fukuyama from the country called "Minaxi" (Menashi) to trade dried salmon and herring, as well as sea otter pelts. Similar to marten pelts sold in Europe, he remarked, these were traded at very high prices. De Angelis wrote that Ainu also came from "Texxo" (Teshio) and brought imported silks from China to trade with Japanese.[4] Diego Carvalho, the missionary who described Matsumae mining practices in chapter 3, observed in 1620 that for Ainu traveling to Matsumae by *nawatojibune* to trade such exotic goods, it was a sixty-three-day journey from the east and a seventy-four-day journey from the west. Following a brief ceremony with the Matsumae lord, Ainu offered everything from silks, sea otter pelts, and eagle feathers to live cranes and hawks.[5] It was these goods that proved symbolically potent as gifts in Japanese political circles, and they appear to have been central to early Japanese trade with Ainu chiefdoms.

From the outset, however, hawks in particular were among Ezo's most noteworthy contributions to early-modern Japan's symbolic economy.

On several occasions, Kakizaki lords presented hawks in Kyoto as valuable gifts, tightening personal bonds between themselves and the hegemons of the late sixteenth century. In the medieval era, falconry had become deeply ingrained in warrior society, both resonating with political authority and appealing strongly to the sentiments of warrior culture.[6] In the early Tokugawa years, hawks for falconry were among the most prized gifts presented by domainal lords to shoguns and their ministers. Falconry was one means with which the shogun and powerful domainal lords could, by hunting throughout their territory, survey their land and make their presence known to their subjects.[7] Thus, as gifts, hawks placed the Kakizaki, and later the Matsumae, in the lucrative position of supplier of a product that symbolized political power in the Japanese society of the day. Supplying hawks for Nobunaga, Hideyoshi, and Ieyasu became such a central part of Matsumae's political ties to Kyoto and Edo that some historians suggest that Matsumae's investiture with exclusive rights to trade in Ezo was largely a result of the demand for hawks in early-modern warrior society.

Kikuchi Isao is just such a historian. He argues that the hawk industry was central to Matsumae's economy and its political authority and that Hideyoshi and Ieyasu placed Matsumae's trade monopoly in Ezo in the same context as the government-controlled distribution of hawks for falconry.[8] Takagi Shōsaku, a historian who studies the Hideyoshi years, argues, only half in jest, that through control of the hawk-distribution system, Hideyoshi sought to extend his hegemony to the skies over the realm.[9] By contrast, the lords of northeastern Japan and Ezo dramatized their submission to the Edo shogunate by presenting hawks to the shogun and his councillors during audiences.

In the late eighteenth century, as mentioned earlier, Lord Michihiro provocatively remarked that his territory should be viewed not as a traditional domain but rather as "similar to foreign lands." However, despite this claim to northern distinctiveness, Wajinchi and its Matsumae lords were integrated into the networks of personal attachment of the Tokugawa polity, although not through rigid borders. Rather, investiture and connections formed with Kyoto and Edo through gifts linked Fukuyama Castle to the political center of early-modern Japan. Harold

Bolitho suggests that these types of gifts should be viewed as "statements of symbolic authority by which the leaders of each *han* [domain] government had been forced to recognize the supremacy of Edo."[10] Mary Elizabeth Berry goes one step further, characterizing early-modern Japan as a "gift society." She writes that gifts "established bonds between the giver and receiver" and that accepting a gift "acknowledges those bonds and fixes relations."[11] This was true not only at the beginning of the early-modern period but later as well. Thus, by means of the exchange of gifts, Lord Norihiro was able to maintain Matsumae's political contacts in Edo during the turbulence of the late seventeenth century, a time when Wajinchi suffered destructive fires and famine. He relied heavily on such gifts as eagle tails, bear gallbladders, and dried salmon, which were distributed to well-connected shogunal officials through the offices of influential figures such as Tsuchiya Masanao and Hōjō Ujihira.[12]

Throughout the Tokugawa years, Matsumae lords offered hawks as gifts during the frequent trips they made to Edo for audiences with the shogun and high-ranking shogunal officials. Admittedly, however, Matsumae lords traveled to Edo for attendance (*sankin*) less often than did other domainal lords, who went about every other year. In the seventeenth century, Matsumae lords traveled to Edo about once every three years, whereas from about 1710 to 1810, they attended only about once every five or six years. After about 1830, the frequency of attendance increased to every other year.[13] During these visits, and even before the establishment of the alternate attendance system that required such visits, Matsumae lords frequently presented hawks in the capital.

To start with, throughout the 1570s hawks served as the impetus for the initial audiences between Nobunaga and members of the Andō and Kakizaki families. In 1578, for example, Nobunaga received five hawks from Andō Chikasue. That same year, Kakizaki Masahiro, the fourth son of Kakizaki Suehiro, attended an audience at Azuchi Castle, Nobunaga's stronghold, where again hawks were likely presented. Illustrating the symbolic value of falconry, Nobunaga issued restrictions to his retainers telling them that they could not "indulge in falconry." Berry suggests that regulations such as these denied "any parity between Nobunaga and the men who represented him." For Nobunaga, falconry was "decorous conduct" symbolic of only the highest levels of military and political power.[14]

In 1591, the Kakizaki family presented hawks to both Hideyoshi and Toyotomi Hidetsugu. It was during this audience with Hideyoshi at the Jurakudai Palace that Yoshihiro was received as the "lord of Ezo Island." Like Nobunaga, Hideyoshi went so far as to prohibit other domainal lords from purchasing hawks in Ezo, which suggests that one of the primary reasons he invested Yoshihiro with such widespread commercial authority was for the purpose of bringing hawks to Kyoto. Hideyoshi even granted the Kakizaki liberal access to post stations between Fukuyama Castle and the capital, removing regional red tape and creating a highway for hawks that led directly to the political core. Later, during his audience with Ieyasu, Yoshihiro met with Maeda Toshinaga of Kaga domain, and in exchange for the services of his second son, Kakizaki Tsuguhiro (who died before he could leave for Kaga), Yoshihiro offered to receive Kaga hawk experts, called *takajō*. These experts eventually gathered under Kakizaki Nagahiro in Wajinchi, and they appear to have played a direct role in the development of the Ezo hawk industry.[15]

When Ieyasu invested Yoshihiro with exclusive rights to trade in Ezo, he (like Hideyoshi) also specified via an official seal that Matsumae lords be permitted direct passage to Edo through the special use of horse-post stations (*gotenma gohan*). Moreover, northeastern lords, whose domains happened to lie between Fukuyama Castle and Edo, were obliged to provide hawk food. Matsumae lords made several trips to Edo to present hawks to the shogun: Yoshihiro to Ieyasu in 1604, Kinhiro to Hidetada in 1624, Kinhiro to Iemitsu in 1634, and Takahiro to Ietsuna in 1664. During the initial mission of 1604, high-ranking shogunal officials oversaw the visits, personally assuring that Yoshihiro was allowed unrestricted use of post stations and received hawk food from northeastern domains.[16] Thus, for Fukuyama Castle, supplying hawks was one way to maintain ties to the political hub of Japan; however, hawks also served as an economic resource that helped strengthen its presence in Ezochi.

In 1669, when Shakushain attacked Japanese in the east, he targeted his initial assaults on people who most frequently entered Ezochi: gold miners, hawk trappers (called *takamachi*), and *takajō*. Of the 273 Japanese killed by Shakushain loyalists, 68 were *takamachi* and 3 were *takajō*, whereas the four Japanese known to have fought alongside the Ainu were either *takamachi* or gold miners.[17] In fact, at least one observer blamed the outbreak of hostilities on *takamachi* and gold miners, whose move into Ezochi had chafed already deteriorating Ainu-Japanese relations.[18] Indeed, the demand for hawks among lords had led to a sizable increase in the number of *takamachi* who traveled into Ezochi. By the mid–seventeenth century, providing hawks for the warrior elite had developed into an industry that comprised a substantial portion of Matsumae's export economy.

In the 1660s, *takamachi* had established about 300 posts, often called *takauchiba*, in Wajinchi. Of these posts, Matsumae lords and high-ranking vassals directly managed about one-third, or 120 to 130 posts. Most posts were built in Wajinchi, but *takamachi* caught most hawks in Ezochi. In the seventeenth century, areas of Ezo such as Lake Shikotsu and Ishikari were particularly productive regions for young hawks, referred to as *sudaka*; and new posts were built in Tokachi, Unbetsu, and Makomahe. Illustrating the importance of hawks to Fukuyama finances, profits from the 1660s ranged from about 1,000 to 2,000 *ryō* from taxes levied on trading vessels (*otebune*), whereas 1,000 to 2,000 *ryō* came from selling hawks. Norita Yasuemon, a shogunal observer, noted that profits from the hawk industry for 1670 were 2,400 to 2,500 *ryō*, whereas taxes levied on trade vessels, a total of about seven or eight vessels, were only 1,000 to 2,000 *ryō*. At least during the mid–seventeenth century, then, profits from the hawk industry rivaled the licensing fees extracted from trading ships.[19]

Almost every aspect of the hawk industry was steeped in ceremony. Once a year, Matsumae vassals ornamented hawk boats, or *takabune*, to retrieve hawks from posts located in Ezochi, and local Ainu were mobilized as porters. Matsumae vassals, moreover, ordered Ainu in villages near these posts to supply dogs, which *takajō* used as food (*esainu*) for the hawks. Considering that the fate of these dogs was to be fed to hungry hawks awaiting transport to Japan, it is hardly surprising that, according to one poem recorded by Saionji Sukekuni, dogs "quaked in fear" at the sight of hawks exported from Ezochi.[20]

However, after Shakushain's War, the practice of trapping live hawks in Ezochi decreased. By 1700, forty *takajō* oversaw only 211 posts, located mainly in Wajinchi. Of these, 136 (64 percent) were managed by members of the Matsumae family. By 1669 most *takamachi* had withdrawn their posts to Wajinchi, where they remained under the direct control of Matsumae officials.[21] As one shogunal inspector reported in 1717, the lord of Matsumae, probably Norihiro, bought up the best-quality hawks for as much as thirty *ryō* apiece, using them for falconry or presenting them as gifts. The remainder of the hawks were sold freely among Matsumae vassals. The inspector also reported that *takamachi* had opened thirty posts on Cape Shirakami and that in the Noshino Mountains in the west eighteen new posts had been built. *Takamachi* also built posts at Ōno, Shiotomari, Monai, Kennichi, and Etomo; in all, the inspector listed some fifty posts located in Wajinchi and Ezochi.[22] But the fact that *takamachi* located their posts in Wajinchi did not mean that they captured their hawks there. The industry was dependent on ecological factors such as migratory habits and seasonal nesting behavior, and *takamachi* often crossed over into Ezochi when necessary to find desirable birds.[23]

When hawks were not being presented as gifts, they were being bought and sold in Ezo. Prospective buyers first approached *takamachi* in Wajinchi and decided what kind of hawk they wanted. Experts divided hawks into two groups: *sudaka* (young hawks) and *kidaka* (one-year-old hawks); the second group was further subdivided into *shō* and *dai* (small and large yearling hawks, respectively). Large yearlings were the most valuable, but sophisticated buyers carefully scrutinized them for signs of quality other than size. Buyers then paid a rice stipend up front. Finally, in late summer or early autumn, *takamachi* set out for their posts. If they managed to capture anything, they received cash payment in gold, on average anywhere from two to five *ryō* per hawk, on top of the rice stipend.[24] To offer some comparative perspective, in the late eighteenth century, a good Nanbu-bred horse, the selling of which supplemented Morioka domain's economy, might bring in between two and eight *ryō*, depending on the quality of the animal.[25]

When *takamachi* went to one of the some three hundred posts in Wajinchi or Ezochi, they paid licensing fees (*unjōkin*) to the Matsumae vassals who controlled the trade fief where the post was located. Fees varied and often depended on the quality of hawks involved. From the revenues generated by these fees, vassals then paid the lord about twenty or thirty *ryō* annually.

The *takamachi* were not the only people involved in the hawk trade. Ainu had become integrally involved in the hawk industry, capturing nesting hawks and trading them directly (see figure 11). After Ainu captured hawks, they traveled to Wajinchi to inform Matsumae officials, who quickly dispatched *takajō*. After Shakushain's War, it became more common for *takamachi* to trade directly with Ainu rather than enter Ezochi themselves.[26]

Hawks were gifts tied to aesthetics connected to the Zen Buddhist culture of many of the ruling elite. Thus, as with other forms of ritualized aesthetics such as the tea ceremony, hawking required expertise that only well-trained *takajō* could provide. Okudaira Sadamori was one such expert. In the early nineteenth century, he wrote at length on the hawk industry and hawking culture in Ezo. He mused, for example, that *takajō* needed to assure that the "spirit of the hawk" remained unbroken during training. In contrast, the writings of Ogasawara Nagatoki and Ogasawara Sadahiro illustrate how the hawk trade was marked by a ceremonial austerity. They remarked that when caged hawks were traded, everything from the placement of the cage to how it was opened was closely shaped by protocol. They also emphasized that trading hawks dramatized the hierarchical status of the participants. Hawk traders first identified upper-level (*sakuhai*) and lower-level (*kahai*) warriors, and their subsequent roles in the trading ceremony were defined by their status. Nagatoki and Sadahiro further noted that certificates accompanied most hawks sold in Ezo.[27] And this protocol even extended beyond the confines of the post. In areas where *takajō* kept hawks, strict edicts prohibited villagers from raising their voices, burning fields, or felling trees and even warned people to keep their horses quiet. Edicts also required each household in the area of a post to donate three dogs to be used for food.[28]

Ecological factors, however, soon led to changes in Matsumae's hawk industry. Hawks were, of course, extracted from the northern landscape, and the supply proved exhaustible and prone to disease. In 1616, for ex-

Figure 11.   An Ainu feeding a hawk to be traded with Japanese. *Bakumatsu ki Mororan fūbutsuzu* [Late-Tokugawa scenes from Muroran]. Courtesy of the Resource Collection for Northern Studies, Hokkaido University Library.

ample, disease wiped out the entire stock of winter hawks for that year.[29] In 1751, *takamachi* complained bitterly that the some three hundred posts in Ezo captured only twenty-two or twenty-three hawks for sale in Japan.[30] The Matsumae family needed to diversify its economic base to replace an industry that suffered from over exploitation and a limited market. They did not have to look far. Matsumae domain did not recreate its economy in Ezo but only refocused on new resources to trade. The demand for hawks remained high, but the hawk industry had always been hampered by ceremonial protocol and a market limited to the ruling elite. However, the demand for salmon, herring, animal skins, and other goods of this sort appeared endless, and Japanese markets, with their merchant-run distribution networks, facilitated a transformation in Matsumae's economic behavior. The hawk industry, part of both the symbolic and the market economies, had only been a first step in Matsumae's intrusion into Ezochi.

TRADE AND PRESTIGE IN AINU SOCIETY

Just as hawks had in Tokugawa political circles, various goods traded in Ezo influenced Ainu political and social behavior. It should be noted that in this respect, Ainu-Japanese trade shares similarities with the trade between early European settlers and Native Americans in New England. For example, William Cronon argues that although Native Americans quickly incorporated European manufactured items such as brass and copper pots, woven fabrics, and iron products into their daily lives, it is "wrong to see the acquisition of European technology as in itself necessitating a revolution in Indian social life." He observes that most of these items "were in fact often reconverted into less utilitarian but more highly valued Indian objects."[31] Similarly, Ainu incorporated Japanese iron pots, clothing, and wooden lacquerware into their daily lives. Yet, these items appear to have been appreciated for both their utilitarian value in domestic life and their value as emblems of prestige.

As early as the Satsumon culture discussed in chapter 1, with the intensification of trade with the Japanese, lacquer cups and iron pots and kettles began to replace items such as the earthenware pots once used by proto-Ainu groups.[32] Products such as iron kettles, which were suspended above fireplaces centrally located in Ainu homes, also might be said to have revolutionized Ainu domestic life. More importantly, however, Japanese items and the domestic space that surrounded them evolved into spiritual hubs for the worship of the fire god, or *ape huci kamuy*. Because it was so closely connected with daily chores such as cooking, *ape huci kamuy* was worshiped frequently by Ainu through domestic ritual. Moreover, *ape huci kamuy* acted as a medium between people and

other gods, making domestic ritual a central part of the Ainu metaphysical order.[33] Illustrating the place of trade in Ainu ritual culture, the entire
spiritual atmosphere surrounding *ape huci kamuy* was built around the
fireplace and the suspended iron kettle. Most items acquired in trade,
along with their utilitarian value, took on new characteristics and became more highly valued objects used in ritual.[34]

In addition to iron kettles, other items were also considered valuable.
Hezutsu Tōsaku observed that small sword hilts, sword pommels (*fuchi-
gashira*), gold utensils, lacquered wooden food and drinking containers
(*jikirō*), and gold and silver lacquer works constituted the majority of
treasures (*ikor*). Matsumae Norihiro remarked that Ainu considered
metal blades for hoes, long swords, cambered swords (*sorigatana*), and
bows to be treasures. Glancing at these brief lists, it might be tempting to
dismiss *ikor* as knickknacks of little value or importance. But, as Cronon
warns of European-manufactured items traded with Native American
tribes, "Indians eventually sought many of the things Europeans offered
in trade, not for what Europeans thought valuable about them, but for
what those things conveyed in Indian schemes of value. In effect, they became different objects. Being rare and exotic, European goods could function as emblems of rank in Indian society and as gifts in the exchanges
that created and maintained alliance networks."[35]

Like the European goods, Japanese goods, in the hands of Ainu, also
became different objects. Many of these goods came to symbolize power
and authority in Ainu society, completely shedding their earlier utilitarian value. Furukawa Koshōken poignantly explained of Ainu schemes of
value that "what Ainu admire as wealth and what Japanese admire as
wealth is very different." He noted that "Ainu who possess grain, saké,
clothing, and various lacquerware containers and utensils (*utsuwamono*)
are considered to be wealthy." He also remarked, illustrating the role of
trading-post distribution in determining Ainu standards of living, that
wealthy Ainu lived in areas where there was active trade with Japanese.
In these areas Ainu often possessed three houses and sometimes even
three to five wives. Matsumae Hironaga noted in his brief comments on
Ainu customs that Ainu chiefs were individuals with household wealth,
presumably meaning they had collected many treasures. He wrote that

wealthy chiefs possessed many servants, called *utar*, and anywhere from ten to twenty mistresses, called *cipanke mat*. He noted one chief in northern Ezo who had sixteen such mistresses.[36]

Some Ainu folktales, or *uepeker*, strengthen the argument that Ainu productive systems and conceptions of personal wealth and prestige underwent a transformation as goods acquired in trade were integrated into Ainu schemes of value. In the late nineteenth and early twentieth centuries, Bronislaw Piłsudski spent time with Sakhalin Ainu collecting and translating Ainu *uepeker*. In one *uepeker*, recited by a Sakhalin Ainu named Sisratoka, the narrative emphasizes that properly conducting ritual and preparing *inaw*, ceremonial fetishes carved from willow, led to good fortune in trade with Japanese. Piłsudski recorded the tale of one Ainu who properly performed rituals: "[W]hatever (he) sold to the Japanese (e.g.) the furs of different animals, (he) received payment (for) that, (and) quickly became a rich man. Hunting, every year he (was) happy, (and) possessed everything (he wanted, and) became a rich man. Thus (runs) the tradition [parentheses in original]."[37]

A second *uepeker*, recited by a Sakhalin Ainu named Jasinoske, celebrated a Turupan Ainu who, upon returning from "Matomai" (Matsumae), possessed a "great cargo," including "various (things)—rice, also saké."[38] Ainu who hunted to "possess everything" and sought to become "rich" were far from a simple bucolic people, hunting and fishing to satisfy basic subsistence needs. Motivated by the desire to acquire goods that symbolized wealth, Ainu hunted and fished according to more-materialistic conceptions of production and personal prestige. In Ainu society, as in early-modern Japan, certain goods accrued value that could be translated into social status and political power.

In 1798, Mutō Kanzō tied personal prestige, embodied by the possession of Japanese goods, to actual political power in Ainu society. Such Ainu chiefs as Sansha of Kunashir, Kotanpiru of Rurumoppe, Kinkiriu of Yoichi, and Wajima of Iwanai were, he explained, "well-known" among Ainu, but they were also wealthy, with "many treasures in their possession." Of Ainu chiefs who had gained wealth and political power in trade, Ikotoi of Akkeshi was among the most powerful and charismatic. Yamazaki Hanzō, from northeastern Japan, wrote of Ikotoi that he had placed himself in the powerful position of middleman for trade between Hidaya merchants, located in eastern Ezo, and Kunashir and Iturup Ainu. Ikotoi commanded fame throughout Ezo, and his ancestors had also profited from trade. Yamazaki wrote that Ikotoi had acquired large amounts of saké, tobacco, and yeast in trade with the Japanese and that as Ainu became wealthy from trade, "the reverence they receive from other Ainu also increases."[39]

A famous portrait by Kakizaki Hakyō visibly dramatizes Ikotoi's wealth and prestige by portraying him with exotic goods acquired in trade. Ikotoi proudly sports a black *jittoku* with red and white embroidered dragons; over the *jittoku* he wears a crimson Russian cloak, acquired by trading pelts with Russians in the Kurils. In his right hand, Ikotoi has gathered the golden hem of the cloak, and in his left hand he is holding a Russian ceremonial lance.[40] Ikotoi adorned himself in clothing and weapons acquired in trade, which were visual symbols of his political prestige.

The items that Ainu acquired in trade remained valuable even after the Meiji Restoration of 1868. When Isabella Bird, an English adventurer, asked Benri of Biratori about the "magnificent pieces of lacquer and inlaying" that he proudly displayed in his home, he explained that the items were "his father's, grandfather's, and great grandfather's at least" and that they were "gifts from the daimyo of Matsumae soon after the conquest of Ezo."[41] Items such as lacquerware cups and bowls translated into personal prestige for many Ainu because of their central place in Ainu ritual; they were symbols that mediated between Ainu and the vast spiritual world. Objects acquired in trade were used as utensils in ritual, adorning ceremonial space or serving as actual tools in ritual performance.

Although Ainu rituals became closely tied to trade, *kamuy*, and the natural environment *kamuy* inhabited, maintained their all-powerful places in Ainu culture.[42] But, how reverence was demonstrated to *kamuy* changed as a result of the import of these new Japanese-manufactured goods. With the intensification of trade, Ainu incorporated Japanese saké and other goods into virtually every important ritual. Whether the *asir-cep-nomi*, a celebration of the coming seasonal salmon harvest (see figure 12); the *kamuy-nomi*, a form of reverence to certain *kamuy* involving saké;

Figure 12. Ainu participating in the *asircep-nomi*, a
celebration of the salmon harvest. Saké and lacquerware,
obtained in trade with Japanese, were generally present
at such rituals. *Ainu tairyō kigan no zu* [Ainu prayers for a
bountiful harvest]. Courtesy of the Resource Collection for
Northern Studies, Hokkaido University Library.

or the *iomante*, "the sending away," a ceremonial killing of a bear, an owl, or even a wolf, Japanese lacquerware, clothing, iron goods, and swords adorned the ritual area.[43] Saké served as the offering that Ainu made to *kamuy*. Although ethnologists point out that Ainu brewed their own millet liquor, the fact that there are few specific examples in Japanese records of its being used in early-modern ceremonies suggests that it had been largely replaced by saké by the seventeenth century.[44]

In 1806, Yamazaki Hanzō noted that among the goods accumulated by the powerful Ikotoi, saké, grain, and yeast (used for brewing saké) remained among the most valuable. In Ezo, the ever-present place of saké in Ainu society shares similarities with the well-documented place of rum in the European trade with Native Americans. Richard White provocatively argues that liquor "controlled the pace of hunting" for certain Native American nations, such as the Choctaw.[45] Although the Pawnee and Navajo nations were less devastated by the introduction of rum into trade, the Choctaw people quickly succumbed to liquor, radically increasing hunting and trapping activity to feed their newly acquired habit. In Ezo, not surprisingly, Japanese merchants understood both the ritual and material value of saké and constructed bogus barrels that actually held less than they were supposed to: merchants insisted that the barrels contained about ten gallons, when in fact they only held about seven. Saké was so valuable to the commercial interests of Japanese merchants that by 1802 a brewery had been built at Kusuri (Kushiro). In 1809, Arai Heibei remarked that of the saké annually produced at the Kusuri brewery, about 3,100 gallons was used in Kusuri while nearby Akkeshi received about 3,600 gallons. This is a fair amount of saké for the roughly 870 Ainu that lived in Akkeshi during the early nineteenth century.[46]

In 1739, Sakakura Genjirō observed how Ainu, during a visit to Fukuyama Castle, incorporated saké into their trade ceremony, called *uymam*. Ainu elders, following their audience (*omemie*) with the Matsumae lord, performed a second ritual—probably the *umusa* (in Ainu, "a greeting") or the *kamuy-nomi*—that involved offering saké to *kamuy* by splashing the saké lightly with a *tukipasuy*, a ceremonial prayer stick used in several Ainu rituals. Matsumae Hironaga remarked that Ainu lightly splashed saké in the direction of the fire god, the sea god, and the mountain god and also used the saké to pay respect to their ancestors during rituals.[47] Saké acquired in trade became the offering that linked Ainu elders to *kamuy-mosir,* the metaphysical plane that gods and ancestors inhabited.

In 1784, Hezutsu Tōsaku observed that in the tenth month of each year Ainu performed the *kamuy-nomi* in preparation for the upcoming *iomante.* Items acquired in trade decorated the *iomante* site, including small lacquerware bowls and cups (Japanese, *kozuka;* Ainu, *tuki*), sword guards and hilts (Japanese, *tsuba;* Ainu, *seppa*), and large lacquerware containers (Japanese, *hokai;* Ainu, *sintoko*). Later, in 1808, Mogami Tokunai wrote that in the *kamuy-nomi,* Ainu lightly splashed saké from lacquerware cups with a *tukipasuy,* making offerings to various *kamuy* before drinking. He wrote elsewhere that before carrying out the *kamuy-nomi,* Ainu adorned the ritual area with swords and other weapons, along with Japanese lacquerware containers, cups, and bowls and other items acquired in trade. He noted that these lacquerware items were important "tools" in Ainu drinking rituals.[48]

In Abuta, Matsuda Denjūrō, a Tokugawa official, observed an *iomante* firsthand. In the *iomante,* Ainu ceremoniously killed a bear cub, believing that they were liberating the *kamuy* from its temporal guise. In the early spring, local Ainu began raising the cub, and the women breast-fed the animal. In the tenth or eleventh month, local elders gathered and prepared for the "sending away." On the day of the ceremony, they first removed the bear from the holding cage and took it to an area near the village center. The bear, after having been shot with both blunted ceremonial arrows (*heperay*) and then more deadly arrows (*isonoreay*), was strangled between two logs. Matsuda wrote that during the ceremony, items acquired in trade adorned the site, along with *inaw* and *nusa,* or groups of Ainu-crafted ceremonial fetishes. They also drank saké from lacquerware cups (see figure 13).[49]

Paintings and other Ainu visual sources similarly illustrate the place of trade in Ainu ritual culture.[50] Kimura Hakō's works on Ainu ritual life, for example, depict how Ainu chiefs used Japanese items to decorate and conduct rituals such as the *iomante.* In one painting, items such as swords, sword pommels, gold and silver lacquerware, red and black lacquered wooden food and drinking containers, iron kettles, and Japanese

Figure 13. The final stage of the *iomante*, or the "sending away" of the bear spirit. Japanese-manufactured items such as lacquerware cups and swords surround the object of worship. *Ezotō kikan* [Strange sights from Ezo Islands]. Courtesy of the Resource Collection for Northern Studies, Hokkaido University Library.

clothing surround the ritual space of the *iomante*. Moreover, according to Kimura's depiction, Ainu elders placed these goods near the bear, the object of veneration, while the participants, some dressed in Japanese clothing, received saké in lacquered bowls (see figure 14).[51] With the intensification of trade, then, many items became inseparably integrated into the *iomante* and other Ainu rituals. As Mogami pointed out, Ainu viewed these goods as the "tools" of ritual. These items linked Ainu to a metaphysical plane inhabited by their gods and ancestors.

Trade became an inseparable part of Ainu domestic life and ritual. Simple goods were often reinvented into hubs of worship, as the case of *ape huci kamuy* illustrates, mediating spiritual relations between Ainu and their broader metaphysical order. Moreover, many of these goods in turn

Figure 14.   The final stage of the *iomante*. Once again, Japanese-manufactured items such as lacquerware cups and swords surround the object of worship. Japanese officials are also present in this version. *Ainu fūzoku kuma matsuri no zu* [Illustration of the Ainu custom of the bear ceremony]. Courtesy of the Resource Collection for Northern Studies, Hokkaido University Library.

altered Ainu material culture and domestic life. The emergence of seventeenth- and eighteenth-century Ainu society, then, with its complex ritual systems and material culture, was closely linked to the intensification of trade with the Japanese.

CHANGES IN THE NORTHERN LANDSCAPE

The environment that comprised the river-based Ainu chiefdoms could not simultaneously sustain hunting and fishing at the pace dictated by the trading post while also supporting the subsistence needs of native Ainu communities. Subsequently, Ainu chiefdoms were transformed

DEPENDENT CHIEFDOMS

from self-sustaining political and ecological regions to production bases for trade. The very nature of Ainu social and economic space changed: Ainu chiefdoms no longer exemplified regions defined by spiritual relationships with the animals and their *kamuy*. It was the intensification of commerce at the trading post, fueled by the demand for goods in cities such as Osaka and Edo, that focused pressure on the natural resources of Ezo, tipping the ecological balance that had once been a defining characteristic of the independent Ainu chiefdom.

Early on, the intensification of trade started to deplete familiar Ainu resources. On the one hand, Ainu living near regions inhabited by fur-bearing animals converted animal skins into improved standards of living and higher levels of subsistence. Ainu who lived on land where these animal species were scarce, on the other hand, found themselves pushed below the subsistence level. The trading post completely reshaped how Ainu interacted with their local environment. Before the intensification of trade, Ainu had demarcated their self-sustaining chiefdoms with the understanding that each designated region contained enough resources to feed and clothe its inhabitants, hence constituting an independent chiefdom. By the early eighteenth century, however, whether an Ainu community was self-sustaining depended on access to the resources necessary for trade.

In 1715, Matsumae Norihiro, in a memorandum to Edo officials, linked Ainu hunting and fishing activity under trade fiefs to regional environmental change. He wrote that whether Ainu were rich or poor was dependent on their industry (*sangyō*). For their industry, he explained, Ainu exploited resources such as eagle tails, bear pelts, various seal pelts, and fisheries such as herring, salmon, codfish, whale, and abalone. He noted that for Ainu in areas with abundant natural resources that could be used in trade, a comfortable subsistence (*tosei*) was possible. He also observed that in recent years natural resources throughout Ezo had become very scarce. Traditionally, for example, Ainu traded many deer pelts. "But recently it is not like it was before," he added. "In all four directions natural resources have become exceedingly scarce." For the majority of Ainu subsistence had become difficult.[52]

In Norihiro's discussion of the social ecology of Ezo, certain terms took on broader meanings. For example, the "industry" that Norihiro tied to Ainu "subsistence" was not simply a reference to hunting as a means to feed Ainu communities. Salmon fishing and deer hunting were subsistence activities; but eagle tails, bear pelts, deer pelts, and seal pelts were all specifically identified by Norihiro as the "industry" of Ainu (what Ōuchi Yoan called "hunted commodities") and were exchanged at trading posts. By associating "hunted commodities" with Ainu subsistence systems, Norihiro implied that by 1715 trade had become part of the Ainu subsistence base or at the very least part of their "livelihood." Naturally, the link between regions with abundant resources and the ability of Ainu to survive led to regional disparities in the standard of living and increased competition between Ainu chiefdoms, such as the disparity that had sparked Shakushain's War.

Norihiro simply jotted down random notes concerning Ainu customs and trade in Ezo. He specifically remarked, however, that among Ezo goods, deer pelts had become scarce. He was not the only observer to note the depletion of deer herds: five years earlier, in 1710, Matsumiya Kanzan had briefly remarked of deer pelts that "in recent years none are traded." Likewise, in 1717, a shogunal inspector wrote that "in past years deer pelts were mainly taken in the Saru River and Yūbetsu areas, but in recent years few pelts are taken at all."[53] These are important observations because healthy deer herds were central to Ainu survival. Much later, for example, in 1879, when Hokkaido deer populations buckled under heavy snowfall and increased hunting for pelts and the two venison canneries built by the Kaitakushi (Hokkaido Development Agency), as many as three hundred Ainu reportedly starved to death.[54]

In 1792, Kushihara Seihō offered some enticing clues as to how deer had come under so much pressure. Illustrating ecological trends in fauna distribution discussed earlier, he observed that in western Ezo the snow became very deep in the winter, and deer found it difficult to forage for food. He wrote that in the autumn, deer from the mountains of the southern section of the Ishikari region migrated east to Shikotsu by crossing the Ishikari River. As the deer approached the river, Ainu concealed themselves and their boats behind reed blinds and waited. When the deer started to swim the river, Ainu overtook them in boats and beat them to death. "In recent years an increasing number of deer have been taken, and none are left. Those deer that did remain have swum across the ocean to Morioka domain," wrote Kushihara. Now, "there are very few if any deer in eastern Ezo."[55] Of course, swimming to Morioka was impossible; the deer had been overhunted.

It is hardly surprising that deer populations were under pressure in the east, considering the amount of trade-related hunting that went on in Ezo. Matsumae Hironaga noted that deer pelts were among the most important commodities that the Matsumae family traded with Japanese provinces.[56] Mogami Tokunai wrote in 1808 that because fishing and hunting proved more profitable than other activities and because ships from Japan frequently picked up Ezo goods, Ainu did "little else other than fish and hunt" for the purpose of trade.[57] He estimated that Japanese merchants had exported a total of 500 koku of animal pelts and atsushi (elm-bark fabric) from different regions throughout Ezo in 1788. At 5,000 pelts per 100 koku, this meant that about 25,000 pelts and pieces of atsushi left Ezo that year.[58] Obviously, there was a market for pelts in early-modern Japan.

In the seventeenth century, there had been what Maehira Fusaaki describes as a deerskin boom. In the first decades of Tokugawa rule, large quantities of deerskins were imported into Japan from Southeast Asia. Once in Japan, they were used to make armor and other specialty crafts. Deerskin items became so popular that Japanese merchants traveled to Southeast Asia in search of more deerskins to bring back and sell. Dutch records from 1624 lament that European traders could not get their hands on any decent deerskins because Japanese had bought them all up. That year alone, 160,000 skins were imported. At one point, Spanish observers worried that deer herds were disappearing from Southeast Asia.[59] The deerskin trade with Japan also became an important part of the Taiwanese economy under early Dutch and Chinese rule.[60] Thus, early-modern Japan had an appetite for animal skins, and as Southeast Asian markets were closed off and as deer became scarce, Ezo began to supply deerskins in place of these other regions.

Although a shogunal inspector noted that members of the warrior elite used bear pelts as decorative saddle coverings, deer pelts, when available, likely made up the majority of animal skins traded in Ezo.[61] In 1853, Kitagawa Morisada wrote that deer pelts were popular among Japanese urbanites (chōnin) and were used for trendy deerskin tabi, a special sock worn with traditional Japanese footwear.[62] Japanese also used deer pelts for leather haori (a kind of overcoat), fabrics, calligraphy and paint brushes, and stencil brushes for printing cotton and silk fabrics.[63] (A deerskin haori remains on display at the rebuilt Fukuyama Castle museum in Matsumae city.) Yet, the market-driven demand for deer pelts appears to have momentarily died out by around the 1830s. One document notes, for example, that only three thousand deer pelts were taken in Ezo in 1839, significantly fewer than in years past.[64]

When deer populations came under pressure in the late eighteenth century, not only did trade suffer but Ainu subsistence practice also completely broke down. Hezutsu Tōsaku observed that in some cases famine was directly related to dramatic declines in the number of deer. He noted that as deer populations decreased under heavy snowfall during the winter of 1784, some three hundred to four hundred Ainu starved to death in the countryside.[65] In 1806, Yamazaki Hanzō wrote that in the Tokachi region "there used to be some 5,000 Ainu" but that a famine in the 1780s had ravaged the Tokachi Ainu. He wrote that before the famine, deer had been abundant in the Tokachi region, but for the purpose of acquiring saké and tobacco in trade, Ainu had carelessly overhunted local deer herds. He speculated that so many Ainu died because the myriad kamuy had become angry and purposely eradicated Tokachi deer.[66]

Yamazaki's comment on the relationship between declining deer herds, kamuy, and famine is worth pursuing. In the context of Ainu chiefdoms, and their agreements with kamuy to hunt and fish within a specified sphere, the idea of kamuy itself often served as a metaphor for the natural environment and the covenant Ainu shared with it. In turn, the covenant that Ainu established with animals and their kamuy-essences was a broader religious justification for the more practical necessities of survival. The Ainu hunted to eat but also to fulfill their obligation as spiritual liberators. In this sense, when he brought down a deer in the forests near the Saru River, an Ainu hunter accomplished two tasks. The first was survival for himself and his family. The deer existed so that it could be hunted, so that its flesh could be used for food, its pelt for clothing. The second was reinforcement of his belief in his spiritual covenant with the land, which shaped his identity as a Saru Ainu. Following the kill, the hunter celebrated the *kamuy*-essence of the deer through ritual while at the same time repaying other debts: to the owl (*kamuy-cikappo*) who had made the hunt successful and to the bear (*kim-un-kamuy*) who had granted the hunter safe passage in the mountains. In the most spiritual sense, then, nature and the hunt inherently depended upon the fulfillment of reciprocal obligations between all participants, but most importantly between the Ainu, the deer, and the *kamuy*.

Barry Lopez, writing about Eskimos, has made insightful observations concerning the relationship between hunting peoples in general and the landscape in which they live. He explains that the "focus of a hunter in a hunting society was not killing animals but attending to the myriad relationships he understood bound him into the world he occupied with them. He tended to those duties carefully because he perceived in them everything he understood about survival."[67] For Eskimos, then, as with other hunting peoples, such as the Ainu, animals were not objectified and separated from the human world and then treated impersonally. Rather, most relationships with animals were "local and personal." As a hunter, Lopez imagines, the "animals one encounters are part of one's community, and one has obligations to them."[68] Although it is an oversimplification to lump all hunting peoples together, as Lopez would be the first to admit, his observations do hold true for the Ainu.

Therefore, if *kamuy* had "eradicated deer," and local obligations had not been met, as Yamazaki suggests, this meant among other things that the environment could no longer sustain hunting and fishing at the pace that either the market, or the newly developed desire among Ainu for certain items acquired in trade, required of it. The market culture of the trading post had caused a breach in the relationship between Ainu and their local animals, destroying the ecological balance between people and animals, and for this reason their overhunting and overfishing for trade struck deeper cultural resonance. A lack of deer drove home the reality that the ritual event that the hunt represented, a symbol of the relationship between people and gods in the Ainu metaphysical order, could be threatened when animals were overhunted to supply the market. The scarcity of animals, in this sense, threatened the entire cultural order upon which Ainu communities were based.[69]

BORDER CONFLICTS AND THE RISE OF *CASI*

The limited supply and changing distribution of resources led to regional diversity and changes in wealth and levels of subsistence among Ainu chiefdoms. Illustrating this new regional distribution of wealth were Ainu-constructed fortifications called *casi* (in Japanese, *chashi*). In Ainu, *casi* meant a "palisade" or a "compound enclosed by a palisade," and the term referred to a structure that was used for a variety of purposes, including rituals, gatherings, and security. However, *casi* served mainly as military fortifications to defend chiefdom borders from being compromised by competing Ainu groups. In recent years, archaeologists have identified about 530 *casi* throughout Hokkaido, almost exclusively located in the eastern section of the island—in the Kusuri, Tokachi, Nemoro (Nemuro), and Hidaka regions, where most hunting for skins took place and where competition over resources was most visibly acute.[70] This competition led to border disputes, such as the early Shibuchari-Hae confrontations, which resulted in the construction of *casi*.

Although the Tōya *casi* (Kusuri) and a handful of others were built sometime during Japan's Muromachi period (1392–1573), archeological evidence suggests that Ainu built most of the *casi* at the beginning of the seventeenth century, at about the same time that the Matsumae family organized the trade-fief system. The Setanai *casi*, the Shibuchari *casi* (Shizunai), and the Abetsu *casi* (Biratori), all in eastern Ezo, were probably built sometime between 1600 and 1667. Utagawa Hiroshi argues that the construction of *casi* was directly linked to the intensification of trade with the Japanese. Among the artifacts discovered from excavated *casi* are Japanese lacquerware, porcelain, ironware, swords, bronze sword ornamentation, and colored beads, probably from Sakhalin.[71]

The primary reason for the construction of *casi* was regional infighting among Ainu chiefdoms. During the conflicts of the 1660s between chiefs

Onibishi and Shakushain, for example, Shakushain had built a *casi* along the Shibuchari River for strategic purposes. Hae Ainu responded by building one along the Atsubetsu River.[72] Fighting then broke out between the two chiefdoms largely because Hae Ainu repeatedly pillaged Shibuchari resources, and many skirmishes actually occurred at the *casi* themselves.[73]

Kaiho Mineo asserts that Ainu built *casi* to resist or assist regional expansion under a single charismatic military figure Japanese observers called the "greater general" (*sōtaishō*). He argues that these greater generals, such as Shakushain and Onibishi, organized trade networks to accumulate valuable commodities from Japan, upon which they were becoming increasingly dependent. Fueled by the materialism inherent in Japanese culture, he continues, Ainu chiefdoms attempted to expand over new production bases that assured a steady flow of resources and thus the Japanese-manufactured goods that accrued prestige.[74]

Some *uepeker*, which often recount the past glory of Ainu battles, support this argument, suggesting that Ainu built *casi* to either protect *ikor* or to defend resources needed for subsistence and access to trade.[75] In one *uepeker* from Utagawa Hiroshi's collection entitled *Ainu denshō to chashi* [Ainu folktales and *casi*], for example, Akkeshi and Nemoro Ainu jointly attacked the Uraike *casi*, hoping to plunder the abundant "fine treasures"; and they ultimately forced the Uraike Ainu to evacuate toward the Sarushina *casi*.[76] Similarly, Ainu chiefdoms threatened by famine attacked other *casi*, demanding supplies of dried salmon and venison. Again, another *uepeker* from the same collection describes how Ishikari Ainu were forced to defend Arashiyama *casi* from Kusuri Ainu "who assaulted it demanding food."[77] And yet another *uepeker* recounts the use of *casi* to defend resources from rival chiefdoms. As one narrative explains, "the Ishikari region was known as a land rich in natural resources," and the living conditions of the Ishikari Ainu were the object of envy among other groups such as the Tokachi Kitami Ainu. Ishikari Ainu were therefore forced to construct *casi* to protect their land from encroachment by other, less fortunate Ainu chiefdoms.[78] In the end, the Ishikari Ainu captured all the Tokachi Ainu and, to add insult to injury, stole their treasures.

Regional infighting between Ainu chiefdoms occurred for various rea-

to be used for trade w/ Japanese.

sons and during various time periods, but competition over animals and fisheries was at the heart of most Ainu conflicts. The best documented example remains the conflict between the Hae and Shibuchari Ainu in the first half of the seventeenth century. As discussed in chapter 2, relations between the two chiefdoms had never been good, and Shibuchari hunting trips into Hae forests and Hae fishing trips down the Shibuchari River aggravated relations to the point of war. The Hae-Shibuchari conflict was not over the demarcation of borders but rather over the animals and fish that lay within the borders; it was the fauna and their environment, after all, that defined political and identity-forming space. Conflicts arose when Ainu knowingly crossed chiefdom borders, which were often unclear because of animal migration patterns, to hunt and fish. The Hae and Shibuchari chiefdoms became locked in competition not only for salmon and deer for their utilitarian needs but also for access to bear cubs for ritual and live cranes for trade. When Shakushain built his *casi* along the Shibuchari River, and Hae Ainu, after the death of Onibishi, built a *casi* along the Atsubetsu River, they were warring over "hunted commodities" and access to trade.[79]

Later, fighting erupted between Tsukinoe, elder of the Kunashir Ainu, and Tashanishi of Kusuri; and *casi* were likely involved in that conflict. Similarly, according to Menkakushi, an elder from Kusuri, his ancestors had constructed *casi* at Harutoru and Sashirui because of fighting that had broken out with Ainu from Nemoro, Akkeshi, and Tokachi, all chiefdoms located in the east.[80] *Casi* such as these were valuable in times of war, but they also resonated with symbolic meaning. Matsumae Hironaga remarked that any chief who held a "large dominion" had a *casi* built upon the highest mountain, suggesting that *casi*, along with their military purpose, could also serve as visible symbols of chiefdom power.[81]

Prior to the construction of trading posts, cooperation might have been possible between chiefdoms. Negotiations likely took place over access to bear cubs and aconite plants, as well as to migrating salmon and deer. A small-scale trade also probably flourished in these early years. However, by the seventeenth century, neither Onibishi nor Shakushain was killing animals simply to feed and clothe his community. The control of natural resources became increasingly competitive, and Hae and Shibuchari Ainu found themselves fighting over animals and fish that migrated through the poorly defined boundaries of their two chiefdoms. Much of eastern Ezo, then, the region that fur-bearing animals predominantly inhabited, was violently ripped apart as Ainu chiefdoms competed over resources and powerful chiefs sought to extend their control over new lands to further strengthen their position in the changing ecological and social landscape of Ezo.

CONCLUSION

With the construction of trading posts, and the market culture that emanated from them, Japanese goods, including grain and saké, became more readily available to Ainu. Of course, Ainu still hunted and fished to meet the immediate utilitarian needs of their families, but they also sought "hunted commodities" to trade for more valuable items with Japanese. It should not be overlooked, for example, that Ainu-crafted items such as salmon-skin boots (*cepker*) and *attus*, being replicable and hence of minimal fixed value, never became emblems of wealth or political power in Ainu chiefdoms. In contrast, as observers such as Furukawa Koshōken, Matsumae Hironaga, and Yamazaki Hanzō have noted, Ainu personal prestige became linked to the emblems of wealth acquired in trade. Even in rituals such as the *iomante* and *kamuy-nomi*, Japanese goods either adorned the ritual site or were integrated into the performance itself as tools that mediated between the metaphysical and temporal worlds. Saké, moreover, became the offering that Ainu elders made to local deities and ancestors during rituals such as the *kamuy-nomi*.

Land and natural resources, especially the "animals of enterprise," took on a new symbolic and commercial value in early-modern Japanese and Ainu culture. Now that at the Kiitappu post, for example, one deer pelt or a live hawk could be traded for rice and tobacco, land became a base from which Ainu produced goods for trade.[82] Autonomous chiefdoms, once defined in large part by their ability to be self-sustaining, became reoriented as production bases for trade, and the ability of Ainu to comfortably feed and clothe themselves became tied to access to resources necessary for trade. As Matsumae Norihiro noted, trade had become the "industry" of Ainu by the seventeenth and eighteenth centuries. Naturally, for Ainu who lived in areas with abundant resources, this "industry" was advantageous, but for others it translated into hardships.

5 The Sakhalin Trade

DIPLOMATIC AND ECOLOGICAL BALANCE

Interaction with the peoples of the Eurasian continent played a crucial role in the creation of the multiethnic and multicultural character of the peoples of Ezo even as far back as the proto-Ainu groups, such as the Satsumon and the Okhotsk, mentioned in chapter 1. This pattern continued into the early-modern period, involved Sakhalin, but later—following Shakushain's War and the construction of trading posts in Ezochi— the Sakhalin relationship to the continent changed, and many communities found themselves navigating new commercial terrain. Fukuyama Castle and later the Edo shogunate conditioned Sakhalin hunting, fishing, and plant-gathering activities to fit the schedules of Ul'ichi traders and the demands of Matsumae trading posts, and this condition deprived Sakhalin peoples of their economic autonomy; this was true particularly after 1809, when the Edo shogunate moved to bail out Ainu who were being taken back to the Ul'ichi homeland as slaves in exchange for massive debts accumulated from serving as middlemen between Qing and Matsumae posts. This chapter explores the early Ainu diplomatic and ecological relationship with Sakhalin and such continental groups as the Chinese and discusses how the Matsumae and early Tokugawa oversight of trade transformed this relationship, further depriving the Ainu of their independence and contributing to their conquest.

THE CONTINENTAL ORBIT

In the *Matsumaeshi*, Matsumae Hironaga, a prolific eighteenth-century scholar from Fukuyama, imagined Ezo as a far-flung commercial expanse and resource-rich landscape. In his mind, Fukuyama Castle was a central gateway fixed between two geographic and ecological spheres: Japan and Ezo. Hironaga believed that Wajinchi, the region under Matsumae rule, was never simply a domain on the edge of the Japanese realm. In fact, he refused to view Fukuyama Castle as being on the edge of anywhere. His maps, representative of Matsumae's regional vision, portrayed Fukuyama Castle as a focal point: a fixed point of reference from which oddly shaped bodies of land stretched out and disappeared beyond a concentric horizon. Moreover, his writings on the natural world focused on the distinctive ecology of Ezo. In part illustrative of the growing natural studies of his day, called *honzōgaku*, he took the time to list more than forty kinds of birds, fifteen fur-bearing mammals, nearly sixty kinds of fish, and more than one hundred types of plants because Ezo was distinct enough, at least in his mind, to merit a taxonomic catalog separate from that of Japan.[1] He had what Michel Foucault describes as the "sharper eye" and "better-articulated language" of the taxonomist. The natural world has no order other than the "grid created by a glance, an examination, a language," writes Foucault, and if natural order "waits in silence for the moment of its expression," it was Hironaga who gave the animal, fish, and plant life of Ezo just such an expression in the Japanese taxonomy.[2]

The regional vision of the Matsumae family was unique within the Tokugawa polity. The Matsumae family, like other warrior households, looked inward to hubs such as Edo and Kyoto for political legitimacy. Its commercial perspective, however, was trained outward toward the vast northern expanse of foreign lands that lay within, and even beyond, its realm of geographic comprehension. The Matsumae world, as represented on maps drawn up by Hironaga, contained only the northernmost tip of Japan; but crude versions of Hokkaido, Sakhalin, and the rest of the north appeared to continue endlessly, and the Russian empire loomed on the eastern border.[3] Matsumae lords acquired this broader commercial and geographic perspective from the Ainu, their counterpart in trade, and through exploration.

It should not be surprising, given the central place of trade in Matsumae finances, that Hironaga also compared commercial activity at Wajinchi ports with the official trade at Nagasaki. The only difference between the ports, he suggested, was the quantity of products exchanged. The Ezo trade, like the Nagasaki trade, evidenced the commercial potential of Japan. He wrote that if the realm rescinded restrictions on trading, a greater variety and quantity of products from throughout the entire world would be coming and going into Japan.[4] Hironaga—a member of the warrior elite, a historian, and a burgeoning naturalist—was no merchant, yet his commercial perspective, born from a life in Fukuyama, favored a less-regulated commercial atmosphere in Japan.

Hironaga possessed a detailed understanding of the geographic and ethnic makeup of Ezo, the northeastern part of the Eurasian continent, and the Kuril Islands, a perspective largely garnered through contact with Ainu. North of Wajinchi, he explained, was Sakhalin Island (called Karafuto by the Japanese), which was inhabited by a variety of foreign peoples and exotic animal life. Sakhalin also served as a pathway for commodities making their way into Wajinchi from the continent. Hironaga explained that ethnic groups such as the Manchu ("the founders of the Qing dynasty"), the Tungus, and the Ugan of Northeast Asia used Sakhalin as a bridge for transporting such merchandise as brocade to the heart of Ezo, and they also crafted many of these goods. "Actually, [the brocade] is produced in Beijing," he wrote, "and now it is used as official uniforms for the Qing dynasty." (Eagle feathers and colored beads, Hironaga explained, were among the other goods produced in foreign countries.) He also tied the natural environment of Sakhalin to this trade, pointing out that Ainu living on Sakhalin brought sea lion, seal, bear, and fox pelts to Manchu posts, where they traded the pelts for textiles. Sakhalin Ainu, their small vessels weighted down with silks and colored beads, transported these goods to Sōya, where they were traded with Japanese.[5] Eventually, with the construction of the trading post in Sōya, northern Ezo and the Okhotsk Sea coast of Hokkaido would be drawn into the commercial and, eventually, ecological orbit of Japan; and the region's strong continental ties would be broken. ??

Providing evidence of early interaction with the continent, Japanese archaeologists have unearthed Chinese bronze mirrors, probably manufactured in Zhejiang Province, from Satsumon archaeological sites near Kusuri (Kushiro) in eastern Hokkaido. The mirrors date from the Song dynasty (960–1279), even before the Mongol conquest, and might have been imported through Sakhalin.[6] Archaeologists have also uncovered bronze and iron decorative medallions manufactured by some continental peoples at grave sites at the Moyoro shell mounds near present-day Abashiri. These items match similar medallions found at Nanai sites at Khabarovsk on the Tungus River, as well as along the banks of the Ussuri and Sungari Rivers in Northeast Asia.[7]

Nanai people wore these medallions, and other decorative pieces recovered at the continental sites, along the lower cuffs of their clothing, and so did women on Sakhalin, according to one nineteenth-century Japanese observer. Mamiya Rinzō sketched Sakhalin women wearing clothing adorned with these same medallions placed along the lower cuffs of their gowns. These medallions also fell into the hands of Hokkaido Ainu. Furukawa Koshōken observed in 1788 that Ainu who acquired these medallions called them *tamasay* and *sitoki* and wore them as pendants on necklaces. They were considered *ikor* by Ainu. These medallions and other decorative items date from about the mid–seventeenth century to the eighteenth century.[8]

After the fall of the Song dynasty, Ezo found itself on the boundary of the Chinese tributary system. Political and commercial ties embodied in tributary trading integrated northern Ezo into the Northeast Asian cultural sphere, shaping Ainu ritual and material culture. In the thirteenth century, for example, with the establishment of the Yuan dynasty (1279–1368), the Mongols adopted the tributary system to manage relations with Northeast Asian and Sakhalin peoples. The Nivkh, Uilta, and Sakhalin Ainu, along with a variety of other continental peoples, were among the groups incorporated into the Yuan diplomatic order. Even Ainu from Sōya, although living on the periphery of the Mongol empire, were affected. Over time, commercial ties formed with people such as the Sakhalin Ainu brought Chinese goods to Sōya, where they became a part of Ainu culture and the Matsumae trade-fief system. It was from here that silks and other goods eventually trickled into Japan.

The Ainu played an active role in shaping the political and commercial landscape of Sakhalin during this early period. In the thirteenth century, at about the time of the Mongol invasion, the Ainu too might have been seen as expansionists, a people who sought to extend their political and cultural influence beyond the traditional confines of northern Hokkaido and southern Sakhalin into the northern part of the latter island and beyond. They also put up a tenacious fight against the Mongol drive into Sakhalin. The Ainu pushed militarily into the Amur region, overrunning some Mongol-controlled posts on northern Sakhalin, but they were eventually expelled by Yuan armies.[9]

Importantly, it was not only Ainu and Yuan military campaigns but also geographic location that encouraged interaction between the Eurasian continent, Sakhalin, and Hokkaido. The distance between Sōya and southern Sakhalin is about twenty-six miles, whereas the distance between Sakhalin and the continent is only about four. During the winter, moreover, Sakhalin is connected to the continent by a bridge of thick, snow-covered ice, further accommodating commercial and cultural exchange.[10] The Ainu cultural order serves as an example of the interaction made possible by this close proximity: the Ainu view of the natural landscape as a space teeming with *kamuy* closely resembled the view held by the hunting cultures of the Tungus and other Northeast Asian peoples. Rituals such as the bear ceremony, a product of continental ties, incorporated Ainu into a natural order upon which their subsistence ultimately depended. This way of ordering the metaphysical and temporal worlds, as discussed in chapters 3 and 4, was widespread among Northeast Asian peoples.[11]

THE EXTENSION OF CHINESE CONTROL

The Mongol invasion of Northeast Asia and Sakhalin reshaped existing trade networks, centering trade at Yuan posts in the Amur Estuary and northern Sakhalin. The Mongol move into the region not only stemmed from a desire to find a passageway into Japan but was also a military response to Ainu attempts at expansion and fighting with other groups on Sakhalin. The *Yuanshi*, for example, the official history of the Yuan dynasty, notes that the Guwei people—a group from south of the Amur Estuary, probably the Ainu—pushed into Sakhalin and every year fought with the Jilimi (the present-day Nivkh), who had been subjugated by the Mongols, sometime in the early thirteenth century. In 1264, in response, Mongol troops made their way to the Amur River region, establishing an outpost at Tyr, along the Amgun River north of Sakhalin; and by 1308 (only after strong resistance in 1264 and 1284), the Mongols had militarily subdued the Ainu. Following their subjugation, Ainu elders made tributary visits to Yuan posts located at Wuliehe, Nanghar, and Boluohe. Much later, in 1409, the Yongle emperor established an outpost at Nurkan and built a large temple near the ruins at Tyr. In brief, then, following the introduction of Chinese political and commercial institutions in the Amur region, by the middle of the fifteenth century the Nivkh, Uilta, and Sakhalin Ainu were making frequent tributary visits to Chinese-controlled outposts, where they presented animal skins in return for textiles and other goods. It was following these developments, that the center of the northern trade shifted to Chinese posts in the Amur Estuary and on Sakhalin.[12] → and then onto Japan

Under the Ming dynasty (1368–1644), following the collapse of Mongol rule, commerce in Northeast Asia and Sakhalin was placed under the "system for subjugated peoples," or *ximin tizhi*. According to the classic *Shujing* [The book of history], Sage Yu subjugated the Miao, a "barbarian" group, by demonstrating the virtue and sincerity of imperial rule, and this system of civilizing peripheral peoples through trade and cultural exchange continued to characterize the administration of the boundaries of the Chinese empire.[13] In theory, integrating "barbarian" headmen into the Chinese administrative structure and conducting tributary trade would civilize all uncivilized peoples. However, recent scholarship demonstrates that this was not always the case and that there was frequently a two-way cultural exchange between the core and borderland peoples.[14] The Ming state, nonetheless, recruited headmen for administrative posts from Sakhalin groups.

These positions consisted of the commander (*zhihuishi*), vice commander (*zhihui tongzhi*), assistant commander (*zhihui qianshi*), and the "official charged with subjugation" (*weizhenfu*).[15] The *Ming shilu* [The veritable record of the Ming dynasty] records several instances in which Chinese officials conducted tributary trade with Sakhalin peoples. In 1431, for example, Alige, who held the title assistant commander, brought tribute in the form of marten pelts to the Wuliehe post. In 1437, four other assistant commanders (including Zhaluha, Sanchiha, Tuolingha, and Alingge) also presented tribute at Ming posts. The *Ming shilu*, besides identifying the officials who presented tribute, also notes that these headman positions were hereditary, passed down along patrilineal lines.[16] During their visits to Wuliehe, many officials also brought their sons, who later inherited the titles and duties of their fathers.

In return for tribute, the Nivkh, Uilta, and Sakhalin Ainu received various silk uniforms from Ming officials, the style of which was directly related to their rank within the tributary order. The Ming state even extended the "system for subjugated peoples" into the Maritime Province area. Between 1465 and 1487, for example, some Tungus groups found themselves integrated into this politicized commercial network, which introduced more continental iron tools into the Sakhalin trade.[17] Under the Ming state, then, Chinese-sponsored political offices were superimposed upon native social hierarchies, changing life at a local level. Yet, the once pervasive view that China's influence on borderland peoples was uniformly "civilizing" is being slowly replaced by a more plausible scenario; that is, a scenario in which a mutual exchange took place between Chinese officials and native peoples, and most headmen recruited by the state actually rose to power according to local political traditions.[18] This was, as we will see later in chapter 8, true of Ainu headmen recruited by Matsumae officials.

Policies of the Qing dynasty (1644–1911) followed a similar pattern.[19] These policies drew Sakhalin peoples further into the "system for subjugated peoples," continuing the modification of native forms of political organization to conform to the Qing order, and forcing local people to pay tribute at Manchurian posts in the Amur Estuary and northern Sakhalin. Qing policy did not completely rob these groups of their native ethnicity and cultural practice, but it proved an effective means of focusing commercial activity toward Chinese posts and managing the boundaries of the Qing state.[20] Qing officials granted titles, such as *haraida* (*xingzhang*, "head of surname group") and *gashanda* or *gashanida* (*xiangzhang*, "village elders"), to local elders and entrusted them with the task of "keeping the peace." By the mid–eighteenth century, Qing officials had registered fifty-six surname groups as *haraida*; of these, Qing sources note that six clans and 148 households were those of Ainu and Nivkh who came under the Qing administrative umbrella on Sakhalin.[21]

Qing officials granted silk textiles to local headmen according to their *wulin*, a form of social status measured by wealth, political prestige, and the position the headmen held in the tributary hierarchy.[22] In the seventeenth and eighteenth centuries, these silk uniforms became trade items in Ezo. The specific terms used to identify these silk uniforms have attracted a great deal of attention among Japanese historians. Briefly, of the roughly thirteen styles of uniforms used by the Qing state, *gunfu* and *longpao* were commonly worn by members of the imperial household, including the Manchu emperor himself. Administrative and military officials commonly wore *mangpao*, *bufu*, and *chaofu*, depending on their governmental positions; these three uniforms were decorated with stylized embroidered dragons or peony patterns. In China, these decorations served as visual communications within Qing society, denoting wealth, education, and political status; and the arrangement of decorations on the uniform itself symbolized the stability and harmony of the Qing state.[23] Of these uniforms, the *mangpao* and *chaofu* comprised the majority of *nishiki* and *jittoku* traded with Japanese at Sōya and Shiranushi.[24] Yet, these uniforms took on a completely different meaning once in the hands of Ainu and Japanese.

Of the products Japanese acquired at trading posts, *nishiki* and *jittoku* were among the most valuable. As dynastic uniforms, they were of considerably higher quality than silks available at Nagasaki, the other gateway through which trade was conducted with China. Furthermore, as exotic clothing, *jittoku* served the local ambitions of the Matsumae family. By at least the late eighteenth century, Matsumae officials had adopted a policy of making Ainu elders wear *jittoku* during audiences, in the same way that the shogunate often made Ryukyuans wear Chinese accoutrements when visiting Edo in an effort to dramatize their place as the foreign "other" and their subordination to the Edo shogunate.[25] Ainu appear to have worn Ezo silks in native rituals only infrequently, and they did not fully incorporate the foreign-manufactured clothing into their own textile culture. Rather, they probably viewed *jittoku* as goods to be imported from abroad and then sold to Matsumae traders. Unlike Japanese lacquerware, silks were never completely integrated into Ainu material culture.[26] Audiences sponsored by Fukuyama Castle, for which the clothing itself was mandated and sometimes distributed by officials, were central to Japanese relations with various Ainu chiefdoms. As discussed in chapter 8, there was no body of water separating Wajinchi from Ezochi, as there was separating Satsuma from the Ryukyu Kingdom, or Tsushima from Korea; so Matsumae officials manufactured borders through ritual, trade, and cultural performance.

With the "system for subjugated peoples" firmly in place, the people of northern Sakhalin and the Amur Estuary viewed Ming and Qing posts as market hubs. And when Japanese constructed trading posts at Sōya and Shiranushi, these posts became a part of this broader commercial landscape that revolved around Chinese tributary posts. In effect, continental networks, carrying everything from elements of Chinese political culture to silk brocade and colored beads, now extended from Beijing to Fukuyama Castle and, ultimately, Japan (see map 3).

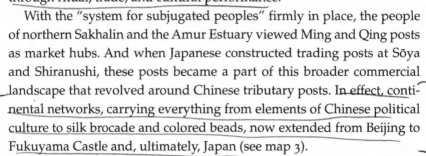

In the fifteenth century and even during the early days of the Matsumae family, the Sakhalin trade route influenced the family's commercial and political perspective. Gifts that would later tie the Kakizaki and Matsumae to Kyoto and Edo, for example, trickled in from the continent through the Sakhalin route. Even items associated with the founding of the Kakizaki family can be tied to the Sakhalin trade. At the Hanazawa fort in southern Ezo, near Kaminokuni, the progenitor of the Matsumae family, Takeda Nobuhiro, obtained a Chinese-manufactured bronze inkstone receptacle, probably through Sakhalin trade channels; and this icon

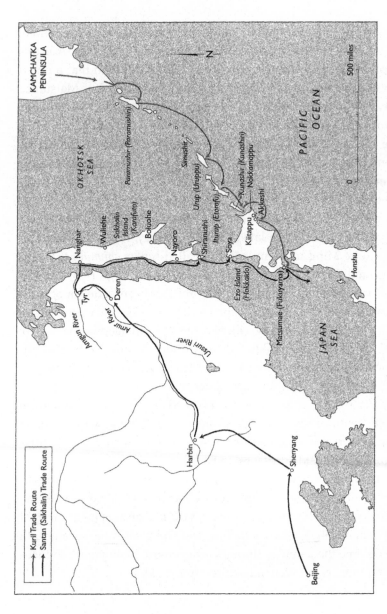

Map 3. Trade routes of North Asia and the North Pacific. Adapted from Emori Susumu, "Ezochi o meguru hoppō no kōryū," in *Nihon no kinsei: Jōhō to kōtsū*, ed. Maruyama Yasunari (Tokyo: Chūō Kōronsha, 1992), 6:387; and Kaiho Mineo, "Hoppō kōeki to chūsei Ezo shakai," in *Nihonkai to hokkoku bunka: Umi to rettō bunka*, ed. Amino Yoshihiko (Tokyo: Shōgakukan, 1990), 274, 280.

later became an important family heirloom of the Matsumae household. Among the first emblems of Kakizaki prominence in Ezo, then, was this bronze piece obtained through the Sakhalin route, an item that accrued local political value in the northern region.[27] The symbol of Matsumae longevity, something passed down through the generations, was a foreign-manufactured item obtained through the Sakhalin trade.

These exotic products from Ezo later attracted attention among the hegemons of seventeenth-century Japan, at about the time that many European products were in vogue. In 1558, for example, Kakizaki Suehiro brought eagle feathers while visiting Kumano in Kii Province. The feathers reportedly came from northern Ezo, probably Sakhalin.[28] While meeting with Ieyasu in the late sixteenth century, Kakizaki Yoshihiro wore an exotic Ming uniform (dōfuku), called santan shimipu, that had been acquired from Ainu. The uniform had been imported through Sakhalin by continental traders and had probably been traded at posts in the Amur Estuary. Yoshihiro explained to Ieyasu, who had expressed an interest in the clothing, that the silk had come "from deep northern Ezo; an island called Karafuto [Sakhalin]." In the end, he offered the silk uniform to Ieyasu, thus extending Sakhalin trading networks all the way to the leading architect of the Tokugawa polity.[29]

Later, Portuguese missionaries confirmed in 1618 that Ainu from Teshio, just south of Sōya, brought Chinese silks to trade with Japanese. Similarly, in 1620, it was noted that the silk textiles traded in Ezochi originated from well outside present-day Hokkaido.[30] However, at that time, only small quantities of Chinese silks entered Japan as gifts. Later, the intensification of exchange at trading posts altered traditional commercial activity at Sōya and Shiranushi by diversifying the kinds of items brought in from Sakhalin. Sōya, where a trading post was built in the seventeenth century, became the gateway through which most continental products, including animal skins, were introduced from Sakhalin.

THE EARLY EXPLORATION OF SAKHALIN

By the early seventeenth century, Matsumae lords had developed commercial interests in Sakhalin that transcended trading-post activity. After all, the Sakhalin route was only a distribution network over which Japanese, at this time, had little control. Fukuyama Castle, which had up to that time conducted trade through intermediaries, developed an interest in nurturing more direct ties to resources on Sakhalin. The seventeenth century witnessed an increase in the volume and variety of trade, and Matsumae expeditions set out to survey the natural resources found on the island. As early as 1635, for example, Murakami Kamonzaemon, Satō Kamoemon, and Kakizaki Hiroshige, all Matsumae vassals, crossed over to southern Sakhalin to conduct commercial and geographical surveys.[31] They sought to determine the feasibility of exploiting salmon and sea cucumber fisheries on southern Sakhalin.[32] Although the cartographic information these three gathered was lost in subsequent fires that flared up in the Matsumae castle town, the information was probably used in the making of the 1644 and 1700 provincial maps that were discussed in the introduction. The next year, in 1636, another Matsumae vassal, Kōdō Shōzaemon, crossed over to southern Sakhalin and spent a harsh winter at Usshamu (possibly being the first Japanese to do so); the following spring he traveled as far as Taraika before turning back.

These short visits improved Matsumae knowledge of Sakhalin considerably. Matsumae officials had surveyed parts of southern Sakhalin, but the whereabouts of the locations and other commercial information were gathered in conversations with Sakhalin and Sōya Ainu during these visits.[33] As Matsumae officials came into more frequent contact with Sakhalin and Sōya Ainu during the eighteenth century, commercial and geographic information was easier to come by. In the mid-1770s, for example, Kudō Chōkyū, a Matsumae vassal from Fukuyama, met with Yōchiteaino, an Ainu elder from Nayoro on Sakhalin, who brought along three pieces of *jittoku* to trade at Sōya; and they exchanged information on both geography and trade.[34]

Immediately following Shakushain's War in 1669, Fukuyama Castle authorized ships to trade in southern Sakhalin. In fact, Matsumae Yasuhiro made reference to ships trading *eburiko*, a medicinal lichen indigenous to southern Sakhalin, just after the heavy fighting in western Ezo. By 1715, Chinese silks were being acquired from Sakhalin, but crossing over to that island remained difficult because of rough seas and low temperatures. The difficult crossing notwithstanding, however, Matsumae

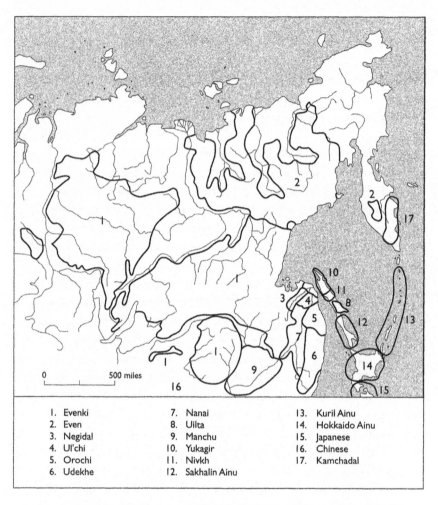

1. Evenki	7. Nanai	13. Kuril Ainu
2. Even	8. Uilta	14. Hokkaido Ainu
3. Negidal	9. Manchu	15. Japanese
4. Ul'chi	10. Yukagir	16. Chinese
5. Orochi	11. Nivkh	17. Kamchadal
6. Udekhe	12. Sakhalin Ainu	

Map 4. Peoples of North Asia and the North Pacific. Adapted from Kikuchi Toshihiko, *Hokutō ajia kodai bunka no kenkyū* (Sapporo: Hokkaidō Daigaku Tosho Kankōkai, 1995), 440.

lords continued to sponsor surveys that were increasingly aimed at opening new fisheries on southern Sakhalin. In the 1750s, Matsumae vassal
Katō Kahei took the merchant ship *Eifuku-maru*, owned by Fukuyama
merchant Hamaya Yozaemon, to investigate sea cucumber and other
fisheries on Sakhalin. Following his visits to Sakhalin he learned a great
deal about the geography and customs of the Sakhalin people. He also
acquired valuable *nishiki* during these voyages. As Akizuki Toshiyuki
observes, Katō's surveys might be viewed as the birth of the Japanese
fishing industry on Sakhalin. In 1771, Fukuyama Castle ordered merchant Murayama Denbei to dispatch two additional ships to investigate
the possibility of expanding fisheries on Sakhalin. Murayama met with
Shimautekan, the Ainu elder from Shiranushi, and exchanged silks, colored beads, fish oil, dried cod, and seal pelts. From the eighteenth century onward, Japanese ships frequented southern Sakhalin to trade or exploit resources, and a permanent Japanese fishery was established in
1790 near Shiranushi.[35]

The Sakhalin route is often called the "Santan trade" in historical documents, as many people of Northeast Asia were frequently lumped together as the Santan in the Japanese mind. The word "Santan" itself probably referred to the Ul'chi people south of the Amur River, as well as to
several other groups, including the Nanai, Orochi, Udekhe, and Negidal,
who inhabited the region near the Mamiya Strait (see map 4). The term
may have also included the Uilta and Nivkh who lived on Sakhalin and
participated in the trade. Regardless of the origins of the term, from the
early eighteenth century onward, the Santan trade described commercial
networks that extended through Sakhalin.[36] In 1737, Sakakura Genjirō
made one of the first references to the Sakhalin route as the Santan trade.
Sakakura remarked, illustrating a broadening geographic and commercial knowledge of the region, that north of Taraika on Sakhalin were
countries called Manchuria and Santan. Various merchants from these
northern countries, he continued, traded silk brocade and colored beads
with the Ainu at Taraikai, who then traded these products with Matsumae domain at Sōya.[37]

Early on, Matsumae lords proved reluctant to divulge information
concerning the Santan trade, and Edo inspectors had become alarmed by

the eighteenth century, fearing Russian advances. In 1761, when inspectors were to arrive at Fukuyama Castle with questions about commerce on Sakhalin, Matsumae officials prepared to answer shogunal inquiries vaguely: Karafuto served as a route for foreign goods coming in from China, and so the imported goods came from "extremely far away." Since acquiring them was "next to impossible," there was "no need to be concerned" that there might be a breach of the maritime prohibitions instituted in the 1630s. Matsumae officials actually knew considerably more about the trade than they led Edo to believe. Through these commercial networks Ainu had been acquiring imported products for many years. Via the trading post a Sōya, these products wound up in Matsumae hands.[38]

In 1785, Tanuma Okitsugu, the shogun's senior councillor, reportedly expressed concern about what he called a "passage way to foreign lands" and about trading commodities "manufactured in foreign countries."[39] To investigate the passageways to foreign lands, the shogunate dispatched Satō Genrokurō, who a year later turned in a report that offered a fairly detailed picture of the Sakhalin route. In 1785, Ibara Yaroku, of the finance magistracy (*kanjō bugyō*), crossed over to Shiranushi together with five Matsumae officials and then traveled west to Tarantomari, surveying much of southern Sakhalin. They returned to Sōya to spend the winter, but, Satō remarked, the five Matsumae officials died of scurvy. According to Satō, the next year, in 1786, shogunal officials under Ōishi Ippei again crossed over to Sakhalin, where they met with twenty-one continental traders (*santanjin*) at Tarantomari. Satō noted that the continental group was led by an elder named Biyanko (also known as Fuyanko), an old hand in the Santan trade, who, through an Ainu interpreter, offered the most detailed explanation to date of the trade route: continental peoples came to Sakhalin for the purpose of trade, the trade originated with tributary visits to Qing posts in the Amur Estuary, and it was from the Qing posts that the silk brocade and colored beads originated.[40]

Satō's report sparked widespread changes in how both Fukuyama Castle and the Edo shogunate viewed trade on Sakhalin. Up to this point, Matsumae officials had understood the Santan trade to be within its broader mandate to control commerce in Ezo: Matsumae Yoshihiro had been invested by Shogun Ieyasu himself with a mandate to oversee trade with the "barbarians," and trade conducted with any and all "barbarians" appeared to be included within this mandate. Whether the Matsumae family obtained the silks directly, through Sōya Ainu, or from Japanese merchants, the Sakhalin trade was thought to be within the sphere of Fukuyama control, at least by the Matsumae family. For almost two hundred years, the shogunate appeared content with this arrangement, until the Russians, the "red barbarians," showed up in the North Pacific.

The Matsumae family had viewed Sakhalin as an area with commercial potential even before the Russian threat, suggesting that the early Japanese interest in Sakhalin was not solely the product of outside pressure. Occasionally local scholars such as Matsumae Hironaga voiced concerns over "the restrictions of the realm" and how those restrictions related to trade on Sakhalin. Nonetheless, the thrust of Matsumae policy was aimed at securing profits at trading posts. Matsumae lords, in this respect, were not seclusionists. Given the situation, their commercial and geographic vision differed from that of many domains in the Tokugawa polity. The Matsumae understood that they were trading with "barbarians" outside the orbit of their influence—Chinese, Manchus, Tungus, Ugan, Santan, and Sakhalin Ainu, all groups specifically mentioned by Matsumae Hironaga in the eighteenth century[41]—but nonetheless they sought to assert their commercial agenda on Sakhalin. Matsumae lords and their vassals approached trade and fisheries on Sakhalin as commercial expansionists. They surveyed, exploited natural resources, set up guard posts, controlled exchange through trading posts, and gradually challenged the weakening Qing order on Sakhalin and in the Amur region, which up until the 1790s had dominated commercial relations on the island.

However, Russian encroachment, discussed in the next chapter, forced both Matsumae lords and the Edo shogunate to pay closer attention to affairs in the North Pacific. From the late eighteenth century onward, the shogunate began to view Russian advances from the north as a realm-threatening problem, a view that eventually led to the abolition of Matsumae control over trade. Tokugawa policy on Sakhalin in the early nineteenth century would depart radically from the previous two hundred years of Matsumae control, and shogunal attempts to redirect all trading on Sakhalin through Tokugawa channels severed the Ainu, Uiltō, and Nivkh from their traditional networks.

ENVIRONMENT AND TRADE ON SAKHALIN

In 1790, the Matsumae lord dispatched Takahashi Seizaemon and Murayama Denbei to conduct surveys and oversee the development of new fisheries on Sakhalin. They constructed a permanent trading post at Shiranushi and had guard posts (*ban'ya*) built at Tonnai and Kushunkotan. Takahashi met with twenty-nine continental traders and acquired information concerning the geography of Northeast Asia and the Chinese origins of many of the items traded on Sakhalin, and he obtained a list of the kinds of products exchanged.[42] The Shiranushi, Tonnai, and Kushunkotan posts were, as Akizuki points out, the first permanent Japanese facilities constructed on Sakhalin.[43]

At the Sōya and Shiranushi posts, some Ainu stood to make a significant profit by trading Chinese textiles with Japanese. In 1786, Yaenkoroaino, an Ainu elder from Nayoro, traded one approximately six-yard length of crimson silk (*akajikire*) for several bales of rice, yeast, barrels of saké, and used clothing. For Kitarakani, another Ainu trader, two colored beads meant two bundles of tobacco. Even trader Kashitaka's steel and flint (*hiuchi*), also acquired from continental traders, bought a bundle of tobacco.[44] Ainu like these became middlemen in a trade that brought them daily necessities such as rice, tobacco, yeast, and saké, only as long as there was a ready supply of fur-bearing animals, which purchased the imported beads and silk. The key, however, remained the natural environment. In time, the productive activity of Sōya and Sakhalin Ainu became conditioned by the market demand emanating from the developing economies of Japan and, to a lesser degree, China, which in turn depleted resources on Sakhalin.

In 1791, Matsumae Heikaku, Aoyama Sonoemon, Suzuki Kumazō, and Takahashi Seizaemon, all Matsumae officials, crossed over to Shira-

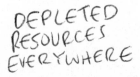

DEPLETED
RESOURCES
EVERYWHERE

nushi to further investigate the Sakhalin route and conduct surveys. The information they brought back to Fukuyama Castle was the most detailed to date. Heikaku traveled only as far as Nayoro, but he met the elder Fuyanko (the same elder who Ōishi Ippei had met in 1786 and who would later meet with Mogami Tokunai in 1792), and their lengthy conversation, preserved in manuscript form, sheds light on ties between the continental peoples and the Qing state. Heikaku's observations also reveal how the trade-fief system had conditioned the productive habits of Sakhalin Ainu in villages such as Shiranushi, Shoni, Machiratsunae, Kunnae, Ueni, Tsunnae, and so on. He explained that the productive systems of all villages in southern Sakhalin relied on hunting fur-bearing animals to exchange with traders from Deren (the Qing post in the Amur) and laboring in Japanese fisheries in the off-season.[45] In short, their subsistence practice had become synchronized to their role as middlemen in trade between Japanese and Qing posts.

As reported by the survey team, Fuyanko understood his subordinate relationship with the Qing state. He explained that the Santan were a "subjugated people" (*itate iyashiku*) and did not possess their own written language. He explained, moreover, that his own people were even more "beastly looking than the Ainu." They ate fish and dogs, he continued, and in matters of commerce were stingy. Fuyanko noted on several occasions that the Santan were under the control of the Qing state, which regulated trade on the continent and northern Sakhalin. Heikaku, the survey-team leader, also observed how the Qing tributary system and the presence of Matsumae trading posts had forced Sakhalin Ainu to intensify the exploitation of fisheries and the killing of fur-bearing animals in their lands (see figure 15). Qing officials, he said, fixed prices in trade on certain animal skins. Fuyanko explained that of animals hunted on Sakhalin, Qing officials regarded black fox as the most valuable, and white fox, sea otter, marten, river otter, and red fox followed in value in that order. Fuyanko also noted that the Santan received eagle feathers, colored beads, silk brocade, pipes, earrings, and other commodities from Qing officials. This merchandise, observed Heikaku, could by that time be found in Japan. In the summer, Fuyanko continued, usually between the fifth and sixth months, the Santan traders departed their homeland

Figure 15. A Sakhalin Islander hunting furs for the Santan trade. Sakhalin Ainu and other groups traded animal skins for silk brocade, which was then traded with the Japanese for saké and other goods. *Kitaezo zusetsu* [Illustrated explanation of northern Ezo]. Courtesy of the Resource Collection for Northern Studies, Hokkaido University Library.

south of the Amur River. In small boats made of salmon skins with birch bark sails, they crossed Mamiya Strait, between the Amur Estuary and Sakhalin Island, with their lucrative cargo. These boats could hold about thirty pieces of clothing, eight bundles of eagle feathers, 160 colored beads, and other merchandise and rations. Fuyanko noted that about four or five boats made the trip annually.[46]

The subsistence practice of many Sakhalin Ainu and some Uilta had become influenced by the pressure that Japanese placed on Ainu to trade. Subsequently, further pressure was leveled on the fur-bearing animals of Sakhalin used to purchase silks. Sakhalin peoples hunted and trapped to acquire merchandise for Japanese traders, who then sold the goods in the burgeoning market economies to the south. Heikaku wrote that in the winter Ainu women from Shiranushi to Nayoro crafted *attus* and *yu-tarube* textiles to trade with the Santan; they also collected plants in the mountains to make colorful dyes. Ainu men hunted and trapped seal, sea lion, whale, bear, marten, river otter, and fox (see figure 16). The skins from these animals were exchanged with the Santan for Chinese and continental products and were often transported via dogsled (see figure 17). In autumn both men and women labored at salmon fisheries, wrote Heikaku, while in the spring they exploited herring runs for Japanese merchants.[47]

However, by the late eighteenth century, Sakhalin was unable to sustain fur hunting at a pace that supported both Japanese and Qing needs. Silks imported through the Santan route were being sold in Japanese cities, and merchants pressured Sakhalin Ainu to increase their hunting and trapping productivity so that more silks could be traded to satisfy Japan's appetite for foreign merchandise. Small wallets (*kamiire*) crafted from the Ezo silks, as well as the colored beads that were used as decorative weights, became emblems of sophisticated taste in Japanese urban society. Buddhist monks used silks for *kesa*, or sacred shoulder scarves, and altar cloths called *uchishiki*; and samurai wore the imported textile as *haori*, a coatlike garb. Smaller pieces of fabric were also used as decorative sword coverings (*naginatabukuro*).[48] Sakhalin and Sōya Ainu, now being squeezed by Japanese markets, overhunted local fur-bearing animals and eventually became unable to pay Santan traders in animal skins.

Mogami Tokunai's reports from Sakhalin highlight the breakdown of any semblance of Ainu and Uilta economic autonomy as a result of trade with Japanese. Mogami, who crossed over to Sakhalin in 1792 with Wada Hyōdayū and Kobayashi Gennosuke, met with several Ainu elders from both Sōya and Sakhalin. He interviewed Ikoibe, an Ainu from Naibo, and Kariyashi (who had also spoken with Heikaku's team), whose parents had been carried off to the Santan homeland because they were unable to repay debts to continental traders. Mogami also surveyed other locations and found that many Ainu villages were deserted; most Ainu had been abducted by continental traders and enslaved because of their

Figure 16. A standard snare used by Sakhalin Islanders to catch fur-bearing animals for trade. *Kitaezo zusetsu* [Illustrated explanation of northern Ezo]. Courtesy of the Resource Collection for Northern Studies, Hokkaido University Library.

inability to repay debts. Mogami placed the blame squarely on the shoulders of Matsumae lords and their trading posts. He wrote,

In 1792, in an official capacity, I crossed over to Sakhalin Island arriving at a place called Shiranushi. Santan people then came, with seven of them riding in one small boat. The captain of the vessel was named Fuyanko. By a Manchu official, Fuyanko had been acknowledged as a Santan chief. The Santan brought along silks and a number of colored beads to sell to the Ainu on credit. If the amount is too high, in exchange, Ainu are taken back to the country of the Santan. In the before-mentioned boat was an Ainu named Ikoibe from a village called Naibo. He was being taken for old debts from four years earlier. Also, I departed Shiranushi for another place called Kushunnai where two more Santan boats arrived. Before long, Kariyashi, who was born in Sōya and later crossed over to Sakhalin

Figure 17. Sakhalin Islanders transporting goods for the northern trade via dog-sled. Sakhalin Islanders had a complex relationship with dogs, which were used both for pulling sleds and for hunting and were also harvested in the winter as an important food source. *Kitaezo zusetsu* [Illustrated explanation of northern Ezo]. Courtesy of the Resource Collection for Northern Studies, Hokkaido University Library.

Island, had also been seized and taken to Santan in exchange for debts. From Kushunnai to the place called Noteto, which serves as the crossover point for Santan, it is about one hundred *ri* [about 244 miles], and I saw two or three Ainu homes, but everybody else, in exchange for debts, had been taken to Santan.[49]

Mogami argued that Sakhalin Ainu found themselves in such debt because they served as middlemen in trade with Japanese. He continued, "Ezo silk is beautiful, and so it is used for making wallets; the glass beads become decorative weights for scroll paintings and calligraphy, and are popular [*aigan*]. If you take notice, the Ainu's body becomes the money [to pay for these items, as it is] sold to a foreign country."[50]

Mogami's interest in the Sakhalin trade intensified when he learned that Yaenkoroaino, the above-mentioned elder from Nayoro, possessed a memorandum written in Manchurian, which stated that the Ainu elder was an official of the Qing state.[51] Later surveys on Sakhalin by shogunal officials such as Takahashi Jidayū and Nakamura Koichirō only confirmed earlier observations: Sakhalin and Sōya Ainu traded foreign goods at trading posts, and because of the pressure to meet quotas, they fell into debt. These goods, the officials confirmed, originated at Qing posts, where continental traders acquired them during tributary ceremonies.[52] The information contained in these types of reports turned out to be a serious blow to the future of Matsumae's trade monopoly in Ezo.

However, if problems for Matsumae domain lurked in the future, the damage had already been done to Sakhalin Ainu. By the end of the eighteenth century, the subsistence practice of Sakhalin Ainu had been conditioned by Japanese trading posts, and this condition transformed the social ecology of Sakhalin trading. Before the Japanese move into Sakhalin, the limited Ainu market, combined with the fact that there appear to have been enough fur-bearing animals to supply continental traders, had sustained an ecological balance between Ainu and the animals they hunted and trapped. However, conditioning Ainu to hunt and trap to supply the trade-fief system and Japanese markets placed new pressure on Sakhalin fur-bearing animals, and their eventual scarcity meant that Ainu became unable to repay their debts. The Japanese move into Sōya and Sakhalin had tipped the ecological balance on the latter island. That Ainu were forced to look to the Edo shogunate to bail them out of their social and economic crisis in the early nineteenth century illustrates this trend. By the late eighteenth century, then, the productive systems of Ainu and Uilta had been refocused away from the continent and the Qing posts there, southward toward Japan.

SHOGUNAL CONTROL

The Edo shogunate took direct control of affairs in Ezo in 1799, after reports of a "secret" trade with Russia surfaced. Following the takeover, Matsuda Denjūrō, of the Matsumae magistracy, oversaw the repayment of Ainu debts to Santan traders. In all, Sōya Ainu owed 2,571 pelts; Sakhalin Ainu 2,975.[53] The shogunate repaid these 5,546 pelts to continental traders between 1809 and 1812, but not without radically restructuring the Sakhalin trade. The shogunate sought to place Sakhalin commercial activity completely under its control by rerouting trade through Tokugawa channels. Edo also reorganized meetings between shogunal officials and continental traders to conform to Tokugawa diplomatic protocol.[54] To start with, the shogunate made Ainu return the merchandise that they had recently received from continental traders. Furthermore, in the presence of a shogunal official, continental creditors and Ainu debtors were forced to confront each other and negotiate a settlement. Upon reaching an agreement, they then sealed the arrangement with their stamps, which were kept on record at Shiranushi. This policy continued until 1812, by which time most of the debts had been settled.

Finally, shortly after Edo repaid these debts in animal skins, shogunal officials forbade Sakhalin and Sōya Ainu to trade with continental peoples who traveled to Sakhalin. This measure severed the commercial and cultural ties that had shaped Ainu maritime activity and material culture for centuries, since as early as the period of the proto-Ainu Okhotsk culture. From about 1799 onward, trade was conducted by shogunal officials at the Shiranushi administrative post, or *kaisho*. Rather than exchanging products directly with Ainu, continental traders were forced to attend audiences with shogunal officials before any commercial exchange could take place. At these audiences, which symbolized Sakhalin and Sōya Ainu subordination to the Edo shogunate, important official edicts, the new laws of the land, were relayed to Ainu elders.[55]

To enforce this new system and deal with the likely scenario of smuggling, the shogunate set up guard posts at Tonnai, on the west coast of Sakhalin, which reported the arrival of continental traders. The transportation of merchandise was overseen by shogunal guards at Kushunnai. Commodities then received an official seal before they were transported to shogunal posts. Continental peoples, while trading in Shiranushi, stayed in guarded temporary houses built under shogunal order, somewhat reminiscent of those at Deshima Islet, where Dutch traders stayed in Nagasaki. To ensure that Ainu did not engage in independent trade,

shogunal inspectors met with elders to warn them against trading outside official channels. Shogunal officials carefully assessed the value of
the commodities brought to Shiranushi and gave continental traders various animal pelts in return.

In this way, direct Tokugawa rule in Ezo further alienated Ainu from
their traditional commercial relations with continental groups. Habuto
Masayasu, of the Hakodate magistracy, writing in the early nineteenth
century, understood that prohibiting Ainu from independently trading
on Sakhalin cut them off from the continent. The shogunate knew, he
wrote, that Sakhalin elders traveled as far as Beijing, where they participated in official tributary visits. Yaenkoroaino from Nayoro, for example,
whom Mogami Tokunai had written about in 1792, had reportedly made
such visits to pay tribute in pelts to Qing officials.[56] But the policy of
rerouting the Sakhalin trade through Japanese-controlled posts cut these
political and commercial ties. The Edo shogunate, implied Habuto, had
knowingly challenged the Qing diplomatic order on Sakhalin, although
by this time Qing officials had largely withdrawn from the region.

To keep the Sakhalin trade flourishing, however, the shogunate encouraged hunting and trapping so that more pelts would be available.
Edo policymakers wanted Ezo silks and other continental goods, but
they wanted acquisition and distribution of these goods under shogunal
control. Toward these ends, the shogunate took measures that assured a
steady supply of continental merchandise. In years when excessive hunting and trapping reduced the number of animal skins available for trade,
for example, the shogunate kept a warehouse outside Shiranushi that
was stocked with iron kettles and other goods, which were sold as sub-
stitutes to the Santan. Mamiya Rinzō, a shogunal official who later traveled to Qing posts, noted the rapid impact of this policy. He wrote that by
the early nineteenth century the use of Japanese iron kettles and other
products, which were sold at the Shiranushi post, had become widespread throughout Sakhalin, with the exception of the northernmost
areas. Sakhalin Ainu and Uilta, he continued, who had once crossed over
to the continent several times a year to acquire iron goods, now made the
trip only once every several years, because Japanese iron products were
readily available.[57] The shogunate also moved to oversee Uilta trading in

the interior of Sakhalin. With the advent of shogunal rule on Sakhalin, Uilta commercial activity was confined to posts at Kushunkotan.[58] By the end of the 1810s, southern Sakhalin peoples were well within the commercial and political orbit of Japan.

The Ainu allowed themselves to be integrated so rapidly into Japanese commercial and diplomatic channels because of their dependence on trade and because of the Japanese military presence on Sakhalin (which will be discussed in chapter 8). For two centuries Fukuyama Castle had pressured Sakhalin Ainu to acquire Chinese silks at trading posts. The incentives for this trade were Japanese-manufactured goods such as lacquerware and iron products, as well as rice, saké, yeast, and tobacco. Records from Sakhalin are scarce, but it can be conjectured that these goods had begun to have the same impact on Sakhalin Ainu as they had had on Ainu from eastern Hokkaido. Japanese goods supplanted traditional subsistence practice and sources of nutrition, making Sakhalin Ainu dependent on grain to support their changing productive systems; they hunted and trapped not only to feed and clothe their families but also to trade. If they had become dependent on the trading posts as a market, they probably had little choice but to conform to shogunal demands.

CONCLUSION

Prior to the construction of trading posts, then, a maritime culture, partially mediated by Qing posts, was one of the hallmarks of the southern Sakhalin and Sōya Ainu. They traded on Sakhalin, but they did so largely as their needs, and the Qing tributary order dictated. However, the expansion of the trade-fief system changed the nature of Ainu subsistence practice. Under Matsumae rule, in the winter Ainu hunted and trapped in anticipation of the arrival of continental traders, not to meet their own cultural needs but to trade at the pace that Japanese markets and Qing tribute demanded. However, Japanese demanded Chinese and other continental products in amounts that neither Ainu nor the Sakhalin environment could consistently sustain, which prompted the shogunate to move into Shiranushi. Subsequently, the shogunate, for its own reasons, tightened its control over the Sakhalin trade, and Ainu there lost one of the last preserves of their maritime autonomy. In the early nineteenth century, by the time Mamiya Rinzō visited Qing outposts in the Amur, the shogunate already controlled trade on southern Sakhalin; and the region and its inhabitants had been integrated into the commercial and, to a certain degree, ecological orbit of Japan.

6 The Kuril Trade

RUSSIA AND THE QUESTION OF BOUNDARIES

From long before 1600, as we have seen, outside groups influenced many aspects of Ainu life, from their cultural order to their subsistence practice. This influence trickled in not only from the Eurasian continent, Sakhalin, and Japan but also from the Kuril Archipelago, from such peoples as the Aleuts, the Kamchadal, the Kuril Ainu, and by the early eighteenth century, the Russians. However, Matsumae trading posts in eastern Ezo, where the Kuril influence was most visible, gradually changed the relationship between the Ainu and trade networks that reached them via the Kurils, just as trading posts had changed the commercial terrain on Sakhalin. In short, these trading posts rerouted Ainu trading activity through Japanese, rather than traditional Ainu, trade channels. As on Sakhalin, moreover, the Edo shogunate, after a lengthy 1780s investigation, ultimately usurped the power to make commercial and political de-

155

cisions related to the Kurils from Fukuyama Castle and enforced maritime restrictions that prohibited Ainu from trading in the Kurils beyond
Iturup Island. This last move severed Ainu from the commercial orbit of
the North Pacific, where they had for a time served as middlemen in an
emerging Russian trade with Matsumae officials and Japanese merchants. Once the Ainu's maritime autonomy had weakened, an earlier
way of life vanished, and many Ainu found themselves resigned to laboring in Japanese-controlled fisheries.

THE EARLY KURIL TRADE

Even after Shakushain's War, many coastal Ainu communities continued
to trade independently, navigating the Japan Sea, the Okhotsk Sea, and
even the North Pacific in *itaomacip*, a small craft equipped with sails.[1]
This maritime trade, like hunting and fishing, was woven into the fabric
of their culture. Powerful Ainu chiefdoms in Nokkamappu, Kiitappu,
and Akkeshi and on Kunashir and Iturup islands had forged commercial
relations that stretched from Hokkaido to as far as the Kamchatka Peninsula. With the appearance of Russian trappers in the North Pacific and
the introduction of the Russian-sponsored tribute system (the *yasak* system), these commercial networks extended all the way to the markets of
Russia. The construction of trading posts in eastern Ezo meant that a variety of new products, ranging from sea otter pelts and eagle feathers to
Russian leather coats and liquor, could be acquired in the Kurils.
Supplying the last link were powerful merchant households such as the
Hidaya, which brought these exotic items to Japan after taking over trad-
ing posts in eastern Ezo.

Similar to trade on Sakhalin, trade in eastern Ezo and the Kurils was
pervasive, multicultural, and multiethnic. Products ranging from sea
otter pelts and eagle feathers to Russian merchandise were traded in eastern Ezo. The distance between Nemoro (Nemuro), on the eastern tip of
Hokkaido, and Kamchatka is over 680 miles, with about twenty-four islands dotting the span between these two larger bodies of land.[2] In the
sixteenth century, before its investiture with the right to control com-

merce in Ezo, the Kakizaki family acquired some goods transported through the Kurils. In the 1560s, for example, "pure white sea otter pelts" were traded in eastern Ezo. Later, in 1594, Kakizaki Yoshihiro reportedly offered three sea otter pelts as gifts to Hideyoshi, after his meeting at Hizen in southwestern Japan.[3] And as we saw in chapter 4, Yoshihiro presented Tokugawa Ieyasu with a sea otter pelt "the size of a bear skin" following the battle for Osaka Castle in 1615. This pelt was only one of several brought to Fukuyama Castle by Nishirain, a Menashi chief from eastern Ezo, who had probably acquired these pelts in the Kurils.

Writing in 1618 about trade between the Ainu and the Japanese merchant ships that came to Fukuyama Castle each year, Portuguese missionary Jeronimo de Angelis remarked that the sea otter pelts that were traded came not from Ezo but from an island called Sea Otter Island (or Urup). Sparking some speculation about the people inhabiting the southern Kurils, he wrote that the inhabitants of Sea Otter Island were unlike Ainu, suggesting that they may have been remnants of the Okhotsk society described in chapter 1.[4] Another missionary report, from Diego Carvalho, noted that Ainu from the east brought sea otter pelts from Urup to trade at Fukuyama Castle.

During Matsumae rule, sea otter pelts became one of the most valuable commodities traded in the Kurils, carrying capital as gifts. In 1720, Arai Hakuseki, in a short ethnography, mentioned sea otter pelts as important products traded in Ezo. In 1739, Sakakura Genjirō remarked of sea otter pelts: "In the eastern seas there is an island called Sea Otter Island, the Ainu [bring sea otter pelts] to Kiitappu where they are traded."[5] Matsumae Hironaga explained that sea otter pelts even had healing properties. He wrote that sea otter skins, when wrapped around the stomach area, relieved abdominal pain, whereas sitting on top of the skins, or using them as a cushion, helped with blood circulation. Even more important, if people suffering from smallpox used the skins as a sleeping cushion, the disease would, at the very least, not get any worse. The Chinese believed that the soft pelts were the "cushion of the emperor," and Japanese merchants traded them at Nagasaki in the late eighteenth century.[6] Mogami Tokunai underscored the value of sea otter pelts when he wrote that "sea otter pelts are the single best product from Ezo.

The ancient precedent is that sea otter pelts are traded with Chinese ships at Hishū Nagasaki."[7] Here again, similar to the skins used in the Sakhalin trade, pelts originating in Ezochi, particularly in the east and from the Kurils, were being integrated into continental export markets.

Sea otter could be trapped or hunted in the northern reaches of the Kurils, from whence they then made their way down the chain of small islands toward trading posts on Hokkaido. A Russian observed in the eighteenth century that Ainu from the northern Kurils brought pelts and eagle feathers to Simushir, where they traded them for Japanese products such as textiles and ironware with Ainu from the south.[8] These Ainu then brought the pelts to Japanese-controlled posts. The French author Jean Baptiste-Barthelemy de Lesseps, who visited Russian posts in Kamchatka, wrote in 1787 that he had met nine Japanese merchants trading sea otter pelts in the Kurils. The merchants had explained to de Lesseps that they had intended to visit Kunashir Island to trade with Ainu but had been blown off course. By questioning the merchants about the commodities that they had brought to trade, de Lesseps determined that the goods consisted chiefly of lacquerware bowls and cups, boxes, and "other commodities of that sort."[9]

Ainu from eastern Hokkaido and the Kurils, as well as Aleuts and the Kamchadals, depended on these trade relations. In eastern Hokkaido, such chiefs as Ikotoi of Akkeshi, Shonko of Nokkamappu, and Tsukinoe of Kunashir Island had built their local hegemonies around the availability of animal skins to trade and the maintenance of commercial ties both to the Japanese and to groups in the Kurils. They profited as middlemen in the Kuril trade, but their position left them vulnerable to well-connected Japanese merchants who moved into eastern Ezo in the early eighteenth century.

In 1702, Hidaya Kyūbei, one such well-connected merchant, left Japan for Ezo, where he contracted outposts from the Matsumae vassal Ōhara Kamegorō.[10] He hoped to gain access to rich timber supplies on Rishiri Island in the north, as well as at Saru, Kusuri, and Akkeshi in the east and Teshio and the Yūbari area in the west. By gaining such access, Hidaya could offer a fresh source of lumber to supplement increasingly depleted stands near Japanese cities.[11] The home of Hidaya Kyūbei, Hida Province, was heavily deforested in the early eighteenth century, according to Conrad Totman. During the seventeenth century, intense monument building had occurred throughout Japan, and it was at this time that most of the castles and palaces that became the architectural symbols of warrior authority had been constructed. Subsequently, rapid deforestation occurred throughout the Japanese Archipelago. Even in the mid–seventeenth century, however, the inner mountains of Hida had still boasted preserves of virgin timber. The Meireki fires of the 1660s, however, had focused shogunal attention on remaining timber supplies to rebuild Japan's wooden cities, and by the 1690s the local domainal family, the Kanamori, had been transferred to another domain in northeastern Japan. At this point, the shogunate had been able to freely exploit the forest reserves of Hida Province. Totman explains that it took the shogunate only three decades to strip the region of its once vast timber supplies. Some local village interests tried to ensure themselves some access to local woodlands, but by 1735 the shogunate had tightened its grip over Hida timber, leaving local lumbermen to fend for themselves with little compensation. The case of Ezo suggests that some shrewd merchants, such as Hidaya Kyūbei, had already begun to look elsewhere for virgin woodlands by 1702.[12]

By exploiting the forests of eastern Ezo and supplying Matsumae lords with badly needed licensing fees (unjōkin) and loans, Hidaya quickly expanded his influence over both local Matsumae policymakers and natural resources throughout Ezo. By 1740, Hidaya had secured a contract that would give him exclusive access to timber in Akkeshi and Shiribetsu.[13] The Matsumae lord approved the request, despite the earlier finding of Fujikura Yūemon of the timber magistracy (hiyama bugyō) that nearly ten thousand trees had been secretly harvested in several areas in western Ezo.[14] The Hidaya household, which may or may not have secretly cut down the trees, had begun to extend its influence over the ruling Matsumae family. However, merchant influence over domain lords, as Mark Ravina illustrates, became a standard feature of early-modern domains as their economies became more dependent on merchant financing.[15]

With a major castle town fire in 1767, the destruction of the Matsumae

Edo residence in the Gyōninzaka fire of 1772, and the expensive obligation of attendance in Edo, it is hardly surprising that Matsumae
Michihiro looked to Hidaya for financial assistance.[16] Shrewdly, Hidaya
seized the opportunity, securing exclusive contracts to exploit resources
that might have otherwise gone to competing merchant interests. For example, after having been fired by the Hidaya household for misconduct,
Nanbuya Kaemon, in league with Matsumae financial official Minato
Genzaemon, maneuvered to take over a deal that had already been
sealed with Hidaya to harvest timber. However, Hidaya quickly re-
claimed what he saw as his rights to resources in Ezochi. Furious, he
threatened to take back the 8,183 *ryō* in money that he had advanced to
the Matsumae if they went through with the inside deal with Nanbuya.
In response, that same year, the Matsumae offered to pay back the advanced money in 500 *ryō* yearly payments, but when Matsumae could
not, they instead extended Hidaya contracts to use trading posts in eastern Ezo, at Etomo, Akkeshi, Kiitappu, and Kunashir Island. Of the over
ten thousand *ryō* in loans extended by the Hidaya, the Matsumae family
appears to have never repaid a single *ryō*. Hidaya, to collect on his in-
vestment in the Matsumae family, extracted a hard price from the Ainu
who lived in the vicinity of eastern trading posts in the form of unfair
trade exchange rates and harsh working conditions at fisheries.[17]
    Under these lucrative contracts, the Hidaya merchants and their
brazen trading-post managers enjoyed uncontested control over eastern
fisheries, animal skins, and timber supplies, without intervention from
Fukuyama Castle or the Edo shogunate. Under Hidaya control, it was ru-
mored that Ainu in the east watched managers threaten to throw their
pregnant wives into boiling kettles; bind the legs of their prized hunting
dogs and toss them in rivers to drown; beat Ainu women to death with
firewood; commit rape; and even threaten to "murder them all."[18]
Hidaya, and other Japanese merchants like him, also forced Ainu to labor
by extracting unfair contracts from elders in the form of what David
Howell calls "communal labor agreements," which shifted their community's commercial activity from hunting and trading to laboring in
Japanese-run herring and salmon fisheries.[19]
    With Ainu increasingly unable to travel between Hokkaido and Kam-

chatka because they were laboring in local fisheries, they became reliant on Hidaya merchants for daily necessities, such as rice to supplement their diet, as well as for tobacco. Once again, the gender dynamics of Ainu communities were crucial: when Ainu women were forced to turn from native forms of shifting agriculture and gathering wild plants to fishery work, as earlier noted, one more component of their productive and self-sustained system was undermined.[20] Laboring in fisheries also meant that their days as a maritime people navigating *ttaomacip* through the Kurils to trade sea otter pelts and other skins and fish were rapidly coming to a close. Some Ainu chiefs still had the time to hunt and trade on Urup Island, but younger Ainu, who had grown up under the sway of Hidaya interests, and probably most women, could not afford to leave the fishery. Hidaya merchants had taken the first step in severing Ainu ties with the North Pacific by forcing them to work under communal labor agreements. More importantly, Hidaya's acquisition of Russian merchandise, with Ainu chiefs acting as middlemen, led to a direct confrontation with the Edo shogunate. Undermining centuries of Ainu maritime activity in the Kurils, Edo policymakers would ultimately react by prohibiting Ainu from trading beyond Iturup, retraining their commercial and political perspective inward toward Japan.

THE APPEARANCE OF RUSSIANS IN THE KURILS

It was the shogunal reaction to the Russian move into the North Pacific that most severely restricted Ainu trading activity in the Kurils. In 1689, following the Treaty of Nerchinsk, which ended border clashes between Russia and China, Russian fur traders moved into the North Pacific and began the exploration of the Kurils.[21] By the end of the seventeenth century, Russians had set up posts in Kamchatka to handle the pelts that they collected as tribute from the native Kamchadal and Kuril Ainu.[22]

Yuri Slezkine argues that as the Russian empire began to emerge as a European power, Russians articulated the eastward push into Siberia and the North Pacific in the abstract political context of "the good of the state," rather than simply justifying the move in commercial terms. In this abstract political context, nurturing "obedient conquered peoples," by collecting *yasak* in the form of animal skins, was construed as bolstering international prestige. Interestingly, the Russian, the Qing, and even the Japanese trade systems shared structural similarities, though Japan was clearly less concerned with garnering international recognition. Following a series of reforms in the eighteenth century, for example, the Russian government, like the Qing, encouraged local native headmen, rather than Russian officials, to collect *yasak*. Unlike the Qing tributary order, the *yasak* system rendered not just the Russian settlers in Siberia and the North Pacific but also the native peoples dependent on the exchange of pelts. In this sense, the relationship between the Russians and Siberia and the North Pacific was much like that between the Matsumae family and Ezo. On the one hand, many native people became reliant on the liquor, tobacco, flour, butter, sugar, and ironware traded by Russian officials. Russian settlers, on the other hand, made their living by acting as middlemen between these native groups and Russian markets. In short, the Russian empire staked much of its prestige on the *yasak* system, which supplied "obedient conquered peoples" to parade before the international community; and settlers depended on the tribute system for their livelihood.[23]

Stepan Krasheninnikov wrote in 1764 that most of the Kuril Ainu and Kamchadal between Kamchatka and Urup Island paid yearly tribute in "sea-beaver" (sea otter), sable, and fox pelts. Despite the fact that the Kamchadal rarely hunted more animals "than what they must pay in tribute, and what will pay their debts," trade in Kamchatka was lucrative because "[t]he sables . . . excel all other sables of *Siberia*, both in largeness, thickness of hair, and brightness." John Stephan, who has written extensively on the North Pacific, points out that the *yasak* system quickly reached the Ainu of the southern Kurils and early on led to confrontations between Ainu and Russians.[24] In the 1760s, for example, Ivan Chernyi visited locations in the Kurils as far south as Iturup, demanding tribute from Ainu at every opportunity. In 1770, violence broke out when Ainu on Urup refused to pay tribute. Several Ainu were killed in the incident.[25] The next year a party of Iturup Ainu ambushed Russian fur trappers on Urup. Satō Genrokurō was told of the Urup incident while in

Ezo. His description offers a dramatic illustration of how Ainu organized themselves to defend hunting grounds against Russian advances southward down the Kuril Islands. Satō wrote that for some time both Ainu and Russians had been coming to Urup Island to hunt sea otter and that the two groups frequently met and even traded with one another. In 1770, while Ainu were hunting near Urup, a large Russian ship arrived with eighty people onboard. After the two groups met, the Russians shot and killed some of the Ainu hunters. The Russians then stole the sea otter skins that the Ainu had taken up to that point and, more importantly, took over their hunting grounds around Urup Island. The Ainu could do little against the eighty armed Russians and so they fled southward. The next year, in response, chiefs from Iturup and Kunashir islands met, organized a large band of Ainu warriors, and, in over fifty boats, traveled to Urup and waited for the Russians to arrive. This time the Russians came in a boat with more than one hundred people onboard; when the Russians disembarked they were surrounded and attacked by the Ainu warriors. More than ten Russians died in the attack, whereas the Ainu casualties were four or five. When the surviving Russians fled back to their ship, they were pursued by Ainu who climbed up the sides of the craft and shot at the Russians with poison arrows, killing another two or three and wounding many others. Although confined to 1770–1, the Urup incident demonstrates that some Ainu were willing to kill and be killed to defend hunting grounds—hunting grounds connected to trade with Japanese and Russians.[26] For this reason, at least in the southern Kurils, Ainu probably never viewed themselves as conquered peoples of the *yasak* system; they were, at least in their view, a maritime people profiting as middlemen in trade.

Some of the earliest examples of Russian traders appearing in the Kuril trade come from the mid–eighteenth century. Fukuda Shinzaburō, a shogunal official, remarked that merchandise transported by Russians was sometimes among the items traded in eastern Ezo. It was brought by Ainu along with other products. Furukawa Koshōken observed that "bound textiles" and "scarlet woolen cloth" were brought to Fukuyama Castle from Urup. Some of this cloth was put on display at a Buddhist temple in the castle town.[27] These products were probably Chinese cloths, but Russians transported them through Kamchatka into the Kurils and traded them with Ainu on Urup.[28]

In the 1780s, however, this dynamic commercial atmosphere in eastern Ezo was threatened by a series of provocative publications in Japan. Works by Kudō Heisuke and Hayashi Shihei, who envisioned a new role for Japan in the North Pacific, forced the shogunate to investigate trading activity on Sakhalin and the Kurils. Briefly, Kudō implicated Matsumae lords in a secret trade that may have included Russians in eastern Ezo.[29] He never presented hard evidence directly linking Fukuyama Castle to the Russian trade, but the implications of his writings were crystal clear to some Edo policymakers, such as Tanuma Okitsugu and Matsumoto Hidemochi.[30] The latter, along with Satō Genrokurō, contributed to the *Ezochi ikken* [Ezochi incident], one of the most comprehensive documents dealing with the Russian trade in eastern Ezo. Tanuma believed that Matsumae trading activity in Sakhalin and the Kurils without any oversight by Edo undermined decades of precedent. The establishment of such precedents had been the lessons of the 1630s, when Japan had brutally expelled most European missionaries and traders. Foreign trade remained a critical element in the shogunal claims to public authority (*kōgi*) over the realm.[31] Moreover, the possibility of a shogunate-controlled trade in Ezo was emerging as part of the financial schemes of Tanuma, who served as the shogun's senior councillor.[32]

Hayashi Shihei advocated a more intrusive approach to the administration of Ezo. He noted that the boundary of the Tokugawa polity extended to Kumaishi, the Wajinchi-Ezochi line near Sekinai, but ultimately suggested that the shogunate should extend its influence as far as Shiranushi in southern Sakhalin.[33] He argued, moreover, that the Russian empire represented the most serious threat to this extension of Japanese influence in the north. The Russians, he cautioned, were in the process of staking their own claims to the Kurils.[34]

Tanuma was swayed by these arguments. In 1786 he dispatched officials to investigate Matsumae trading activity. As it turned out, this initial shogunal interest was short lived. In 1787, when Matsudaira Sadanobu became the shogun's new senior councillor, he discontinued the investigation. He believed, as Herman Ooms points out, that "a barren and un-

developed island [Ezo] would tempt the Russians less than an economically developed one."[35] However, the writings of Kudō and Hayashi and
the subsequent shogunal investigation, combined with the 1789 Menashi-
Kunashir War, triggered the confiscation of trade under Matsumae control in the late eighteenth century.

RUSSIAN GOODS IN THE KURIL TRADE

During the Tanuma investigation, Satō Genrokurō, Yamaguchi Tetsugorō,
and Aoshima Shunzō traveled to Fukuyama Castle, where they interviewed Ujiie Shinbei and Shimonokuni Toneri, both of the Matsumae
town magistracy, or *machi bugyō*.[36] The initial investigation centered
around a 1778 incident in which two Russians (probably Ivan Antipin and
Dmitrii Shabalin) had landed in eastern Ezo.[37] Later questions were aimed
at Asari Kōbei, the Matsumae official who had initially investigated the incident. The final report explains that in 1778 Niida Daihachi, a Matsumae
trade official, or *uwanoriyaku*, was in Nokkamappu, on the eastern tip of
Hokkaido, when Russians landed and explained that they wanted to open
trade with Japan. He told the Russians that he would consult the Matsumae lord and that Ainu would be dispatched to Urup to relay the answer
to the Russian traders. "But it is best that you leave Nokkamappu," he reportedly told the Russians several times. Before departing, however, the
Russians presented Niida with a formal written request to open trade and
offered several exotic gifts for the Matsumae lord.[38]

Lord Michihiro, according to the report, decided that opening trade
with Russia was out of the question. He dispatched Matsui Mohei, Kudō
Seiemon, and Asari Kōbei, all Matsumae *uwanoriyaku*, to relay the official
denial to the Russians. The three officials also told the Russians to go to
Nagasaki, and then returned the gifts. Asari explained that he was un-
sure what the gifts even were because they had never been unwrapped.
After sending the Russians away, Matsumae officials met to decide
whether the incident should be reported to Edo. In the end, Michihiro decided against reporting the incident because no trading had actually occurred. Sakai Izaemon, another Matsumae official, was dispatched to

Edo to meet with Matsumae political allies in the capital, where again it was decided that the shogunate should not be informed. *Uwanoriyaku* were then dispatched periodically to eastern Ezo following the incident, but no additional contact with Russians was reported.[39]

Although Satō Genrokurō learned little from his first encounter with the tight-lipped Matsumae officials, his questions reveal that the shogunate's fundamental interest was not simply trade but also foreign relations. According to the Matsumae officials interviewed, Lord Michihiro had refused to trade with Russians in the 1778 incident, had refused even to unwrap the gifts. One might think that the matter would be closed, but what appeared on the surface to be a harmless exchange of gifts on the barren coastline of eastern Ezo was a serious matter in the eyes of Edo policymakers. In the shogunate's view of foreign diplomacy and trade, gifts and commercial overtures from foreign envoys should have been presented to Edo, not dealt with at a local level. That foreign trade was overseen by the shogunate had been another lesson of the 1630s, when the European missionaries were expelled. Lord Michihiro had refused to trade with the Russians, but that he had made the decision at a local level without informing Edo must have worried Satō. To decide whether a foreign country should be granted trading privileges was the purview of the shogun. Although Michihiro had given the correct answer, the Matsumae lord should not, in Satō's view, have answered at all. Satō's reaction is an indication that the two centuries of relative commercial and political independence that the Matsumae family had enjoyed in Ezo were quickly coming to a close.

After interviewing tight-lipped Matsumae officials and gathering only limited information, Satō soon found more effective ways of extracting information about the possibilities of a Russian trade in the Kurils. In effect, he sought out weaker links in the chain of command. In the seventh month of 1786, according to the manuscript *Kiitappu basho shihainin Shōjirō jinmonsho* [The interrogation of Kiitappu fishery manager Shōjirō], Satō interrogated Kasajima Shōjirō, Yadomataemon, and Heihachi, all Kiitappu trading-post managers of the Hidaya household. The questions were primarily aimed at Shōjirō and at first had to do with Japanese sailors (Rihachirō, Chōmatsu, Katsuzaemon, Miyakomura no Chōsuke, and Takeuchi Tokubei) who had reportedly had contact with Russians in the North Pacific. Shōjirō explained that he had heard of the men but knew no specifics of their whereabouts.[40] Satō also grilled Shōjirō concerning a merchant ship out of Saimura, in northeastern Japan. The ship, which had had seventeen hands onboard and had been carrying soybean and fish mulch, had been blown off course in bad weather and wound up in Kamchatka. Shōjirō, as before, explained that he had heard of the incident but could offer no details.

Satō then moved on to the 1778 incident in eastern Ezo. "About 1778," asked Satō, "is it the truth that you had no kind of trade contact with the Russians?" Shōjirō replied, "I did not trade. When the Russians came during the ban [on trade], because I was given one bottle of liquor that held about one gō [0.384 pints] and refined sugar, I accepted it. [However], from the start I shared [these items] with the other guards to eat and drink. According to what the Ainu say, this liquor is called shaku no sake, which refers to the fact that it is made from grass. The flavor was bad. I gave all the sugar away to the guards to eat."[41]

Satō continued, "Is the Russian's translator an Ainu? [Or is the translator] a Russian?" Shōjirō replied, "The translator [used in trade] discussions is an Ainu named Shikeita." Satō then asked: "This translator [Shikeita], he cannot speak Japanese [ningen no kotoba]?" Shōjirō replied: "Of course, he only understands a little Japanese, but because he does not understand enough, some of the discussions were translated into the Ainu language." Satō, his curiosity piqued, then pressed on: "Did the translator [Shikeita] not know Russian? And did the Russians know the Ainu language?" Shōjirō replied, "I remember that this Ainu [Shikeita] knows Russian. Negotiations to our side [the Japanese side] are done in the Ainu language, [whereas] negotiations to the Russian side are done in Russian. From this point I had dropsy and stayed in a small drinking hut, [however, and so] I do not know if this is accurate."[42]

Keeping with the theme of the 1778 incident, Satō continued the questioning: "At that time, what were the names of the [Matsumae] officials [who were present]?" Shōjirō answered that they were "Matsui Mohei and Kudō Seiemon." Satō then asked: "Was not Asari Kōbei there?" Shōjirō replied, "Now that you mention it, he was there. Because all this happened a long time ago, I am extremely sorry to say that I have forgotten [much of these events]." Satō then shouted, "You are a fool who quickly forgets things! The Ainu do remember these past events, [which makes you] an idiot even inferior to the Ainu. Now, with this sugar, at this time, was any of it sent to [Matsumae] officials as a gift?" Shōjirō replied, "I remember that that is what happened." Satō then said, "Just as I thought, didn't you trade cotton cloth?" But Shōjirō again denied that he had done any trading. Satō then burst out,

> I already have in my hands the evidence, as I have been investigating, [and so] for you to say that you have had no connection [with the secret trade] makes you an insolent man. The evidence that I am speaking of is this: [Hidaya] Kyūbei and [Hidaya] Kyūjirō have sent textiles (habahiro chōjaku) as gifts to Hidaya no kuni, their home province. Moreover, the shogunate knows that these goods were being sold in Edo. Did this stuff just fly down from the heavens? Who brought [these goods]? I think that you probably traded [with the Russians], and then sent the goods to your boss, Hidaya Kyūbei?

Satō then snapped at Shōjirō, "Return to your lodgings!"; however, before Shōjirō could, Satō started questioning him about buying firearms from the Russians.[43] Shōjirō replied that he absolutely did not buy firearms from the Russians. Satō then asked, "If you did not trade, then why is [there a gun] at your boss's house?" Shōjirō explained that he was only a low-level employee of the Hidaya and thus did not know about any gun in the Hidaya house.

The Edo shogunate, starting at about the end of the seventeenth century, had reduced firearms manufacturing in Japan to a mere trickle, at least when compared with the number produced in Europe.[44] The shogunate considered unauthorized firearms a threat to its hold on power; Satō's implication that the Hidaya or Matsumae family might be acquiring foreign-made weapons on the sly was a serious charge. Satō, focusing on the firearms issue, asked Shōjirō whether an Ainu named Nochikusa owned a Russian-manufactured weapon. Satō also asked several questions related to the firing mechanism, but Shōjirō could answer none of them.[45]

The interrogation of Shōjirō illustrates several important points about the Russian place in Ainu maritime behavior, about trade with Hidaya merchants, and ultimately, about the reaction of the shogunate. Satō's questions revealed that neither Fukuyama Castle nor Hidaya merchants were at the center of the "secret" Russian trade; it was an open trade conducted by Ainu. They had traditionally traded on Urup, and Russians were easily integrated into the existing commercial terrain. In fact, at least according to Shōjirō, the trade language of the region was Ainu. Matsumae lords and Hidaya Kyūbei tapped into this trade between Ainu and Russians, hoping to capitalize on the sale of European merchandise. What precise role Fukuyama Castle played in the trade remains unknown. *Uwanoriyaku* such as Matsui Mohei, Kudō Seiemon, and Asari Kōbei admitted to being on the scene in 1778, and they were placed there by Shōjirō. In addition, they acknowledged receiving Russian gifts but claimed that the gifts had been returned. The most damaging accusation, then, was that the Hidaya household was directly shipping Russian merchandise to Japan, perhaps even firearms, and then selling goods right under the shogunate's nose in Edo.

Accusations aside, however, the Matsumae family had reached an impasse in its authority over trade in Ezo. The Russians represented a new, more powerful kind of northern "barbarian," one which was thought to threaten the security of the realm. Kudō Heisuke and Hayashi Shihei had warned of Russian designs in Ezo, and the interrogation of Shōjirō must have confirmed Satō's worst fears. Matsumae evasiveness, rumors of a secret trade, wily merchant lies, bilingual Ainu, the dissemination of muskets—all this added up to a threat to Tokugawa power.

It was interviews with Ainu chiefs Ikotoi of Akkeshi and Shonko of Nokkamappu that proved the most unsettling for Satō. Interviewing Ainu chiefs to gather the necessary information on the Russian trade was no easy matter. Prior to Satō's arrival in eastern Ezo, Matsumae officials had issued a series of deadly serious warnings to local Ainu advising them to listen to shogunal questions carefully but not to say anything about Russians or Russian goods. Matsumae officials had reportedly lied to Ainu, saying that Ainu would be killed by Satō and the others if the trade was discovered. The officials had added that Satō would likely prohibit all commercial activity in the Kurils. Because Ainu in the east were so dependent on trade, these threats must have struck a chord with many Ainu.[46]

However, one night in the second month of 1786, while Satō was staying in eastern Ezo, Ikotoi came to his lodgings. There, he implicated Matsumae lords in an attempt to cover up trading with Russians in eastern Ezo. In his testimony, recorded in the original Ainu with a partial Japanese translation, he said:

> From this autumn, you Edo officials have asked [Ainu] questions about the Russians. Matsumae officials and merchants from the trading post warned us not to say anything with regard to the Russians; if we talked they threatened to cut off our heads and stop dispatching trade ships. [They will be] very severe. Up to now, we have said nothing [regarding the Russians]. [In truth], every year Russians come to Urup Island. The beautiful silks, the calico and cotton textiles, as well as sugar and medicines, [we Ainu] acquire in trade. From last year to this summer, [Russians] have been staying on Urup. This summer we went to Urup and met the Russians. We traded rice [for goods] they had brought; we brought [these goods] home. [However, because] this autumn Edo officials were coming, we were told by Matsumae officials, trading post merchants, and translators, that this is not good; and that we should look as if we had not been trading [with the Russians on Urup]. We [thus] closed up all of these items out of sight. [This is sad because] the fabric that my mother has is extremely beautiful.[47]

Shonko, the chief of Nokkamappu, also spoke with Satō that night.

> This year I went to Iturup, [but] the Russians did not come. I went to Iturup with Shamushari, an Ainu translator, and brought back silk fabric, cotton textiles, and other items, which I traded at the Nokkamappu trading post. [However], the [Hidaya] translators have told us that the textiles at the Nokkamappu trading post should not be shown to the Edo officials. Mitsuemon, the translator, and Kojirō, the trading-post manager, burned [the Russian goods]. [They also] weighted them down with rocks and tossed them into the ocean. I am not sure what goods they were, but items were also hidden in the mountains. [Moreover], this autumn, officials had told the chief of Kunashir, Tsukinoe, to go as far as Urup to see if the Russians had arrived. He returned the same day to Shibetsu. At this time,

the [Edo] lords were in the vicinity of Shibetsu, and Tsukinoe [explained that he] wanted to meet with them. [But] Matsumae officials replied that this was not a good idea. They also warned [Tsukinoe that if he] met with them he would be gouged to death with a spear. [In the end], Tsukinoe was very sorry [not to be able to meet with the shogunal officials]. Matsumae officials are villains![48]

Satō confirmed these testimonies in an interview with Kondō Kichizaemon, a Matsumae vassal. Moreover, he linked the burning of the Russian merchandise in Nokkamappu to orders that had originated at the Hidaya branch shop (demise). Managers at the Hidaya shop, he alleged, had ordered that all Russian merchandise be sent to Fukuyama and that the remaining goods, one Russian leather coat and a Russian sword, be hidden in the mountains.[49]

To be sure, this trade with the Russians in eastern Ezo was conducted on a small scale. Ainu acquired Russian merchandise by trading on Urup and then brought these goods to the Nokkamappu trading post, which was under the control of Hidaya interests. Whether Ainu from eastern Ezo understood themselves to be "conquered peoples" in the Russian tribute system is difficult to determine. From what can be gathered from Ainu testimony, they saw themselves as independent middlemen in a maritime trade between the Hidaya in eastern Ezo and the Russians on Urup. Because Ainu used their own language and served as interpreters in their homelands, they probably viewed themselves as the center of this trade rather than as "peripheral barbarians" on the frontiers of Russia and Japan. Ainu elders, however, appear to have conducted the Kuril trade; most other Ainu were by this time laboring in fisheries. Matsumae officials and Hidaya employees used Ainu dependency on trade as leverage against Ainu chiefs; they warned that if Ainu talked to Satō Genrokurō, they would stop dispatching trade ships.

That the Matsumae family participated in a trade that included Russians in the Kurils was natural. Their commercial perspective, born from nearly two centuries of trading in Ezo, was focused northward. Lord Michihiro may not have wanted to trade openly with Russians, but a small-scale Russian trade, with Ainu functioning as middlemen, meant that exotic European merchandise could be found in Fukuyama. In addition, Hidaya profits translated into the regular payment of licensing fees and even the extension of generous loans to the Matsumae family.

Even though the shogunal reaction to Satō's report contributed to the confiscation of control over trade from Fukuyama Castle, the implications of shogunal direct rule were even more damaging to Ainu maritime independence than Matsumae control had been. New shogunal edicts prohibited Ainu from trading north of Iturup, severing their traditional commercial relations and undermining centuries of maritime activity that had contributed to Ainu subsistence practice. As with Qing-controlled trade on Sakhalin, the shogunate moved to challenge Russian commercial and political designs (symbolized by the Russian tribute system) on Iturup and Kunashir islands, placing Ainu under their own trade system. The Ainu may once have viewed themselves as at the center of trading in eastern Ezo, but that all changed after 1799. The Edo shogunate asserted its own vision of foreign relations and trade, depriving the Ainu of the ability to trade independently in the North Pacific.

as what e in the happine Sakhalin trade

THE MENASHI-KUNASHIR WAR

The Menashi-Kunashir War of 1789 was the final blow to the Matsumae family's exclusive right to oversee trade in Ezo. The war broke out in the fifth month of 1789, when Ainu from Furukamafu attacked Japanese at Tomari, Hetoka, Memakirae, Chifukaruhetsu, and Furukamafu on Kunashir Island. When the dust settled, twenty-two Japanese lay dead. Six days later, Ainu in the east attacked Japanese at Shibetsu, Chiurui, Kotanuka, Kunnehetsu, Sakimai, and Uenhetsu. They also assaulted Japanese sailors aboard the *Ōdōri-maru*, killing forty-nine.

A younger generation of Ainu, the sons of powerful chiefs, planned and executed the attacks. They anticipated a strong Matsumae response and thus built fortifications and trenches to defend themselves. They also appear to have been well organized when attacking Japanese: they reportedly counted bodies in the midst of the fighting to make sure that all Japanese aboard the *Ōdōri-maru* had been executed (although they did miss one). Only four Japanese survived the assaults. Two trading-post managers, Denshichi and Kichibei from Morioka domain, had been caught on Kunashir during the fighting but were granted clemency by Ikotoi. Kichitarō, another merchant, was eventually rescued at Shari; and Shōzō, from Morioka domain, survived because of his relationship with Horoemeki, an Ainu elder from Chiurui. Despite such brief moments of sympathy, Ainu managed to kill seventy-one Japanese in the two quick assaults.[50]

Sukeemon, a Hidaya manager, reported the uprising to Matsumae officials in the sixth month of 1789, and an armed force of Matsumae troops commanded by Niida Magosaburō, Matsui Mohei, and Matsumae Heikaku was quickly dispatched, as were translators for dealing with the Ainu. When the force arrived in Nokkamappu in the seventh month, Tsukinoe, who had hurried back from Iturup to defuse the conflict, presented the commanders with a written pledge, presumably to stop the fighting, and compensatory gifts in the form of two sea otter pelts.[51]

Matsumae forces were not interested in compensation, however, and they quickly rounded up Ainu who had reportedly participated in the attacks. Shimochi, an elder from Akkeshi, was ordered to gather Ainu from Kunashir. About two weeks later, 183 Ainu "suspects" from eastern Ezo arrived in Nokkamappu for questioning; 131 came from Kunashir. The results of the official investigation, at least according to Matsumae documents, were as follows: from Kunashir, military officials identified 5 Ainu "ringleaders," 9 Ainu connected with the murders, and 27 others, for a total of 41 "conspirators." From eastern Ezo, they singled out 3 ringleaders, 21 Ainu connected with murders, and 65 others, for a total of 89 conspirators.[52] Most of the ringleaders—Mamekiri, Honishiainu, Nochiutokan, Sakechire, Inukuma, Shitonue, Keutomohishike, and Horoemeki—were young Ainu. It appears that no major political figures, such as Ikotoi or Shonko, were connected with the attacks.

Of the 130 men linked to the attacks, 37 were directly tied to the murders, imprisoned, and scheduled to be beheaded by Matsumae warriors; the others gave *tsugunai*.[53] On the appointed day, one by one the young men were taken from their holding cell. Mamekiri, from Furukamafu village, was the first executed. However, when it was the turn of the sixth Ainu, somebody from inside the cell screamed *"Pewtanke!"* a call used by

Ainu to alert others of an emergency. According to some reports, the remaining conspirators became so agitated that it looked as if they might rip down the prison itself. Matsumae officials, in one of the most brutal acts of their two centuries in Ezo, ordered guards to shoot through the bars of the prison or thrust with their lances to kill the others as they tried to break out. By the ninth month of 1789, the 37 heads, carefully pickled in salt, were on display at Fukuyama, a spectacle designed to illustrate Matsumae military superiority.[54]

A brief analysis of the underlying causes of the 1789 war is worth pursuing. The Hidaya household, with its unrestricted exploitation of resources in eastern Ezo, had helped spark the war. At least this was the conclusion reached by Aoshima Shunzō, a shogunal official who later investigated the war. He wrote that before Matsumae had contracted out trading posts to Hidaya, trade ships had traveled to the east only once a year. Following the Hidaya takeover, however, merchants started setting up permanent shops at the trading posts, conducting business throughout the year. The permanent trading post, and its thriving market culture, redirected the productive activity of the Ainu, deepening their need for trade and thus forcing them to work in fisheries rather than hunt for their own subsistence needs.[55]

Moreover, the number of merchant ships transporting goods to Japan from eastern Ezo grew after the Hidaya takeover, placing more pressure on Ainu to increase production. Under the Matsumae family, Ainu had been able to subsist because they traded in the Kurils and hunted to feed and clothe their families, but Hidaya stipends at the fisheries were not enough to support these families, and increasing commercialization led to immiserization for many in the east. In the old days, Aoshima remarked, Ainu had kept some of the game and fish they took from their lands, which had allowed them to survive the winter. Trading skins and fish products with Japanese, Kuril Ainu, and even Russians had allowed them to retain some semblance of economic independence. But with the large number of merchant ships picking up goods at trading posts in the east, they no longer had the time to hunt and fish for their own subsistence needs, and they became dependent on Hidaya merchants for providing food and clothing. They came to resemble fishery laborers.[56]

Ainu elders explained to Aoshima that it would have done little good to lodge a complaint about Hidaya practices with Matsumae officials, because the officials' only response would have been to threaten to completely halt trade. Fukuyama Castle, Aoshima said angrily, knew nothing of proper government anyway. Greed and shoddy administration had agitated Ainu in the east, sparking the bloody war. In 1789, after a few suspicious deaths that Ainu blamed on poisoned saké received from Hidaya managers, a contentious generation of young Ainu decided to throw Hidaya merchants out of eastern Ezo.[57] Aoshima concluded that the conduct of some merchants, such as those on the Hidaya payroll, had sparked the 1789 war. Some chiefs such as Tsukinoe, Ikotoi, and Shonko could hunt on Urup and Iturup, but the majority of Ainu from the east spent their time supplying fish and animal skins to Japanese merchants. By the end of the eighteenth century, trade in Ezo had undergone a final transformation, and Ainu almost completely relied on the trading post for their food and clothing.

This reliance also meant that Ainu were no longer the trade-oriented people they had once been. Ikotoi could still enhance his personal prestige by acting as middleman in trade between the Japanese and groups in the Kurils, but the future of most young Ainu, the "ringleaders" of the 1789 war, was tied to trade at fisheries. Hidaya merchants were what David Howell aptly refers to as "superficial capitalists." Howell suggests that contractor merchants represented a transitional stage between the "feudal economy" of the Tokugawa period and the "capitalist economy" of the Meiji period (1868–1912).[58] Hidaya Kyūbei and his descendants were masters at maneuvering within the Tokugawa economy. They financed projects such as the reconstruction of the Matsumae Edo residence and offered a variety of other loans to the Matsumae family. In return for these loans, they received exclusive rights to oversee the development of fisheries in eastern Ezo. In this respect, their claims to timber, animal skins, fisheries, and Russian goods were contingent upon the powers of oversight granted to Fukuyama Castle, which were in turn based on earlier investiture by the shogunate. The Hidaya merchants were, as Howell argues of other merchants, capitalists "who needed feudalism to survive."[59]

By 1789 Ainu had recognized that the Matsumae family and Japanese merchants threatened to completely destroy their way of life and what remained of their autonomy. Their productive activity had come to mirror Japanese expansion in Ezo, and as each year passed they forfeited more of their economic independence. The process was not uniform throughout Ezo, and remote chiefdoms held out for longer periods of time. Yet, in the late eighteenth century, many Ainu communities were in desperate straits. Two centuries of harsh trade policies had forced many Ainu below subsistence levels, threatening many communities with dislocation and famine.

CONCLUSION

Aoshima Shunzō's report on the Menashi-Kunashir War triggered a series of shogunal policy initiatives that, combined with Adam Laxman's arrival in 1792, eventually led to the first period of shogunal rule in Ezo.[60] The independent commercial landscape of Ezo, where Ainu and Japanese traded with groups throughout the Kurils and in Kamchatka, changed under the direction of the Hakodate magistracy, which oversaw Ezo affairs for the shogun. Under shogunal rule, Ainu were cut off from their traditional trade sphere and forced to look inward to Japan for their livelihood, which underscored the fact that Ainu could no longer assert maritime independence in the North Pacific. Habuto Masayasu, of the Hakodate magistracy, shut down trading between Iturup and Urup and even prohibited Ainu from hunting sea otter in the waters surrounding Urup. This move redefined the borders of the Tokugawa polity in the north. Severing Ainu from North Pacific trading networks contributed to their dependency on Japan by establishing new political borders that carved up the pre-1780s ethnic and commercial landscape of Ezo.[61]

7 Epidemic Disease, Medicine, and the Shifting Ecology of Ezo

Commenting on epidemic diseases and the medical condition of the Ainu in the eighteenth century, Mogami Tokunai noted that there was a lack of medicine and medical care in Ezo and that no attempts were made to comfort infected Ainu or prevent the spread of contagions from village to village, which forced many Ainu to live like animals. He wrote,

> Essentially, like Japanese, Ainu are a kind of human, and so like Japanese they also get sick. Because they are without medicine, if a smallpox [*hōsō*] epidemic breaks out, they fear the disease spreading, [and] deserting their homes, they evade the disease deep in the mountains. When the epidemic subsides, they return to their village residences. Among mothers and children, husbands and wives, and among brothers, they nurse and look after one another, but other people, because they have been abandoned by everybody, eventually die. Even if they get better, many people die of starvation."[1]

Because of these practices, which other reports confirm, many Ainu succumbed to epidemic diseases and died in astonishing numbers following the creation of Matsumae's trade-fief system, although not like animals but rather like other peoples around the world subjected to newly imported killers such as smallpox in a colonial setting. This chapter explores the spread of some epidemic diseases in Ezo, as well as the Japanese and Ainu responses. In 1590, before the intensification of trade between the Japanese and the Ainu, epidemiologic trends in Ezo were distinct from those in Japan. Contact between the Japanese and the Ainu was neither regular enough nor widespread enough to completely transform disease patterns in Ainu communities. By about 1800, however, following two centuries of trade, war, economic development, and cultural exchange, Ezo lay firmly within the realm of Japan's disease ecology.

THE IMPACT OF SMALLPOX IN EZO

On the surface, the introduction of epidemic disease to Ezo follows a fairly standard pattern in global epidemiology in which a disproportionately powerful society, through trade, war, and other forms of human interaction, extends its epidemiologic range over lands inhabited by a semi-independent peripheral people. Ultimately, following centuries of exchange, the peripheral people finds itself incorporated into the "civilized disease pools" of the more powerful society. The classic treatment of this model remains *Plagues and Peoples,* in which William McNeill illustrates how this process forever altered the native disease ecology of certain groups (largely non-European societies) and often weakened their autonomy in the face of foreign colonization.[2]

This chapter looks at the cultural, social, and political history of the years between 1590 and 1800—that is, the years between the pre–regularized contact period and the post-conformity period—as they relate to the incorporation of the Ainu into global disease pools. During this transitional period, contact between Japanese and Ainu spawned in Ezo an altogether new disease ecology and cultural order. Japanese who settled

in Wajinchi often came from cities in Japan where diseases such as smallpox had become largely endemic, and these settlers relocated to lands
where their children proved vulnerable to more-potent smallpox epidemics. Over time, smallpox spread beyond Japanese settled areas in
Wajinchi to Ainu communities in Ezochi, and as a result Ainu disease
patterns underwent a transformation as the population was introduced
to new epidemics.

Ann Bowman Jannetta, a pioneer in the study of the epidemiology of
early-modern Japan, observes that with the establishment of the Edo
shogunate in 1603, and the subsequent restrictions on foreign trade and
travel that took the form of maritime prohibitions, few new diseases actually entered Japan. Nonetheless, population growth and the rapid development of cities such as Edo and Osaka caused certain diseases to
flourish. Jannetta points out that smallpox remained the most common
cause of premature death among early-modern Japanese and reminds
historians that even as late as 1850 at least 10 percent of the Japanese population died from this devastating contagion.[3]

The lack of evidence indicating that new diseases entered Japan has
led Jannetta to challenge some long-standing assumptions regarding
Japanese history. She questions the interpretation of historians, such as
Thomas Smith, who suggest that epidemic disease contributed in a major
way to population stabilization and the subsequent emergence of sur-
plus goods and the commercialization of the rural economy.[4] Following a
lengthy quantitative analysis, Jannetta concludes that "pestilence was not
responsible for the population stability of the late Tokugawa period."[5]
She argues that because early-modern Japan remained "relatively isolat-
ed geographically, and her people had little association with population
centers outside East Asia," epidemics played only a minor role in the
population stability of the Tokugawa period. Pointing to evidence such as
the absence of bubonic plague and epidemic typhus, Jannetta argues that
"Japan's geography and her isolation from the major world trade routes
provided a cordon sanitaire that prevented major diseases from penetrat-
ing Japan until the mid–nineteenth century." Japan contrasts sharply
with southwestern China, where the plague raged throughout the nineteenth century.[6]

To date, most discussions of the place of early-modern Japan in global epidemiology have focused primarily on its experiences in receiving new diseases—that is, whether new contagions entered or failed to enter Japan, who introduced them, and what their ultimate demographic impact was—rather than on the possible role that Japan played in the dissemination of diseases to foreign peoples such as the Ainu. In light of the frequency of epidemic outbreaks in Ezo, and the relationship of these epidemics to trade and other forms of interaction between Japanese and Ainu, it is evident that Japan has not remained exclusively on the receiving end of disease exchange.[7] Rather, epidemics in Ezo illustrate that pathogens traveled in both directions: early-modern Japan contributed to the dissemination of deadly contagions in East Asia as it extended its commercial and political interests outward into Ezo.

Despite the severe limitations of available data, medical historians have demonstrated that a basic chronology and geography of disease dissemination in Ezo can be traced (see table 1).[8] This chronology illustrates that smallpox and measles first appeared in Wajinchi, where both Japanese and Ainu suffered from the disease. There are two brief references to epidemics in Wajinchi prior to the fifteenth century, both associated with natural disasters, but the first recorded epidemic to hit Ezo in the early-modern period was a smallpox epidemic in 1624. Matsumae Kagehiro, a scholar from the north, wrote that the epidemic killed many children. Kagehiro noted that among the "great number of children" who perished in this epidemic was the ten-year-old Matsumae Kanehiro, heir to Lord Kinhiro. Similarly, Matsumae Mitsuhiro, son of Yoshihiro, died at the age of eighteen.[9] The fact that Kagehiro specified that children made up the majority of the victims in the 1624 epidemic has led Takashita Taizō to speculate that there might have been a smallpox epidemic about twenty years earlier, say in 1600; the survivors of this earlier epidemic, who by the time of the 1624 epidemic would have been adults more than twenty years old, would have developed immunity. By contrast, children not yet born during the earlier epidemic would have developed no such immunity.[10]

As the seventeenth century advanced, smallpox spread beyond Wajinchi and began to extract a heavy toll from Ainu in the form of disease-

Table 1   Recorded Epidemics in Ezo, 1624–1862

Year	Interval	Location	Disease
1624	—	—	smallpox
1658	34	—	smallpox
1669	11	Oshamanbe	smallpox
1698	29	western Ezo	smallpox/measles
1710	12	Tazawa/Otobe	smallpox/measles
1733	23	—	influenza
1753	20	—	measles
1776–77	23–24	western Ezo	measles, then smallpox
1779	2–3	Mashike	smallpox
1780	1	—	smallpox
1788	8	Tazawa/Otobe	smallpox/measles
1798–99	10–11	eastern Ezo	smallpox
1800	1–2	Usu/Abuta/Horobetsu	smallpox
1805–6	5–6	Sōya/Rebun/Rishiri	smallpox
1809	3–4	Osatsube	smallpox
1817–19	8–10	Ishikari	smallpox
1824	5–7	Matsumae	—
1834	10	—	smallpox
1844–45	10–11	Shizunai-Mitsuishi	smallpox
1855	10–11	—	smallpox
1857	2	Oshamanbe	smallpox
1861–62	4–5	Fukushima	rabies

SOURCE: Matsuki Akitomo, Hokkaidō no ishi (Hirosaki: Tsugaru Shobō, 1970), 124–31; and Takashita Taizō, "Kinsei Ezochi no shippeishi," in Ezochi no iryō, ed. Sapporo Ishigaku Kenkyūkai (Sapporo: Hokkaidō Shuppan Kikaku Sentā, 1988), 84, 98.

related mortality and the social dissolution of infected communities. Early demographic figures for Ezo are sketchy, but some scattered numbers are available. The earliest reference to the Ainu population of Ezo placed the number for the entire island of Hokkaido at about 20,000 during the 1670s.[11] However, this number surely underestimates the total Ainu population. In fact, the figure 20,000 might represent a decent guess at the population in southwestern and eastern Ezo, but much of the north and the inland areas in the Ishikari region (under the control of the defiant Haukase) remained largely unexplored by Japanese. Takakura Shin'ichirō explains that early estimates range from 20,000 to 40,000 and so must be considered unreliable.[12] In the late eighteenth century, more accurate data became available as shogunal officials in Edo grew alarmed by the Ainu demographic slide. In 1807, officials estimated the total population of Hokkaido Ainu at 26,256. Forty-seven years later that number had been reduced to 17,810, a 32 percent decline.[13]

Moreover, some local demographic information—although from the nineteenth century and, thus, strictly speaking outside the scope of this analysis—tends to support the argument that smallpox caused population decline, disrupted Ainu seasonal subsistence activity, and led to social dissolution. Observations made by Matsuura Takeshirō, for example, illustrate concretely the dramatic decline of Ainu populations caused by epidemic diseases. Writing in the mid–nineteenth century, he noted that the 1809 population of Akkeshi, in eastern Ezo, had been 177 households with 874 people. By 1822, Akkeshi's population had fallen to 164 homes with 804 Ainu. By 1856, the Akkeshi population had fallen even more dramatically and stood at 53 households with 217 people, roughly a 75 percent decline in forty-seven years.[14] Matsuura noted that in the early nineteenth century, more than 1,200 Ainu lived in the Nemoro (Nemuro) area, also in the east. However, by the 1850s, the population there stood at 511 people, a total 57 percent decline.[15]

THE SHIZUNAI-MITSUISHI EPIDEMIC OF 1845

Even more valuable than Matsuura's observations is the information contained in the *Hōsō ikken* [The matter of smallpox], a series of official memoranda on a smallpox epidemic that ravaged the Shizunai-Mitsuishi region in 1845.[16] The *Hōsō ikken* is singular among the remaining sources related to disease in Ezo. It adds color, if very bleak color, to an otherwise monochromatic picture of the disease ecology of Ezo. It too is from the nineteenth century, but in the absence of hard demographic numbers from the seventeenth and eighteenth centuries, the *Hōsō ikken* is useful in illustrating the destructive capabilities of smallpox in Ainu communities. In the memoranda, fishery and trading-post supervisors recorded the names of the infected, the date they contracted the disease, and the outcome of the infection (see table 2). Unfortunately, the supervisors did not include the ages of the victims. What this record reveals is that once a smallpox epidemic struck an Ainu community, mortality rates could be as high as 60 percent, with virtually every family in a given community affected. As family members were incapacitated by fever and disfigured with pustules, basic subsistence-related activity became impossible. Just building a fire to keep warm in the winter required an extraordinary act of will. In 1799, Japanese physicians had begun to provide medical care for infected Ainu and their families under shogunal order; however, during the previous two centuries of Matsumae rule, the Ainu, as Mogami Tokunai observed earlier, had been left to starve or to die from exposure and infections.

Information in the *Hōsō ikken* illustrates that local Matsumae and shogunal officials, as well as private merchants, responded quickly to the Shizunai-Mitsuishi smallpox epidemic. Within one day after the "fever illness" had been discovered, fishery managers, working with local Japanese state and merchant leaders, called for physicians to diagnose the disease and then to advise on the best course of action. The next step was isolating the infected Ainu. Later on that same day, supervisors ordered that relief huts be built for moving uninfected Ainu. Local supervisors also appreciated the need to care for the infected; they requested supplies of rice, fish, and tobacco. Infected Ainu and their families stayed in houses where supervisors and family members could most effectively administer care. The quick response time probably limited the number of Ainu ultimately infected, but it did little for those who had already contracted smallpox; and the data contained in the *Hōsō ikken* demonstrate that mortality rates were high.

Even Ainu leaders were not spared, which undoubtedly caused social disruption. Renkafu, an Ainu sō-otona from Kamuikotan, who had recovered at one point, became ill again and died on the twenty-first day of the sixth month despite the efforts of fishery supervisors, merchants,

Table 2   Shizunai-Mitsuishi Smallpox Epidemic, 1845, by Ainu Name

Ainu Name	Title	Kotan	Sex	Date Contracted	Result (died or recovered)
Chisekaruha	—	Beuri	f	5/25	d 6/5
Irakesan	—	Beuri	m	5/26	r
Nefukiha	—	Beuri	f	5/27	r
Kakai	—	Beuri	f	5/27	r
Chiyarekean	—	Beuri	f	5/27	d 6/5
Shirikaroku	—	Beuri	m	5/17	d 5/27
Chiekaruha	—	Beuri	f	5/26	d 6/5
Irotoku	—	Beuri	m	5/18	d 5/27
Karenha	—	Beuri	f	6/1	r
Shintotsuka	—	Beuri	m	6/2	r
Ihetekan	—	Beuri	f	—	r
Itekani	—	Beuri	f	—	d 6/11
Isashunka	—	Beuri	f	—	d 6/11
Iroku	—	Beuri	f	—	d 6/11
Irakani	—	Beuri	f	6/5	d 6/11
Iwaku	—	Beuri	m	6/6	d 6/11
Renkafu	sō-otona	Kamui	m	5/17	d 6/21
Konhei	kozukai	Hehau	m	5/19	d 6/21
Arioku	—	Hehau	m	5/21	d 6/1
Morikonochiyu	—	Hehau	f	5/23	r
San	—	Hehau	f	5/24	r
Konhei's child	—	Hehau	m	5/25	r
Itakishikoro	—	Hehau	f	5/14	d 5/24
Isen	—	Hehau	f	5/16	d 5/26
Konhei's child	—	Hehau	f	5/19	d 5/25
Yōsa	—	Hehau	f	6/7	d 6/15
Ikafunte	—	Hehau	f	6/7	d 6/15

SOURCE: *Hōsō ikken* [1845], RCNS.

local officials, and the physician Ogawa Eisetsu. Moreover, Konhei, an Ainu *kozukai* from Hehau, who had also nearly recovered from smallpox, caught a severe cold and died on the morning of the twenty-first day of the sixth month, again despite the efforts of Ogawa and a second physician named Sakai Gendō.

The premature death of such village elders weakened the political vitality of Ainu communities. Physiologist Jared Diamond points out that for a people without a written language, village elders act as "repositories of information" and oral traditions and play a critical role in preserving social and cultural autonomy.[17] Such was the case with the Ainu society of the day. With the premature death of their elders, Ainu villagers became unable to transmit much of the information necessary for the continuation of their cultural traditions and hunting and fishing techniques, and this problem led to social change and a weakening of their autonomy.

The Shizunai-Mitsuishi epidemic undoubtedly also disrupted essential seasonal work, including the harvest of local herring fisheries and subsistence activity. William Cronon, writing about Native Americans, notes that epidemics often force people to miss critical seasons in their subsistence cycle. In describing the widespread effects of disease, he explains, "Social disorganization compounded the biological effects of disease. Once villages were attacked by a new pathogen, they often missed key phases in their annual subsistence cycles—the corn planting, say, or the fall hunt—and so were weakened when the next infection arrived."[18]

The *Hōsō ikken* notes that the Shizunai-Mitsuishi epidemic hit six households in Hehau village and five in Beuri village (see table 3). The percentage of the entire village, or the larger Shizunai-Mitsuishi region, that was infected during the course of the epidemic can only be guessed at, but information gathered from a census taken in 1809, thirty-six years before the epidemic, is instructive. According to the census, Hehau, which was in the vicinity of Mitsuishi, possessed a total of eleven households in about 1809. There are not enough data to estimate the average population of individual villages in the region, but for the villages located along the Mitsuishi and Kerimappu rivers, the average number of Ainu households per village was about five.[19]

Beuri was not among the twenty-one villages in the Shizunai vicinity

Table 3   Shizunai-Mitsuishi Smallpox Epidemic, 1845, by Household

Household	Kotan	Number of Members	Contracted Smallpox	Died	Recovered
Shirikaroku	Beuri	7	4	3	1
Irakesan	Beuri	8	5	2	3
Kamuichin	Beuri	4	1	0	1
Shintotsuka	Beuri	3	1	0	1
Kuesanke	Beuri	7	2	2	0
Itakishikoro	Hehau	2	1	1	0
Shiafushita	Hehau	2	1	1	0
Konhei	Hehau	—	6	3	3
Tamayuri	Hehau	4	1	1	0
Ikafunte	Hehau	2	1	1	0
Renkafu	Kamuikotan	5	1	1	0

SOURCE: *Hōsō ikken* [1845], RCNS.

listed in the otherwise detailed 1809 census. However, for the villages that were listed, the average number of households was about six.[20] If Beuri and Hehau had been average villages (with between five and eleven households), then half to all the households in both villages would have been touched by the epidemic. In both Beuri and Hehau, 40.2 percent of individual household members contracted smallpox. Based on table 3, the mortality rate for those who contracted the disease was 62.5 percent; the rate of recovery was 37.5 percent; and 34.1 percent of total village populations died. Obviously, with a mortality rate of 62.5 percent among the infected in some villages, a smallpox epidemic could have wiped out an entire generation of Ainu village leadership, making unified military resistance to Japanese intrusion, not to mention independent subsistence, nearly impossible.

What demographic impact the 1845 epidemic had on the Shizunai-Mitsuishi region as a whole is also difficult to determine. On the one hand, Matsuura Takeshirō noted of Mitsuishi that between the 1820s and the 1850s there was virtually no decline in the Ainu population, although the number of Ainu households fell from fifty-six to forty-nine.[21] Shizunai, on the other hand, underwent population declines as high as 26 percent, from 523 Ainu in 1822 to 386 in 1854, and one suspects that losses in 1845 were a major part of this decline. However, census data from Shizunai are extremely inconsistent.[22] Regardless of what these faceless numbers say, once a village became infected by smallpox, the scale and abruptness of social disruption that is suggested by the *Hōsō ikken* surely meant that basic subsistence activity became impossible, which brought the threat of starvation, as well as death from the disease itself or from secondary infections.

By the early nineteenth century, these devastating epidemics were occurring more often, and the epidemiologic trends of Ezo came increasingly to resemble the epidemiologic trends of early-modern Japan as outlined by Jannetta. In short, this transformation toward more frequent but, one suspects, less deadly epidemics in Ezo indicates the confluence of disease pools within the expanding perimeters of Japan's range of contacts. In this way the history of smallpox in Ezo reveals a variation on the broader theme in the classic case of disease dissemination, as articulated in McNeill's *Plagues and Peoples,* which focuses on the role of European expansion and the subjection of peripheral peoples to global disease pools. The case of Ezo shows how inter-regional contact in East Asia spread smallpox from a populous core to a more sparsely settled territory, a process which ultimately aided the expansion of Japan.

TRADE AND DISEASE IN EZO

Most of the exchange of communicable diseases in Ezo was a direct by-product of growing commercial activities, and contagions were transmitted widely during trade between Ainu and Japanese. Commerce in Ezo was quite far-flung, and evidence suggests that smallpox was carried along the Santan trade route, by which goods moved from China, through Sakhalin, and eventually to Ezo and even to Japanese cities. In light of Alfred Crosby's observations that "disease can tag along with commerce just as effectively as with any other kind of human intercourse," it would not be surprising if contagions were exchanged among participants in the Santan trade.[23] However, other forms of human intercourse frequently occurred in Ezo, and diseases associated with commerce included not only smallpox but also sexually transmitted diseases such as syphilis, which flourished with the rise of seasonal commercial ports in Wajinchi. Illustrating the festive atmosphere at such seasonal ports, David Howell has translated a colorful description by Mutō Kanzō, who wrote, "[The women of Fukuyama] are all as beautiful and fair as the courtesans of Kyoto—Edo women could never compare. Whether they have husbands or not, but especially if they do not, they readily sell themselves to anyone. This is quite routine and is not considered shameful. . . . Esashi . . . is as lively a port as Matsumae [Fukuyama] or Hakodate. In the huts on the seashore countless *gannoji* [prostitutes] play the shamisen and sing."[24]

Commercial growth in Wajinchi ports brought prostitution to Ezo, and syphilis followed shortly. Syphilis is a chronic disease that probably entered Japan in the early sixteenth century and spread quickly thereafter. The first record of syphilis in Japan comes from 1512, when continental traders introduced the disease to southern Japan.[25] Unlike smallpox and measles rates, syphilis rates among Ainu remain difficult to illustrate by means of historical documents, but its presence in Ezo seems quite clearly to have been a result of the Japanese intrusion into Ezochi. Medical historians conjecture that syphilis was probably introduced to Ezo in the later part of the eighteenth century, with the creation of the trade-fief system. However, some skeletal remains excavated from Katsuyamadate, at Kaminokuni in southern Hokkaido, suggest that the disease could have been introduced from Japan as early as the mid–sixteenth century. This is not inconceivable, considering the early trade and routine banishment of prisoners to Ezo discussed in chapter 1.[26]

Once introduced, syphilis spread quickly across Ezo as Ainu men came into contact with Japanese prostitutes and as Ainu women, through both prostitution and rape, introduced syphilis to the general Ainu population. In the 1790s, Kushihara Seihō mentioned a Sōya Ainu man whose name, Uenchi *(wenci)*, literally meant "bad penis" *(wen,* "something bad," and *ci,* "penis"). Kushihara explained that this man had syphilis and noted that other Ainu frequently had a good laugh at poor Uenchi's expense. In the 1850s, Matsuura Takeshirō noted that a fishery supervisor in the Ishikari River region had infected a nineteen-year-old Ainu woman with syphilis after sending her husband to work at a distant fishery in Otarunai. The supervisor then refused to offer her medical care. Matsuura also noted that of the forty-one Japanese supervisors in Kusuri, in eastern Ezo, thirty-six had taken Ainu women as "concubines" after sending their husbands to work at fisheries in nearby Akkeshi.[27]

Instances of rape and adultery were also documented. Kimura Kenji, from Mito domain, wrote in 1793 that Japanese sailors making the voyage to and from Ezo sometimes raped or committed adultery with Ainu women. The husbands of these women then went to the merchant ships to demand *tsugunai* but usually received only small amounts of tobacco in return.[28] Kimura also observed widespread prostitution in Wajinchi ports. He wrote that in Hakodate Japanese prostitutes sold themselves to Ainu men; and in the Ishikari region, Ainu prostitutes made themselves available to Japanese merchants.[29] Yamazaki Hanzō observed in 1808 that syphilis was particularly prevalent in Fukuyama, where "tea houses," such as those mentioned by Mutō Kanzō, sprouted up every year during the fishing seasons.[30]

The spread of syphilis mattered: as Crosby argues, it is "important in the history of a people in jeopardy, because it cripples their ability to reproduce" and contributes to their inability to resist foreign conquerors. In the Western Districts of Australia, for example, Jan Critchett points out that by the mid–nineteenth century venereal diseases had begun to ravage aboriginal women, leading to a decline in birthrates and facilitating European colonialism in that region. Moreover, in an even better known example, historians speculate that venereal diseases decimated the postcontact Hawaiian populations. As David Stannard explains, "The devastating effect of gonorrhea on fertility is well known; what is less known is that, even today, there is virtually 'no chance that an infant will be born normal and healthy' if its mother has primary or secondary syphilis during her pregnancy and that about one out of three fetuses infected with syphilis will either miscarry or be stillborn."[31]

Infant mortality and birth defects likely occurred among the Ainu, whose well-documented demographic decline in the nineteenth century was nothing short of astonishing. Okuyama Ryō, among the first to un- earth the root causes for the decline of Ainu society, argued that syphilis was a major contributor to this decline and a factor in the weakening of Ainu autonomy in Ezo.[32] Ainu could never recover from other diseases, or from the crippling influence of trade, as long as reproductive activity and the general health of their children were threatened by syphilis.

We have already seen that syphilis was not the only disease spread through trade. Smallpox also tagged along with traders, and even a short visit by a stranger from an outside village could bring the airborne killer and ignite a deadly epidemic. The shogunal official Matsuda Denjūrō noted how easily smallpox was spread by both Japanese and Ainu fur seal traders during the 1800 epidemic in the village of Usu, in southeast- ern Ezo. He wrote that a Japanese soldier (ashigaru) from Fukuyama and an Ainu had traveled to Usu from Oshamanbe to trade fur seals at the post there. In Usu, the two lodged at a local home. It was soon discovered that the Ainu visitor had smallpox. Local Ainu quickly protested, lodging a complaint with their headman; however, the damage had already been done. Matsuda wrote that "as is the nature of the disease," only a few days elapsed before signs of smallpox began appearing in the village, de- spite the fact that Ainu, according to custom, had burned the house where the disease first appeared. Usu Ainu forcefully lodged a second complaint about the epidemic with the headman, and Japanese supervi- sors in charge of local fisheries exhausted themselves helping the infect- ed. These efforts notwithstanding, the victims, after running high fevers, began to die. Matsuda noted that grief and despair began spreading among other Usu Ainu.[33]

Matsuda wrote that Ainu not yet infected with the disease had be- come alarmed and "without exception took cover in the surrounding mountains, dispersing in various directions" to escape the scourge. Upon arriving in the mountains, the infected ones simply fell in place and died, according to Matsuda. He estimated that of the some 250 Ainu in the vil- lage, about 40 died. The epidemic soon spread with the scattering Ainu into nearby villages, next appearing in Abuta, a village with a population of more than 500 people. Matsuda wrote that Abuta Ainu, like those of

Usu, also hid in the mountains following the outbreak. The epidemic then spread to Horobetsu, and deaths from the epidemic there were reportedly high. Horobetsu Ainu were observed smearing kettle soot on their faces and running frantically into the mountains, hoping to evade the epidemic.[34]

Fukuyama Castle took few steps to deter these epidemics in Ezo. Ezochi was, after all, outside Matsumae responsibilities, a foreign land inhabited by foreign people. To contain the spread of certain contagions, however, local physicians and officials warned Japanese to steer clear of infected Ainu. The officials' aim was to prevent the spread of smallpox and measles into Wajinchi villages where sparse population, at least when compared with cities in Japan, had transformed smallpox into an epidemic, rather than an endemic, disease. In the eighteenth century, however, nonstate interests, such as trading-post managers, attempted to deal with smallpox. In 1792, for example, Kushihara Seihō, like Matsuda, alluded to the relationship between trade and the spread of smallpox. He wrote that in 1779, Ainu from Mashike, north of the Ishikari plain in western Ezo, had died in a deadly smallpox epidemic. At that time, the Ainu of Rurumoppe, located in the Ishikari plain between the Teshio Mountains and the Japan Sea coast, obtained information concerning the epidemic and quickly became alarmed at the prospect of the disease's spreading. When Murayama Chōsaburō, the trading-post manager of Rurumoppe, returned from a trip to Sōya, the village headman, Kotan-piru, warned Murayama that some of the local Ainu were contemplating taking shelter in the mountains to escape the disease.[35]

Murayama reasoned that if Ainu hid in the mountains, they would be without food and medical supplies, whereas they would have these necessities if they remained at Rurumoppe. He recited a Japanese proverb, "although a net has many holes it still protects against the wind" (*ami no me nimo kaze fusegu*), and proceeded to set up an old herring net around the borders of Rurumoppe. He insisted that it would stop the epidemic from spreading. He also erected an edict placard with "prohibited" written in large characters to keep traders, possibly infected with the disease, from entering the area. Murayama even posted supervisors at the entrances to make sure that nobody came in.[36]

At the same time, local Ainu drew on their own medical culture to challenge the disease. They began by placing *inaw* around the village boundary.[37] These were likely *sinna inaw*, "abnormal fetishes," used by Ainu to placate the god of smallpox. In the early twentieth century, both John Batchelor and Neil Munro, following their respective research on Ainu culture, described *sinna inaw* as holding important places in Ainu medical culture and as being able to protect a village from smallpox.[38]

Ultimately, the Mashike epidemic bypassed Rurumoppe. Kushihara wrote that "not one person" from Rurumoppe died of smallpox. "In my humble opinion," he wrote, the fact "that the Ainu remained ignorant, and trusted Japanese like gods" explained why Rurumoppe Ainu never contracted smallpox. He conjectured that Murayama was a particularly "benevolent" fishery manager and that local Ainu never questioned what he told them to do.[39] Murayama also speculated that Ainu died in such high numbers from smallpox elsewhere because they had "no knowledge of medicine" or of basic forms of "medical treatment." He argued that Ainu women infected with congenital syphilis transmitted pathogens, or the "poisons in the mother's abdomen," to their children in the form of smallpox. The disease then quickly spread from village to village.[40] Kushihara was no physician, and his speculations reveal as much. However, his portrayal of how smallpox spread illustrates that Ainu were under assault by several diseases for which they had no cure. As medical historian Sekiba Fujihiko observed in the Meiji period, syphilis often caused stunted development and even death among Ainu children shortly after birth, and this could have been what Kushihara was alluding to.[41] Moreover, the condition of the Ainu resembles the situation described by Stannard among postcontact Hawaiian populations.

During the early nineteenth century, smallpox also appears to have traveled with the Santan trade to Sakhalin Island. In 1801, shogunal official Nakamura Koichirō stated that a massive smallpox epidemic in the Santan homeland, just south of the Amur Estuary, had made it uncertain whether traders from there would arrive in Shiranushi. In the sixth month of 1801, however, Aririnko, an Ainu elder from Sakhalin, informed the Shiranushi fishery supervisor that four trading vessels, with thirty-one traders, had arrived from Santan.[42] The captains of these vessels were old hands in trading with Shiranushi Ainu and Japanese.

Fuyanko and Tonko, for example, captains of two of the trade vessels, had been making the trip to southern Sakhalin for over thirty years.[43] Seven of their crew members had scars on their faces and bodies from smallpox. The origin of their disease is unclear however. The Santan homeland, which was inhabited largely by the Ul'chi people, lay at the intersection of three major empires: the Chinese, the Russian, and to a limited degree, the Japanese. The traders could have contracted smallpox from the Chinese who had operated a trade post at Deren or possibly from Russian fur trappers who were moving through Siberia in large numbers in search of animal skins. The traders could also have contracted smallpox from Ainu or Japanese at Shiranushi.

Historians document how Russians moving through Siberia and eventually into Kamchatka frequently introduced smallpox to indigenous groups, often decimating local populations. Indeed, Crosby observes that smallpox cut through Siberian peoples such as the Ostyak, Tungus, Yakut, Samoyed, and even the Kamchadal like a "scythe through standing grain."[44] Moreover, some records even suggest that in the winter of 1805–6 Russian sailors aboard Nikolai Rezanov's ship introduced smallpox to the islands of Rebun and Rishiri, off northwestern Hokkaido, although inconsistencies exist in the two primary sources involved.[45] In a similar vein, Takakura has pointed out that when the Russians moved into the Amur region in 1857, taking over what was a major trade center for the Ul'chi and forcing Qing officials to relocate upstream from Deren, a massive smallpox epidemic hit the Ul'chi, nearly bringing the Sakhalin trade to an end.[46] Regardless of their source, however, ecological "commodities" such as smallpox became permanent fixtures in Ainu lands, even on Sakhalin Island. Among the marten pelts, Chinese silks, and colored beads traded on Sakhalin was the airborne killer smallpox.

AINU MEDICAL CULTURE
AS JAPANESE POLITICAL CAPITAL

In an ironic twist, it was not only epidemic diseases such as smallpox but also the medications Ainu used to combat these contagions that ultimately spurred Japan's conquest of Ezo by heightening shogunal interest in the region. By at least the mid–seventeenth century, Japanese officials in both Fukuyama and Edo had begun to demonstrate an interest in pharmaceuticals extracted from the natural environment of Ezo. Later, in 1799, the practice of surveying for medicinal plant and animal products, many of which were associated with Ainu medical culture, became shogunal policy; and subsequently many Ainu medicines were integrated into the culture of gift giving that delineated hierarchical relations and cemented personal alliances in the early-modern Japanese state. For centuries Japanese merchants had viewed Ezo as rich in resources such as herring and salmon, but in time Ezo also became valued for the medicines that attracted the attention of Japanese physicians, some of whom eventually departed for Ezo under shogunal order to catalog plants and animals.

These shogunal-sponsored physicians, through their official taxonomical catalogs and notebooks of the fauna and flora of the north, recast Ezo's environment to fit a Japanese conception of natural order; and this process reminds one of an argument advanced by Max Horkheimer and Theodor Adorno. In their critique of the Enlightenment, they suggest that this type of cataloging of resources facilitates the domination of the environment and its inhabitants by objectifying the spirit of both nature and people. "What men want to learn from nature," they argue, "is how to use it in order wholly to dominate it and other men."[47] They continue that this objectification destroys animistic belief systems in favor of a more rational view of nature. Whereas animistic belief systems "spiritualized" the environment, the more ordered, or exploitative, approach of cataloging the environment "objectified" it for the more methodological use of resources. In much the same manner, during the early nineteenth century, after taking direct control of Ezo, the shogunate began to define the ecology of Ezo to fit the early-modern Japanese vision of natural order. The Japanese expansion into Ezochi, then, was in part motivated by this interest in materia medica and the desire to reshape the natural environment of Ezo to fit within Japanese conceptions of nature and its domination.

However, the Japanese version of natural order, at least as it related to medical culture and pharmaceuticals, was different from the European order described by Horkheimer and Adorno. In Japan, Neo-Confucianism dominated theories related to the natural world. Even in the late eighteenth century, and despite an accelerating influx of Dutch Learning, Japanese medical culture was still influenced primarily by medical thought imported from China.[48] That thought stressed a "holistic," or "physiological," approach to the body, which was seen as a microcosm of the universe, as a cosmos of well-balanced elements that corresponded to anatomical organs that needed to be kept in good order to prevent illness. Disease was understood to be a product of imbalances among the elements within the body, and it was treated by counterbalancing the excesses with opposing elements through acupuncture, preventative therapy, moxibustion, and certain pharmaceuticals. Surgery was ruled out because it interfered with the natural order of the body. Moreover, Chinese cosmology did not isolate the body in medical treatment but rather viewed medical therapy within the broader context of the "five evolutionary phase" theory, the yin-yang cycle, and the system of numerical emblems. Medicines were given to counter symptoms; for example, hot medicines were used to treat cool afflictions. Pharmaceuticals prevented disease, and because prevention was emphasized over finding a cure, pharmaceuticals were highly sought after by Japanese physicians.[49] Thus, the Neo-Confucian order that Japanese officials imposed on the resources of Ezo was based on a conception of the world and its competing elements that differed substantially from that of European medical culture. However, the Japanese and the Europeans were similar in that shogunal-sponsored physicians imposed the Neo-Confucian order over the natural environment of Ezo as assiduously as Enlightenment figures imposed their conceptual order on the European medicine and natural world of their day.

but had the same effect

The Edo shogunate first showed an interest in surveying Ezo pharmaceuticals decades before it took direct control in 1799. In 1727, for example, officials dispatched the physician Abe Tomonoshin to collect and categorize medicinal plant and animal products in Ezo. Abe, born in Morioka in 1670, had lived in Fujian Province for eighteen years after his Osaka-bound vessel drifted off course and wound up in China. Not one to squander an opportunity, he had studied Chinese medicine during his lengthy stay. Subsequently he had returned home to Japan to practice medicine, acquiring the solid reputation that led to his appointment by the shogunate. While in Ezo, he wrote the *Saiyaku shiki* [A record of a pharmaceutical collector], a catalog that lists over 107 different pharmaceuticals available in the north.[50]

After 1799, shogunal officials continued to dispatch physicians to Ezo for the purpose of collecting plant- and animal-based pharmaceuticals. That same year, physicians Sō Senshun and Shibue Chōhaku arrived in the north for that purpose. Some historians argue that these physicians were part of the government effort to provide medical treatment for Ainu and Japanese living in Ezo, but their activities were confined, at least initially, to collecting medicines under government order.[51] Neither Sō nor Shibue described the medical conditions of Ainu or Japanese, although both kept detailed notebooks of medicinal plants. They also sketched the austere eastern coastline of the island and included occasional references to Ainu customs.[52] These lengthy accounts, which were later made available to shogunal officials, became the lens through which Japanese officialdom viewed the northern landscape and its political and economic potential. The process of cataloging pharmaceuticals, in other words, contributed to defining the basic character of this sharply escalating Japanese intrusion into Ezo.

Of medicines used by Ainu, Japanese explored the healing properties of *kuma no i* (bear gallbladder), *takeri* (dried fur seal penis), *eburiko* (Ainu, *siw karus* or *kuy karus; Fomitopsis officinalis*, a bracket fungus), *ikema* (Ainu, *ikema; Cynanchum caudatum (Miq.) Maxim*), *okurikankiri* (Ainu, *tekunbeko-rube; Cambariodes japonicus;* a shellfish product), and others. In the mid–seventeenth century, some of these medicines quickly became gifts exchanged during official audiences between Ainu and Matsumae officials, or domainal lords and the shogun (see figures 18–20). According to Matsumae Hironaga, for example, shogunal officials ordered in 1669 that *eburiko* be sent to Edo as annual gifts. Matsumae Yasuhiro, the shogunal vassal who led Matsumae forces in Shakushain's War, noted that of four merchant vessels that traveled to western Ezo to trade that year, one went as far as Sakhalin to pick up *eburiko*. This occurred despite the violent fighting that convulsed parts of Ezo at the time. Officials also exchanged bear gallbladder as gifts.[53]

Figure 18.   Ainu fur seal hunters. Ainu and Japanese ate fur seal meat, processed the pelts, and dried the penis, which was used as a pharmaceutical and traded in Ezo. Such medicines were an important part of trading in Ezo throughout the Edo period. *Ezotō kikan* [Strange sights from Ezo Islands]. Courtesy of the Resource Collection for Northern Studies, Hokkaido University Library.

An understanding of the politics of gift giving in Ezo requires that something be said of the Ainu medical culture from which Japanese physicians drew much of their information.[54] The Ainu response to smallpox and other diseases was shaped by the environment they inhabited and by how diseases were perceived within their cultural order. In general, Ainu medical rituals were shaped by the notion that the natural environment was a realm alive with *kamuy*, which assumed many forms.[55] Simply put, diseases were like all other living things: they were *kamuy* that existed in the natural world but possessed an inner, spiritual essence that was linked to a plane of existence transcending the temporal world. John Batchelor, an English missionary writing around 1900, observed of

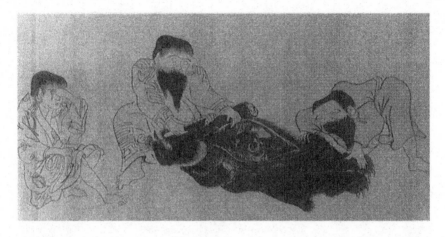

Figure 19. Ainu skinning a bear after the *iomante*. Bear gallbladder was considered an important pharmaceutical among Ainu and Japanese and was traded in both market and symbolic economies. *Ezo kokufū zue* [Illustrations of the provincial customs of Ezo]. Courtesy of the Resource Collection for Northern Studies, Hokkaido University Library.

Ainu medical culture that unlike nineteenth-century Western medicine, which tended to portray disease as an "adventitious, blind, irrational force," Ainu believed contagions had a "personal and spiritual existence." He remarked that Ainu believed diseases were able to "think, will and act."[56]

Payoka kamuy, the god of smallpox, was among the most feared and respected of these *kamuy,* and Ainu believed that it appeared in villages or individual households in many forms.[57] To deal with *payoka kamuy,* diviner-physicians, called *uepotarakur,* administered medicine, carved special *inaw* (ceremonial fetishes), and oversaw the process of exorcizing *kamuy* from the body of the ailing.[58] Ainu believed the effectiveness of a medicine depended on its ability to expel contagions from the body of the victim, and they included a variety of plant- and animal-based medicines in their pharmacopoeia. Exorcisms (*uepotara*) were also important to Ainu medical practice because people who died from smallpox were thought to linger as ghosts (*tukap*) who spread pestilence to other villages. One tale from Nibutani, a village in eastern Hokkaido, emphasizes

Figure 20.   Ritualized gift giving between Ainu and Japanese. At this post, Ainu are trading fur seal for clothing, tobacco, and rice. *Ezotō kikan* [Strange sights from Ezo Islands]. Courtesy of the Resource Collection for Northern Studies, Hokkaido University Library.

the tenaciousness of smallpox, even in the land of the ancestors. Long ago, as Kayano Shigeru recounted in 1987, an outbreak of smallpox in Nibutani killed so many Ainu that the area of Kankan was "virtually annihilated." However, among the survivors of Kankan was an elderly man named Iruekashi, who cautioned the surviving children of Kankan: "People who die of this disease called smallpox are not like the people who die from other ailments. People who die from smallpox do not go to the place of our ancestors." Rather, they roamed the earth in the form of ghosts, spreading smallpox to other unsuspecting Ainu villages.[59]

Of these exorcisms, Neil Munro, who researched Ainu *uepotara* in the early twentieth century, observed that Ainu used terms such as *kasi-kik*, literally "striking down from above," to describe the process of exorcizing *payoka kamuy* from the bodies of the infected. He wrote that in preparation for exorcisms, *uepotarakur* carved *sinna-inaw*, "abnormal fetishes," such as those used in Rurumoppe, and constructed "houses of evil" from sticks, which they used to hold *payoka kamuy* once it had been exorcized. They also built traps from hollow plants such as the *kuttar* (*Polygonum sachalinensis*), which captured the "ghosts and spirits of pestilence." In other cases, the *uepotarakur* beat the infected person with switches of brush clover (*sinkep*) or made slight incisions on the body of the victim to let out the "bad blood." Munro also remarked that Ainu who died from smallpox were understood to take ghostly form and wander the earth touching off other epidemics rather than resting peacefully in the "land of their ancestors."[60] Batchelor observed one exorcism in the early twentieth century during which the *uepotarakur* "was in a trance and much excited. His eyes were wide open but they appeared to be glazed over with a sort of film, and he seemed to be looking far away into the world of spirits, without seeing anything material."[61]

In 1715, Lord Norihiro confirmed in a memorandum to Edo that Ainu used a variety of medicines, including fur seal gallbladder and *ikema*. He also noted that Ainu even ate whale feces to combat certain ailments. This practice is consistent with Ainu medical culture, in which pharmaceuticals that expelled contagions, or *kamuy*, from the body were thought to be the most effective; whale feces would surely have revolted even the most stubborn *kamuy*. Norihiro also observed that when smallpox, measles, and other epidemic diseases first struck the Ainu, they abandoned their sick, and scattered into the "mountains and valleys." But Norihiro also observed changes in Ainu attitudes toward epidemic diseases, noting that Ainu had even started to administer medical care.[62] Later, in 1850, Matsuura Takeshirō remarked of the Ainu on Kunashir and Iturup that medicinal plants such as *eburiko* and *ikema* were commonly used to combat diseases.[63] He also noted that Ainu possessed herbal medicines for colds, eye diseases, dizziness from childbirth, chest pains, abscesses or boils, colds with fever, and even nosebleeds.[64] Some Ainu even understood that, when consumed, fish such as the Gasterosteidae, as well as diatomaceous earth, possessed certain healing properties.[65]

Matsumae Hironaga, in the *Matsumaeshi*, was among the first Japanese to attempt to categorize and quantify the natural environment of Ezo, and he cataloged hundreds of plants, mammals, birds, and fish in Ezo. Writing in the 1780s, he revealed the practical "objectifying" impulse of the day when he characterized many of these items as *Ezo sanbutsu*, "Ezo products." He also included a lengthy section on pharmaceuticals that contained well over one hundred entries outlining brief histories, some explanations of Ainu medical practice, and the known medicinal properties of the pharmaceuticals.[66] Of these pharmaceuticals, he wrote that plants such as *eburiko* and *ikema* were medicines used by both Ainu and Japanese. He remarked that Terashima Ryōan mentioned *eburiko* in the *Wakan sansai zue*, and he noted that it grew on the larch trees of Sakhalin. He refuted the assertion of noted botanist Hiraga Gennai, who wrote that *eburiko* could be found on pine trees throughout Japan. "If this is the case," Hironaga blithely asked, "then why isn't *eburiko* produced on Honshu?" Hironaga claimed that Ainu believed *eburiko* to be a source of physical strength, whereas some Japanese understood it to be effective against fever and eye infections when mixed with iris tea and used to wash out the infected eye. He also reported that the head priest of the Shinzenhōji Temple in Sanshō Hachiman, in central Japan, had suggested that *eburiko* could even be effective against bites from rabid dogs.[67] Toki Shinpo, a student of Shibue Chōhaku who also traveled in eastern Ezo cataloging pharmaceuticals, remarked in his writings that the plant both Ainu and Japanese referred to as *ikema* had important medicinal qualities.[68]

Hironaga, for his part, ended his discussion of *ikema* on a skeptical note: "These days people insist that virtually every plant is a medicine of some kind, so you need to be careful."[69] For Fukui Yoshimaro, however, a student of Dutch Learning, the outlook was more positive, and he wrote at length on the medicinal properties of *eburiko*, as well as *ikema* and *okurikankiri*. He explained that while in Nagasaki the physician Katsuragawa Hoshū had asked Swedish scientist C. P. Thunberg, who served as physician at the Dutch factory at Deshima in 1775–6, about the medicinal properties of *eburiko*.[70] Thunberg had noted that it was effective against gastrointestinal disorders and intestinal roundworm. Fukui also wrote that physician Ōtsuki Gentaku, also a student of Dutch Learning, suggested that *eburiko* could be used for sore throat and for menstrual pain. Like Hironaga, Fukui himself believed that *eburiko* helped prevent certain eye diseases, among other maladies.[71]

Ainu probably used *okurikankiri, ikema*, and *eburiko* as medicines before the seventeenth century and may have introduced them to the Japanese. However, some of these medicines may have been introduced to the Japanese by the Dutch at Deshima. Ōtsuki Gentaku, for example, wrote about *okurikankiri* in two treatises on Dutch Learning, noting that in Japan only crawfish from Ezo and northeastern Japan produced *okurikankiri*.[72] During the nineteenth century, the Dutch physician Philipp Franz von Siebold prescribed *okurikankiri* while he was in Japan. *Eburiko*, moreover, was widely used by Europeans, as well as by Ainu, Native Americans, Siberian groups, Japanese, and Chinese. How Japanese physicians first came in contact with *eburiko* is unclear, but it is probable that, like *okurikankiri*, it was first introduced by Dutch physicians at Deshima. There is a good chance, however, that Ainu introduced *eburiko* through trade. To begin with, Ainu likely acquired knowledge of *eburiko* very early through contacts with the East Asian continent.[73] Moreover, *eburiko* was being presented as a gift in Edo as early as 1669, before the heyday of Dutch influence at Nagasaki. Indeed, by then, both *okurikankiri* and *eburiko* were pharmaceuticals considered to be among "Ezo products" and were later listed in catalogs such as those written by Matsumae Hironaga and Abe Tomonoshin, linking Ainu medical practice to the politicized "gift society," as Mary Elizabeth Berry describes it, of early-modern Japan.

With increasing contact between Ainu and Japanese in Ezo, then, there was a spread of deadly contagions, as well as an exchange of medical knowledge, that altered the relationship of these people with one another and with their local ecosystem. In the seventeenth century, *eburiko* was being brought to Edo as a gift, and with it came tidbits of Ainu culture and the northern environment. With the subsequent Japanese expansion into Ezo, including the southern section of Sakhalin, medicinal plants theretofore not widely found in Japan, such as *eburiko*, became available in Japanese population centers. These pharmaceuticals then attracted the attention of Katsuragawa Hoshū and Ōtsuki Gentaku, two of the leading medical scholars of Japan's early-modern period. It was the

ECOLOGICAL IMPERIALISM

exchange of medical culture between Ainu and Japanese, perhaps even the Ainu reaction to contagions such as smallpox itself, that alerted Edo to the medicinal value of many of these products.

and of the Ezo environment

CONCLUSION

In Ezo, the breaching of epidemic boundaries, or what Alfred Crosby calls "ecological imperialism," created an altogether new epidemiology, one that weakened Ainu autonomy and ultimately undermined their ability to resist the Japanese incorporation of their lands.[74] In 1590, the regularization of trade relations in Ezo allowed pathogens to secure a prominent place among the unseen commodities being exchanged, sparking far-flung changes in the epidemiology of Ainu communities and even in communities on Sakhalin and possibly beyond.

The new epidemic patterns in Ezo led in turn to changes in Ainu medical practice, which then transformed trade. Some of the materia medica that Ainu *uepotarakur* used to combat contagions caught the attention of Japanese who were interested in exploiting the region's pharmaceuticals. The Ainu reaction to new diseases resonated both culturally and politically in Ezo. Contemporary observers noted that Ainu used medicinal plants to combat smallpox. In time these medicines attracted the attention of Dutch Learning scholars in Japan (who specialized in Western medical technology), such as Katsuragawa Hoshū and Ōtsuki Gentaku, who had up to this point centered their activities in Nagasaki; and Ainu medicines became valued medical products for official gift giving. Along with exotic eagle feathers and animal pelts, pharmaceuticals such as bear gallbladder and certain fungi were exchanged as gifts at the highest levels of the early-modern Japanese state, and these exchanges of medicines helped forge the ties of personal attachment so critical to politics in the Tokugawa polity.

8 The Role of Ceremony in Conquest

Following Shakushain's War in 1669, Fukuyama Castle, through yearly audiences and ceremonies, sought to establish a tradition of Ainu subservience and, subsequently, to create a precedent for Matsumae rule in Ezo by polarizing Ainu-Japanese relations according to the Confucian-based dichotomy that pitted the "civilized center" against the "barbarian edge" (*ka'i chitsujo*). In a manner typical of the Tokugawa approach to foreign relations, Matsumae officials highlighted, or even manufactured, the barbarian features of the Ainu, emphasizing their exotic customs (*fū-zoku*) and then contrasting these to the civilized customs of the Japanese. These differences in customs, particularly in Ezo, where the Wajinchi-Ezochi line was largely an artificial one, helped to delineate the borders of the Tokugawa polity. These borders proved flexible and dynamic, however, and yearly audiences and ceremonies were performed throughout Ezochi as part of a larger policy to bolster Matsumae prestige and power in more distant regions. As this chapter shows, in Ezo, sometimes the line between the "civilized center" and the "barbarian edge" eroded as Ainu and Japanese incorporated the ceremonial practices of the other to form altogether new ritual experiences: the experiences of the middle ground,

DIPLOMATIC ORDER AND THE AINU

Starting about sixteen years after the defeat of Shakushain, in the fourth month of 1685 and then again in the second month of 1686, Matsumae lords conducted what they called barbarian audiences (*ijin raiheki*) with Ainu from western Ezo (possibly Ainu chiefs from Sōya). During these audiences Lord Norihiro wore ceremonial dress when meeting with Ainu.[1] Generally speaking, Matsumae officials referred to these ceremonies as *uimamu* (Ainu, *uymam*) when conducted at Fukuyama Castle and as *omusha* (Ainu, *umusa*) when conducted at trading posts. The *uimamu*, on the one hand, developed from trade at the castle town into audiences and gift exchanges that had more political connotations than did simple exchanges of goods. Early references to *uimamu* can be found in documents dating to the 1610s, but the documents offer few details as to the protocol or political motivations of these ceremonies. The *omusha*, on the other hand, developed from an Ainu greeting into an event during which Japanese regulations and prohibitions could be communicated to Ainu leaders throughout Ezo. The *omusha* also became a valuable administrative device for the military occupation of distant posts in southern Sakhalin, as well as on Kunashir and Iturup islands.

After Shakushain's War, at least in principle, these ceremonies developed into tools for the management of trade and fisheries in Ezo. Holding audiences and participating in the process of confirming Ainu elders allowed Matsumae lords to influence Ainu affairs at a local level. Although elders, called village headman (*otona*) and lesser–village headman (*kozukai*), continued to be selected within Ainu communities according to Ainu criteria of leadership qualities, they were at least nominally approved by Matsumae officials during *uimamu,* a practice that (according to Fukuyama officialdom) incorporated them into the Matsumae administrative structure. These headmen then represented their villages at audiences during which interpreters communicated new edicts to Ainu leaders, and these affairs were followed by ritualized saké drinking and gift exchanges. With the introduction of audiences, Matsumae lords began to participate directly in interchiefdom politics, something they had not done before Shakushain's War.

The policy reflected governance elsewhere in early-modern Japan. Herman Ooms observes that the Edo shogunate, by confirming village leadership at the local level, established and maintained a certain degree of administrative influence within peasant communities. Such shogunal investiture, he points out, sometimes became a source of legitimization for headmen, often replacing local selection criteria. Ooms writes that headmen, "as stipended agents for the city-bound warriors, were an integral part of the dominant class in not only structural but also economic terms."[2] Similarly, Stephen Vlastos notes how headmen in the peasant villages of Aizu "possessed great power over political and economic affairs of the village" because they had been confirmed by the local warrior elite. Many headmen even possessed sanctioned symbols of social status and the trappings of warrior culture, such as swords, which made them easy targets for disgruntled peasants.[3] In part, the positions of Ainu and Japanese headmen were based on similar notions of village administration in that these leaders functioned as the "crucial nexus of state-society contact."[4] Contemporary observers recognized this familiar relationship that Ainu headmen shared with peasant-village heads in Japan. Sakakura Genjirō, following his visit to Ezo, remarked that Ainu *otona* resemble village headmen (*shōya*) in Japan. He also explained that orders might be relayed to them by Matsumae officials because of their influence at the local level.[5] In the eyes of Matsumae officials, in other words, *otona* were meant to serve as local governing agents in Ainu communities.

However, yearly audiences and ceremonies appear only to have officially approved, according to Japanese political practice, headmen who had already risen to power within Ainu political circles, illustrating that the middle ground extended into the political arena.[6] This fact suggests that a kind of consensus was reached among Ainu communities and

Fukuyama Castle, exposing the limitations of Matsumae influence in Ezochi even after Shakushain's War. Friendly ties to Fukuyama Castle might have helped those who wanted to be chiefs, but as Iwasaki Naoko has emphasized, wealth acquired in trade, powerful ancestors, and other criteria, such as physical strength and manliness, were important qualities in eastern Ezo.[7] Matsumiya Kanzan noted that Ainu headman oversaw affairs at the village level, and that for the most part *otona* were the strongest and so they naturally become leaders (*kashira*). Hezutsu Tōsaku remarked that headmen were usually manly figures with full beards, whereas Mogami Tokunai remarked of these manly chiefs that they "used to travel once in their lifetime to Fukuyama for an audience with the lord. At this time, they brought with them various gifts produced in the regions they came from." *Otona* came in special trade boats, called *uymamcip*, when making the journey to Fukuyama Castle.[8] Viewed from the perspective of Fukuyama Castle, then, attending audience with the Matsumae lord was one of the most important duties of an Ainu *otona*. It authenticated his position as overseer of his village; however, from the perspective of these villages, at least in the seventeenth and eighteenth centuries, these *otona* naturally assumed positions of leadership because of qualities admired by Ainu.

Otona and *kozukai*, then, rose to power within Ainu villages. Yet, these positions were authenticated when the headmen attended audience at Fukuyama Castle. In this way, Matsumae audiences in Ezochi resembled the Ming and Qing approaches to foreign affairs in the Amur Estuary and northern Sakhalin. For example, one of the first steps that Qing authorities took to secure control of commercial activity in northern Sakhalin was to give titles such as *haraida* (*xingzhang*) and *gashanida* (*xiangzhang*), both meaning "headman," to local elders. These official positions were confirmed at audiences, and ranks were identified through silk uniforms. In the Chinese world order, all "uncivilized barbarians" on the outskirts of China had the potential to become "civilized barbarians" through this type of exchange. Many of these headmen, however, rose to power within the context of their local communities. Matsumae officials assumed a similar posture following Shakushain's War, assigning titles to Ainu elders and constructing their administrative framework in Ezochi on a firm foundation of ritualized trade.

This policy reflected the Tokugawa approach to foreign affairs in general. The shogunate, by selling Tokugawa rule as the realization of "civilized government," sought to garner international and domestic respect for the shogun. Subsequently, all foreign trade and diplomacy was approved in Edo under the guise of maritime prohibitions. Maritime prohibitions placed the right to regulate and conduct diplomatic relations with foreign countries in the hands of the shogunate, yielding both financial and political benefits.[9] In 1633, for example, the shogunate invested the Nagasaki magistracy with rights to oversee trading with the Dutch and Chinese at Nagasaki. Similarly, local warrior houses such as the Sō of Tsushima and the Shimazu of Satsuma were allowed to conduct foreign trade with Korea and the Ryukyu Kingdom. In this way, Japan was not the closed country (*sakoku*) that it is so often portrayed as being, but rather a country with "four windows" through which shogunal-endorsed exchange was conducted with the outside world.[10]

JAPAN-CENTERED TRADITIONS IN EZO

By the end of the eighteenth century, audiences at Fukuyama Castle had become an established yearly tradition in Ainu-Japanese relations and a part of the ceremonial landscape in Ezo. One reason that these audiences were probably so successful was the native Ainu roots of both the *uymam* and *umusa*. In the eyes of most Ainu chiefs, this fact may have further legitimized the ceremonies, despite their political ramifications. Mogami Tokunai wrote in 1808 that the linguistic origin of *uimamu* was unknown and that the closest Japanese word might be *uimamie* (or *shoken*), "to see for the first time."[11]

Some Ainu epic poetry speaks of the *uymam* and the implications of ceremonial trade and audiences at Fukuyama Castle. In 1936, Hirame Karepia recited a *yukar* that illustrates the anxiety provoked by ceremonial trading at Fukuyama Castle. Of course, the *uimamu* was long gone by the early twentieth century, so one can only assume that at least some elements of this epic can be traced to earlier times; and for this reason, I will explore the poem at some length. It starts out with the female narrator being told that she will accompany her two elder brothers on a trading mission to Fukuyama Castle. Her eldest brother explains,

Listen well
to what I have to say!
I have gone through
many hardships
in raising both of you.
Even though
we often used to go
trading with the Japanese [tono-ko-uymam],
we have not done so
until now.
Now at last
I want to go trading.
Let us make a boat
in preparation for it![12]

The uymamcip (a vessel also described by Mogami Tokunai) is then beautifully adorned by the eldest brother, who leads the trade expedition. The sister continues,

On the side of the boat,
that big boat,
he had carved
many pictures,
countless pictures
of the gods dwelling in the mountains,
both the good ones
and the evil ones.
On the other side of the boat
he had carved
many pictures,
countless pictures
of the gods dwelling in the sea,
both the evil ones
and the good ones.
It was a delightful sight,
and my heart leaped with pleasure.[13]

En route to Wajinchi aboard the *uymamcip*, the three receive an ominous warning from birds flying overhead. The birds shed tears like rain, and the sound of their wings speaks the following,

> I also
> went off
> to go trading
> but a wicked Japanese interpreter
> gave me poisoned wine
> to drink.
> After a while,
> I died and this
> is my dead soul
> which is now going homeward.
> Do not go on!
> Turn back at once![14]

Despite the warning, the three continue onward until they reached the "land of the Japanese." The younger sister offers an extremely rare Ainu perspective on trade in Wajinchi:

> After that,
> my elder brothers
> landed the boat
> and built
> a large hut of matting.
> After that,
> they unloaded the trade goods.
> After a while,
> they finished the unloading.
> After they were finished,
> my elder brothers
> attired themselves
> in the best garments
> which I had embroidered
> in order to have an audience
> with the Japanese lord.
> I also
> dressed myself
> in the best garments

which I had embroidered.
Then we set out.[15]

Fukuyama seems lavish to the Ainu visitors. The sister explains,

The Japanese town,
of which I had heard,
went stretching out
far in the distance.
As we walked on,
a large wooden house
stood there
majestically.
We went inside it.
Then
the wicked Japanese interpreter,
of whom we had heard,
came out.
After my elder brothers
had finished their audience
with the Japanese lord,
my elder brothers
were seated
on the entrance porch,
where a single mat
had been spread.[16]

Despite the warnings borne on the wings of birds, the two elder brothers drink the saké offered by the interpreter and die. Ultimately, after being admonished by gods and suffering intense anguish, the sister is saved by her brothers, who have taken the form of birds, and she is taken back home.

Some elements of this *yukar* appear to be quite early. First, the ceremonial nature of the visit suggests a certain degree of anticipation, as well as fear and anxiety; and the smartly decorated *uymamcip*, adorned with the icons of the Ainu metaphysical order, nicely illustrates the ritual importance of the trading mission. Second, the timing of the visit appears to coincide with the transition to adulthood, or some other kind of coming of age: perhaps the eldest brother demonstrates his bravery in making the trading visit, a gesture symbolic of his ascendancy to head of the family. At a later point in the poem, while in the form of a bird, he expresses concern over the continuation of his ancestral line. Third, the small hut, or *marugoya*, built at Fukuyama by the two brothers resembles huts built in the early seventeenth century, before trading posts became a standard feature in Ezochi. However, in other ways, this trading expedition resembles *uimamu* of later years. For example, the three Ainu appear to distinguish between trade (*uymam*) and the audience; in practice the two are combined. The three receive their trade goods on the entrance porch (*ogenkan*) while seated on a "single mat," features which are typical of later *uimamu*.

Japanese sources suggest that whatever form they took, audiences changed a great deal over time.[17] One of the earliest references to ritualized trade in Ezo comes from a Portuguese missionary, who noted in 1620 that when Ainu from the west arrived in Fukuyama to trade, they undertook a ceremony that the Matsumae lord attended. Ainu brought *coromos* (silks) and *jitocus* (*jittoku*) to this ceremony, which they presented to the lord.[18] The only other pre-1660s reference to *uimamu* was in 1633, when Ainu from Otobe and Kuroiwa performed an *uimamu* for a shogunal inspector.[19]

The defeat of Shakushain let Matsumae officials impose their hierarchical model of foreign relations over the "vanquished barbarians," particularly in the realm of the *uimamu*. In 1685 and 1686, as mentioned, Matsumae Norihiro conducted audiences with Ainu from western Ezo. Later, in 1692, Matsumae Hirotoki noted that Ainu from fifteen different locations attended audiences at Fukuyama Castle.[20] Similarly, between 1684 and 1755, members of the Wada family recorded that Ainu from Futoro attended audiences thirty-one times, a little more than once every two years. Although exact details of these early audiences remain unknown, the participants conducted a *sakazuki*, or a ceremonial saké drinking, while Ainu presented *kenjōbutsu*, "gifts presented upward," to the lord and in return received *kudasaremono*, "gifts bestowed from above."[21] In Japan, *sakazuki* with a domainal lord was considered a "signal honor"; João Rodrigues, a European translator, recalled his *sakazuki* with Hideyoshi as one of the most moving moments of his lengthy stay in Japan.[22]

Satō Genrokurō noted in 1786 that Ainu from nearby locations traveled to Fukuyama Castle for audiences. He explained that arrangements for the visits were first made between Ainu headmen and trade officials, *uwanoriyaku*, at the local level. He noted that Ainu referred to the visits as *musharei*, or the *omusha*, and brought local products or gifts such as Ezo silks to Fukuyama Castle and in return received saké and tobacco from officials.[23] Following the Menashi-Kunashir War of 1789 and shortly after the execution of the thirty-seven Ainu conspirators, Niida Magosaburō, a Matsumae military commander, ordered that thirty-nine Ainu—including Ikoriyakani, the son of Tsukinoe of Kunashir—come back to Fukuyama Castle with Matsumae armies for an audience with Lord Michihiro.[24] Matsumae warriors gave these Ainu a crash course on their culture of violence, displaying the salted heads of the Ainu conspirators and parading the vanquished through the streets of Fukuyama.[25] Hoping to avoid other Ainu uprisings, officials Shimonokuni Toneri and Ujiie Shinbei issued orders specifying that "regardless of where they live," Ainu headmen were to attend audience at least once a year. The officials also added that no special arrangements should be made for presenting gifts. In short, in the context of these audiences in Fukuyama, commercial trade had almost completely given way to trade conducted solely for its political value.[26]

Matsumae officials believed that audiences strongly deterred Ainu uprisings. As yearly events, audiences created a precedent for Matsumae rule in Ezo, providing symbolic reminders of Matsumae power and prestige. Before the audience with the lord, Matsumae officials directed Ainu under the Fukuyama Castle entrance, which was adorned with unsheathed swords and lances.[27] Officials also decorated the audience chamber with samurai armor, lances, rifles, and even cannons.[28] In one painting, Ainu elders, made to hold hands, are portrayed as children when on their way to visit the Matsumae lord (see figure 21).

After Shakushain's War, then, Fukuyama Castle asserted control over Ainu affairs by authenticating the appointment of village headmen at audiences. More than simply an audience between lord and vassal, however, these meetings were construed by Matsumae officials as symbolic of the "subjugation of the barbarians." Ainu chiefs traveled "great distances," accounts often stress, to present gifts to the lord of Matsumae.

Figure 21.   Ainu being led hand-in-hand to an audience with a Matsumae lord. With Ainu holding hands and crouched over, these audiences emphasized Ainu subordination to Japanese. *Ezojin omemie zu* [Illustration of an Ainu audience]. Courtesy of the Resource Collection for Northern Studies, Hokkaido University Library.

These audiences had been occurring since "ancient times," accounts add, creating a tradition of Matsumae rule. In this way, Matsumae officials tried to place Fukuyama Castle at the center of Ainu political and ritual life.

CEREMONY AT FUKUYAMA CASTLE

Once Ainu arrived at Fukuyama Castle, audiences were performed according to meticulously designed ritual protocol, and everything from the decor of the room to the seating arrangements was arranged to dramatize Matsumae supremacy. Kakizaki Orindo's guide to castle events, the *Matsumae jōnai nenjū gyōji* [The annual events of Matsumae Castle], although written during the second period of Matsumae rule, between

1821 and 1854, sheds light on how carefully audiences at Fukuyama Castle were performed.[29] This manual for yearly rituals illustrates the attempts made by Matsumae officials to organize Ainu ceremonial behavior while providing a yearly reminder of Matsumae power and prestige.

The ceremony begins, writes Orindo, with an official briefing of Ainu elders on the protocol for attendance at the castle (*tojō*). After the briefing, Ainu elders are shown to their waiting room. Once Matsumae officials have gone over the ceremonial procedures with Ainu, the lord enters the audience chamber, or *ozashiki*. Beforehand, insists Orindo, the chamber needs to be carefully decorated with hanging curtains (*onmaku*) bearing the Matsumae household crest (*gomon*). In addition, military weaponry, including samurai armor (*gogusoku*), should be placed in the center of the chamber. Before the participants are led into the chamber, the *tōyaku*, an official charged with tending to Ainu elders, formally greets the lord. He then departs to escort the town magistrates, or *machi bugyō*, to the audience chamber. Following his departure, several low-ranking officials, or *okachi*, bring gifts into the audience chamber; these items are placed in the lower section of the audience chamber called the *naien*.[30]

Orindo's guide points out that the lord occupies the raised section of the chamber, or the *gojōdan*. An official then leads Ainu elders into the audience chamber. At this time, individual elders introduce themselves by announcing their names and official titles. The elders then line up near the wooden decorative seam, called the *onhashiragiwa*, that divides the larger outer chamber, or *sotojikii*. The master of ceremonies, here referred to as the *goyōban*, then escorts the town magistrates and the elders into the audience chamber. The magistrates, once all present, assemble along a wall within the inner chamber, and Matsumae elders assemble along the other.[31]

An official interpreter then reads the edicts, and after confirming that the Ainu understand the contents of the regulations, he passes the document to the magistrates, who then hand it to the master of ceremonies. He approaches the lord and explains that the Ainu understand the contents of the document; then both the master of ceremonies and the magistrates depart the audience chamber after formally paying respect to the lord.[32] At this point, two officials charged with pouring the ceremonial saké, or *ochōshikata*, enter the chamber. They place lacquered trays and cups (*zenbu*) in front of the lord and the Ainu, and the lord drinks with the elders. Following a short meal, the Ainu are escorted to inspect the various displays, such as swords and rifles (*okazaritsuke*), that decorate the chamber. They are then taken on a tour of the entire castle. Ainu finally withdraw to the *ogenkan* (entrance porch), where they are told by the interpreter that they will receive *kudasaremono*.[33] (Note that the receipt of gifts on the entryway porch matches the above cited Ainu *yukar* perfectly, minus the poisoned saké.)

Although somewhat smaller in scale, the audiences held at Fukuyama Castle share similarities to the Korean envoys to Edo in the seventeenth century. Ronald Toby writes that the "presentation of greetings" and the "presentation of gifts" were part of the "central ceremony" of Korean envoys. Toby continues that with Korean and Ryukyuan envoys, protocol such as seating arrangements was meant to draw attention to "ceremonial distinctions" that delineated "a hierarchical ordering of Japan, Korea, and Ryukyu." In Edo, during a 1665 audience, the Dutch envoys "presented their obeisance from the veranda furthest from the Upper Stage, and withdrew by the same route."[34] Similarly, Ainu elders, as dictated by protocol, were made to sit in the *sotojikii*, or outer chamber, below the Matsumae lords, who occupied the *gojōdan*. Other Ainu, such as the three siblings in the *yukar*, were forced to sit in the entry area. Orindo went into great detail about the seating arrangements at Matsumae audiences, making sure they fit the description of audiences typical of the day.

In the Ainu language, *uymam* might have meant simply "trade," but by 1841 there could be little doubt in the minds of either Ainu elders or Matsumae officials that audiences at Fukuyama Castle resonated with political symbolism. Ainu elders made yearly visits to Fukuyama Castle, where they participated in a carefully orchestrated ceremony which emphasized Matsumae power and prestige in five ways. First, Fukuyama Castle, the administrative center of Matsumae rule, was a massive fortification that served as a visual symbol of Matsumae's military strength.[35] Second, the tours of the castle and displayed weaponry ensured that these visual reminders of military power stayed fresh in the memory of Ainu elders. (Orindo even included simple illustrations in his manual on the placement of weaponry.) Third, the hierarchical organization of space in the audience chamber emphasized Ainu subordination. Ainu elders were seated in the outer chamber, and other Ainu were placed on the entrance porch. Ainu were seated below, and distant from, the focal point of political authority, the Matsumae lord. Fourth, even trade terminology resonated with political nuances. Ainu brought *kenjōbutsu*, gifts presented "upward" to superior officials. In contrast, Ainu were given *kudasaremono*, gifts bestowed "downward" to subordinates. And fifth, the administrative practicality of the audiences should not be overlooked. In a procedure overseen by Matsumae officialdom, interpreters read new edicts to the Ainu. Whether Ainu officials understood the regulations was reported by the master of ceremonies to the lord himself. In this way, audiences at Fukuyama Castle again were similar to shogunal audiences in Edo during which replies from foreigners were reported to the shogun through an official master of ceremonies, or *sōshaban*, because "they would be too base directly to enter the 'August Hearing.'"[36]

One last point should be made about the *uimamu* at Fukuyama Castle. These audiences also served to strengthen the position of Matsumae lords in Tokugawa political circles. In the context of diplomatic visits to Edo, Toby stresses that envoys from Korea and the Ryukyu Kingdom helped bolster shogunal prestige and legitimacy in the eyes of competing political interests at home.[37] Like the shogun, the Matsumae lords had their own image to consider. For example, following Shakushain's War, questions were raised concerning the ability of Fukuyama Castle to control trade in Ezo. Remember that one of Matsumae Yasuhiro's greatest fears was that Hirosaki spies collecting information from Ainu chiefs in Ezo might spread reports throughout the realm that Ezo was a place "without order."[38] Conducting audiences with chiefs throughout Ezo in the wake of Shakushain's War helped bolster Matsumae prestige and stake out its political terrain within the Tokugawa polity.

CEREMONY AT TRADING POSTS

If the *uimamu* fit within the Japanese diplomatic order because Ainu elders attended audiences at Fukuyama Castle, the *omusha* was something different. *Omusha* were ceremonies performed on a local level at trading posts rather than at Fukuyama Castle. The linguistic origins of *omusha*, like those of *uimamu*, remain unclear, but the term most likely originated from the Ainu term *umusa*, "greeting."[39] Although the *omusha* retained many of its Ainu characteristics, Matsumae lords reshaped it to fit within the confines of the Tokugawa diplomatic order; and Matsumae officials still construed the ceremony as a formal acknowledgment of their supremacy.

Originally, the *omusha* probably retained much of its flavor as a simple greeting between Ainu elders and Japanese, but later its protocol came to stress Ainu subordination. Hezutsu Tōsaku noted in the late eighteenth century that in the early years of the *omusha*, when Ainu received Matsumae officials, who arrived by boat, they patted each other on the back and even embraced.[40] Matsuda Denjūrō remarked that the Ainu who participated in *omusha* were the headmen (*otona*) and the Ainu in charge of gifts (*miyagetori*). He wrote that local fishery managers and interpreters relayed edicts to the assembled Ainu notables. The Ainu and Japanese participants dressed formally and drank saké after the reading of the edicts.[41] As is typical in many native ceremonies, Ainu elders drank saké from lacquered wooden cups called *takaysara* or *tuki* while using a ritual piece called the *tukipasuy* to show homage to their deities. Kushihara Seihō described an *omusha* in Sōya during which all of the approximately twenty-three elders in attendance were bestowed such gifts as rice, yeast, and saké.[42] As these accounts suggest, in particular Hezutsu Tōsaku's, the *omusha* differed from the *uimamu* in that it retained many of its original Ainu features.

In 1791, Mogami Tokunai observed an *omusha* held in eastern Ezo. He noted that Ainu headmen even crossed over from Kunashir to attend the ceremony; leaders such as Shimochi from Akkeshi and Shonko from Nokkamappu, as well as Sankichi and Tsukinoe from Kunashir, represented Ainu from all over the eastern region. Ainu wore *attus* or *jinbaori* that they had received from Matsumae officials prior to the ceremony. The Ainu officials who attended the ceremony were described as *otona* and *kozukai*, which Mogami compared to Japanese headmen, *nanushi* and *kumigashira*, and the interpreters were Ainu from Wajinchi.[43]

When the ceremony began, Ainu were led into the trading post hand-in-hand, again like children. Mogami confidently observed them as "trembling with fear" and "crouched over in submission," awed to be in the presence of Matsumae officials. After Ainu elders were seated, they crawled one-by-one toward the raised platform where the officials were seated. Then they put their hands together in a praying motion and bowed their heads. Mogami described how one Ainu chief took the hand of an official and placed it on the chief's chest; when the official removed his hand, the Ainu elder stroked his beard and murmured prayers to himself. Mogami explained that Ainu performed this act because Japanese officials were like "living gods" to them. He continued that even their faces revealed the expressions of somebody who had just seen a divine presence. The Ainu chiefs then returned to their proper seats, saying under their breath that they were grateful.[44]

Ainu performed such obvious forms of obeisance because, according to the Matsumae leadership, this was traditionally how meetings with officials were conducted. However, *omusha* were multilayered events, and other factors also played a role in their pervasive performance. Fear, in the form of the vivid memories of Ainu being shot down by Matsumae troops following the Menashi-Kunashir War of 1789, was probably still fresh in the minds of elders at the 1791 *omusha* described by Mogami. Yet, at the same time, Ainu also knew that by performing this ceremony, even if it meant demonstrating obeisance, they would be receiving saké and other goods in return. Mogami Tokunai observed that following the 1791 *omusha*, Ainu were seen sticking their fingers in the saké, testing to see whether it was good quality.[45] The *omusha* represented many things to Ainu, including a chance to get their hands on decent saké.

The *Ezo Matsumae kenbunki* [Recorded observations of Ezo and Matsumae], a manuscript probably written by a shogunal observer in 1798, provides another detailed description of an *omusha* held in eastern Ezo.[46] According to this observer, Matsumae officials scheduled *omusha* during the summer and autumn of every year. At this time, he continued, they brought various gifts, including rice, yeast, saké, and tobacco; and strict ceremonial protocol was observed during the distribution of these items. The order in which Ainu elders were seated during the ceremony was determined by rank. The greater headman, or *sō-otona*, sat at the head of the Ainu delegation, closest to the Matsumae official; next were the *otona*, the *kozukai*, and the *miyagetori*. These positions were described as being hereditary, similar to official posts filled by natives in the Qing system on Sakhalin. As one of the customs of Ezo, the shogunal official explained, the ceremony was considered by Ainu to be a special occasion, and they often took time off from the fisheries to attend. Even the elderly, women, and children, he observed, traveled from distances of twenty-four miles to witness the event.

Greater headmen wore formal *jittoku*—"Qing uniforms acquired from Manchurian traders," as the shogunal official noted—over their silk garments; the *otona*, *kozukai*, and *miyagetori* wore formal silk garments with vests and *haori*. These uniforms, including the *jittoku*, were assigned by Matsumae officials. It is fascinating that Ainu elders were made to wear *jittoku*, exotic clothing acquired in the Santan trade, because similar requirements were imposed on Ryukyuan envoys in Edo. In Ezo, where ethnic and political lines were difficult to draw, audiences served to construct a "Japanese" identity for the Matsumae family. That Ainu were made to wear Chinese silks highlighted their role as the recognized foreign other, contributing to the creation of a Japanese self on the northern borders of the Tokugawa polity. The determination of what clothing chiefs wore also placed them in a subordinate position to the Japanese, setting visible limits on their degree of self-determination.[47]

In the *omusha*, the organization of ceremonial space closely resembled that of the *uimamu*: Ainu seating was divided into *kamiza*, or upper seating, where elders sat, and *shimoza*, or lower seating, where common Ainu were placed. Even more revealing, however, was how Matsumae officials situated Ainu and Japanese within the trading post. Both the *kamiza* and *shimoza* were located on straw mats placed on the earthen floor, but the Japanese sat on the raised platform, or *ozashiki*, regardless of their rank.[48] Likewise, following a brief introduction, during which Japanese officials praised Ainu for working so hard during the fishing season, new domain edicts were read in translation. Ainu officials reacted to these edicts "similar to the way we [the Japanese] react when we pay reverence to Shinto gods or the Buddha." Following the reading of each item, the Ainu spoke among themselves, stroking their beards. The interpreter explained to Matsumae officials that these gestures (which as ethnologists point out were typical of the native *umusa*) symbolized Ainu gratitude to Matsumae officials for all that they had done.[49]

The *omusha* was also accompanied by saké drinking. The shogunal observer explained that fishery supervisors poured saké into lacquered cups and placed a *tukipasuy* across the rim; the Matsumae official then took the tray in his left hand, steadying the cup with his right, and handed it to the Ainu elder. The Ainu, having received the tray, dipped the *tukipasuy* into the saké, made libations to *kamuy*, and lightly splashed the saké three or four times to the right and left. He then lifted his beard with the *tukipasuy* and drank. This ceremonial exchange (*kenshū*) of saké cups, as the shogunal observer described it, was repeated twice, and then the next Ainu approached the raised platform. After the elders had participated in the *kenshū*, the rest of the Ainu participants were given two cups each.[50] Some sketches, possibly by Mogami Tokunai, depict Japanese officials also using a *tukipasuy* during the *omusha* and even embracing Ainu chiefs (also typical of the native *umusa* and mentioned by Hezutsu Tōsaku), illustrating that a ceremonial middle ground had been retained in the performance of this ceremony (see figures 22 and 23).[51] The event stood somewhere between the *kenshū* and *umusa*. Or, in an intriguing possibility, perhaps the participants failed to realize that two different rituals were being conducted at once. In the minds of Ainu elders, they were offering saké to their various gods, and greeting Matsumae officials after a long absence. In contrast, Matsumae representatives understood Ainu to be participating in a *kenshū*, or a ritual exchange of saké cups, which solidified newly forged loyalties. One might argue that in the ceremonial space of the *omusha*, Ainu and Japanese had, as White describes of the Great Lakes region, distorted the "values and practices of those they deal with" to create altogether new cultural practices.

In a last ironic note, of the gifts given to Ainu, only tobacco was a real gift, because Matsumae officials made Ainu pay for the rest of the items with animal skins and labor in fisheries. The shogunal official noted that Ainu worked hard throughout the fishing season so that they could pay back debts acquired during the previous year's *omusha*; it was an endless cycle of debt.[52]

Figure 22. Ainu and Japanese participating in an *omusha*. The author of this illustration (and the document from which it comes) remains unknown, but the work is thought to be by Mogami Tokunai. The illustration shows the ceremonial "middle ground" during the *omusha*. Ainu are seated on mats located on the floor, while Japanese officials are seated on a raised platform. Interestingly, at least one Japanese official is depicted using an Ainu ceremonial piece, *tukipasuy*. *Ezochi e chakugan no akahito ikken* [The matter of the Russian landing in Ezochi]. Courtesy of the Resource Collection for Northern Studies, Hokkaido University Library.

Figure 23. A Japanese official embracing an Ainu elder in a traditional Ainu *umusa* (*omusha* in Japanese), or "greeting." One suspects that such physical gestures were rare among Japanese warriors, at least in these public contexts. This rare image, however, further illustrates the possible existence of a ceremonial "middle ground" in Ezo, where Ainu and Japanese incorporated the practices of each other to form entirely new ritual experiences. *Ezochi e chakugan no akahito ikken.* Courtesy of the Resource Collection for Northern Studies, Hokkaido University Library.

CEREMONY AND CONQUEST

Probably the most distinctive difference between the *uimamu* and the *omusha* was that the latter was used to legitimize the Japanese presence in distant regions. Under Matsumae rule, *omusha* were frequently conducted by officials at newly opened trading posts, such as the one at Shiranushi on Sakhalin, as well as the posts on Kunashir and Iturup. Here, the Japanese diplomatic order was refitted to function on a local level, and it served as a ceremonial template for Japanese relations with distant Ainu groups. Rather than make Ainu chiefs submit to Matsumae authority at Fukuyama Castle, Matsumae officials held audiences at trading posts, where interpreters read edicts and Ainu submitted to the new Japanese hegemony.

Observations of *omusha* tend to come from eastern Ezo, Kunashir, and Sakhalin, but there are some exceptions. One reason might be that *omusha* conducted in the west simply received less attention. A more compelling reason, however, is that Matsumae officials intensified *omusha* ceremonies in areas where their authority was not taken for granted. Both the 1669 and 1789 wars had erupted in the east, and this region had always been viewed as more independent from Matsumae influence than the west. In the east, the *omusha* served as a visual reminder of Matsumae, and later Tokugawa, power and prestige; and the ritual also introduced administrative and commercial priorities to Ainu communities. Similarly, *omusha* conducted on Sakhalin and in the Kurils fit this model.

Hirate Hidekatsu's journey to Sakhalin in 1808 illustrates this point. He accompanied Aizu troops who had been dispatched to Sakhalin by the shogunate to defend the region from Russian attack. Following a two-month journey from Kyoto aboard the *Seikichi-maru*, Hirate set out for Sakhalin in the fourth month of 1808. He possessed a vivid imagination and placed his journey in the context of past Japanese conquests. He conjured up images of the eighth-century pacification of northeastern Honshu, discussed briefly in chapter 1, likening his sojourn to Sakhalin to the campaigns of Ōno Azumando, the *Mutsu chinjufu shōgun*, who had been ordered by the court to Taga Castle, near Sendai, to subjugate the

Emishi. At another point Hirate evoked images of Japanese foreign military campaigns on the Eurasian continent, likening the Aizu camp to Katō Kiyomasa's camp in Korea.[53]

In the fourth month of 1808, Hirate and a sizable Aizu force of about 730 soldiers arrived in Kushunkotan, in southern Sakhalin. After setting up camp, in the sixth month of 1808, Matsumae officials, probably acting under shogunal orders, held an *omusha* at Kushunkotan to introduce Aizu military leaders and shogunal officials to local Ainu notables. About eighty Ainu "from as far as 200 miles away," he hyperbolically explained, attended the audience with officials, where new edicts were relayed. During the audience, many gifts were bestowed upon Ainu elders. The *omusha* was led by military generals as a celebration of landing and setting up camp (*gochakujin gagi*), but there was a more symbolic reason for the ceremony as well. Several Tokugawa officials—including Yamaoka Denjūrō Kagekaze (probably Matsuda Denjūrō), Arai Heibei, and Mogami Tokunai—were in the region, and Aizu commanders probably wanted to put on a good show. Hirate noted, moreover, that the work of these officials and the Aizu troops was to subjugate (*chingyo*) Sakhalin in the face of encroaching "maritime barbarians" (*kaikoku no ijin*).[54] The *omusha* was placed within the context of subjugating these "barbarian lands."

Three years later, the kinds of edicts relayed during *omusha* in the southern Kurils were nicely listed in an 1811 manuscript.[55] For the most part, the edicts focused on Neo-Confucian conceptions of the relationship between ruler and ruled and on how Ainu should fit into this political order. However, the edicts also reveal the ways in which the shogunate asserted its administrative agenda over newly subjugated peoples. Edicts specified that public authority, or *kōgi*, was to be respected; parents and children, husbands and wives, and brothers and sisters were to live in peace; Ainu were not to gather in large groups; Iturup Ainu were not to travel to Urup; Russian vessels spotted in the area were to be reported to the administrative office; and if the Russians landed, all Ainu men between the ages fifteen and sixty were to immediately report to the administrative office with their bows and arrows.[56]

These edicts also explain that the reason that the shogunal officials had crossed over to Iturup was to protect the island from foreign invasion. Ainu, to demonstrate their appreciation for Japanese "benevolence" (*gojinkei*), were to labor diligently for their Japanese supervisors. Moreover, trading outside Japanese-endorsed channels was prohibited; Ainu were to use the same language as their supervisors; they were forbidden to have disheveled hair; and elders were allowed to take only one wife. Finally, Ainu were required to visit physicians at the administrative post if they became sick.[57]

By the 1820s, *omusha* edicts were being standardized throughout Ezo, most being similar to the above example from Iturup; and fishery supervisors used standard Ainu translations of these edicts.[58] There were edicts that related to the reporting of foreign vessels; calling for increased pelt production for trade; strictly prohibiting trading outside Japanese-endorsed channels and unauthorized travel; and emphasizing Neo-Confucian notions of filial piety and harmony.[59] Even after the collapse of the Edo shogunate, troops dispatched to Hokkaido by the fledgling Meiji government used *omusha* to communicate edicts related to stipends. In 1869, for example, troops from Ichinoseki used *omusha* to relay important information to Ainu in the Shiraoi region.[60] However, in 1875 the Meiji government totally abolished the *omusha* and other Ainu audiences.[61]

CONCLUSION

It has been over a decade since Ronald Toby argued that the early-modern Japanese diplomatic order was characterized not by a "cowering, passively isolationist stance" toward the international environment, but rather by a "positive, constructive one . . . that sought actively to reconstitute Japanese relations with the outside world in ways that advanced both international and domestic goals."[62] Matsumae's use of ceremonial gift giving and yearly audiences with the Ainu fits this model. With an anything-but-passive stance toward trading with Ainu, both the Matsumae and Tokugawa regimes actively modified the form of ritual trading so that Japan was placed at the center of the local political landscape. Moreover, as edicts and prohibitions relayed at *omusha* illustrate, this version of ceremonial trading in Ezo advanced both the international and domestic goals of Matsumae and, later, shogunal policymakers. Modifying Ainu rituals to conform to Tokugawa diplomatic standards served as a potent reminder of Japanese cultural and military superiority in these contested lands. It created a tradition of Japanese control such that Ainu eventually reached a point in the mid–nineteenth century when it became difficult for them to imagine an Ainu-centered past in Ezo. Yet, conduct during the *omusha,* in particular, demonstrates that the ceremonial landscape in Ezo was not entirely a product of Japanese designs. The images of Japanese and Ainu embracing, and drinking saké according to Ainu custom, are indeed powerful ones, and they suggest that a ceremonial middle ground had taken shape in Ezo, in which both Japanese and Ainu negotiated their ritual differences in the arena of cultural performance.

Epilogue

In 1802, after nearly two centuries of regional oversight by the Matsumae family, the shogunate established the Hakodate magistracy (*bugyō*), a colonial office of sorts; and the affairs of Ezo were administered by the political core in Edo. Although the Matsumae family was again put in charge of Ezo between 1821 and 1854, its days of unrestricted trade with Ainu were effectively over in 1802. Importantly, at this juncture, to the degree that such historical boundaries remain useful, the administration of Ezo departed from its previous "early-modern" form, characterized by domainal administration and strictly feudal economic decision making, to a more "modern" form, with the central government participating in the planning of economic policy and overseeing the deculturation and assimilation of the Ainu. Direct rule by the shogunate, for example, eventually included everything from the building of an early infrastructure, including roads and more elaborate trading posts, to forms of state-sponsored medicine such as Jennerian smallpox vaccinations in 1857.[1] When viewed from the perspective of Ezo and its Ainu inhabitants, *kinsei*, or the early-modern period in Japan, began to phase out around 1800.

At this time, moreover, foreign policy aimed at containing the threat posed by Western nations occupied the time of the shogunate. Territory that had once been under Matsumae rule was gradually integrated into a larger administrative bulwark, the thrust of which was to protect the northern border against Russian encroachment. However, as the Russian threat ebbed and flowed, so too did the intensity of Tokugawa interest in the northern region. Only with the advent of the Meiji state did Japan make outright, and internationally recognized, claims to much of the area known as Ezo. However, this delay in formally claiming Hokkaido was indicative less of political complacency on the part of the shogunate than of the fact that it was only after the Meiji Restoration that Japan adopted the Western notions of diplomacy and international law that made such formal declarations meaningful.[2] Ceremonial trade and other forms of submission, such as the *uimamu* and *omusha*, had resonated with implications of Japanese claims during Matsumae rule. Moreover, such claims to Hokkaido were intrinsic to the Edo shogunate's program, beginning in 1802, to alter the customs of the Ainu and assimilate them into the realities of Japanese life. Therefore, these post-Meiji claims to Hokkaido aside, it was during the centuries of trade between 1644 and 1838—that historical core sample taken in the introduction—that we find evidence for what proved to be the ecological and cultural roots of the Japanese conquest of Ainu lands.

Importantly, by the time of the Meiji Restoration of 1868, the settlement of Hokkaido could be conducted with little resistance from local inhabitants because Ainu society had weakened to the point that the Japanese intrusion went virtually uncontested, making it, ironically, all the more legitimate. Japanese officials, in other words, came to see themselves as rescuing the Ainu from a barbaric oblivion characterized by disease and starvation. Officials believed that through enlightened Confucian policy they were saving a people who lay on the brink of extinction because of poor hygienic and medical practices, not to mention problems rooted in their primitive means of providing sustenance for their communities. The word that best symbolizes the tenor of this new post-1802 shogunal policy regarding the Ainu was *buiku*, "to care, tend to, or show benevolence toward."[3]

THE MARCH OF BENEVOLENT RULE

The new strategy of *buiku*, which served as the moral justification for shogunal direct rule, requires some elaboration because it is a product of the historical events outlined in this book. Indeed, as a historical description of Japanese attitudes toward Ainu in the early nineteenth century, *buiku* was forged at the intersection of ecological upheaval, cultural change, and semicolonial activity. As Richard White argues, ecological factors are central in understanding the conquest of certain Native American nations: unlike strictly political or cultural explanations, ecological factors expose the historical reasons behind such phenomena as disease and starvation among native communities and call into question the bogus rhetoric of a dominant civilization that many Europeans employed to explain and justify colonialism in Native American lands. To European settlers, colonialism "cared" for Native Americans by bringing civilization to their disease-ridden and famished communities; and in early-nineteenth-century Japan, *buiku* developed into the Confucian equivalent of these Western notions of the march of civilization.

However, the conditions in many Native American nations, like those in Ezo, were historical products of centuries of ecological and cultural exchange between conquerors and borderland groups. White observes, for example, that European settlers explained away massive starvation in Native American communities as an indication of their dependency on the hunt or as a by-product of their primitive agricultural practices, and such explanations bolstered the European case for colonial control on the grounds that it promised to halt suffering among the less civilized. Any recognition of the fact that Native Americans starved because of trade with European settlers, or that they died in such astonishing numbers from diseases actually brought from the Old World, would have "subverted the more beneficial rationale that colonialism brought a better life to all," writes White.[4] Similarly, the rhetoric of *buiku* in Japan cast shogunal direct rule as bringing a better life to the Ainu.

Kuwata Ryūsai, for example, a physician hired by the shogunate to vaccinate Ainu for smallpox, imagined state-sponsored medicine to be a civilizing force among "barbaric" Ainu communities, particularly in the realm of diseases and their treatment. In the *Ezo no kyōkai* [The boundary of Ezo], a short tract he wrote after returning to Edo, Kuwata put a Neo-Confucian spin on the vaccination effort. He wrote that state-sponsored medicine represented the extension of "benevolence" to the "barbarians" of Ezo. The shogunate, he believed, sought to introduce the Ainu to a more healthy—at least as Japanese defined notions of "healthy"—way of life. He was highly critical of Ainu homes, which he described as similar to "dog houses," and he argued that clothing crafted from deerskins or elm bark was inadequate for the northern climate.[5] For Kuwata, as for most Japanese officials, the dire condition of Ainu communities was seen not as the by-product of two centuries of ecological and cultural changes resulting from trade with Matsumae domain but as a symbol of the need for more aggressive policy measures by the shogunate. The Japanese argument that the upheaval in Ainu communities was a product of their primitive customs exposed, as White argues of European settlers, a preference for "imaginary pasts and more benign presents."[6]

Post-1802 shogunal policy in Ezo illustrates this ahistorical "imaginary past" in regards to the Ainu; the *buiku* policy was a state celebration of a "benign present" in which the Japanese, the most civilized ethnic group on the archipelago, needed to care for Ainu. The ahistorical spin put on the policy of supplying medical care and vaccinating all inhabitants of Ezo, including the Ainu, not only betrays these forms of cultural chauvinism, which ignored fundamental historical and ecological realities, but also stands as a vivid example of this shift to more-modern forms of administration in what were once Ainu lands. I argue elsewhere that "[s]tate-sponsored medicine in Ezo, as part of a more broadly cast assimilationist agenda, transformed the relationship of Ainu to the Japanese state, reshaping native Ainu conceptions of personal health and weakening their political autonomy." Edo policymakers increasingly came to view Ainu as wards of the state, people under the administrative umbrella and paternalistic care of the Tokugawa regime, thus illustrating the role of disease and public medicine in "crafting the ethnic and cultural boundaries of Japan" in the early nineteenth century.[7]

In 1802, in a broad-ranging policy statement, the Hakodate magistracy spelled out its new priorities in Ezo, which included *buiku*. Pointing to advances in the region made by the Russian empire, the magistracy warned that "some twenty islands" off the coast of "our country" were already under Russian sway and that the Russians were aiming at the very heart of Ezo itself. The magistracy recommended, therefore, realizing the logistical difficulties of extending Tokugawa military control over Ezo, that the shogunate should take the more Confucian approach of projecting its benevolent rule over the native inhabitants. This being done, submitted the magistracy, "Ainu will be satisfied in their hearts with the [early-modern Japanese] state (*kokka*) and not be tempted to flee Ezo for foreign lands."[8] In 1811, only a decade later, this vague notion of benevolent rule became specific administrative reality when the magistracy pushed a series of edicts designed to oversee the affairs of Ezo and assimilate the Ainu. Edict thirteen, specifically, boasted that the shogunate had made physicians available to ailing Ainu, so those in need of medical attention should report to posts. Later, illustrating that some Ainu obeyed these orders, documents tell of the state-sponsored distribution of prescription "ointments," "decoctions," pills, lily-root pharmaceuticals, and other medications; and in addition there is evidence, provided by Vasilii Golovnin, a Russian prisoner captured by Japanese, of experimental surgery being carried out on Ainu afflicted with scurvy.[9] Dealing with the poor state of Ainu health emerged as the cornerstone of the new *buiku* strategy.

In 1857, the shogunal commitment to providing medical care for the Japanese and Ainu in Ezo culminated with Jennerian smallpox vaccinations. Two notable physicians, Kuwata Ryūsai and Fukase Yōshun, led the expedition to Ezo. Interestingly, from the outset, it was the officials who decided where and whom to vaccinate; in doing so, they were, in the arena of public medicine, consciously mapping out the ethnic and political bodies within the Japanese polity. The ecological and cultural im-

plications of Jennerian vaccinations, moreover, resonated throughout
Ezo. After 1600, as mentioned in chapter 7, with the intensification of
trade between Ainu and Japanese, diseases such as smallpox and syphilis
were introduced to communities in Ezochi, unleashing demographic
havoc among Ainu. However, Ainu projected smallpox through the lens
of their cultural order, viewing the airborne killer as a god, *payoka kamuy*,
who visited death on unsuspecting communities. Powerful healers tried
to deal with the disease, but their efforts, as demographic evidence suggests, met only with failure. However, the fact that Japanese physicians,
"with the prick of an arm, could succeed where Ainu medicine had
failed, providing a medicine so potent that it destroyed one of the most
powerful gods in the Ainu pantheon, must have challenged the very
foundation of their cultural order, as well as their autonomy in Ezo."[10]
Once again, cultural change—sparked by an ecological phenomenon
and, in this case, its medical treatment—translated into a weakening of
Ainu society in the face of Japanese advances.

The critical point is that shogunal officials cast the poor state of Ainu
health as an intrinsic condition of Ainu society, as a product of their primitive lifestyle rather than as a condition caused by interaction with
Japanese. For this reason, *buiku* could be sold to Ainu as an unprecedent-
ed show of benevolence on the part of the Edo shogunate or as a moral
justification for direct rule in Ezo, when in fact it was the ecological and
cultural result of centuries of interaction between Ainu and Japanese.
Shogunal authorities dehistoricized the situation in Ezo and articulated a
benign present that set up the late-nineteenth- and early-twentieth-cen-
tury reputation of the Ainu as a "dying race," an image readily embraced
by Western observers.[11]

AINU AMIABILITY

In the early Meiji years, Western employees of the Kaitakushi (Hokkaido
Development Agency) viewed what they called the "submissive" traits
of the Ainu as a partial explanation for their wretched condition and thus
agreed with their Japanese counterparts that Ainu were in desperate

PATERNALISM

need of assistance. Horace Capron, for example, hired by the Meiji government to oversee the Western-style colonization of Hokkaido, observed an Ainu community while making his rounds on the northern island. He compared the Ainu to Native Americans, explaining that he thought Ainu might be more easily assimilated into the Japanese state because of their docile nature.[12] In an 1874 letter to Kuroda Kiyotaka, the governor of Hokkaido, Capron explained, "It would seem that the same difficulties are to be encountered in efforts to civilize these people [Ainu] which are met in similar attempts with the North American Indians. The Aino [or Ainu], however, possesses more amiable and attractive traits of character than the Indian, and greater capacity to appreciate the advantages of higher civilization."[13]

That Capron believed Ainu possessed a greater capacity to appreciate the higher civilization embraced by Meiji intellectuals and policymakers, many enamored by the slogan "civilization and enlightenment," must have been good news for Governor Kuroda. However, the amiability that Capron saw in the eyes of Ainu was not their "character," nor did it make them better prepared to appreciate "higher civilization." Rather, what Capron mistook as a "benign present" was actually the historical result of two centuries of trade with Matsumae domain, an exchange that had unraveled the social fabric of Ainu communities and undermined their ability, not to mention their basic will, to resist Japanese claims to what was once their homeland. John Batchelor, a sympathetic spokesperson for the Ainu, wrote in 1901: "Upon asking an experienced medical man a short time since as to what he considered the chief cause of the decrease in the Ainu population, he replied that he was of the opinion that the race was worn out. This is the true state of the case, for vitality appears to have truly died out."[14]

Henry Landor, an English traveler to Hokkaido—and unfortunately a notorious liar—also wrote about the Ainu in the early Meiji years. Commenting on Ainu hygienic practice and health, he said, "On visiting an Ainu village what impressed me most were the miserable and filthy huts, compared with the neat and clean Japanese houses; the poverty and almost appalling dirt of the people and their gentle, submissive nature." He later wrote of diseases among the Ainu: "One hardly sees one creature out of ten that is not covered with a repulsive eruption of some sort. Leprosy, too, has found its way among the fishermen; and my readers can easily imagine how pleasant it was for me, when I was sketching, to be surrounded by a crowd of these loathsome people." Clearly Landor was unsympathetic to Ainu decline.[15]

Despite the picture painted by Landor, I have argued that the Ainu had not always been such amiable and submissive people. The stark contrast between the sixteenth century, when such powerful figures as Koshamain contested Japanese intrusions into southern Ezo, or the seventeenth century, when Shakushain forged a pan-Ainu alliance to slash his way to Matsumae, and the nineteenth century, when Ainu evoked images of a "dying race," was a product of the centuries of trade with Japanese described in this book.

RETURN TO KUNNUI

One can only assume that the piercing battle cries of Shakushain and his Ainu warriors in 1669 struck fear into the hearts of the increasingly urbanized warriors of Japan. Even the Edo shogunate, which dispatched a vassal to halt the threat of an Ainu march on Fukuyama Castle, was forced to act decisively and sacrifice men on the battlefield near Kunnui. It is difficult to know what the Ainu warriors thought as they raced across the cold, drenched fields outside Kunnui, nearby rivers flooding over from the massive rains, engaging the cold steel of Japanese swords, bows and arrows, and firearms, but whatever thoughts gripped their imaginations proved important enough at the time for them to sacrifice their lives. Ainu resolve, galvanized by the charismatic leadership of Shakushain, threatened the very foundation of the Japanese presence in southern Ezo. The Ainu appeared determined to expel the Japanese from Wajinchi, to cleanse the island of Japanese via the sword; and the shogunate, equally resolved, reacted by defeating the Shibuchari Ainu in battle, treacherously murdering Shakushain and his generals, burning Japanese collaborators at the stake, and violently suppressing flash points of Ainu resistance for the next couple years. Neither side was interested in "caring" for or "tending" to the other, because they were competing in a life-and-death struggle for the right to exist in Ezo. By the nineteenth century, however, and the initiation of what would have been an unthinkable policy in 1669—*buiku*—the battle cries of Ainu fighters and their defiant leader echoed only as the distant memory of a past age, replaced by Japan's benign present.

Notes

The following abbreviations have been used for works cited frequently in the notes:

HMSS Ōtomo Kisaku, ed. *Hokumon sōsho.* 6 vols. Tokyo: Hokkō Shobō, 1943–4.

MCS Matsumae Chōshi Henshūshitsu, ed. *Matsumae chōshi.* 7 vols. Hakodate: Daiichi Insatsu, 1974–93.

MTKS Yoshida Takezō, ed. *Matsuura Takeshirō kikōshū.* 3 vols. Tokyo: Fūzanbō, 1977.

NSSSS Takakura Shin'ichirō, ed. *Nihon shomin seikatsu shiryō shūsei.* Vol. 4. Tokyo: San'ichi Shobō, 1969.

RCNS Resource Collection for Northern Studies, Hokkaido University Library.

SHS Hokkaidō, ed. *Shin Hokkaidōshi.* 9 vols. Sapporo: Shin Hokkaidō-shi Insatsu Shuppan Kyōdō Kigyōtai, 1969–81.

SSHS Hokkaidō Chō, ed. *Shinsen Hokkaidōshi.* 7 vols. Sapporo: Hokkaidō Chō, 1936–7. Reprint, Osaka: Seibundō, 1990–91.

SSKS Takakura Shin'ichirō, ed. *Saisenkai shiryō.* Sapporo: Hokkaidō Shuppan Kikaku Sentā, 1982.

INTRODUCTION

1. Enomoto Morie, *Hokkaidō no rekishi* (Sapporo: Hokkaidō Shinbunsha, 1981), 8–9.

2. In this introduction I gloss the complex history of the cartographic exploration of the North Pacific to dramatize a point about the changing place of Ezo in relation to early-modern Japan. For a history of the exploration of Hokkaido and Sakhalin Island, and the important relationships between Japanese maps, see Akizuki Toshiyuki, *Nihon hokuhen no tanken to chizu no rekishi* (Sapporo: Hokkaidō Daigaku Tosho Kankōkai, 1999). About the *Genroku kuniezu* [1700], Akizuki explains that the original map, which was held at the Tokyo Imperial University Library, was destroyed in the Great Kantō earthquake. However, prior to its destruction, the Ezochi portion of the map was replicated (18–9). On the early cartography and exploration of Ezo, also see John J. Stephan, *Sakhalin: A History* (Oxford: Clarendon Press, 1971), 33–41.

3. Akizuki, *Nihon hokuhen no tanken to chizu no rekishi*, 18–9.

4. *Shōhō Nihon sōzu* [1644], in *Ezo chizushō*, ed. Narita Shūichi (Tokyo: Sara Shobō, 1989), 20–21. For a more general study of the use of maps in historical analysis, see Denis Wood, *The Power of Maps* (New York: Guilford Press, 1992).

5. *Ezochi zenzu* [1830s], RCNS. For the Tenpō-era provincial map, see *Tenpō okuniezu* [1838], in *Ezo chizushō*, ed. Narita Shūichi (Tokyo: Sara Shobō, 1989), 177.

6. Frederick Jackson Turner, *The Significance of the Frontier in American History*, ed. Harold P. Simonson (New York: Frederick Ungar, 1963), 27.

7. Kerwin Lee Klein, *Frontiers of Historical Imagination: Narrating the European Conquest of Native America, 1890–1990* (Berkeley: University of California Press, 1997), 13–22. For more on Turner's frontier thesis, see Richard White, "Frederick Jackson Turner," in *Historians of the American Frontier: A Bio-Bibliographical Sourcebook*, ed. John R. Wunder (Westport, Conn.: Greenwood Press, 1988); William Cronon, "Turner's First Stand: The Significance of Significance in American History," in *Writing Western History: Essays on Major Western Historians*, ed. Richard Etulain (Albuquerque: University of New Mexico Press, 1991); and Patricia Nelson Limerick, "Turnerians All: The Dream of a Helpful History in an Intelligible World," *American Historical Review* 100 (1995): 697–716.

8. Takakura Shin'ichirō, *Ainu seisakushi* (Tokyo: Nihon Hyōronsha, 1942; reprint, Tokyo: San'ichi Shobō, 1972), 17.

9. John A. Harrison, *Japan's Northern Frontier: A Preliminary Study in Colonization and Expansion with Special Reference to the Relations of Japan and Russia* (Gainesville: University of Florida Press, 1953).

10. Yamamoto Hirofumi, *Sakoku to kaikin jidai* (Tokyo: Azekura Shobō, 1995), 1–9.

11. Patricia Nelson Limerick, *The Legacy of Conquest: The Unbroken Past of the*

American West (New York: W. W. Norton, 1987), 26; and Limerick, "What on Earth Is the New Western History?" in *Trails: Toward a New Western History*, ed. Patricia Nelson Limerick et al. (Lawrence: University of Kansas Press, 1991), 85–6.

12. Richard White, *The Middle Ground: Indians, Empires, and Republics in the Great Lakes Region, 1650–1815* (Cambridge: Cambridge University Press, 1991), x. Piper Rae Gaubatz makes a similar point while surveying urban development on the multiethnic and multicultural frontiers of China. Gaubatz writes that although "each of the settlements began as a small enclave for the Chinese, they became increasingly multicultural as non-Chinese people came to live in or near them during the course of their development (Piper Rae Gaubatz, *Beyond the Great Wall: Urban Form and Transformation on the Chinese Frontiers* [Stanford: Stanford University Press, 1996], 2).

13. On the historiography related to Japanese contact with the Ainu, see Emori Susumu et al., "Chihōshi kenkyū no genjō: Hokkaidō," parts 1 and 2, *Nihon rekishi* 561 (February 1995): 34–51; 562 (March 1995): 33–66.

14. For critiques of *sakoku*, I am thinking of works by such historians as Asao Naohiro (*Sakoku: Nihon no rekishi 17* [Tokyo: Shōgakukan, 1975]), Ronald Toby (*State and Diplomacy in Early Modern Japan: Asia in the Development of the Tokugawa Bakufu* [Princeton: Princeton University Press, 1984; reprint, Stanford: Stanford University Press, 1991]), and Arano Yasunori (*Kinsei Nihon to higashi ajia* [Tokyo: Tōkyō Daigaku Shuppankai, 1988]).

15. Kikuchi Isao, *Bakuhan taisei to Ezochi* (Tokyo: Yūzankaku, 1984), 12–3, 92–3. Others, including myself, have emphasized the *ka'i chitsujo* as well. See my "Reappraising the *Sakoku* Paradigm: The Ezo Trade and the Extension of Tokugawa Political Space into Hokkaidō," *Journal of Asian History* 30, no. 2 (1996): 169–92. On the use of the *ka'i chitsujo* in creating a Japanese identity in the northern frontier, see Tessa Morris-Suzuki, "The Frontiers of Japanese Identity," in *Asian Forms of the Nation*, ed. Stein Tonnesson and Hans Antlov (Surrey: Curzon Press Ltd., 1996). On the role of the foreign "other" in creating national identity in early-modern Japan, see Ronald P. Toby, "Carnival of the Aliens: Korean Embassies in Edo-Period Art and Popular Culture," *Monumenta Nipponica* 41, no. 4 (winter 1988): 423; Ronald P. Toby, "The 'Indianness' of Iberia and Changing Japanese Iconographies of Other," in *Implicit Understandings: Observing, Reporting, and Reflecting on the Encounter between Europeans and Other Peoples in the Early Modern Era*, ed. Stuart B. Schwartz (Cambridge: Cambridge University Press, 1994), 323–351; and Ronald P. Toby, "The Birth of the Hairy Barbarian: Ethnic Pejorative as Cultural Boundary-Marker" (paper prepared for presentation at the Conference on Society and Popular Culture in Medieval and Early-Modern Japan, Princeton, N.J., October 25–27, 1995).

16. David L. Howell, "Ainu Ethnicity and the Boundaries of the Early Modern Japanese State," *Past and Present* 142 (February 1994): 79–80.

17.   David L. Howell, "Kinsei Hokkaidō ni okeru midoru-gurando no kanōsei," in *Basho ukeoisei to Ainu*, ed. Hokkaidō-Tōhokushi Kenkyūkai (Sapporo: Hokkaidō Shuppan Kikaku Sentā, 1998), 417–8, 420.

18.   Toby, *State and Diplomacy in Early Modern Japan*, 3–22.

19.   Susan B. Hanley, *Everyday Things in Premodern Japan: The Hidden Legacy of Material Culture* (Berkeley: University of California Press, 1997), 53.

20.   Conrad Totman, *The Lumber Industry in Early Modern Japan* (Honolulu: University of Hawai'i Press, 1995), 5.

21.   Alfred W. Crosby, *Ecological Imperialism: The Biological Expansion of Europe, 900–1900* (Cambridge: Cambridge University Press, 1986); and Peter Duus, *The Abacus and the Sword: The Japanese Penetration of Korea, 1895–1910* (Berkeley: University of California Press, 1995), 23–4.

22.   Nishimura Saburō, *Bunmei no naka no hakubutsugaku* (Tokyo: Kinokuniya Shoten, 1999), 1:98–185.

23.   I use the term "chiefdom" in this study for several reasons. To start with, "nation," or any term that denotes modern political organization or rigidly defined borders, is inappropriate for the Ainu. Yet, "community" or "group" fails to capture the strong hierarchical social organization that evolved around chiefs and the powerful households that produced chiefs. These chiefs appear to have been charismatic figures who sometimes extended their spheres of influence over neighboring communities. They were often called "generals" (*taishō*) in Japanese manuscripts, a title that evokes a sense of authority based on military might and personal leadership qualities. Thus, in many cases, chiefs were at the center of Ainu political life. The term "chiefdom" embodies this sense of organization around a particular household or personality rather than around permanent "communal" borders. In addition, the term "community" also relays a sense of egalitarianism, which appears to have been lacking in Ainu society, particularly after the normalization of trade with the Japanese. Robert Carneiro defines a chiefdom as "an autonomous political unit comprising a number of villages or communities under the permanent control of a paramount chief" (Robert Carneiro, "The Chiefdom: Precursor of the State," in *The Transition to Statehood in the New World*, ed. G. D. Jones and R. R. Kautz [Cambridge: Cambridge University Press, 1981], 47).

24.   Kayano Shigeru, *Ainugo jiten* (Tokyo: Sanseidō, 1996).

CHAPTER 1.   THE CONSOLIDATION OF THE
EARLY-MODERN JAPANESE STATE IN THE NORTH

1.   Furukawa Koshōken, *Tōyū zakki* [1788], ed. Ōtō Tokihiko (Tokyo: Tōyō Bunko, 1964), 115.

2.   The region of southern Ezo, or the present-day Oshima Peninsula, which

was inhabited by Japanese settlers in the seventeenth and eighteenth centuries, was referred to with a variety of telling names, including Japanese land (Wajinchi), human land (Ningenchi), and Matsumae land (Matsumaechi). Henceforth, this study uses the term Wajinchi to describe this area.

3.   Emori Susumu, *Ainu no rekishi: Hokkaidō no hitobito* 2 (Tokyo: Sanseidō, 1987), 9–10.

4.   Joan R. Piggott, *The Emergence of Japanese Kingship* (Stanford: Stanford University Press, 1997), 117, 143.

5.   On occasion, the Japanese state found itself involved in a tributary relationship with China. On the relationship between Himiko, paramount of Wa, and China, see ibid., 24–8. On Ashikaga Yoshimitsu and the Ming tributary order, see Tanaka Takeo with Robert Sakai, "Japan's Relations with Overseas Countries," in *Japan in the Muromachi Age*, ed. John Whitney Hall and Toyoda Takeshi (Berkeley: University of California Press, 1977), 163–8; and Kawazoe Shoji, "Japan and East Asia," in *The Cambridge History of Japan*, vol. 3, *Medieval Japan*, ed. Kozo Yamamura (Cambridge: Cambridge University Press, 1990), 432–8.

6.   John Whitney Hall has argued that dispatching Sakanoue no Tamuramaro to northeastern Japan was part of the larger effort of Emperor Kanmu to solidify political power in the newly established capital of Heian. See John Whitney Hall, *Japan: From Prehistory to Modern Times* (New York: Delta, 1970), 62.

7.   Kikuchi Isao, *Ainu minzoku to Nihonjin: Higashi ajia no naka no Ezochi* (Tokyo: Asahi Sensho 510, 1994), 28–30; and Emori, *Ainu no rekishi*, 20. For more on the fighting in northeastern Japan, see Karl F. Friday, "Pushing beyond the Pale: The Yamato Conquest of the Emishi and Northern Japan," *Journal of Japanese Studies* 23, no. 1 (winter 1997): 1–24; and Friday, "The Taming of the Shrewd: The Conquest of the Emishi and Northern Japan," *The Japan Foundation Newsletter* 21, no. 6 (March 1994): 17–21. Bruce Batten has provided a broader perspective on the formation of boundaries in early Japan, and he links the demarcation of borders to state consolidation in the Nara, Heian, and Kamakura periods. See Bruce Batten, "Frontiers and Boundaries of Pre-modern Japan," *The Journal of Historical Geography* 25, no. 2 (1999): 166–82.

8.   Emori, *Ainu no rekishi*, 17–8.

9.   Ibid., 13–7.

10.   Mimi Hall Yiengpruksawan, "The House of Gold: Fujiwara Kiyohira's Konjikidō," *Monumenta Nipponica* 48, no. 1 (spring 1993): 45–7. This argument is covered more fully in Yiengpruksawan, *Hiraizumi: Buddhist Art and Regional Politics in Twelfth-Century Japan* (Cambridge: Harvard University Press, 1998), 51–120.

11.   Emori, *Ainu no rekishi*, 22–4. On the origins of the reading of "Ezo," see Kaiho Mineo, *Ezo no rekishi: Kita no hitobito to Nihon* (Tokyo: Kōdansha, 1996), 34–6. One of the most widely accepted explanations has been offered by Kindaichi

Kyōsuke, who suggests that "Ezo" might be from the term *enjū*, which sounds something like Ezo and was a term that some Sakhalin Ainu used to describe themselves. See Kindaichi Kyōsuke, *Kindaichi Kyōsuke zenshū* (Tokyo: Sanseidō, 1993), 12:462–71. However, Ezo might also be an alternative pronunciation of *kai*, which is an alternative reading of the Chinese ideographs used to write Ezo. This position is supported by an obscure reference made by Tokugawa official Satō Genrokurō that Ainu described themselves as *kai*. See Satō Genrokurō, *Ezo shūi* [1786], in HMSS, 1:249.

12.   Emori, *Ainu no rekishi*, 24–5.

13.   Ibid., 25–9.

14.   The debate concerning where exactly to locate the birth of medieval Japan has recently been reopened. For essays dealing with this topic, see Jeffrey P. Mass, ed., *The Origins of Japan's Medieval World: Courtiers, Clerics, Warriors, and Peasants in the Fourteenth Century* (Stanford: Stanford University Press, 1997).

15.   Emori, *Ainu no rekishi*, 34–7.

16.   For more on the relationship between the Andō and the Emishi or Ainu, as well as other aspects of pre-Ainu history, see David L. Howell, *Geographies of Japanese Identity: Polity, Status, and Civilization in the Nineteenth Century* (forthcoming).

17.   Emori, *Ainu no rekishi*, 30–1, 37–41.

18.   Kaiho, *Ezo no rekishi*, 18–9, 140–1.

19.   For more on the conflicts of the Era of the Warring States, see H. Paul Varley, *The Ōnin War: History of Its Origins and Background, with a Selective Translation of The Chronicle Of Ōnin* (New York: Columbia University Press, 1967); and Mary Elizabeth Berry, *The Culture of Civil War in Kyoto* (Berkeley: University of California Press, 1994).

20.   On behalf of Andō Chikasue, Tsugaru-no-Nanbu Kunaishōyū frequently brought hawks as gifts to Nobunaga at Azuchi Castle. See *Shinchō kōki*, in *Chūsei Ezo shiryō*, ed. Kaiho Mineo (Tokyo: San'ichi Shobō, 1983), 169–70; Matsumae Kagehiro, *Shinra no kiroku* [1646], in SHS, 7:30; Kaiho Mineo, *Chūsei no Ezochi* (Tokyo: Yoshikawa Kōbunkan, 1987), 228–35; and Asao Naohiro, *Taikei Nihon no rekishi: Tenka no ittō* (Tokyo: Shōgakukan, 1993), 8:307–9.

21.   Matsumae Kagehiro, *Shinra no kiroku* [1646], in SHS, 7:39–40.

22.   Asao, *Taikei Nihon no rekishi*, 309–10.

23.   Fujii Jōji, "Jūnana seiki no Nihon: Buke no kokka no keisei," in *Iwanami kōza Nihon tsūshi: Kinsei 2*, ed. Asao Naohiro et al. (Tokyo: Iwanami Shoten, 1994), vol. 12, bk. 2, 34–49.

24.   Mark Ravina, "State-Building and Political Economy in Early-Modern Japan," *The Journal of Asian Studies* 54, no. 4 (November 1995): 1008.

25.   Asao, *Taikei Nihon no rekishi*, 382–3. See also Takagi Shōsaku, *Nihon kinsei kokkashi no kenkyū* (Tokyo: Iwanami Shoten, 1990), 33–4.

26.   Matsumae Kagehiro, *Shinra no kiroku* [1646], in SHS, 7:41.

27. Philip Brown points out that the cadastral surveys of Hideyoshi's day were not as effective as once believed. He argues that "the evidence for the implementing of nationally standardized land surveys is very weak" [Philip C. Brown, *Central Authority and Local Autonomy in the Formation of Early Modern Japan: The Case of Kaga Domain* (Stanford: Stanford University Press, 1993), 60]. However, my point here is that dispatching magistrates to intrude on domainal affairs, despite their inability to reshape local survey practices or proprietorship, served as a potent reminder of the strength of the emerging political order being crafted by Hideyoshi.

28. Mary Elizabeth Berry, *Hideyoshi* (Cambridge: Harvard University Press, 1982), 147–67. For more on the Hideyoshi years and the formation of the early-modern Japanese state, see Berry, "Restoring the Past: The Documents of Hideyoshi's Magistrate in Kyoto," *Harvard Journal of Asiatic Studies* 43, no. 1 (June 1983): 57–95; and Berry, "Public Peace and Private Attachment: The Goals and Conduct of Power in Early Modern Japan," *Journal of Japanese Studies* 12, no. 2 (summer 1986): 237–71.

29. Berry, "Public Peace and Private Attachment," 258.

30. Matsumae Kagehiro, *Shinra no kiroku* [1646], in SHS, 7:41–2.

31. This meeting with Hideyoshi, as well as a second in 1593, is covered in Kaiho Mineo, *Kinsei Ezochi seiritsushi no kenkyū* (Tokyo: San'ichi Shobō, 1984), 180–5.

32. Herman Ooms, *Tokugawa Ideology: Early Constructs, 1570–1680* (Princeton: Princeton University Press, 1985), 45–6.

33. Kaiho, *Kinsei Ezochi seiritsushi no kenkyū*, 182–5.

34. Akizuki Toshiyuki, *Nihon hokuhen no tanken to chizu no rekishi* (Sapporo: Hokkaidō Daigaku Tosho Kankōkai, 1999), 15–8. For more on what is called the *Toyotomi Hideyoshi shoji senmen chizu*, see Maruyama Yasunari, "Kinsei jōhōka shakai no keisei," in *Nihon no kinsei: Jōhō to kōtsū*, ed. Maruyama Yasunari (Tokyo: Chūō Kōronsha, 1992), 6: plates 1 and 11. See also Kamiya Nobuyuki, "Japanese Control of Ezochi and the Role of Northern Koryŏ," *Acta Asiatica* 67 (1994): 52–3.

35. Takahashi Kimiaki, "Ezogachishima ō kara no Chōsen kenshi ni tsuite," *Hokkaidōshi kenkyū* 28 (December 1981): 1–5. For the best discussion to date of the king of Ezogachishima envoy, see Kaiho, *Ezo no rekishi*, 112–7; and Kenneth R. Robinson, "The Jiubian and Ezogashima Embassies to Chōsen, 1478–1482," *Chōsenshi kenkyūkai ronbunshū* 35 (October 1997): 56–86.

36. Kaiho Mineo, "'Chūsei' hoppōshi yori mita 'Ezogachishima ō' no Chōsen kenshi," *Hokkaidōshi kenkyū* 28 (December 1981): 11. See also *Furoisu Nihonshi*, in *Chūsei Ezo shiryō*, ed. Kaiho Mineo (Tokyo: San'ichi Shobō, 1983), 197.

37. *Kiyomasaki* (n.d.), in *Zoku gunsho ruijū*, ed. Hanawa Hokiichi and Ōta Toshirō (Tokyo: Zoku Gunsho Ruijū Kanseikai, 1924), vol. 23, no. 1, 337, 341–2.

38. *Kiyomasa Orankai no shiro o otoshiiruru no koto*, in *Tsūzoku Nihon zenshi*, ed. Waseda Daigaku Henshūbu (Tokyo: Waseda Daigaku Shuppanbu, 1913), 14:610–2.

39.   Matsumae Kagehiro, *Shinra no kiroku* [1646], in SHS, 7:43.

40.   Kamiya, "Japanese Control of Ezochi and the Role of Northern Koryŏ," 55.

41.   "Shima" in Shima-no-kami is based on two Chinese ideographs that, despite their different meanings, were homonymous with the single ideograph for "island." This courtesy title, one suspects, may have been a pun on the reading "protector of the island" and may have originated from Yoshihiro's having first been received as the lord of Ezogashima when he met with Hideyoshi (Kaiho, *Kinsei Ezochi seiritsushi no kenkyū*, 184).

42.   Matsumae Kagehiro, *Shinra no kiroku* [1646], in SHS, 7:43-4.

43.   The original passage related to shipping duties in the vermilion-seal order reads *Narabi (ni) funayaku no koto*. See Matsumae Kagehiro, *Shinra no kiroku* [1646], in SHS, 7:43; and Matsumae Hironaga, *Fukuyama hifu* [1780], in SSHS, 5:83.

44.   Matsumae Kagehiro, *Shinra no kiroku* [1646], in SHS, 7:46.

45.   Kasaya Kazuhiko, "Shōgun to daimyō," in *Nihon no kinsei: Shihai no shikumi*, ed. Fujii Jōji (Tokyo: Chūō Kōronsha, 1991), 3:49, 66, 74-5. See also Kasaya Kazuhiko, *Kinsei buke shakai no seiji kōzō* (Tokyo: Yoshikawa Kōbunkan, 1993).

46.   Harold Bolitho, "The Han," in *The Cambridge History of Japan*, vol. 4, *Early Modern Japan*, ed. John Whitney Hall (Cambridge: Cambridge University Press, 1991), 192. On the map and genealogical chart, see Matsumae Kagehiro, *Shinra no kiroku* [1646], in SHS, 7:46. The name "Matsumae" came from an earlier name for southern Ezo, the area that later became known as Wajinchi (Kaiho, *Kinsei Ezochi seiritsushi no kenkyū*, 185).

47.   Matsumae Hironaga, *Fukuyama hifu* [1780], in SSHS, 5:21, 96; and Kaiho, *Kinsei Ezochi seiritsushi no kenkyū*, 185.

48.   Kaiho Mineo, "Matsumae han no nidaime: Wakasa-no-kami Morihiro ni tsuite," *Hokkaidō no bunka* 37 (1977): 30; and Kaiho, *Kinsei Ezochi seiritsushi no kenkyū*, 190.

49.   *Matsumae Morihiro shojō* (n.d.), Hokkaido Prefectural Library, Ebetsu, Hokkaido.

50.   Matsumae Hironaga, *Fukuyama hifu* [1780], in SSHS, 5:23-24; and *Tokugawa jikki* [1809-43], in *Bakusei shiryō to Ezochi*, ed. Kaiho Mineo (Tokyo: Miyama Shobō, 1980), 101. On the conflicting dates, see Kaiho, *Kinsei Ezochi seiritsushi no kenkyū*, 185.

51.   Matsumae Kagehiro, *Shinra no kiroku* [1646], in SHS, 7:47.

52.   The black-seal order, or *kokusei no kokuin*, was granted on Keichō 9.1.27; see Matsumae Hironaga, *Fukuyama hifu* [1780], in SSHS, 5:80; *Tokugawa jikki* [1809-43], in *Bakusei shiryō to Ezochi*, 101; and "Tokugawa Ieyasu kokuinjō" [1604], in *Chūsei Ezo shiryō*, ed. Kaiho Mineo (Tokyo: San'ichi Shobō, 1983), 222-3.

53.   Hidetada in 1617, Iemitsu in 1634, Ietsuna in 1664, Tsunayoshi in 1682, Ienobu in 1711, and Yoshimune in 1719. In 1715, when Chinese trading was redirected through the Nagasaki *kaisho*, Matsumae control over trade in Ezo re-

mained essentially untouched [Matsumae Hironaga, *Fukuyama hifu* [1780], in SSHS, 5: 82–4]. For the correct dates, see Hokkaidō, ed., *Shin Hokkaidōshi nenpyō* (Sapporo: Hokkaidō Shuppan Kikaku Sentā, 1989), 25, 28, 33, 37, 47, 49.

54. Robert K. Sakai, "The Satsuma–Ryūkyū Trade and the Tokugawa Seclusionist Policy," *The Journal of Asian Studies* 23, no. 3 (May 1964): 398; and John Whitney Hall, "Notes on the Ch'ing Copper Trade with Japan," *Harvard Journal of Asiatic Studies* 12 (1949): 456.

55. Matsumae Chō Chōshi Henshūshitsu, ed., *Gaisetsu Matsumae no rekishi* (Tokyo: Gyōsei, 1994), 59–60.

56. David L. Howell, *Capitalism from Within: Economy, Society, and the State in a Japanese Fishery* (Berkeley: University of California Press, 1995), 27–8. For more on the origins and nature of Matsumae domain, see ibid., 27–35.

57. Kamiya, "Japanese Control of Ezochi and the Role of the Northern Koryŏ," 57–8.

58. Ronald P. Toby, *State and Diplomacy in Early Modern Japan: Asia in the Development of the Tokugawa Bakufu* (Princeton: Princeton University Press, 1984; reprint, Stanford: Stanford University Press, 1991), 110.

59. Matsumae Kagehiro, *Shinra no kiroku* [1646], in SHS, 7:49–50.

60. Howell, *Capitalism from Within*, 33.

61. William Cronon, *Changes in the Land: Indians, Colonists, and the Ecology of New England* (New York: Hill and Wang, 1983), 71–2.

62. Takakura Shin'ichirō, *Ainu seisakushi* (Tokyo: Nihon Hyōronsha, 1942; reprint, Tokyo: San'ichi Shobō, 1972), 94.

63. For *ikoku jinbutsu* and *gai'i jinbutsu*, see Terashima Ryōan, comp., *Wakan sansai zue* [1713], vols. 13–15, RCNS. See also Emori Susumu, "Ezochi o meguru hoppō no kōryū," in *Nihon no kinsei: Jōhō to kōtsū*, ed. Maruyama Yasunari (Tokyo: Chūō Kōronsha, 1992), 6:371, 374.

64. Matsumae Kagehiro, *Shinra no kiroku* [1646], in SHS, 7:45.

65. Matsumae was remote enough to serve as an ideal location to exile Kazan'in Tadanaga, a member of the imperial household, in the wake of a 1609 adultery incident (Herschel Webb, *The Japanese Imperial Institution in the Tokugawa Period* [New York: Columbia University Press, 1968], 91). On the incident itself, see *Tokugawa jikki* [1809–43], in *Bakusei shiryō to Ezochi*, 102; and Matsumae Kagehiro, *Shinra no kiroku* [1646], in SHS, 7:50–1.

66. Arai Hakuseki [1702], *Hankanpu*, in *Arai Hakuseki zenshū*, ed. Imaizumi Sadasuke (Tokyo: Kokusho Kankōkai, 1905), 1:458–63.

67. *Ezokoku shiki* [1751–63], RCNS; and Kaiho, *Kinsei Ezochi seiritsushi no kenkyū*, 178.

68. Yamada Sansen, *Sansen zakki*, ed. Tomimura Toboru (Tokyo: Yoshikawa Kōbunkan, 1972), 304; and Kaiho, *Kinsei Ezochi seiritsushi no kenkyū*, 178.

69. Jeronimo de Angelis, "Carta de algumas novas de Japam" [1618], in *Hoppō*

tankenki: Genna nenkan ni okeru gaikokujin no Ezo hōkokusho, ed. Hubert Cieslik (Tokyo: Yoshikawa Kōbunkan, 1963), 6, 53.

70. Ōhara Sakingo, *Chihoku gūdan* [1797], in HMSS, 3: 225; and Kaiho, *Kinsei Ezochi seiritsushi no kenkyū*, 179.

71. Mukoyama Seisai, *Seisai zakki* [1856], in *Dai Nippon shiryō*, ed. Tōkyō Teikoku Daigaku (Tokyo: Tōkyō Teikoku Daigaku Insatsukyoku, 1901), vol. 12, bk. 1, 934-5; and Kaiho, *Kinsei Ezochi seiritsushi no kenkyū*, 177.

72. Akizawa Shigeru, "Taikō kenchi," in *Iwanami kōza Nihon tsūshi: Kinsei 1*, ed. Asao Naohiro et al. (Tokyo: Iwanami Shoten, 1994), vol. 11, bk. 1, 133.

73. *Tōōgunki* [1711], in *Zoku gunsho ruijū*, ed. Hanawa Hokiichi and Ōta Toshirō (Tokyo: Zoku Gunsho Ruijū Kanseikai, 1924), 22:415.

74. Matsumae Hironaga, *Fukuyama hifu* [1780], in SSHS, 5:98.

75. *Matsumae nennenki* [1742], in MCS, 1:68.

76. Takayanagi Shinzō and Ishii Ryōsuke, eds., *Ofuregaki kanpō shūsei* (Tokyo: Iwanami Shoten, 1976), 93; and Naitō Chisō, ed., *Tokugawa jūgodaishi* (Tokyo: Jinbutsu Ōraisha, 1968), 4:93. See also Kaiho, *Kinsei Ezochi seiritsushi no kenkyū*, 197-201.

77. *Hansei ichiran* (n.d.), in *Nihon shiseki kyōkai sōsho*, ed. Nihon Shiseki Kyōkai (Tokyo: Tōkyō Daigaku Shuppankai, 1928), 173:223.

78. George H. Kerr, *Okinawa: The History of an Island People* (Tokyo: Charles E. Tuttle, 1958), 157-8.

79. Toby, *State and Diplomacy in Early Modern Japan*, 45-6.

80. Gregory Smits, *Visions of Ryukyu: Identity and Ideology in Early-Modern Thought and Politics* (Honolulu: University of Hawai'i Press, 1999), 108-11.

81. Matsumae Hironaga, *Fukuyama hifu* [1780], in SSHS, 5:201; and *Matsumae Fukuyama sho okite zen* (n.d.), in MCS, 1:583.

82. Habuto Masayasu, *Kyūmei kōki* [1807], in SSHS, 5:432, 1111.

83. Kaiho Mineo, "'Wajinchi' seiritsu no shodankai," *Matsumae han to Matsumae* 12 (July 1979): 1-13. Kaiho Mineo refers to the establishment of these boundaries, particularly those in the nineteenth century, as the "total implementation of the *sakoku* policy" (*sakoku taisei no kantetsu*; Kaiho Mineo, "Hoppō kōeki to chūsei Ezo shakai," in *Nihonkai to hokkoku bunka: Umi to rettō bunka*, ed. Amino Yoshihiko [Tokyo: Shōgakukan, 1990], 1:282-4). See also Kaiho Mineo, *Bakuhansei kokka to Hokkaidō* (Tokyo: San'ichi Shobō, 1978), 11-18; and Kaiho, *Kinsei Ezochi seiritsushi no kenkyū*, 207-25.

84. *Tsugaru ittōshi*, bk. 10 [1731], in SHS, 7:191; and Richard Louis Edmonds, "Northern Frontiers of Qing China and Tokugawa Japan: A Comparative Study of Frontier Policy" (research paper no. 213, Department of Geography, University of Chicago, 1985), 96.

85. Constantine Vaporis, *Breaking Barriers: Travel and the State in Early Modern Japan* (Cambridge: Harvard University Press, 1994), 257.

86. Sugimoto Fumiko, "Kuniezu sakusei jigyō to kinsei kokka," *Rekishigaku*

kenkyū 586 (October 1988): 126–38; and Sugimoto Fumiko, "Kuniezu," in *Iwanami kōza Nihon tsūshi: Kinsei 2*, ed. Asao Naohiro et al. (Tokyo: Iwanami Shoten, 1994), vol. 12, bk. 2, 303–6.

87. *Shōhō Nihon sōzu* [1644], in *Ezo chizushō*, ed. Narita Shūichi (Tokyo: Sara Shobō, 1989), 20–1. On the early Ainu-Japanese trade, see Takakura, *Ainu seisakushi*, 59–60.

88. *Genroku okuniezu chū Matsumae Ezozu* [1700], RCNS; and *Matsumae jima gōchō* [1700], in *Zokuzoku gunsho ruijū*, ed. Ichijima Kenkichi (Tokyo: Naigai Insatsu Kabushikigaisha Bunkōjō, 1906), 9:323. For the Tenpō era survey, see *Tenpō gōchō*, bk. 2, in *Naikaku bunko shozō shiseki sōkan*, ed. Shiseki Kenkyūkai (Tokyo: Kyūko Shoin, 1984), 56:363–5.

89. *Ezo shōko kikigaki* [1739], in MCS, 3:5–12.

90. Brown, *Central Authority and Local Autonomy*, 111.

91. *Ezo shōko kikigaki* [1739], in MCS, 3:5–12.

92. John W. Hall, *Tanuma Okitsugu, 1719–1788: Forerunner of Modern Japan* (Cambridge: Harvard University Press, 1955), 100–5.

93. Kondō Jūzō, *Nishi Ezochi bunken* [1786], RCNS.

94. Brown, *Central Authority and Local Autonomy*, 6–7.

CHAPTER 2.   SHAKUSHAIN'S WAR

1. Jill LePore, *The Name of War: King Philip's War and the Origins of American Identity* (New York: Alfred A. Knopf, 1998), xiii.

2. Ibid., 240, xiv.

3. See Andrew Knaut, *The Pueblo Revolt of 1680: Conquest and Resistance in Seventeenth-Century New Mexico* (Norman: University of Oklahoma Press, 1995).

4. Emori Susumu, "Ainu no shihai to teikō," in *Sakoku: Kōza Nihon kinseishi*, ed. Katō Eiichi and Yamada Tadao (Tokyo: Yūhikaku, 1981), 2:443–4.

5. Matsumae Yasuhiro, *Ezo hōki gairyakuki* [1669–72], in NSSSS, 4:643–4.

6. Kaiho Mineo, "Shakushain no tatakai: Ainu shakaishi ni taisuru bakuhansei kokka seiritsu no igi," in *Kinsei no shihai taisei to shakai kōzō*, ed. Kitajima Masamoto (Tokyo: Yoshikawa Kōbunkan, 1983), 64–6.

7. *Tsugaru ittōshi*, bk. 10 [1731], in SHS, 7:185.

8. Ibid., 126. On the placement of Onibishi's chiefdom, see ibid., 7:126, 130.

9. Ibid., 176–7.

10. Ibid., 177.

11. Ibid., 126.

12. Matsumae Yasuhiro, *Ezo hōki gairyakuki* [1669–72], in NSSSS, 4:641.

13. *Tsugaru ittōshi*, bk. 10 [1731], in SHS, 7:127.

14. Ibid., 127–8.

15. Norita Yasuemon, *Kanbun jūnen Ezo hōki atsumegaki* [1670], in NSSSS, 4:660.

16. *Tsugaru ittōshi*, bk. 10 [1731], in SHS, 7:128.

17. Ibid., 128.

18. Ibid. For a summary of these events, see also Shizunai Yakuba, ed., *Shizunai chōshi* (Shizunai: Shizunai Yakuba, 1975), 178–83; and Okuyama Ryō, *Ainu suibōshi* (Sapporo: Miyama Shobō, 1966), 65–9.

19. Matsumae Yasuhiro, *Ezo hōki gairyakuki* [1669–72], in NSSSS, 4:641.

20. *Tsugaru ittōshi*, bk. 10 [1731], in SHS, 7:129.

21. Ibid., 129–30.

22. Ibid.

23. Ibid.; Matsumae Yasuhiro, *Ezo hōki gairyakuki* [1669–72], in NSSSS, 4:641; Shizunai Yakuba, ed., *Shizunai chōshi*, 183–6; and Okuyama, *Ainu suibōshi*, 68–74.

24. Tawara Hiromi, *Hokkaidō no shizen hogo* (Sapporo: Hokkaidō Daigaku Tosho Kankōkai, 1979), 67.

25. Ōi Haruo, " 'Shakushain no ran (Kanbun kyūnen Ezo no ran)' no saikentō," parts 1 and 2, *Hoppō bunka kenkyū* 21 (1992): 1–66; 22 (1995): 1–116.

26. *Tsugaru ittōshi*, bk. 10 [1731], in SHS, 7:187.

27. Ibid., 181.

28. Luke S. Roberts, *Mercantilism in a Japanese Domain: The Merchant Origins of Economic Nationalism in Eighteenth-Century Tosa* (Cambridge: Cambridge University Press, 1998), 1.

29. Ibid., 135.

30. Mark Ravina, *Land and Lordship in Early Modern Japan* (Stanford: Stanford University Press, 1999), 2.

31. Matsumae Yasuhiro, *Ezo hōki gairyakuki* [1669–72], in NSSSS, 4:642; and Norita Yasuemon, *Kanbun jūnen Ezo hōki atsumegaki* [1670], in NSSSS, 4:661.

32. Matsumae Yasuhiro, *Ezo hōki gairyakuki* [1669–72], in NSSSS, 4:643.

33. Ibid., 642.

34. Umenai Yūkun, *Bunrō iji* [1822], in *Nanbu sōsho*, ed. Nanbu Sōsho Kankōkai (Morioka: Nanbu Sōsho Kankōkai, 1927), 2:491.

35. *Tsugaru ittōshi*, Book 10 [1731], in SHS, 7:101–2.

36. *Tokugawa jikki* [1809–43], in *Bakusei shiryō to Ezochi*, ed. Kaiho Mineo (Tokyo: Miyama Shobō, 1980), 109.

37. Ibid.

38. Kikuchi, *Bakuhan taisei to Ezochi*, 52–3.

39. Hayashi Shunsai, *Honshō tsugan*, cited in Kamiya Nobuyuki, "Japanese Control of Ezochi and the Role of Northern Koryŏ," *Acta Asiatica* 67 (1994): 66–7.

40. Ibid.

41. Matsumae Yasuhiro, *Ezo hōki gairyakuki* [1669–72], in NSSSS, 4:646.

42. Nakamura Mitsunori, *Uin shiryaku*, in *Shin Akita sōsho*, ed. Inoue Takaaki et al. (Tokyo: Rekishi Toshosha, 1971), 1:142–3; and Kikuchi, *Bakuhan taisei to Ezochi*, 57–8.

43. Onodera Michikore, *Nagano sensei yawashū*, in *Shin Akita sōsho*, ed. Inoue

Takaaki et al. (Tokyo: Rekishi Toshosha, 1971), 3:218–9; and Kikuchi, *Bakuhan tai-sei to Ezochi,* 57–8.

44. Kikuchi, *Bakuhan taisei to Ezochi,* 57–8.

45. Matsumae Yasuhiro, *Ezo hōki gairyakuki* [1669–72], in NSSSS, 4:644.

46. Matsumae Hironaga, *Fukuyama hifu* [1780], in SSHS, 5:36; and Matsumae Yasuhiro, *Ezo hōki gairyakuki* [1669–72], in NSSSS, 4:644.

47. Matsumae Yasuhiro, *Ezo hōki gairyakuki* [1669–72], in NSSSS, 4:646; *Matsumae kaki* [1878], in MCS, 1:16; and *Matsumae nennenki* [1742], in MCS, 1:61.

48. Matsumiya Kanzan, *Ezo dan hikki* [1710], in NSSSS, 4:395; and Matsumae Yasuhiro, *Ezo hōki gairyakuki* [1669–72], in NSSSS, 4:645.

49. *Tsugaru ittōshi,* bk. 10 [1731], in SHS, 7:184.

50. Ibid., 188.

51. Ibid., 185.

52. Kaiho Mineo, "Akinaiba chigyōsei no mittsu no kinō: Tōitsu seiken-Matsumae han-Ezochi ni taishite," *Hokkaidōshi kenkyū* 19 (August 1979): 6–7.

53. *Tsugaru ittōshi,* bk. 10 [1731], in SHS, 7:185.

54. Ibid., 186–7.

55. Ibid., 186.

56. Ibid.

57. Matsumae Yasuhiro, *Ezo hōki gairyakuki* [1669–72], in NSSSS, 4:643.

58. *Tsugaru ittōshi,* bk. 10 [1731], in SHS, 7:185.

CHAPTER 3.   THE ECOLOGY OF AINU
AUTONOMY AND DEPENDENCE

1. Richard White, *The Roots of Dependency: Subsistence, Environment, and Social Change among the Choctaws, Pawnees, and Navajos* (Lincoln: University of Nebraska Press, 1983), xiv.

2. Ibid., 239.

3. Richard White, "Animals and Enterprise," in *The Oxford History of the American West,* ed. Clyde A. Milner II et al. (New York: Oxford University Press, 1994), 238.

4. Ronald P. Toby, "Both a Borrower and a Lender Be: From Village Money-lender to Rural Banker in the Tempō Era," in *Monumenta Nipponica* 46, no. 4 (winter 1991): 483; and Saitō Osamu, *Puroto kōgyōka no jidai: Seiō to Nihon no hikakushi* (Tokyo: Hyōronsha, 1985). Although Thomas Smith did not use the term "proto-industrialism" in *The Agrarian Origins of Modern Japan,* as Saitō Osamu argues, Smith was in fact heading in that direction (Saitō Osamu, "Bringing the Covert Structure of the Past to Light," *Journal of Economic History* 49, no. 4 [1989]: 992–9). See Thomas C. Smith, *The Agrarian Origins of Modern Japan* (Stanford: Stanford University Press, 1959; reprint, New York: Atheneum, 1966). See also Kären Wigen,

The Making of a Japanese Periphery, 1750–1920 (Berkeley: University of California Press, 1995), 25–136; and David L. Howell, *Capitalism from Within: Economy, Society, and the State in a Japanese Fishery* (Berkeley: University of California Press, 1995), 1–23. On the protoindustrialists, see Anne Walthall, *The Weak Body of a Useless Woman: Matsuo Taseko and the Meiji Restoration* (Chicago: University of Chicago Press, 1998), 38–99; and Edward E. Pratt, *Japan's Proto-Industrial Elite: The Economic Foundations of the Gōnō* (Cambridge: Harvard University Press, 1999).

5. Norihisa Kondo, "Mammal Fauna and Its Distribution in Hokkaidō," in *Biodiversity and Ecology in Northernmost Japan*, ed. Seigo Higashi et al. (Sapporo: Hokkaido University Press, 1993), 83.

6. *Ezo shōko kikigaki* [1739], in MCS, 3:5–12.

7. Teruaki Hino, "Bird Fauna and Its Distribution in Hokkaidō," in *Biodiversity and Ecology in Northernmost Japan*, ed. Seigo Higashi et al. (Sapporo: Hokkaido University Press, 1993), 90–5.

8. *Ezo shōko kikigaki* [1739], in MCS, 3:5–12.

9. Sakakura Genjirō, *Hokkai zuihitsu* [1739], in NSSSS, 4:408.

10. Sannyo-Aino Toyo'oka, "The Future of Humans and the Creation of a Third Philosophy: An Ainu Viewpoint," trans. Takeshi Osanai and Richard Siddle, in *Indigenous Minorities and Education: Australian and Japanese Perspectives of Their Indigenous Peoples, the Ainu, Aborigines, and Torres Strait Islanders*, ed. Noel Loos and Takeshi Osanai (Tokyo: Sanyusha Publishing, 1993), 353.

11. Kaiho Mineo, *Nihon hoppōshi no ronri* (Tokyo: Yūzankaku, 1974), 100.

12. Kōno Hiromichi, "Bohyō no keishiki yori mitaru Ainu no shokeitō," *Ezo ōrai* 4 (August 1931): 101–21; and Utagawa Hiroshi, *Ainu bunka seiritsushi* (Sapporo: Hokkaidō Kikaku Sentā, 1988), 314–6.

13. Takashi Irimoto, "Ainu Territoriality," *Hoppō bunka kenkyū* 21 (1992): 69–71, 78.

14. Honda Katsuichi, *Harukor: An Ainu Woman's Tale*, trans. Kyoko Selden (Berkeley: University of California Press, 2000), 124–8. For the original Japanese, see Honda Katsuichi, *Ainu minzoku* (Tokyo: Asahi Shinbunsha, 1993), 122–5.

15. Honda, *Harukor*, 124–8.

16. James Serpell, *In the Company of Animals: A Study of Human-Animal Relationships* (Cambridge: Cambridge University Press, 1986), 181.

17. Takeshirō noted, for example, that a piece of driftwood marked the border between Yamakoshinai and Abuta chiefdoms (Matsuura Takeshirō, *Shinpan Ezo nisshi: Higashi Ezo nisshi*, ed. Yoshida Tsunekichi [Tokyo: Jiji Tsūshinsha, 1984], 1:41).

18. Hitoshi Watanabe, *The Ainu Ecosystem: Environment and Group Structure* (Tokyo: University of Tokyo Press, 1972), 56, 69–70, 77–8.

19. Inukai Tetsuo, "Hokkaidō no shika to sono kōbō," *Hoppō bunka kenkyū hōkoku* 7 (March 1952): 1–22.

20. SSHS, 2:466; and Kadosaki Masaaki and Inukai Tetsuo, *Higuma: Hokkaidō no shizen* (Sapporo: Hokkaidō Shinbunsha, 1993), 272-352.

21. Deriha Kōji, "Shuryōgu kara mita Hokkaidō Ainu oyobi hokutō ajia shominzoku no kogata mōhijū shuryō katsudō no imi," in *Kita no rekishi-bunka kōryū kenkyū jigyō*, ed. Hokkaidō Kaitaku Kinenkan (Sapporo: Hokkaidō Kaitaku Kinenkan, 1995), 305-30.

22. Watanabe, *The Ainu Ecosystem*, 26-7; and Chiri Mashiho, "Ainu no sake ryō," *Hoppō bunka kenkyū hōkoku* 12 (March 1959): 245-65.

23. *Matsumae nennenki* [1742], in MCS, 1:56-7; and Matsumae Hironaga, *Fukuyama hifu* [1780], in SSHS, 5:30.

24. SSHS, 2:127.

25. Robert Leroy Innes, "The Door Ajar: Japan's Foreign Trade in the Seventeenth Century" (Ph.D. diss., University of Michigan, 1980), 533.

26. Ibid., 543.

27. Yanaga Yoshiko, *Ezo no sakin* (Sapporo: Hokkaidō Shuppan Kikaku Sentā, 1981), 134-46.

28. Michael Cooper, comp., *They Came to Japan: An Anthology of European Reports on Japan, 1543-1640* (Berkeley: University of California Press, 1965), 235-6; and Diego Carvalho, "Copia de huma [carta] que o Padre Diogo Carvalho me escreveo acerca da missam que fez a Yezo e outras partes" [1620], in *Hoppō tankenki: Genna nenkan ni okeru gaikokujin no Ezo hōkokusho*, ed. Hubert Cieslik (Tokyo: Yoshikawa Kōbunkan, 1963), 13, 64.

29. Tawara Hiromi, *Hokkaidō no shizen hogo* (Sapporo: Hokkaidō Daigaku Tosho Kankōkai, 1979), 66-7.

30. "Kyōhō kyūnen shichigatsu jūrokunichi Edo e Ezojin gashi tsukamatsuri sōrō nitsuki mōshitsukawashi sōrō kakitsuke" [1724], cited in SSHS, 2:301.

31. *Tsugaru ittōshi*, bk. 10 [1731], in SHS, 7:127-8.

32. Tawara, *Hokkaidō no shizen hogo*, 67-8.

33. Asakura Yūko, "Ezo ninshiki no keisei: Toku ni keiki to shite no jōhō o megutte," in *Kita kara no Nihonshi*, ed. Hokkaidō-Tōhoku Kenkyūkai (Tokyo: Sanseidō, 1990), 2:136.

34. *Tsugaru ittōshi*, bk. 10 [1731], in SHS, 7:188.

35. Ibid.

36. Yamamoto Tadashi, *Kinsei Ezochi nōsakumotsu nenpyō* (Sapporo: Hokkaidō Daigaku Tosho Kankōkai, 1996), 111-5. For an interesting look at Ainu agricultural practices in historical perspective, see Tessa Morris-Suzuki, "Creating the Frontier: Border, Identity, and History in Japan's Far North," *East Asian History* 7 (June 1994): 18-23.

37. Matsumae Norihiro, *Shōtoku gonen Matsumae Shima-no-kami sashidashi sōrō kakitsuke* [1715], in SSKS, 134.

38. Yamamoto Tadashi, "Ezo nōkō kinshi kō," *Monbetsu shiritsu kyōdo hakubut-*

sukan hōkoku 5 (1992): 18. For more complete studies of "Ainu plants," see Fukuoka Itoko, *Ainu shokubutsushi* (Tokyo: Sōfūkan, 1995); Hayashi Yoshishige, "Ainu no shokuryō shokubutsu saishū," *Hoppō bunka kenkyū* 2 (1967): 157–72; and Hayashi Yoshishige, "Ainu nōgyō no keiei keitai," *Hoppō bunka kenkyū hōkoku* 17 (March 1962): 39–60. See also John Batchelor and Miyabe Kingo, "Ainu Economic Plants," *Transactions of the Asiatic Society of Japan* 21 (1893): 197–240.

39.   Mogami Tokunai, *Ezokoku fūzoku ninjō no sata* [1791], in NSSSS, 4:444.

40.   *Ezochi ikken* [1784–90], in SHS, 7:87, 330, 333, 341.

41.   *Gojunkenshi ōtō mōshiawasesho* [1761], in MCS, 1:406.

42.   Mogami Tokunai, *Ezo sōshi betsuroku* [1781–8], in MCS, 3:36.

43.   For more on the Ainu relationship with dogs, see Hatakeyama Saburōta, "Hokkaidō no inu ni tsuite no oboegaki: Senshi jidai kaizuka ken to Ainu ken no hikaku," *Hokkaidōshi kenkyū* 1 (December 1973): 41–68.

44.   Morris-Suzuki, "Creating the Frontier," 18–21.

45.   MCS, 1:559.

46.   *Ezochi ikken* [1784–90], in SHS, 7:483.

47.   Shirayama Tomomasa, *Matsumae Ezochi basho ukeoiseido no kenkyū* (Hako-date: Hokkaidō Keizaishi Kenkyūjo, 1961), 1:155–7.

48.   *Ezochi ikken* [1784–90], in SHS, 7:335–6.

49.   Ibid., 334–5.

50.   Maehira Fusaaki, "'Sakoku' Nihon no kaigai bōeki," in *Nihon no kinsei: Sekaishi no naka no kinsei*, ed. Asao Naohiro (Tokyo: Chūō Kōronsha, 1991), 1:159; and Tashiro Kazui, "Bakumatsuki nitchō shibōeki to wakan bōeki shōnin: Yunyū yonhinmoku no torihiki o chūshin ni," in *Tokugawa shakai kara no tenbō*, ed. Hayami Akira et al. (Tokyo: Dōbunkan Shuppan, 1989), 300.

51.   Maehira, "'Sakoku' Nihon no kaigai bōeki," 159.

52.   *Ezochi ikken* [1784–90], in SHS, 7:336–7.

53.   *Higashi Ezochi kakubasho yōsu taigaigaki* [1808–11], in SHS, 7:577, 544.

54.   Ibid., 544. See also Tani Gentan, *Ezo kikō* [1799], ed. Satō Keiji (Tokyo: Asahi Shuppan, 1973), 35. For paintings of trading posts in eastern Ezo, see Tani Gentan, *Ezo kishō zue* [1799], ed. Satō Keiji (Tokyo: Asahi Shuppan, 1973).

55.   Ōuchi Yoan, *Tōkai yawa* [1854–59], in HMSS, 5:461.

56.   Kunitomo Zen'an, *Hokusui taimon* [1838], RCNS.

57.   Innes, "The Door Ajar," 77–243.

58.   Mogami Tokunai, *Ezo sōshi betsuroku* [1781–8], in MCS, 3:36–7; *Ezochi ikken* [1784–90], in SHS, 7:301; and Sakakura Genjirō, *Hokkai zuihitsu* [1739], in NSSSS, 4:404.

59.   Kaiho Mineo, "Shakushain no tatakai: Ainu shakaishi ni taisuru bakuhansei kokka seiritsu no igi," in *Kinsei no shihai taisei to shakai kōzō*, ed. Kitajima Masamoto (Tokyo: Yoshikawa Kōbunkan, 1983). See also Fukusawa Yuriko, "Ainu Archaeology as Ethnohistory: Iron Technology among the Saru Ainu of Hokkaidō in the Seventeenth Century" (Ph.D. diss., Cambridge University, 1995).

60. Matsumiya Kanzan, *Ezo dan hikki* [1710], in NSSSS, 4:392.
61. Furukawa Koshōken, *Tōyū zakki* [1788], ed. Ōtō Tokihiko (Tokyo: Tōyō Bunko, 1964), 164–6.
62. Kaiho, "Shakushain no tatakai," 48.
63. *Matsumae Ezoki* [1717], in MCS, 1:386; Sakakura Genjirō, *Hokkai zuihitsu* [1739], in NSSSS, 4:404; Matsumiya Kanzan, *Ezo dan hikki* [1710], in NSSSS, 4:392; and *Ezo banashi* [1798], RCNS, or *Ezo Matsumae kenbunki* [1798], RCNS. (This manuscript also appears under the title *Ezo miyage*.) For salmon and herring products, see Murayama Denbei, *Matsumae sanbutsu daigaikan* [1804–17], in *Hokkaidō kyōdo kenkyū shiryō* 6 (December 1960). For a list of animal, fish, and bird products, or the general fauna of Hokkaido, mentioned in pre-1868 manuscripts on Ezo, see Kadosaki Masaaki and Seki Hideshi, "Ezochi ni okeru dōbutsu no bunkengakuteki kenkyū," *Hokkaidō kaitaku kinenkan chōsa hōkoku* 38 (1999): 96–108.
64. Hezutsu Tōsaku, *Tōyūki* [1784], in NSSSS, 4:429.
65. Innes, "The Door Ajar," 77–243; John W. Hall, "Notes on the Ch'ing Copper Trade with Japan," *Harvard Journal of Asiatic Studies* 12 (1949): 456; Kate Wildman Nakai, *Shogunal Politics: Arai Hakuseki and the Premises of Tokugawa Rule* (Cambridge: Harvard University Press, 1988), 108; and Maehira, "'Sakoku' Nihon no kaigai bōeki," 155–6.
66. Harold Bolitho, *Treasures among Men: The Fudai Daimyo in Tokugawa Japan* (New Haven: Yale University Press, 1974), 195–6; and Maehira, "'Sakoku' Nihon no kaigai bōeki," 156.
67. Abuya Mohei and Abuya Senpachi, *Nagasaki tawaramono no ikken: Tenmei hachinen saru jūgatsu Ōsaka omote e sashidasu nari* [1788], in *Hidaya Takekawa-ke monjo*, vol. 9, no. E 7, RCNS.
68. Hōraiya Chūbei and Ōtsuya Buzaemon, *Tenmei hachi saru toshi Matsumae Ezochi mawari tawaramono kaiire daikin ukeharai kanjōchō* [1788], in *Hidaya Takekawa-ke monjo*, vol. 9, no. E 1, RCNS.
69. Kushihara Seihō, *Igen zokuwa* [1792], in NSSSS, 4:491–2.
70. Purchase rates were standardized at 250 *mon* of gold per 1 *kin* per *tawaramono*. At this rate, the 300 *tawaramono* that were put together in one month were worth 1,562 *ryō* 2 *bu* in gold (ibid.).
71. Ibid., 492–4.
72. *Kiitappu hitsuji no haru uketori nimotsu no bun* [1788], in *Hidaya Takekawa-ke monjo*, vol. 9, no. D 6, RCNS.
73. *Matsumae Ezoki* [1717], in MCS, 1:389.
74. Kushihara Seihō, *Igen zokuwa* [1792], in NSSSS, 4:492–4.
75. Mogami Tokunai, *Ezo sōshi betsuroku* [1781–8], in MCS, 3:28–9.
76. Kushihara Seihō, *Igen zokuwa* [1792], in NSSSS, 4:491–2.
77. Toby, "Both a Borrower and a Lender Be," 486–7.

CHAPTER 4.   SYMBOLISM AND
ENVIRONMENT IN TRADE

1. Kushihara Seihō, *Igen zokuwa* [1792], in NSSS, 4:505.

2. Pierre Bourdieu, *Distinction: A Social Critique of the Judgement of Taste*, trans. Richard Nice (Cambridge: Harvard University Press, 1984), 260.

3. *Matsumae kaki* [1878], in MCS, 1:12; and Matsumae Kagehiro, *Shinra no kiroku* [1646], in SHS, 7:72–3.

4. Jeronimo de Angelis, "Carta de algumas novas de Japam" [1618], in *Hoppō tankenki: Genna nenkan ni okeru gaikokujin no Ezo hōkokusho*, ed. Hubert Cieslik (Tokyo: Yoshikawa Kōbunkan, 1963), 56, 8–9.

5. Diego Carvalho, "Copia de huma [carta] que o Padre Diogo Carvalho me escreveo acerca da missam que fez a Yezo e outras partes" [1620], in *Hoppō tankenki: Genna nenkan ni okeru gaikokujin no Ezo hōkokusho*, ed. Hubert Cieslik (Tokyo: Yoshikawa Kōbunkan, 1963), 68–9, 17.

6. Akutagawa Tatsuo, "Sengoku bushō to taka: Taikō Hideyoshi no hinata takasu bugyō setchi o megutte," in *Nihon no chūsei no seiji to bunka*, ed. Toyota Takeshi (Tokyo: Yoshikawa Kōbunkan, 1980), 543–4.

7. Tsukamoto Manabu, *Edo jidai jin to dōbutsu* (Tokyo: Nihon Editā Sukūru Shuppanbu, 1995), 196–216.

8. Kikuchi Isao, "Taka to Matsumae han: Kinsei zenki o chūshin ni," in *Ezochi-Hokkaidō: Rekishi to seikatsu*, ed. Chihōshi Kenkyū Kyōgikai (Tokyo: Yūzankaku, 1983), 122–3; Kikuchi Isao, *Ainu minzoku to Nihonjin: Higashi ajia no naka no Ezochi* (Tokyo: Asahi Sensho 510, 1994), 72–3; and Kikuchi Isao, *Bakuhan taisei to Ezochi* (Tokyo: Yūzankaku, 1984), 26–49.

9. Takagi Shōsaku, *Nihon kinsei kokkashi no kenkyū* (Tokyo: Iwanami Shoten, 1990), vii.

10. Harold Bolitho, "The Han," in *The Cambridge History of Japan*, vol. 4, *Early Modern Japan*, ed. John Whitney Hall (Cambridge: Cambridge University Press, 1991), 197.

11. Mary Elizabeth Berry, "Public Peace and Private Attachment: The Goals and Conduct of Power in Early Modern Japan," *Journal of Japanese Studies* 12, no. 2 (summer 1986): 263, 267.

12. *Norihiro no shojō* (n.d.), Hokkaido Prefectural Library, Ebetsu, Japan. This manuscript appears at the end of *Matsumae Morihiro shojō*.

13. Kaiho Mineo, *Kinsei Ezochi seiritsushi no kenkyū* (Tokyo: San'ichi Shobō, 1984), 199–200.

14. For the receipt of hawks from Andō Chikasue, see "Shinchō kōki," in *Chūsei Ezo shiryō*, ed. Kaiho Mineo (Tokyo: San'ichi Shobō, 1983), 169 (Andō Chikasue appears in this document as Nanbu Kunaishōyū). For Kakizaki Masahiro's audience at Azuchi Castle, see Matsumae Kagehiro, *Shinra no kiroku* [1646], in SHS, 7:62

(Kakizaki Masahiro appears in this document as Uemontayū Masahiro). For Nobunaga's restrictions on falconry, see Okuno Takahiro, ed., *Oda Nobunaga monjo no kenkyū* (Tokyo: Yoshikawa Kōbunkan, 1958), 2:87–92. For Mary Elizabeth Berry's comment on Nobunaga's restrictions, see her *Hideyoshi* (Cambridge: Harvard University Press, 1982), 55–6.

15. Kikuchi Isao, "Taka to Matsumae han," 132–3; and Kikuchi Isao, *Ainu minzoku to Nihonjin*, 72. See also 44, 48; and Matsumae Hironaga, *Fukuyama hifu* [1780], in SSHS, 5:83–4. The reading of *takajō* comes from the 1681 *Buke setsuyōshū*, Hokuga Library, Hokkai Gakuen, Sapporo, Hokkaido.

16. On the seal provided to use the horse-post stations, see *Matsumae nennenki* [1742], in MCS, 1:55; and Matsumae Kagehiro, *Shinra no kiroku* [1646], in SHS, 7:47. The officials were Aoyama Narikazu, Andō Shigenobu, Doi Toshikatsu, Sakai Tadayo, and Honda Masanobu (Matsumae Hironaga, *Fukuyama hifu* [1780], in SSHS, 5:80–5).

17. Matsumae Yasuhiro, *Ezo hōki gairyakuki* [1669–72], in NSSSS, 4:643.

18. Matsumiya Kanzan, *Ezo dan hikki* [1710], in NSSSS, 4:395.

19. Takakura Shin'ichirō, *Ainu seisakushi* (Tokyo: Nihon Hyōronsha, 1942; reprint, Tokyo: San'ichi Shobō, 1972), 59; and Kikuchi Isao, "Taka to Matsumae han," 122. See also Norita Yasuemon, *Kanbun jūnen Ezo hōki atsumegaki* [1670], in NSSSS, 4:662; and *Tsugaru ittōshi*, bk. 10 [1731], in SHS, 7:166–7.

20. Saionji Sukekuni, ed., *Taka hyakushu ogura mondō* (n.d.), RCNS.

21. Kikuchi Isao, "Taka to Matsumae han," 123.

22. *Matsumae Ezoki* [1717], in MCS, 1:383–4.

23. Kikuchi Isao, "Taka to Matsumae han," 123–4.

24. Kunaishō Shikibushoku, *Hōyo* (Tokyo: Yoshikawa Kōbunkan, 1933), 701; and SSHS, 2:121. See also Maki Bokusen, *Hitoyo banashi* [1810], RCNS; and *Matsumae Ezochi oboegaki* (n.d.), RCNS.

25. Susan B. Hanley and Kozo Yamamura, *Economic and Demographic Change in Preindustrial Japan, 1600–1868* (Princeton: Princeton University Press, 1977), 136.

26. *Matsumae Ezochi oboegaki* (n.d.), RCNS.

27. Okudaira Sadamori, *Taka tsukaiyō no sho* [1824], RCNS; and Ogasawara Nagatoki and Ogasawara Sadahiro, *Taka no sho* (n.d.), RCNS.

28. *Matsumae Fukuyama shojō* [1756], in MCS, 1:610; and Kikuchi Isao, "Taka to Matsumae han," 124–5.

29. Matsumae Hironaga, *Fukuyama hifu* [1780], in SSHS, 5:30.

30. *Matsumae Ezoki* [1717], in MCS, 1:384–89. See also SSHS, 2:123.

31. William Cronon, *Changes in the Land: Indians, Colonists, and the Ecology of New England* (New York: Hill and Wang, 1983), 93.

32. Utagawa Hiroshi, *Ainu bunka seiritsushi* (Sapporo: Hokkaidō Shuppan Kikaku Sentā, 1988), 312–29; and Emori Susumu, "Ezochi o meguru hoppō no kōryū," in *Nihon no kinsei: Jōhō to kōtsū*, ed. Maruyama Yasunari (Tokyo: Chūō Kōronsha, 1992), 6:388.

33. Miyajima Toshimitsu, *Ainu minzoku to Nihon no rekishi* (Tokyo: San'ichi Shobō, 1996), 39–42.

34. Iwasaki Naoko, "Zenkindai Ainu no 'takara' to sono shakaiteki kinō," *Shirin* 78, no. 5 (September 1995): 124.

35. Hezutsu Tōsaku, *Tōyūki* [1783], in NSSSS, 4:423; Matsumae Norihiro, *Shōtoku gonen Matsumae Shima-no-kami sashidashi sōrō kakitsuke* [1715], in SSKS, 134–5; and Cronon, *Changes in the Land*, 94. Carolyn Merchant, in the context of North America, also investigates trade goods as prestige items in Native American society and the ultimate transformation of animals into commodities (Carolyn Merchant, *Ecological Revolutions: Nature, Gender, and Science in New England* [Chapel Hill: University of North Carolina Press, 1989], 29–68).

36. Furukawa Koshōken, *Tōyū zakki* [1788], ed. Ōtō Tokihiko (Tokyo: Tōyō Bunko, 1964), 174, 169–70; and Matsumae Hironaga, *Matsumaeshi* [1781], in HMSS, 2:117.

37. Bronislaw Pilsudski, *Materials for the Study of the Ainu Language and Folklore* (Cracow: Spolka Wydawnicza Polska, 1912), 93–4. Himself a victim of changing times, Pilsudski had been exiled to Siberia for his involvement in the Narodniki revolutionary movement (Katō Kyūzō, "Dawn of Russian Ethnology-Researchers and Convicts around Bronislaw Pilsudski," in *European Studies on Ainu Language and Culture*, ed. Josef Kreiner [München: Alle Rechte Vorbehalten Druck und Bindearbeiten, 1993], 105).

38. Pilsudski, *Materials for the Study of the Ainu Language and Folklore*, 190.

39. Mutō Kanzō, *Ezo nikki* [1798], in NSSSS, 4:19; and Yamazaki Hanzō, *Mōi tōkanki* [1806], part 2, ed. Namikawa Kenji, *Hirosaki daigaku kokushi kenkyū* 97 (October 1994): 59.

40. Kakizaki Hakyō, *Ishū retsuzō* [1790], in *Ainu-e shūsei*, ed. Takakura Shin'-ichirō (Tokyo: Banchō Shobō, 1973), 2: plates 1–14; and Matsumae Hironaga, *Ishū retsuzō furoku* [1790], in *Ainu-e shūsei*, ed. Takakura Shin'ichirō (Tokyo: Banchō Shobō, 1973), 1:86–9.

41. Isabella Bird, *Unbeaten Tracks in Japan* (London: J. Murray, 1880; reprint, Boston: Beacon Press, 1984), 287.

42. Yamada Takako, *Ainu no sekaikan: 'Kotoba' kara yomu shizen to uchū* (Tokyo: Kōdansha, 1994).

43. On bear, wolf, and owl ceremonies, see Sarashina Genzō and Sarashina Kō, *Kotan seibutsuki* (Tokyo: Hōsei Daigaku Shuppankyoku, 1976), 2:341–80, 289–95, 3:546–58.

44. Satō Tadao, "Ainu no Amam-sake (kokumotsushu) no jittai to sono kigen," *Senshū daigaku Bibai nōkō Tanki daigaku nenpō* 1 (March 1970): 118–24.

45. Richard White, *The Roots of Dependency: Subsistence, Environment, and Social Change among the Choctaws, Pawnees, and Navajos* (Lincoln: University of Nebraska Press, 1983), 83–4.

46.   Kushiro Chōshi Henshū Iinkai, ed., *Kushiro chōshi* (Tokyo: Gyōsei, 1990), 253; and "Hokkaidō," bk. 2, in *Kadokawa Nihon chimei daijiten*, ed. Takeuchi Rizō (Tokyo: Kadokawa Shoten, 1978), 1:800–1. See also *Ezokoku shiki* [1751–63], RCNS; and Arai Heibei, *Tōkō manpitsu* [1806], RCNS.

47.   Sakakura Genjirō, *Hokkai zuihitsu* [1739], in NSSSS, 4:409; and Matsumae Hironaga, *Matsumaeshi* [1781], in HMSS, 2:117.

48.   Hezutsu Tōsaku, *Tōyūki* [1784], in NSSSS, 4:423; Mogami Tokunai, *Watarishima hikki* [1808], in NSSSS, 4:527; and Mogami Tokunai, *Ezokoku fūzoku ninjō no sata* [1791], in NSSSS, 4:452.

49.   Matsuda Denjūrō, *Hokuidan* (n.d.), in NSSSS, 4:83.

50.   Sasaki Toshikazu, "Ainu-e ga egaita sekai," in *Ainu bunka ni manabu*, ed. Sapporo Gakuin Daigaku Jinbutsu Gakubu (Sapporo: Hokkaidō Daigaku Tosho Kankōkai, 1990), 168.

51.   Kimura Hakō, *Ainu fūzoku kuma matsuri no zu* (n.d.), RCNS.

52.   Matsumae Norihiro, *Shōtoku gonen Matsumae Shima-no-kami sashidashi sōrō kakitsuke* [1715], in SSKS, 133.

53.   Ibid., 139; Matsumiya Kanzan, *Ezo dan hikki* [1710], in NSSSS, 4:392; and *Matsumae Ezoki* [1717], in MCS, 1:387.

54.   For an interesting discussion of the relationship between deer and Ainu, see Inukai Tetsuo, *Waga dōbutsuki* (Tokyo: Kurashi No Techōsha, 1970), 114–5.

55.   Kushihara Seihō, *Igen zokuwa* [1792], in NSSSS, 4:504.

56.   Matsumae Hironaga, *Matsumaeshi* [1781], in HMSS, 2:195.

57.   Mogami Tokunai, *Watarishima hikki* [1808], in NSSSS, 4:523.

58.   Mogami Tokunai, *Ezo sōshi betsuroku* [1781–8], in MCS, 3:34–5.

59.   Maehira Fusaaki, "'Sakoku' Nihon no kaigai bōeki," in *Nihon no kinsei: Sekaishi no naka no kinsei*, ed. Asao Naohiro (Tokyo: Chūō Kōronsha, 1991), 166.

60.   The deerskin trade emerged as a major part of the initial Chinese economic interest in Taiwan (John Robert Shepherd, *Statecraft and Political Economy on the Taiwan Frontier, 1600–1800* [Stanford: Stanford University Press, 1993], 57, 73–9, 100).

61.   *Matsumae Ezoki* [1717], in MCS, 1:387.

62.   Kitagawa Morisada, *Kinsei fūzokushi* or *Morisada mankō* [1853], ed. Muromatsu Iwao (Tokyo: Bunchōsha Shoin, 1928), 499–500.

63.   Miyoshi Kazumitsu, ed., *Edo-Tōkyō seigyō bukka jiten* (Tokyo: Seiabō, 1960), 73–5; and Inukai Tetsuo, "Hokkaidō no shika to sono kōbō," *Hoppō bunka kenkyū hōkoku* 7 (March 1952): 18.

64.   *Matsumae hisetsu* [1839], RCNS.

65.   Hezutsu Tōsaku, *Tōyūki* [1784], in NSSSS, 4:432.

66.   Yamazaki Hanzō, *Mōi tōkanki* [1806], ed. Namikawa Kenji, *Hirosaki daigaku kokushi kenkyū* 96 (March 1994): 46; and SSHS, 2:301–2.

67.   Barry Lopez, *Arctic Dreams: Imagination and Desire in a Northern Landscape* (New York: Bantam Books, 1986), 200.

68. Ibid., 200–1.

69. For a similar discussion in the context of New England tribes, see Merchant, *Ecological Revolutions*, 44–68.

70. Toyohara Shōji, "Chashi to sono kinō," in *Menashi no sekai: Nemuro shinpojiumu 'kita kara no Nihonshi,'* ed. Hokkaidō-Tōhokushi Kenkyūkai (Sapporo: Hokkaidō Shuppan Kikaku Sentā, 1996), 78–9, 83.

71. Utagawa, *Ainu bunka seiritsushi*, 346; and Utagawa Hiroshi, *Hokkaidō no kōkogaku* (Sapporo: Hokkaidō Shuppan Kikaku Sentā, 1995), 279–85.

72. Kaiho Mineo, *Nihon hoppōshi no ronri* (Tokyo: Yūzankaku, 1974), 134; and *Tsugaru ittōshi*, bk. 10 [1731], SHS, 7:128.

73. Matsumae Yasuhiro, *Ezo hōki gairyakuki* [1669–72], in NSSSS, 4:641–2.

74. Kaiho, *Nihon hoppōshi no ronri*, 139.

75. Hirayama Hiroto, *Ainushi o mitsumete: Ainushi kenkyū-Ainushi gaikan* (Sapporo: Hokkaidō Shuppan Kikaku Sentā, 1996), 132; and Hirayama Hiroto, "Chashi bunka to kōeki," in *Ainu no chashi to sono sekai*, ed. Hokkaidō Chashi Gakkai (Sapporo: Hokkaidō Shuppan Kikaku Sentā, 1994), 309–12.

76. Utagawa Hiroshi, *Ainu denshō to chashi* (Sapporo: Hokkaidō Shuppan Kikaku Sentā, 1981), 143–4.

77. Ibid., 23.

78. Ibid., 23–4.

79. *Tsugaru ittōshi*, bk. 10 [1731], in SHS, 7:127–30.

80. Toyohara, "Chashi to sono kinō," 104–6.

81. Matsumae Hironaga, *Matsumaeshi* [1781], in HMSS, 2:118.

82. Mogami Tokunai, *Ezo sōshi betsuroku* [1781–8], in MCS, 3:33.

CHAPTER 5.   THE SAKHALIN TRADE

1. Matsumae Hironaga, *Matsumaeshi* [1781], in HMSS, 2:124–5, 136, 165–316. For a look at the birth of the study of natural history, or *honzōgaku*, in Japan, see Nishimura Saburō, *Bunmei no naka no hakubutsugaku* (Tokyo: Kinokuniya Shoten, 1999), 1:98–185.

2. Michel Foucault, *The Order of Things: An Archaeology of the Human Sciences* (New York: Vintage Books, 1970), xix.

3. Matsumae Hironaga, *Matsumaeshi* [1781], in HMSS, 2:125; and *Gukō shinzu tairyaku* [1781], in *Ezo chizushō*, ed. Narita Shūichi (Tokyo: Sara Shobō, 1989), 40.

4. Matsumae Hironaga, *Matsumaeshi* [1781], in HMSS, 2:121.

5. Ibid., 2:120–1, 307, 127–8.

6. Kaiho Mineo, "Hoppō kōeki to chūsei Ezo shakai," in *Nihonkai to hokkoku bunka: Umi to rettō bunka*, ed. Amino Yoshihiko (Tokyo: Shōgakukan, 1990), 270.

7. Kikuchi Toshihiko, "Ainu minzoku to hoppō kōeki," in *Hoppōshi no shin*

shiza: Taigai seisaku to bunka, ed. Chihōshi Kenkyū Kyōgikai (Tokyo: Yūzankaku, 1994), 107–8.

8. Mamiya Rinzō, *Hokui bunkai yowa sōkō* [1811], ed. Hora Tomio and Tanisawa Shōichi (Tokyo: Tōyō Bunko, 1988), 36; Furukawa Koshōken, *Tōyū zakki* [1788], ed. Ōtō Tokihiko (Tokyo: Tōyō Bunko, 1964), 124–5; and Kikuchi Toshihiko, "Ainu minzoku to hoppō kōeki," 99.

9. John J. Stephan, *Sakhalin: A History* (Oxford: Clarendon Press, 1971), 21; and Emori Susumu, "Jūsan-jūroku seiki no higashi ajia to Ainu minzoku: Gen-Minchō to Saharin-Ainu no kankei o chūshin ni," in *Kita Nihon chūseishi no kenkyū*, ed. Haga Norihiko (Tokyo: Yoshikawa Kōbunkan, 1990), 223–4, 360–1.

10. Kikuchi Toshihiko, "Hokkaidō o meguru hoppō shominzoku no kōryū," in *Kodai no Nihon: Tōhoku-Hokkaidō*, ed. Sudō Takashi et al. (Tokyo: Kadokawa Shoten, 1992), 9:371–2.

11. Ogihara Shinko, *Hoppō shominzoku no sekaikan* (Tokyo: Sōfūkan, 1996), 326–477.

12. See Stephan, *Sakhalin*, 21; Emori, "Jūsan-jūroku seiki no higashi ajia to Ainu minzoku," 234–60; Emori, "Ezochi o meguru hoppō no kōryū," in *Nihon no kinsei: Jōhō to kōtsū*, ed. Maruyama Yasunari (Tokyo: Chūō Kōronsha, 1992), 385–7; Akizuki Toshiyuki, *Nichiro kankei to Saharin tō: Bakumatsu Meiji shonen no ryōdo mondai* (Tokyo: Chikuma Shobō, 1994), 9; and Kaiho Mineo, "Santan kōeki to henmin seido: Shoki roshin kankeishi no shiten yori," in *Kita no rekishi: Bunka kōryū kenkyū jigyō*, ed. Hokkaidō Kaitaku Kinenkan (Sapporo: Hokkaidō Kaitaku Kinenkan, 1995), 194–8.

13. "The Shoo King," in *The Chinese Classics*, trans. James Legge (Hong Kong: Hong Kong University Press, 1960), 3:64–7.

14. For an older and somewhat Sinocentric version of the tributary trade, see Lien-sheng Yang, "Historical Notes on the Chinese World Order," in *The Chinese World Order*, ed. John King Fairbank (Cambridge: Harvard University Press, 1968), 21. For more-recent scholarship, see Richard Von Glahn, *The Country of Streams and Grottoes: Expansion, Settlement, and the Civilizing of the Sichuan Frontier in Song Times* (Cambridge: Harvard University Press, 1988).

15. For definitions of the titles *zhihuishi, zhihui tongzhi*, and *zhihui qianshi*, see Charles O. Hucker, *A Dictionary of Official Titles in Imperial China* (Stanford: Stanford University Press, 1985), 159.

16. Emori, "Ezochi o meguru hoppō no kōryū," 404–5.

17. Ibid.

18. Von Glahn, *The Country of Streams and Grottoes;* and Charles Patterson Giersch, "Qing China's Reluctant Subjects: Indigenous Communities and Empire along the Yunnan Frontier" (Ph.D. diss., Yale University, 1988).

19. John K. Fairbank and S. Y. Têng, "On the Ch'ing Tributary System," *Harvard*

Journal of Asiatic Studies 6 (1941): 135-246; Mark Mancall, "The Ch'ing Tribute System: An Interpretive Essay," in *The Chinese World Order,* ed. John K. Fairbank (Cambridge: Harvard University Press, 1968), 63-89; Robert H. G. Lee, *The Manchu Frontier in Ch'ing History* (Cambridge: Harvard University Press, 1970); and Mark Mancall, *China at the Center: Three Hundred Years of Foreign Policy* (New York: The Free Press, 1984), 13-39.

20.   Sasaki Shirō, "Shinchō shihai to Amūru kawashimo ryūiki jūmin no esunishiti," in *Minzoku bunka no sekai: Shakai no tōgō to dōtai,* ed. Abe Toshiharu et al. (Tokyo: Shōgakukan, 1990), 2:510.

21.   Emori, "Ezochi o meguru hoppō no kōryū," 406-7; and Stephan, *Sakhalin,* 25.

22.   Emori, "Ezochi o meguru hoppō no kōryū," 408.

23.   John E. Vollmer, *Decoding Dragons: Status Garments in Ch'ing Dynasty China* (Eugene: University of Oregon Museum of Art, 1983), 12, 58.

24.   Yajima Satoshi, "Santan kōekihin Ezo nishiki no meishō to keitai," in *Kita no rekishi: Bunka kōryū kenkyū jigyō,* ed. Hokkaidō Kaitaku Kinenkan (Sapporo: Hokkaidō Kaitaku Kinenkan, 1995), 292; and Nakamura Kazuyuki, "Ezo nishiki to Santan kōeki," *Hokkaidō kōtō gakkō kyōiku kenkyūkai kenkyū kiyō* 24 (March 1987): 45-6.

25.   Kikuchi Isao, *Hoppōshi no naka no kinsei Nihon* (Tokyo: Azekura Shobō, 1991), 23.

26.   Nakamura Kazuyuki, "Santan fuku to Ainu no ibunka," in *Shinpojiumu: Ainu no ifuku bunka,* ed. Ainu Minzoku Hakubutsukan (Shiraoi: Ainu Minzoku Hakubutsukan, 1994), 27.

27.   Kaiho, "Hoppō kōeki to chūsei Ezo shakai," 271; and Akizuki, *Nichiro kankei to Saharin tō,* 33.

28.   Matsumae Hironaga, *Fukuyama hifu* [1780], in SSHS, 5:10.

29.   Matsumae Kagehiro, *Shinra no kiroku* [1646], in SHS, 7:44.

30.   Jeronimo de Angelis, "Carta de algumas novas de Japam" [1618], in *Hoppō tankenki: Genna nenkan ni okeru gaikokujin no Ezo hōkokusho,* ed. Hubert Cieslik (Tokyo: Yoshikawa Kōbunkan, 1963), 56, 8-9; and Diego Carvalho, "Copia de huma [carta] que o Padre Diogo Carvalho me escreveo acerca da missam que fez a Yezo e outras partes" [1620], in *Hoppō tankenki: Genna nenkan ni okeru gaikokujin no Ezo hōkokusho,* ed. Hubert Cieslik (Tokyo: Yoshikawa Kōbunkan, 1963), 68-9, 17.

31.   Akizuki, *Nichiro kankei to Saharin tō,* 34. See also Matsumae Hironaga, *Matsumaeshi* [1781], in HMSS, 2:122-6. For a brief review of the earliest Japanese exploration of Sakhalin, see Stephan, *Sakhalin,* 45.

32.   *Shōhō Nihon sōzu* [1644], in *Ezo chizushō,* ed. Narita Shūichi (Tokyo: Sara Shobō, 1989), 20-1.

33.   Akizuki, *Nichiro kankei to Saharin tō,* 35.

34. Matsumae Hironaga, *Matsumaeshi* [1781], in HMSS, 2:130–31.
35. Akizuki, *Nichiro kankei to Saharin tō*, 36. See also Matsumae Yasuhiro, *Ezo hōki gairyakuki* [1669–72], in NSSS, 4:644; Matsumae Norihiro, *Shōtoku gonen Matsumae Shima-no-kami sashidashi sōrō kakitsuke* [1715], in SSKS, 140; Matsumae Hironaga, *Matsumaeshi* [1781], in HMSS, 2:126; and Murayama Denbei, *Ishikari ukeoinin Murayama-ke kiroku*, in *Ishikari chōshi shiryō*, ed. Hokkaidō Ishikari Chōshi Henshū Iinkai (Sapporo: Seibunsha Insatsujo, 1969), 3:11.
36. Kikuchi Toshihiko, *Hokutō ajia kodai bunka no kenkyū* (Sapporo: Hokkaidō Daigaku Tosho Kankōkai, 1995), 441; and Kikuchi, "Hokkaidō o meguru hoppō shominzoku no kōryū," 375–81. The origins of the word "Santan" are nearly impossible to trace, but some speculation is possible. Kaiho Mineo has offered three possible explanations: One, that the term simply referred to the Nivkh (Gilyak); two, that Ainu called Tungus groups *samorkur* and that Matsumae traders picked this up as "Santan"; and three, that "Santan" might be a corruption of an Ul'chi word. For example, Mamiya Rinzō claimed that Santan was in fact a mispronunciation of the word *janta*, which is what the Ul'chi may have called themselves in their local dialect (Kaiho, "Hoppō kōeki to chūsei Ezo shakai," 269).
37. Sakakura Genjirō, *Hokkai zuihitsu* [1739], in NSSS, 4:405; and Kaiho, "Hoppō kōeki to chūsei Ezo shakai," 273.
38. *Gojunkenshi ōtō mōshiawasesho* [1761], in MCS, 1:405, and Kaiho, "Hoppō kōeki to chūsei Ezo shakai," 273–4.
39. Kaiho, "Hoppō kōeki to chūsei Ezo shakai," 274.
40. Akizuki, *Nichiro kankei to Saharin tō*, 36–7; and Satō Genrokurō, *Ezo shūi* [1786], in HMSS, 1:308–9.
41. Matsumae Hironaga, *Matsumaeshi* [1781], in HMSS, 2:121.
42. Takahashi Seizaemon, *Karafuto tō zakki* [1790], RCNS.
43. Akizuki, *Nichiro kankei to Saharin tō*, 38.
44. Mogami Tokunai, *Ezo sōshi betsuroku* [1781–8], in MCS, 3:31–2.
45. Matsumae Heikaku, *Karafuto tō Shiranushi to mōsu tokoro yori nishikata kenbun tsukamatsuri sōrō tokoro sa no tōri gozasōrō* [1791], RCNS.
46. Ibid.
47. Ibid.
48. Sasaki Shirō, *Hoppō kara kita kōekimin: Kinu to kegawa to Santanjin* (Tokyo: Nihon Hōsō Shuppan Kyōkai, 1996), 22.
49. Akizuki, *Nichiro kankei to Saharin tō*, 40. See also Mogami Tokunai, *Ezo sōshi kōhen* [1800], in HMSS, 3:462–3.
50. Mogami Tokunai, *Ezo sōshi kōhen* [1800], in HMSS, 3:462–3.
51. Ibid., 3:468. For an annotated Japanese translation of this document, see Ikegami Jirō, "Karafuto no Nayoro monjo no Manshūsho," *Hoppō bunka kenkyū* 3 (1968): 179–96.
52. Takahashi Jidayū and Nakamura Koichirō, *Karafuto tō kenbun tsukamatsuri*

sōrō omomuki sa ni mōshiage tatematsuri sōrō [1801], in SSHS, 5:816–37; and Nakamura Koichirō, *Karafuto zakki* [1801], in SSKS, 611.

53.   Akizuki, *Nichiro kankei to Saharin tō*, 49. See also Matsuda Denjūrō, *Hokuidan* (n.d.), in NSSSS, 4:133.

54.   Takakura Shin'ichirō, "Kinsei ni okeru Karafuto o chūshin to shita Nichiman kōeki," *Hoppō bunka kenkyū hōkoku* 1 (March 1940): 175; and Akizuki, *Nichiro kankei to Saharin tō*, 49.

55.   Takakura, "Kinsei ni okeru Karafuto o chūshin to shita Nichiman kōeki," 176; and Emori, "Ezochi o meguru hoppō no kōryū," 408–12.

56.   Habuto Masayasu, *Kyūmei kōki* [1807], in SSHS, 5:386–7.

57.   Mamiya Rinzō, *Kitaezo zusetsu* (n.d.), in HMSS, 5:318, 335–6.

58.   Takakura, "Kinsei ni okeru Karafuto o chūshin to shita Nichiman kōeki," 176; and Akizuki, *Nichiro kankei to Saharin tō*, 47–55.

CHAPTER 6.   THE KURIL TRADE

1.   Ōtsuka Kazuyoshi, *Ainu kaihin to mizube no tami* (Tokyo: Shinjuku Shobō, 1995), 73–80, 121–34.

2.   Kaiho Mineo, "Hoppō kōeki to chūsei Ezo shakai," in *Nihonkai to hokkoku bunka: Umi to rettō bunka*, ed. Amino Yoshihiko (Tokyo: Shōgakukan, 1990), 1:276. The name Kamchatka itself probably came from the Ainu language. Ikotoi, the elder from Akkeshi, told Satō Genrokurō in 1785 of a land called Kamsakka, an Ainu word that alluded to the large amounts of fish and game that were harvested, dried, and stored there (from *kam*, "meat," and *satke*, "to dry"; see Satō Genrokurō, *Ezo shūi* [1786], in HMSS, 1:267). "Kuril," the term used for the archipelago that spans the waters between Hokkaido and Kamchatka, probably originated from the Ainu word *kur*, "people" (Murayama Shichirō, *Kuriru shotō no bunkengakuteki kenkyū* [Tokyo: San'ichi Shobō, 1987], 18–21). For more on the geography and early history of the Kurils, see John J. Stephan, *The Kuril Islands: Russo-Japanese Frontier in the Pacific* (Oxford: Clarendon Press, 1974) 11–30.

3.   On the trade of white sea otter pelts in the 1560s, see Matsumae Hironaga, *Matsumaeshi* [1781], in HMSS, 2:188. On the sea otter pelts offered to Hideyoshi, see Kaiho, "Hoppō kōeki to chūsei Ezo shakai," 276.

4.   Jeronimo de Angelis, "Carta de algumas novas de Japam" [1618], in *Hoppō tankenki: Genna nenkan ni okeru gaikokujin no Ezo hōkokusho*, ed. Hubert Cieslik (Tokyo: Yoshikawa Kōbunkan, 1963), 8–9, 56.

5.   Arai Hakuseki, *Ezoshi* [1720], in *Arai Hakuseki zenshū*, ed. Imaizumi Sadasuke (Tokyo: Kokusho Kankōkai, 1905–7), 3:685; and Sakakura Genjirō, *Hokkai zuihitsu* [1739], in NSSSS, 4:404.

6.   On sea otter pelts and smallpox, see Matsumae Hironaga, *Matsumaeshi*

[1781], in HMSS, 2:188. On Chinese beliefs about the pelts, see Kikuchi Isao, *Ainu minzoku to Nihonjin: Higashi ajia no naka no Ezochi* (Tokyo: Asahi Sensho 510, 1994), 160.

7. Mogami Tokunai, *Ezokoku fūzoku ninjō no sata* [1791], in NSSSS, 4:466–7.

8. A. S. Polonskii, *Chishimashi* [1875], trans. Enomoto Takeaki, in *Hoppō mikōkai komonjo shūsei*, ed. Terasawa Hajime et al. (Tokyo: Sōbunsha, 1981), 7:67–9.

9. Jean Baptiste-Barthelemy de Lesseps, *Travels in Kamtschatka* (New York: Arno Press and the New York Times, 1970), 208–16.

10. *Ezochi ikken* [1784–90], in SHS, 7:332.

11. Conrad Totman, *The Lumber Industry in Early Modern Japan* (Honolulu: University of Hawai'i Press, 1995), 74–6.

12. Conrad Totman, *The Green Archipelago: Forestry in Pre-industrial Japan* (Berkeley: University of California Press, 1989; reprint, Ohio University Press, 1998), 77, 110–13.

13. *Hidaya Ezoyama ukeoi kankei monjo* [1718–67], in SHS, 7:239–40.

14. Matsumae Hironaga, *Fukuyama hifu* [1780], in SSHS, 5:69.

15. Mark Ravina, *Land and Lordship in Early Modern Japan* (Stanford: Stanford University Press, 1999), 53–69.

16. Matsumae Hironaga, *Kyūki shōroku* [1781], in MCS, 1:428; and *Matsumae kujiki* [1827], RCNS. On the Gyōninzaka fire, see William W. Kelly, "Incendiary Actions: Fires and Firefighting in the Shogun's Capital and the People's City," in *Edo and Paris: Urban Life and the State in the Early Modern Era*, ed. James L. McClain et al. (Ithaca: Cornell University Press, 1994), 311.

17. Hirose Takahito, "Kunashiri-Menashi no tatakai: Gaisetsu," in *Sanjūnana hon no inau*, ed. Nemuro Shinpojiumu Jikkō Iinkai (Sapporo: Hokkaidō Shuppan Kikaku Sentā, 1990), 26–8.

18. Ibid., 30.

19. David L. Howell, *Capitalism from Within: Economy, Society, and the State in a Japanese Fishery* (Berkeley: University of California Press, 1995), 48.

20. Tessa Morris-Suzuki, "Creating the Frontier: Border, Identity and History in Japan's Far North," *East Asian History* 7 (June 1994): 18–21.

21. George Alexander Lensen, *The Russian Push toward Japan: Russo-Japanese Relations, 1697–1875* (Princeton: Princeton University Press, 1959), 31–95.

22. Stephan, *The Kuril Islands*, 48–9.

23. Yuri Slezkine, *Arctic Mirrors: Russia and the Small Peoples of the North* (Ithaca: Cornell University Press, 1994), 60–3.

24. S. P. Krasheninnikov, *The History of Kamchatka*, trans. James Grieve (Gloucester: R. Raikes, 1764; reprint, Richmond: Richmond Publishing, 1973), 34–8, 97; and Stephan, *The Kuril Islands*, 48–9.

25. Stephan, *The Kuril Islands*, 48–9.

26. Satō Genrokurō, *Ezo shūi* [1786], in HMSS, 1:298.

264 NOTES TO PAGES 163–167

27. Fukuda Shinzaburō, *Tenmei hei go otameshi kōeki no shimatsu* [1786], in *Bakusei shiryō to Ezochi*, ed. Kaiho Mineo (Sapporo: Miyama Shobō, 1980), 275; and Furukawa Koshōken, *Tōyū zakki* [1788], ed. Ōtō Tokihiko (Tokyo: Tōyō Bunko, 1964), 163.

28. Kaiho, "Hoppō kōeki to chūsei Ezo shakai," 280.

29. Kudō Heisuke, *Akaezo fūsetsu kō* [1783], in HMSS, 1:213–23.

30. John W. Hall, *Tanuma Okitsugu, 1719–1788: Forerunner of Modern Japan* (Cambridge: Harvard University Press, 1955), 67; John J. Stephan, "Ezo under the Tokugawa Bakufu, 1799–1821: An Aspect of Japan's Frontier History" (Ph.D. diss., University of London, 1969), 38–40; Stephan, *The Kuril Islands*, 66–7; and Akizuki Toshiyuki, *Nichiro kankei to Saharin tō: Bakumatsu Meiji shonen no ryōdo mondai* (Tokyo: Chikuma Shobō, 1994), 36.

31. Ronald P. Toby, *State and Diplomacy in Early Modern Japan: Asia in the Development of the Tokugawa Bakufu* (Princeton: Princeton University Press, 1984; reprint, Stanford: Stanford University Press, 1991), 53–109; and Fujii Jōji, "Jūnana seiki no Nihon: Buke no kokka no keisei," in *Iwanami kōza Nihon tsūshi: Kinsei 2*, ed. Asao Naohiro et al. (Tokyo: Iwanami Shoten, 1994), vol. 12, bk. 2, 34–49.

32. Harold Bolitho, *Treasures among Men: The Fudai Daimyo in Tokugawa Japan* (New Haven: Yale University Press, 1974), 193–8.

33. Hayashi Shihei, *Sangoku tsūran zusetsu* [1786], in *Shinpen Hayashi Shihei zenshū*, ed. Yamagishi Tokuhei and Sano Masami (Tokyo: Daiichi Shobō, 1979), 2:39–40; and Bob Tadashi Wakabayashi, *Anti-foreignism and Western Learning in Early-Modern Japan: The New Thesis of 1825* (Cambridge: Harvard University Press, 1991), 73–4.

34. Donald Keene, *The Japanese Discovery of Europe, 1720–1830* (reprint, Stanford: Stanford University Press, 1969), 39–41.

35. Herman Ooms, *Charismatic Bureaucrat: A Political Biography of Matsudaira Sadanobu, 1758–1829* (Chicago: University of Chicago Press, 1975), 120.

36. *Ezochi ikken* [1784–90], in SHS, 7:338–9.

37. Stephan, *The Kuril Islands*, 62.

38. *Ezochi ikken* [1784–90], in SHS, 7:339.

39. Ibid.

40. *Kiitappu basho shihainin Shōjirō jinmonsho* [1786], in *Hidaya Takekawa-ke monjo*, vol. 14, no. I 6, RCNS. Under the year 1785 in northeastern histories, Kasajima Shōjirō is mentioned as having been questioned by Tokugawa authorities concerning a "secret" trade in eastern Ezo; see Aomori-ken Bunkazai Hogo Kyōkai, ed., *Genshi manpitsu fūdo nenpyō michinoku sōsho* (Aomori: Aomori-ken Bunkazai Hogo Kyōkai, 1960), 14:143.

41. *Kiitappu basho shihainin Shōjirō jinmonsho*, in *Hidaya Takekawa-ke monjo*, RCNS.

42. Ibid.

43. Ibid.

44. Noel Perrin, *Giving Up the Gun: Japan's Reversion to the Sword, 1543–1879* (Boston: David R. Godine, 1979).

45. *Kiitappu basho shihainin Shōjirō jinmonsho*, in *Hidaya Takekawa-ke monjo*, RCNS.

46. *Ezochi ikken* [1784–90], in SHS, 7:340.

47. Ibid., 340–1.

48. Ibid., 341–2.

49. Ibid.

50. Hirose, "Kunashiri-Menashi no tatakai," 35–6.

51. The Matsumae force included 260 men, eighty-five rifles, three cannons, and twenty horses (ibid., 36).

52. Niida Magosaburō, *Kansei Ezo ran torishirabe nikki* [1789], in NSSSS, 4:699–729; and Hirose, "Kunashiri-Menashi no tatakai," 37.

53. Niida Magosaburō, *Kansei Ezo ran torishirabe nikki* [1789], in NSSSS, 4:709–10.

54. Hirose, "Kunashiri-Menashi no tatakai," 38, 40.

55. *Ezochi ikken* [1784–90], in SHS, 7:450.

56. Ibid.

57. Ibid.

58. Howell, *Capitalism from Within*, 47–9.

59. Ibid.

60. On Laxman's arrival in Japan, see Lensen, *The Russian Push toward Japan*, 113–14; and Conrad Totman, *Early Modern Japan* (Berkeley: University of California Press, 1993), 484–7.

61. Kikuchi, *Ainu minzoku to Nihonjin*, 161.

CHAPTER 7.   EPIDEMIC DISEASE, MEDICINE, AND THE SHIFTING ECOLOGY OF EZO

1. Mogami Tokunai, *Ezokoku fūzoku ninjō no sata* [1791], NSSSS, 4:460.

2. William H. McNeill, *Plagues and Peoples* (New York: Anchor Books, 1976).

3. Ann Bowman Jannetta, "Disease of the Early Modern Period in Japan," in *The Cambridge World History of Human Disease*, ed. Kenneth F. Kiple (Cambridge: Cambridge University Press, 1993), 385, 386–7.

4. Thomas C. Smith, *Nakahara: Family Planning and Population in a Japanese Village, 1717–1830* (Stanford: Stanford University Press, 1977), 53.

5. Ann Bowman Jannetta, *Epidemics and Mortality in Early Modern Japan* (Princeton: Princeton University Press, 1987), 15. See also Susan B. Hanley, *Everyday Things in Premodern Japan: The Hidden Legacy of Material Culture* (Berkeley: University of California Press, 1997), 176–98.

6. Jannetta, *Epidemics and Mortality*, 5–6; and Carol Benedict, *Bubonic Plague in Nineteenth-Century China* (Stanford: Stanford University Press, 1996), 17–48.

7. On the introduction of smallpox to Japan, see William Wayne Farris, *Population, Disease, and Land in Early Japan, 645–900* (Cambridge: Harvard University Press, 1985), 50–73. Whether smallpox from Korean fishermen in the eighth century or new strains of tuberculosis from Western visitors in the nineteenth century, as currently portrayed in the mainstream historiography, disease has always been imported into Japan. For thoughts on foreigners and tuberculosis in Japan, see William Johnston, *The Modern Epidemic: A History of Tuberculosis in Japan* (Cambridge: Harvard University Press, 1995), 50. Alfred Crosby observes that throughout the world syphilis, in particular, has been associated with foreign countries. In Japan it was sometimes called the "Tang sore." See Alfred W. Crosby, *The Columbian Exchange: Biological and Cultural Consequences of 1492* (Westport, Conn.: Greenwood Press, 1972), 124–5.

8. Takahashi Shinkichi, *Ezo tōbai shikō* (Tokyo: Nankōdō, 1937), 2–11; Matsuki Akitomo, *Hokkaidō no ishi* (Hirosaki: Tsugaru Shobō, 1970), 124–31; and Takashita Taizō, "Kinsei Ezochi no shippeishi," in *Ezochi no iryō*, ed. Sapporo Ishigaku Kenkyūkai (Sapporo: Hokkaidō Shuppan Kikaku Sentā, 1988), 78–98.

9. On the epidemic that claimed the lives of these members of the Matsumae family, see Matsumae Kagehiro, *Shinra no kiroku* [1646], in SHS, 7:65–6.

10. Takashita, "Kinsei Ezochi no shippeishi," 81.

11. *Tsugaru ittōshi*, bk. 10 [1731], in SHS, 7:136; and Shirayama Tomomasa, *Hokkaidō Ainu jinkōshi* (Sapporo: Hokkaidō Keizaishi Kenkyūjo, n.d.), 29.

12. Takakura Shin'ichirō, *Ainu seisakushi* (Tokyo: Nihon Hyōronsha, 1942; reprint, Tokyo: San'ichi Shobō, 1972), 289.

13. Emori Susumu, *Ainu no rekishi: Hokkaidō no hitobito (2)* (Tokyo: Sanseidō, 1987), 103. For similar numbers, see E. A. Hammel, "A Glimpse into the Demography of the Ainu," *American Anthropologist* 90, no. 1 (March 1988): 28; and Shirayama, *Hokkaidō Ainu jinkōshi*, 35–6.

14. Matsuura Takeshirō, *Nosappu nisshi* [1858], in MTKS, 3:424. Later, in the Meiji era, Henry Landor wrote of the Ainu in Akkeshi, at one time a militantly defiant region, that "few of them are left now, and those few are indeed poor specimens of their race. They have nearly all become bald, and they seem to suffer very severely from Rheumatism" (A. Henry Savage Landor, *Alone with the Hairy Ainu; or, 3,800 Miles on a Pack Saddle in Yezo and a Cruise to the Kurile Islands* [London: John Murray, 1893; reprint, New York: Johnson Reprint Corporation, 1970], 104).

15. Matsuura Takeshirō, *Shiretoko nisshi* [1858], in MTKS, 3:457.

16. *Hōsō ikken* [1845], RCNS. This manuscript is a compilation of official memoranda (*Osorenagara kakitsuke o motte otodoke mōshiage tatematsuri sōrō*) sent between fishery supervisors in Shizunai, Mitsuishi, and an administrative post. The

copy of this manuscript available at Hokkaido University appears to have been recopied by Satō Masuo in 1929, on Hokkaidō Chō letterhead. However, there is no reason to question the authenticity of the information.

17.   Jared Diamond, *The Third Chimpanzee: The Evolution and Future of the Human Animal* (New York: Harper Perennial, 1992), 123.

18.   William Cronon, *Changes in the Land: Indians, Colonists, and the Ecology of New England* (New York: Hill and Wang, 1983), 88.

19.   *Higashi Ezochi kakubasho yōsu taigaigaki* [1808–11], in SHS, 7:551–2.

20.   Ibid., 548–9; and "Hokkaidō," bk. 2, in *Kadokawa Nihon chimei daijiten*, ed. Takeuchi Rizō (Tokyo: Kadokawa Shoten, 1978), 1:1163.

21.   Matsuura Takeshirō, *Shinpan Ezo nisshi: Higashi Ezo nisshi*, ed. Yoshida Tsunekichi (Tokyo: Jiji Tsūshinsha, 1984), 1:181.

22.   "Hokkaidō," bk. 2, in *Kadokawa Nihon chimei daijiten*, 1:1164.

23.   Alfred W. Crosby, *Ecological Imperialism: The Biological Expansion of Europe, 900–1900* (Cambridge: Cambridge University Press, 1986), 214.

24.   David L. Howell, *Capitalism from Within: Economy, Society, and the State in a Japanese Fishery* (Berkeley: University of California Press, 1995), 50–1.

25.   Fujikawa Yū, *Nihon shippeishi* (Tokyo: Tōyō Bunko, 1969), 65; and W. Wayne Farris, "Disease of the Premodern Period in Japan," in *The Cambridge World History of Human Disease*, ed. Kenneth F. Kiple (Cambridge: Cambridge University Press, 1993), 383–4.

26.   Tanda Hitoshi, "Ezochi no shippei shōshi: Baidoku," in *Hokkaidō no iryō: Sono ayumi*, ed. Nihon Ishigaku Kenkyūkai (Sapporo: Hokkaidō Iryō Shinbunsha, 1996), 50–1.

27.   Kushihara Seihō, *Igen zokuwa* [1792], in NSSSS, 4:507; and Matsuura Takeshirō, *Kinsei Ezo jinbutsushi* [1858], in MTKS, 3:19, 158.

28.   Kimura Kenji, *Hokkō nichiroku* [1793], ed. Yamazaki Eisaku (Aomori: Daiichi Insatsu, 1983), 83; and Takakura, *Ainu seisakushi*, 106–7.

29.   Kimura, *Hokkō nichiroku*, 83; and Kaiho Yōko, *Kindai hoppōshi: Ainu minzoku to josei to* (Tokyo: San'ichi Shobō, 1992), 210–11.

30.   Yamazaki Hanzō, *Sōya tsumeai Yamazaki Hanzō nisshi* (n.d.), RCNS. On the pervasiveness of syphilis among Japanese prostitutes, see Sone Hiromi, "Prostitution and Public Authority in Early Modern Japan," trans. Akiko Terashima and Anne Walthall, in *Women and Class in Japanese History*, ed. Hitomi Tonomura, Anne Walthall, and Wakita Haruko (Ann Arbor: Center for Japanese Studies, The University of Michigan, 1999), 176–9.

31.   Crosby, *Ecological Imperialism*, 231; Jan Critchett, *A Distant Field of Murder: Western District Frontiers, 1834–1848* (Carlton, Victoria: Melbourne University Press, 1990), 31, 38–9; and David Stannard, *Before the Horror: The Population of Hawai'i on the Eve of Western Contact* (Honolulu: University of Hawai'i Press, 1989), 72–3.

32. Okuyama Ryō, *Ainu suibōshi* (Sapporo: Miyama Shobō, 1966), 146–8.

33. Matsuda Denjūrō, *Hokuidan* (n.d.), in NSSSS, 4:98–9.

34. Ibid.

35. Kushihara Seihō, *Igen zokuwa* [1792], in NSSSS, 4:490.

36. Ibid.

37. Ibid., 490–1.

38. Neil Gordon Munro, *Ainu Creed and Cult* (Westport, Conn.: Greenwood Press, 1962), 99–102; and John Batchelor, *The Ainu and Their Folklore* (London: The Religious Tract Society, 1901), 103.

39. Kushihara Seihō, *Igen zokuwa* [1792], in NSSSS, 4:491.

40. Ibid., 491.

41. Sekiba Fujihiko, *Ainu ijidan* (Tokyo: Tōzai Shooku Zōhan, 1896), 122.

42. Nakamura Koichirō, *Karafuto zakki* [1801], in SSKS, 611–3.

43. Mogami Tokunai, *Ezo sōshi kōhen* [1800], in HMSS, 3:462–3.

44. Crosby, *Ecological Imperialism*, 38–9. Although Yuri Slezkine is less concerned with the relationship of disease and Russian expansion, see his *Arctic Mirrors: Russia and the Small Peoples of the North* (Ithaca: Cornell University Press, 1994).

45. Yamazaki, *Sōya tsumeai Yamazaki Hanzō nisshi* (n.d.), RCNS; SSHS, 2:535–6; and Takashita, "Kinsei Ezochi no shippeishi," 96–7.

46. Takakura Shin'ichirō, "Kinsei ni okeru Karafuto o chūshin to shita nichiman kōeki," *Hoppō bunka kenkyū hōkoku* 1 (March 1940): 181.

47. Max Horkheimer and Theodor W. Adorno, *Dialectic of Enlightenment*, trans. John Cumming (New York: Continuum Publishing, 1976), 5. For excerpts of this work related to critical-ecological theory, see Carolyn Merchant, ed., *Ecology: Key Concepts in Critical Theory* (New Jersey: Humanities Press, 1994), 44–50.

48. Paul U. Unschuld, *Medicine in China: A History of Ideas* (Berkeley: University of California Press, 1985); and Joseph Needham, *Science in Traditional China* (Cambridge: Harvard University Press, 1981), 57–106.

49. Margaret M. Lock, *East Asian Medicine in Urban Japan: Varieties of Medical Experience* (Berkeley: University of California Press, 1980), 27–49; Manfred Porkert, "Epistemological Fashions in Interpreting Disease," *Nihon ishigaku zasshi* 23, no. 1 (1977): 1–18; Shizu Sakai, "A History of Ophthalmology before the Opening of Japan," *Nihon ishigaku zasshi* 23, no. 1 (1977): 19–43; Hans Agren, "Empiricism and Speculation in Traditional East Asian Medicine," *Nihon ishigaku zasshi* 23, no. 2 (1977): 4–21. For some discussion of the impact of Dutch Learning on medical practice in Japan, see Yū Fujikawa, *Japanese Medicine*, trans. John Ruhräh (New York: P. B. Hoeber, 1934), 34–62; and Donald Keene, *The Japanese Discovery of Europe, 1720–1830* (reprint, Stanford: Stanford University Press, 1969), 1–30.

50. Hokkaidō Iryō Shinbunsha, ed., *Hokkaidō no iryōshi* (Sapporo: Seibunsha Insatsujo, 1976), 2; and Abe Tomonoshin, *Saiyaku shiki* [1758], RCNS.

51. Habuto Masayasu, *Kyūmei kōki* [1802], in SSHS, 5:334; and Sekiba, *Ainu ijidan*, 2.

52. Sō Senshun, *Ezo sōmoku shiryō* [1799], RCNS; Shibue Chōhaku, *Tōyō kisho* [1799], RCNS; and Shibue Chōhaku, *Ezo sōmoku sakuyōchō* [1799], RCNS.

53. Matsumae Hironaga, *Fukuyama hifu* [1780], in SSHS, 5:36; Matsumae Yasuhiro, *Ezo hōki gairyakuki* [1669–72], in NSSSS, 4:644; and *Norihiro no shojō* (n.d.), Hokkaido Prefectural Library, Ebetsu, Japan. Bear gallbladder is frequently listed in records such as the *Karumono sonohoka sōbasho* [1857], RCNS. The author of the *Ezokoku shiki*, written in the 1750s, explained that bear gallbladder produced in Ezo was inferior to that produced in locations such as Tateyama in Etchū Province, on the Japan Sea coast. He wrote that the bears in Etchū were off limits to all but the lord of Kaga domain, illustrating the place of materia medica in the gift society of early-modern Japan. That bears from Ezo were considered to be of inferior quality may have had something to do with the fact that bears indigenous to Ezo (*higuma* in Japanese; *Ursus arctos*) differ from the Asian black bear (*tsukinowaguma* in Japanese; *Ursus thibetanus*), which is indigenous to most of Japan, except Kyushu, where they are now extinct. See Kadosaki Masaaki and Inukai Tetsuo, *Higuma: Hokkaidō no shizen* (Sapporo: Hokkaidō Shinbunsha, 1993), 12–23. Bear gallbladder was produced in both powder and pill form, and imposter medicines appear to have been a problem: the *Ezokoku shiki* offers lengthy explanations on how to detect phony medications. Although bear gallbladder was available in general pharmacies during Japan's early-modern period, it was also traded among the ruling warrior elite as cultural capital. See *Ezokoku shiki* [1751–63], RCNS.

54. For a short explanation of Ainu medical culture, see my "Foreign Contagions, Ainu Medical Culture, and Conquest," in *Ainu: Spirit of a Northern People*, ed. William W. Fitzhugh and Chisato O. Dubreuil (Washington, D.C.: Arctic Studies Center, National Museum of National History, Smithsonian Institution, in association with the University of Washington Press, 1999), 102–7.

55. Yamada Takako, *Ainu no sekaikan: 'Kotoba' kara yomu shizen to uchū* (Tokyo: Kōdansha, 1994).

56. Batchelor, *The Ainu and Their Folklore*, 108.

57. Munro, *Ainu Creed and Cult*, 25; Takashita, "Kinsei Ezochi no shippeishi," 90; and Sekiba, *Ainu ijidan*, 29.

58. Sekiba, *Ainu ijidan*, 5.

59. Kayano Shigeru, *Ainu no sato: Nibutani ni ikite* (Sapporo: Hokkaidō Shinbunsha, 1987), 53–4.

60. Munro, *Ainu Creed and Cult*, 99–102.

61. John Batchelor, *Ainu Life and Lore: Echoes of a Departing Race* (Tokyo: Kyobunkan, 1927), 277.

62. Matsumae Norihiro, *Shōtoku gonen Matsumae Shima-no-kami sashidashi sōrō*

kakitsuke [1715], in SSKS, 135–6; and Tsuda Harumi, "Ainu no yakusō," in *Ezochi no iryō*, ed. Sapporo Ishigaku Kenkyūkai (Sapporo: Hokkaidō Shuppan Kikaku Sentā, 1988), 35–6.

63. Matsuura Takeshirō, *Sankō Ezo nisshi* [1850], ed. Yoshida Takezō (Tokyo: Yoshikawa Kōbunkan, 1971), 2:438–9.

64. Matsuura Takeshirō, *Tokachi nisshi* [1858], in MTKS, 3:346.

65. Matsuura Takeshirō, *Yūbari nisshi* [1857], in MTKS, 3:308–9; and Matsuura Takeshirō, *Shiretoko nisshi* [1858], in MTKS, 3:482.

66. Matsumae Hironaga, *Matsumaeshi*, in HMSS, 1:165–316.

67. Ibid., 272–3.

68. Toki Shinpo, *Tōi bussanshi* [1799], RCNS; Tsuda, "Ainu no yakusō," 37–8; and Yoshihiro Kinoshita and Haruo Takemura, *Studies on Disease and the Medical Treatments of Ainu People* (Sapporo: Takeuchi Publishing, 1993), 8–9.

69. Matsumae Hironaga, *Matsumaeshi* [1781], in HMSS, 2:273.

70. Keene, *The Japanese Discovery of Europe*, 9, 55.

71. Fukui Yoshimaro, *Tōi shūran* [1801], RCNS.

72. Ōtsuki Gentaku, *Ransetsu benwaku* [1799], in *Edo kagaku koten sōsho*, ed. Kikuchi Toshiyoshi (Tokyo: Kōwa Shuppan, 1979), 17:36.

73. Yamagishi Takashi, "Ezochi yakubutsushi," in *Hokkaidō no iryō: Sono ayumi*, ed. Nihon Ishigaku Kenkyūkai (Sapporo: Hokkaidō Iryō Shinbunsha, 1996), 82–5.

74. Crosby, *Ecological Imperialism*.

CHAPTER 8.   THE ROLE OF CEREMONY
IN CONQUEST

1. Matsumae Hironaga, *Fukuyama hifu* [1780], in SSHS, 5:42; and Kaiho Mineo, *Nihon Hoppōshi no ronri* (Tokyo: Yūzankaku, 1974), 215.

2. Herman Ooms, *Tokugawa Village Practice: Class, Status, Power, Law* (Berkeley: University of California Press, 1996), 106.

3. Stephen Vlastos, *Peasant Protests and Uprisings in Tokugawa Japan* (Berkeley: University of California Press, 1986), 147–8.

4. James W. White, *Ikki: Social Conflict and Political Protest in Early Modern Japan* (Ithaca: Cornell University Press, 1995), 300.

5. Sakakura Genjirō, *Hokkai zuihitsu* [1739], in NSSSS, 4:409.

6. Takakura Shin'ichirō, *Ainu seisakushi* (Tokyo: Nihon Hyōronsha, 1942; reprint, Tokyo: San'ichi Shobō, 1972), 84.

7. Iwasaki Naoko, "Ainu 'otona' kō," in *Nihon shakai no shiteki kōzō: Kinsei-kindai*, ed. Asao Naohiro Kyōju Taikan Kinenkai (Tokyo: Shibunkaku, 1995); and Iwasaki Naoko, *Nihon kinsei no Ainu shakai* (Tokyo: Azekura Shobō, 1998), 106–10. For more on the Ainu *otona*, see Emori Susumu, *Hokkaidō kinseishi no kenkyū*:

Bakuhan taisei to Ezochi (Sapporo: Hokkaidō Shuppan Kikaku Sentā, 1982), 178–80.

8. Matsumiya Kanzan, *Ezo dan hikki* [1710], in NSSSS, 4:389; Hezutsu Tōsaku, *Tōyūki* [1784], in NSSSS, 4:424; and Mogami Tokunai, *Watarishima hikki* [1808], in NSSSS, 4:525.

9. Arano Yasunori, *Kinsei Nihon to higashi ajia* (Tokyo: Tōkyō Daigaku Shuppankai, 1988), iv.

10. Tsuruta Kei, "Kinsei Nihon no yottsu no 'kuchi,'" in *Ajia no naka no Nihonshi: Gaikō to sensō*, ed. Arano Yasunori et al. (Tokyo: Tōkyō Daigaku Shuppankai, 1992), 2:297–9.

11. Mogami Tokunai, *Watarishima hikki* [1808], in NSSSS, 4:525.

12. Donald L. Philippi, ed., *Songs of Gods, Songs of Humans: The Epic Tradition of the Ainu* (San Francisco: North Point Press, 1982), 247–8.

13. Ibid., 248–9.

14. Ibid., 249–50.

15. Ibid., 250.

16. Ibid.

17. For a history of the *uimamu* and *omusha*, see Inagaki Reiko, "Kinsei Ezochi ni okeru girei shihai no tokushitsu: Uimamu-omusha no hensen o tōshite," in *Minshū seikatsu to shinkō-shisō*, ed. Minshūshi Kenkyūkai (Tokyo: Yūzankaku, 1985), 113; and Inagaki Reiko, "Ainu minzoku ni taisuru girei shihai: 'uimamu'-'omusha' ni tsuite," in *Kita kara no Nihonshi*, ed. Hokkaidō-Tōhoku Kenkyūkai (Tokyo: Sanseidō, 1988), 315–21. On the role of the *uimamu* in the communication networks of Tokugawa Japan, see Maruyama Yasunari, *Nihon kinsei kōtsūshi no kenkyū* (Tokyo: Yoshikawa Kōbunkan, 1989), 542–3.

18. Diego Carvalho, "Copia de huma [carta] que o Padre Diogo Carvalho me escreveo acerca da missam que fez a Yezo e outras partes" [1620], in *Hoppō tankenki: Genna nenkan ni okeru gaikokujin no Ezo hōkokusho*, ed. Hubert Cieslik (Tokyo: Yoshikawa Kōbunkan, 1963), 17, 68.

19. Inagaki, "Kinsei Ezochi ni okeru girei shihai no tokushitsu," 114.

20. Matsumae Hironaga, *Fukuyama hifu* [1780], in SSHS, 5:42; and Matsumae Hirotoki, *Matsumae mondo Hirotoki nikki* [1692], in SHS, 7:213–8.

21. Inagaki, "Kinsei Ezochi ni okeru girei shihai no tokushitsu," 115–6.

22. Michael Cooper, *Rodrigues the Interpreter: An Early Jesuit in Japan and China* (New York: Weatherhill, 1974), 79.

23. *Ezochi ikken* [1784–90], in SHS, 7:336–7.

24. Hirose Takahito, "Kunashiri-Menashi no tatakai: Gaisetsu," in *Sanjūnana hon no inau*, ed. Nemuro Shinpojiumu Jikkō Iinkai (Sapporo: Hokkaidō Shuppan Kikaku Sentā, 1990), 40–1.

25. Kikuchi Isao, "Tsugunai, kishōbun, omemie, hōki chin'atsu to Ainu no seiyaku," *Miyagi gakuin joshi daigaku kenkyū ronbunshū* 16 (1988): 17–8.

26. Niida Magosaburō, *Kansei Ezo ran torishirabe nikki* [1789], in NSSSS, 4:688.

27. *Tsugaru kibun* [1758], RCNS.

28. Takakura Shin'ichirō, "Omusha kō," *Minzokugaku kenkyū* 1, no. 3 (July 1935): 491.

29. Kakizaki Orindo, *Matsumae jōnai nenjū gyōji* [1841], RCNS.

30. Ibid.

31. Ibid.

32. Ibid.

33. Ibid.

34. Ronald P. Toby, *State and Diplomacy in Early Modern Japan: Asia in the Development of the Tokugawa Bakufu* (Princeton: Princeton University Press, 1984; reprint, Stanford: Stanford University Press, 1991), 185, 188.

35. William H. Coaldrake, *Architecture and Authority in Japan* (London: Routledge, 1996).

36. Toby, *State and Diplomacy in Early Modern Japan*, 186.

37. Ibid., 67.

38. *Tsugaru ittōshi*, bk. 10 [1731], in SHS, 7:187.

39. For more on the *omusha*, see Takakura, "Omusha kō," 496; and Takakura, *Ainu seisakushi*, 85-7.

40. Takakura, *Ainu seisakushi*, 85.

41. Matsuda Denjūrō, *Hokuidan* (n.d.), in NSSSS, 4:129.

42. Kushihara Seihō, *Igen zokuwa* [1792], in NSSSS, 4:516-7.

43. Mogami Tokunai, *Ezokoku fūzoku ninjō no sata* [1791], in NSSSS, 4:450-1.

44. Ibid.

45. Ibid.

46. *Ezo Matsumae kenbunki* [1798], *Ezo miyage* [1800], or *Ezo banashi* [1798], RCNS.

47. For more on the relationship between Ainu clothing and the Tokugawa system, see Kikuchi Isao, *Hoppōshi no naka no kinsei Nihon* (Tokyo: Azekura Shobō, 1991), 23.

48. For a detailed illustration of an *omusha* ceremony with many of these hierarchical characteristics, see Ōuchi Yoan, *Tōkai yawa* [1854-9], in HMSS, 5:447-9.

49. *Ezo Matsumae kenbunki* [1798], RCNS.

50. Ibid.

51. See Mogami Tokunai, *Ezochi e chakugan no akahito ikken* (n.d.), RCNS.

52. *Ezo Matsumae kenbunki* [1798], RCNS.

53. Hirate Hidekatsu, *Ezo Karafuto hokusei jūgunki* [1808], RCNS.

54. Ibid.

55. For the original manuscript, see *Etorofu tō omusha mōshiwatashisho* [1811], RCNS. See also Takakura, *Ainu seisakushi*, 172-4.

56. Ibid.

57. Ibid.

58. For standard Ainu translations, see *Man'en nisai shoyōtome* [1861], in *Shakotan chōshi shiryō*, ed. Shakotan Chōshi Hensan Iinkai (Shakotan: Shakotan Chō, 1977), 2:56–61.

59. *Goseisatsu no utsushi narabi ni nenjū gyōji omusha mōshiwatashi osonaemono rui* [1860], RCNS; and *Yoichi unjōya omusha toriatsukai nenjū gyōjiki [1824]*, in *Yoichi chōshi shiryō sōsho*, vol. 4 (1972), RCNS.

60. *Ichinoseki han Iburinokuni Shiraoi gun kaitaku goyōtome* [1869–70], RCNS.

61. Inagaki, "Kinsei Ezochi ni okeru girei shihai no tokushitsu," 123.

62. Toby, *State and Diplomacy in Early Modern Japan*, 186.

EPILOGUE

1. Brett L. Walker, "The Early Modern Japanese State and Ainu Vaccinations: Redefining the Body Politic, 1799–1868," *Past and Present* 163 (May 1999): 121–60.

2. Ronald P. Toby, *State and Diplomacy in Early Modern Japan: Asia in the Development of the Tokugawa Bakufu* (Princeton: Princeton University Press, 1984; reprint, Stanford: Stanford University Press, 1991), 240–1.

3. Habuto Masayasu, *Kyūmei kōki* [1807], in SSHS, 5:326.

4. Richard White, *The Roots of Dependency: Subsistence, Environment, and Social Change among the Choctaws, Pawnees, and Navajos* (Lincoln: University of Nebraska Press, 1983), 314.

5. Walker, "The Early Modern Japanese State and Ainu Vaccinations," 157. See also Ninomiya Mutsuo, *Kuwata Ryūsai sensei* (Tokyo: Kuwata Ryūsai Sensei Kenkyūkai Jimukyoku, 1998).

6. White, *The Roots of Dependency*, 315.

7. Walker, "The Early Modern Japanese State and Ainu Vaccinations," 121.

8. Ibid., 124.

9. Ibid., 132–3.

10. Ibid., 158.

11. John Batchelor, *Ainu Life and Lore: Echoes of a Departing Race* (Tokyo: Kyobunkan, 1927).

12. Kuwabara Masato, "Hokkaidō no keiei," *Iwanami kōza Nihon tsūshi* 16 (January 1994): 351.

13. Horace Capron, *Reports and Official Letters to the Kaitakushi* (Tokei: Kaitakushi, 1875), 266–7.

14. John Batchelor, *The Ainu and Their Folklore* (London: The Religious Tract Society, 1901), 17.

15. A. Henry Savage Landor, *Alone with the Hairy Ainu; or, 3,800 Miles on a Pack Saddle in Yezo and a Cruise to the Kurile Islands* (London: John Murray, 1893; reprint, New York: Johnson Reprint Corporation, 1970), 5, 42.

Works Cited

UNPUBLISHED DOCUMENTARY SOURCES

Abe Tomonoshin. *Saiyaku shiki* [1758]. Resource Collection for Northern Studies, Hokkaido University Library, Sapporo, Hokkaido.

Abuya Mohei and Abuya Senpachi. *Nagasaki tawaramono no ikken: Tenmei hachi-nen saru jūgatsu Ōsaka omote e sashidasu nari* [1788]. In *Hidaya Takekawa-ke monjo.* Vol. 9, no. E 7. Resource Collection for Northern Studies, Hokkaido University Library, Sapporo, Hokkaido.

Arai Heibei. *Tōkō manpitsu* [1806]. Resource Collection for Northern Studies, Hokkaido University Library, Sapporo, Hokkaido.

Buke setsuyōshū [1681]. Hokuga Library, Hokkai Gakuen, Sapporo, Hokkaido.

Etorofu tō omusha mōshiwatashisho [1811]. Resource Collection for Northern Studies, Hokkaido University Library, Sapporo, Hokkaido.

Ezo banashi [1798]. Resource Collection for Northern Studies, Hokkaido University Library, Sapporo, Hokkaido.

Ezochi zenzu [1830s]. Resource Collection for Northern Studies, Hokkaido University Library, Sapporo, Hokkaido.

Ezokoku shiki [1751–63]. Resource Collection for Northern Studies, Hokkaido University Library, Sapporo, Hokkaido.

Ezo Matsumae kenbunki [1798]. Resource Collection for Northern Studies, Hokkaido University Library, Sapporo, Hokkaido.

Ezo miyage [1800]. Resource Collection for Northern Studies, Hokkaido University Library, Sapporo, Hokkaido.

Fukui Yoshimaro. *Tōi shūran* [1801]. Resource Collection for Northern Studies, Hokkaido University Library, Sapporo, Hokkaido.

Genroku okuniezu chū Matsumae Ezozu [1700]. Resource Collection for Northern Studies, Hokkaido University Library, Sapporo, Hokkaido.

Goseisatsu no utsushi narabi ni nenjū gyōji omusha mōshiwatashi osonaemono rui [1860]. Resource Collection for Northern Studies, Hokkaido University Library, Sapporo, Hokkaido.

Hirate Hidekatsu. *Ezo Karafuto hokusei jūgunki* [1808]. Resource Collection for Northern Studies, Hokkaido University Library, Sapporo, Hokkaido.

Hōsō ikken [1845]. Resource Collection for Northern Studies, Hokkaido University Library, Sapporo, Hokkaido.

Ichinoseki han Iburinokuni Shiraoi gun kaitaku goyōtome [1869–70]. Resource Collection for Northern Studies, Hokkaido University Library, Sapporo, Hokkaido.

Kakizaki Orindo. *Matsumae jōnai nenjū gyōji* [1841]. Resource Collection for Northern Studies, Hokkaido University Library, Sapporo, Hokkaido.

Karumono sonohoka sōbasho [1857]. Resource Collection for Northern Studies, Hokkaido University Library, Sapporo, Hokkaido.

Kiitappu basho shihainin Shōjirō jinmonsho [1786]. In *Hidaya Takekawa-ke monjo*. Vol. 14, no. I 6. Resource Collection for Northern Studies, Hokkaido University Library, Sapporo, Hokkaido.

Kiitappu hitsuji no haru uketori nimotsu no bun [1788]. In *Hidaya Takekawa-ke monjo*. Vol. 9, no. D 6. Resource Collection for Northern Studies, Hokkaido University, Sapporo, Hokkaido.

Kimura Hakō. *Ainu fūzoku kuma matsuri no zu* (n.d.). Resource Collection for Northern Studies, Hokkaido University Library, Sapporo, Hokkaido.

Kondō Jūzō. *Nishi Ezochi bunken* [1786]. Resource Collection for Northern Studies, Hokkaido University Library, Sapporo, Hokkaido.

Kunitomo Zen'an. *Hokusui taimon* [1838]. Resource Collection for Northern Studies, Hokkaido University Library, Sapporo, Hokkaido.

Maki Bokusen. *Hitoyo banashi* [1810]. Resource Collection for Northern Studies, Hokkaido University Library, Sapporo, Hokkaido.

Matsumae Ezochi oboegaki (n.d.). Resource Collection for Northern Studies, Hokkaido University Library, Sapporo, Hokkaido.

Matsumae Heikaku. *Karafuto tō Shiranushi to mōsu tokoro yori nishikata kenbun tsukamatsuri sōrō tokoro sa no tōri gozasōrō* [1791]. Resource Collection for Northern Studies, Hokkaido University Library, Sapporo, Hokkaido.

Matsumae hisetsu [1839]. Resource Collection for Northern Studies, Hokkaido University Library, Sapporo, Hokkaido.

Matsumae kujiki [1827]. Resource Collection for Northern Studies, Hokkaido University Library, Sapporo, Hokkaido.

Matsumae Morihiro shojō (n.d.). Hokkaido Prefectural Library, Ebetsu, Hokkaido.

Mogami Tokunai(?). *Ezochi e chakugan no akahito ikken* (n.d.). Resource Collection for Northern Studies, Hokkaido University Library, Sapporo, Hokkaido.

Murakami Shimanojō. *Ezotō kikan* [1800]. Resource Collection for Northern Studies, Hokkaido University Library, Sapporo, Hokkaido.

Norihiro no shojō (n.d.). Hokkaido Prefectural Library, Ebetsu, Hokkaido.

Ogasawara Nagatoki and Ogasawara Sadahiro. *Taka no sho* (n.d.). Resource Collection for Northern Studies, Hokkaido University Library, Sapporo, Hokkaido.

Okudaira Sadamori. *Taka tsukaiyō no sho* [1824]. Resource Collection for Northern Studies, Hokkaido University Library, Sapporo, Hokkaido.

Saionji Sukekuni, ed. *Taka hyakushu ogura mondō* (n.d.). Resource Collection for Northern Studies, Hokkaido University Library, Sapporo, Hokkaido.

Shibue Chōhaku. *Ezo sōmoku sakuyōchō* [1799]. Resource Collection for Northern Studies, Hokkaido University Library, Sapporo, Hokkaido.

———. *Tōyō kisho* [1799]. Resource Collection for Northern Studies, Hokkaido University Library.

Sō Senshun. *Ezo sōmoku shiryō* [1799]. Resource Collection for Northern Studies, Hokkaido University Library, Sapporo, Hokkaido.

Takahashi Seizaemon. *Karafuto tō zakki* [1790]. Resource Collection for Northern Studies, Hokkaido University Library, Sapporo, Hokkaido.

Terashima Ryōan, comp. *Wakan sansai zue* [1713]. 105 vols. Resource Collection for Northern Studies, Hokkaido University Library, Sapporo, Hokkaido.

Toki Shinpo. *Tōi bussanshi* [1799]. Resource Collection for Northern Studies, Hokkaido University Library, Sapporo, Hokkaido.

Tsugaru kibun [1758]. Resource Collection for Northern Studies, Hokkaido University Library, Sapporo, Hokkaido.

Yamazaki Hanzō. *Sōya tsumeai Yamazaki Hanzō nisshi* (n.d.). Resource Collection for Northern Studies, Hokkaido University Library, Sapporo, Hokkaido.

Yoichi unjōya omusha toriatsukai nenjū gyōjiki [1824]. In *Yoichi chōshi shiryō sōsho.* Vol. 4. 1972. Resource Collection for Northern Studies, Hokkaido University Library, Sapporo, Hokkaido.

PUBLISHED DOCUMENTARY SOURCES

Aomori-ken Bunkazai Hogo Kyōkai, ed. *Genshi manpitsu fūdo nenpyō michinoku sōsho.* Vol. 14. Aomori: Aomori-ken Bunkazai Hogo Kyōkai, 1960.

Arai Hakuseki. *Ezoshi* [1720]. In *Arai Hakuseki zenshū*. Vol. 3. Edited by Imaizumi Sadasuke. Tokyo: Kokusho Kankōkai, 1906.

———. *Hankanpu* [1702]. In *Arai Hakuseki zenshū*. Vol. 1. Edited by Imaizumi Sadasuke. Tokyo: Kokusho Kankōkai, 1905.

Capron, Horace. *Reports and Official Letters to the Kaitakushi*. Tokei: Kaitakushi, 1875.

Carvalho, Diogo (Diego). "Copia de huma [carta] que o Padre Diogo Carvalho me escreveo acerca da missam que fez a Yezo e outras partes" [1620]. In *Hoppō tankenki: Genna nenkan ni okeru gaikokujin no Ezo hōkokusho*. Edited by Hubert Cieslik. Tokyo: Yoshikawa Kōbunkan, 1963.

De Angelis, Jeronimo. "Carta de algumas novas de Japam" [1618]. In *Hoppō tankenki: Genna nenkan ni okeru gaikokujin no Ezo hōkokusho*. Edited by Hubert Cieslik. Tokyo: Yoshikawa Kōbunkan, 1963.

De Lesseps, Jean Baptiste-Barthelemy. *Travels in Kamtschatka*. New York: Arno Press and the New York Times, 1970.

Ezochi ikken [1784–90]. In *Shin Hokkaidōshi*. Vol. 7. Edited by Hokkaidō. Sapporo: Shin Hokkaidōshi Insatsu Shuppan Kyōdō Kigyōtai, 1969.

Ezo shōko kikigaki [1739]. In *Matsumae chōshi*. Vol. 3. Edited by Matsumae Chōshi Henshūshitsu. Hakodate: Daiichi Insatsu, 1979.

Fukuda Shinzaburō. *Tenmei hei go otameshi kōeki no shimatsu* [1786]. In *Bakusei shiryō to Ezochi*. Edited by Kaiho Mineo. Sapporo: Miyama Shobō, 1980.

Furoisu Nihonshi. In *Chūsei Ezo shiryō*. Edited by Kaiho Mineo. Tokyo: San'ichi Shobō, 1983.

Furukawa Koshōken. *Tōyū zakki* [1788]. Edited by Ōtō Tokihiko. Tokyo: Tōyō Bunko, 1964.

Gojunkenshi ōtō mōshiawasesho [1761]. In *Matsumae chōshi*. Vol. 3. Edited by Matsumae Chōshi Henshūshitsu. Hakodate: Daiichi Insatsu, 1979.

Gukō shinzu tairyaku [1781]. In *Ezo chizushō*. Edited by Narita Shūichi. Tokyo: Sara Shobō, 1989.

Habuto Masayasu. *Kyūmei kōki* [1807]. In *Shinsen Hokkaidōshi*. Vol. 5. Edited by Hokkaidō Chō. Sapporo: Hokkaidō Chō, 1936. Reprint, Osaka: Seibundō, 1991.

Hansei ichiran (n.d.). In *Nihon shiseki kyōkai sōsho*. Vol. 173. Edited by Nihon Shiseki Kyōkai. Tokyo: Tōkyō Daigaku Shuppankai, 1928.

Hayashi Shihei. *Sangoku tsūran zusetsu* [1786]. In *Shinpen Hayashi Shihei zenshū*. Vol. 2. Edited by Yamagishi Tokuhei and Sano Masami. Tokyo: Daiichi Shobō, 1979.

Hezutsu Tōsaku. *Tōyūki* [1784]. In *Nihon shomin seikatsu shiryō shūsei*. Vol. 4. Edited by Takakura Shin'ichirō. Tokyo: San'ichi Shobō, 1969.

Hidaya Ezoyama ukeoi kankei monjo [1718–67]. In *Shin Hokkaidōshi*. Vol. 7. Edited by Hokkaidō. Sapporo: Shin Hokkaidōshi Insatsu Shuppan Kyōdō Kigyōtai, 1969.

Higashi Ezochi kakubasho yōsu taigaigaki [1808–11]. In *Shin Hokkaidōshi*. Vol. 7.
    Edited by Hokkaidō. Sapporo: Shin Hokkaidōshi Insatsu Shuppan Kyōdō
    Kigyōtai, 1969.

Kakizaki Hakyō. *Ishū retsuzō* [1790]. In *Ainu-e shūsei*. Vol. 1. Edited by Takakura
    Shin'ichirō. Tokyo: Banchō Shobō, 1973.

Kimura Kenji. *Hokkō nichiroku* [1793]. Edited by Yamazaki Eisaku. Aomori:
    Daiichi Insatsu, 1983.

Kitagawa Morisada. *Kinsei fūzokushi* or *Morisada mankō* [1853]. Edited by
    Muromatsu Iwao. Tokyo: Bunchōsha Shoin, 1928.

Kiyomasaki (n.d.). In *Zoku gunsho ruijū*. Vol. 23, no. 1. Edited by Hanawa
    Hokiichi and Ōta Toshirō. Tokyo: Zoku Gunsho Ruijū Kanseikai, 1924.

Kiyomasa Orankai no shiro otoshiiruru no koto. In *Tsūzoku Nihon zenshi*. Vol. 14.
    Edited by Waseda Daigaku Henshūbu. Tokyo: Waseda Daigaku Shuppanbu,
    1913.

Kudō Heisuke. *Akaezo fūsetsu kō* [1783]. In *Hokumon sōsho*. Vol. 1. Edited by
    Ōtomo Kisaku. Tokyo: Hokkō Shobō, 1943.

Kushihara Seihō. *Igen zokuwa* [1792]. In *Nihon shomin seikatsu shiryō shūsei*. Vol.
    4. Edited by Takakura Shin'ichirō. Tokyo: San'ichi Shobō, 1969.

Mamiya Rinzō. *Hokui bunkai yowa sōkō* [1811]. Edited by Hora Tomio and
    Tanisawa Shōichi. Tokyo: Tōyō Bunko, 1988.

————. *Kitaezo zusetsu* (n.d.). In *Hokumon sōsho*. Vol. 5. Edited by Ōtomo Kisaku.
    Tokyo: Hokkō Shobō, 1944.

Man'en nisai shoyōtome [1861]. In *Shakotan chōshi shiryō*. Vol. 2. Edited by
    Shakotan Chōshi Hensan Iinkai. Shakotan: Shakotan Chō, 1977.

Matsuda Denjūrō. *Hokuidan* (n.d.). In *Nihon shomin seikatsu shiryō shūsei*. Vol. 4.
    Edited by Takakura Shin'ichirō. Tokyo: San'ichi Shobō, 1969.

Matsumae Ezoki [1717]. In *Matsumae chōshi*. Vol. 1. Edited by Matsumae Chōshi
    Henshūshitsu. Hakodate: Daiichi Insatsu, 1974.

Matsumae Fukuyama shojō [1756]. In *Matsumae chōshi*. Vol. 1. Edited by
    Matsumae Chōshi Henshūshitsu. Hakodate: Daiichi Insatsu, 1974.

Matsumae Fukuyama sho okite zen (n.d.). In *Matsumae chōshi*. Vol. 1. Edited by
    Matsumae Chōshi Henshūshitsu. Hakodate: Daiichi Insatsu, 1974.

Matsumae Hironaga. *Fukuyama hifu* [1780]. In *Shinsen Hokkaidōshi*. Vol. 5. Edited
    by Hokkaidō Chō. Sapporo: Hokkaidō Chō, 1936. Reprint, Osaka: Seibundō,
    1991.

————. *Ishū retsuzō furoku* [1790]. In *Ainu-e shūsei*. Vol. 1. Edited by Takakura
    Shin'ichirō. Tokyo: Banchō Shobō, 1973.

————. *Kyūki shōroku* [1781]. In *Matsumae chōshi*. Vol. 1. Edited by Matsumae
    Chōshi Henshūshitsu. Hakodate: Daiichi Insatsu, 1974.

————. *Matsumaeshi* [1781]. In *Hokumon sōsho*. Vol. 2. Edited by Ōtomo Kisaku.
    Tokyo: Hokkō Shobō, 1943.

Matsumae Hirotoki. *Matsumae mondo Hirotoki nikki* [1692]. In *Shin Hokkaidōshi*. Vol. 7. Edited by Hokkaidō. Sapporo: Shin Hokkaidōshi Insatsu Shuppan Kyōdō Kigyōtai, 1969.

Matsumae jima gōchō [1700]. In *Zokuzoku gunsho ruijū*. Vol. 9. Edited by Ichijima Kenkichi. Tokyo: Naigai Insatsu Kabushikigaisha Bunkōjō, 1906.

Matsumae Kagehiro. *Shinra no kiroku* [1646]. In *Shin Hokkaidōshi*. Vol. 7. Edited by Hokkaidō. Sapporo: Shin Hokkaidōshi Insatsu Shuppan Kyōdō Kigyōtai, 1969.

Matsumae kaki [1878]. In *Matsumae chōshi*. Vol. 1. Edited by Matsumae Chōshi Henshūshitsu. Hakodate: Daiichi Insatsu, 1974.

Matsumae nennenki [1742]. In *Matsumae chōshi*. Vol. 1. Edited by Matsumae Chōshi Henshūshitsu. Hakodate: Daiichi Insatsu, 1974.

Matsumae Norihiro. *Shōtoku gonen Matsumae Shima-no-kami sashidashi sōrō kakitsuke* [1715]. In *Saisenkai shiryō*. Edited by Takakura Shin'ichirō. Sapporo: Hokkaidō Shuppan Kikaku Sentā, 1982.

Matsumae Yasuhiro. *Ezo hōki gairyakuki* [1669–72]. In *Nihon shomin seikatsu shiryō shūsei*. Vol. 4. Edited by Takakura Shin'ichirō. Tokyo: San'ichi Shobō, 1969.

Matsumiya Kanzan. *Ezo dan hikki* [1710]. In *Nihon shomin seikatsu shiryō shūsei*. Vol. 4. Edited by Takakura Shin'ichirō. Tokyo: San'ichi Shobō, 1969.

Matsuura Takeshirō. *Kinsei Ezo jinbutsushi* [1858]. In *Matsuura Takeshirō kikōshū*. Vol. 3. Edited by Yoshida Takezō. Tokyo: Fūzanbō, 1977.

———. *Nosappu nisshi* [1858]. In *Matsuura Takeshirō kikōshū*. Vol. 3. Edited by Yoshida Takezō. Tokyo: Fūzanbō, 1977.

———. *Sankō Ezo nisshi* [1850]. Vol. 2. Edited by Yoshida Takezō. Tokyo: Yoshikawa Kōbunkan, 1971.

———. *Shinpan Ezo nisshi* [1856–8]. 2 vols. Edited by Yoshida Tsunekichi. Tokyo: Jiji Tsūshinsha, 1984.

———. *Shiretoko nisshi* [1858]. In *Matsuura Takeshirō kikōshū*. Vol. 3. Edited by Yoshida Takezō. Tokyo: Fūzanbō, 1977.

———. *Tokachi nisshi* [1858]. In *Matsuura Takeshirō kikōshū*. Vol. 3. Edited by Yoshida Takezō. Tokyo: Fūzanbō, 1977.

———. *Yūbari nisshi* [1857]. In *Matsuura Takeshirō kikōshū*. Vol. 3. Edited by Yoshida Takezō. Tokyo: Fūzanbō, 1977.

Mogami Tokunai. *Ezokoku fūzoku ninjō no sata* [1791]. In *Nihon shomin seikatsu shiryō shūsei*. Vol. 4. Edited by Takakura Shin'ichirō. Tokyo: San'ichi Shobō, 1969.

———. *Ezo sōshi betsuroku* [1781–8]. In *Matsumae chōshi*. Vol. 3. Edited by Matsumae Chōshi Henshūshitsu. Hakodate: Daiichi Insatsu, 1979.

———. *Ezo sōshi kōhen* [1800]. In *Hokumon sōsho*. Vol. 3. Edited by Ōtomo Kisaku. Tokyo: Hokkō Shobō, 1944.

———. *Watarishima hikki* [1808]. In *Nihon shomin seikatsu shiryō shūsei*. Vol. 4. Edited by Takakura Shin'ichirō. Tokyo: San'ichi Shobō, 1969.

Mukoyama Seisai. *Seisai zakki* [1856]. In *Dai Nippon shiryō*. Vol. 12, bk. 1. Edited by Tōkyō Teikoku Daigaku. Tokyo: Tōkyō Teikoku Daigaku Insatsukyoku, 1901.

Murayama Denbei. *Ishikari ukeoinin Murayama-ke kiroku*. In *Ishikari chōshi shiryō*. Vol. 3. Edited by Hokkaidō Ishikari Chōshi Henshū Iinkai. Sapporo: Seibunsha Insatsujo, 1969.

———. *Matsumae sanbutsu daigaikan* [1804–17]. In *Hokkaidō kyōdo kenkyū shiryō* 6 (December 1960): 5–32.

Mutō Kanzō. *Ezo nikki* [1798]. In *Nihon shomin seikatsu shiryō shūsei*. Vol. 4. Edited by Takakura Shin'ichirō. Tokyo: San'ichi Shobō, 1969.

Naitō Chisō. *Tokugawa jūgodaishi*. Tokyo: Jinbutsu Ōraisha, 1968.

Nakamura Koichirō. *Karafuto zakki* [1801]. In *Saisenkai shiryō*. Edited by Takakura Shin'ichirō. Sapporo: Hokkaidō Shuppan Kikaku Sentā, 1982.

Nakamura Mitsunori. *Uin shiryaku* (n.d.). In *Shin Akita sōsho*. Vol. 1. Edited by Inoue Takaaki, Taguchi Shōichirō, and Watanabe Kōjirō. Tokyo: Rekishi Toshosha, 1971.

Niida Magosaburō. *Kansei Ezo ran torishirabe nikki* [1789]. In *Nihon shomin seikatsu shiryō shūsei*. Vol. 4. Edited by Takakura Shin'ichirō. Tokyo: San'ichi Shobō, 1969.

Norita Yasuemon. *Kanbun jūnen Ezo hōki atsumegaki* [1670]. In *Nihon shomin seikatsu shiryō shūsei*. Vol. 4. Edited by Takakura Shin'ichirō. Tokyo: San'ichi Shobō, 1969.

Ōhara Sakingo. *Chihoku gūdan* [1797]. In *Hokumon sōsho*. Vol. 3. Edited by Ōtomo Kisaku. Tokyo: Hokkō Shobō, 1944.

Okuno Takahiro, ed. *Oda Nobunaga monjo no kenkyū*. Tokyo: Yoshikawa Kōbunkan, 1958.

Onodera Michikore. *Nagano sensei yawashū* (n.d.). In *Shin Akita sōsho*. Vol. 3. Edited by Inoue Takaaki, Taguchi Shōichirō, and Watanabe Kōjirō. Tokyo: Rekishi Toshosha, 1971.

Ōtsuki Gentaku. *Ransetsu benwaku* [1799]. In *Edo kagaku koten sōsho*. Vol. 17. Edited by Kikuchi Toshiyoshi. Tokyo: Kōwa Shuppan, 1979.

Ōuchi Yoan. *Tōkai yawa* [1854–9]. In *Hokumon sōsho*. Vol. 5. Edited by Ōtomo Kisaku. Tokyo: Hokkō Shobō, 1944.

Polonskii, A. S. *Chishimashi* [1875]. Translated by Enomoto Takeaki. In *Hoppō mikōkai komonjo shūsei*. Vol. 7. Edited by Terasawa Hajime, Wada Toshiaki, and Kuroda Hidetoshi. Tokyo: Sōbunsha, 1981.

Sakakura Genjirō. *Hokkai zuihitsu* [1739]. In *Nihon shomin seikatsu shiryō shūsei*. Vol. 4. Edited by Takakura Shin'ichirō. Tokyo: San'ichi Shobō, 1969.

Satō Genrokurō. *Ezo shūi* [1786]. In *Hokumon sōsho*. Vol. 1. Edited by Ōtomo Kisaku. Tokyo: Hokkō Shobō, 1943.

Shinchō kōki. In *Chūsei Ezo shiryō*. Edited by Kaiho Mineo. Tokyo: San'ichi Shobō, 1983.

Shōhō Nihon sōzu [1644]. In *Ezo chizushō*. Edited by Narita Shūichi. Tokyo: Sara Shobō, 1989.

Takahashi Jidayū and Nakamura Kooihirō. *Karafuto tō kenbun tsukamatsuri sōrō omomuki sa ni mōshiage tatematsuri sōrō* [1801]. In *Shinsen Hokkaidōshi*. Vol. 5. Edited by Hokkaidō Chō. Sapporo: Hokkaidō Chō, 1936. Reprint, Osaka: Seibundō, 1991.

Takayanagi Shinzō and Ishii Ryōsuke, eds. *Ofuregaki kanpō shūsei*. Tokyo: Iwanami Shoten, 1976.

Tani Gentan. *Ezo kikō* [1799]. Edited by Satō Keiji. Tokyo: Asahi Shuppan, 1973.

———. *Ezo kishō zue* [1799]. Edited by Satō Keiji. Tokyo: Asahi Shuppan, 1973.

Tenpō gōchō. Bk. 2. In *Naikaku bunko shozō shiseki sōkan*. Vol. 56. Edited by Shiseki Kenkyūkai. Tokyo: Kyūko Shoin, 1984.

Tenpō okuniezu [1838]. In *Ezo chizushō*. Edited by Narita Shūichi. Tokyo: Sara Shobō, 1989.

"Tokugawa Ieyasu kokuinjō" [1604]. In *Chūsei Ezo shiryō*. Edited by Kaiho Mineo. Tokyo: San'ichi Shobō, 1983.

Tokugawa jikki [1809–43]. In *Bakusei shiryō to Ezochi*. Edited by Kaiho Mineo. Tokyo: Miyama Shobō, 1980.

Tōōgunki [1711]. In *Zoku gunsho ruijū*. Vol. 22. Edited by Hanawa Hokiichi and Ōta Toshirō. Tokyo: Zoku Gunsho Ruijū Kanseikai, 1924.

Tsugaru ittōshi. Bk. 10 [1731]. In *Shin Hokkaidōshi*. Vol. 7. Edited by Hokkaidō. Sapporo: Shin Hokkaidōshi Insatsu Shuppan Kyōdō Kigyōtai, 1969.

Umenai Yūkun. *Bunrō iji* [1822]. In *Nanbu sōsho*. Vol. 2. Edited by Nanbu Sōsho Kankōkai. Morioka: Nanbu Sōsho Kankōkai, 1927.

Yamada Sansen. *Sansen zakki*. Edited by Tomimura Toboru. Tokyo: Yoshikawa Kōbunkan, 1972.

Yamazaki Hanzō. *Mōi tōkanki* [1806]. Part 1. Edited by Namikawa Kenji. *Hirosaki daigaku kokushi kenkyū* 96 (March 1994): 34–47.

———. *Mōi tōkanki* [1806]. Part 2. Edited by Namikawa Kenji. *Hirosaki daigaku kokushi kenkyū* 97 (October 1994): 58–68.

OTHER SOURCES

Akutagawa Tatsuo. "Sengoku bushō to taka: Taikō Hideyoshi no hinata takasu bugyō setchi o megutte." In *Nihon no chūsei no seiji to bunka*. Edited by Toyota Takeshi. Tokyo: Yoshikawa Kōbunkan, 1980.

Agren, Hans. "Empiricism and Speculation in Traditional East Asian Medicine." *Nihon ishigaku zasshi* 23, no. 2 (1977): 4–21.

Akizawa Shigeru. "Taikō kenchi." In *Iwanami kōza Nihon tsūshi: Kinsei 1*. Vol. 11, bk. 1. Edited by Asao Naohiro, Amino Yoshihiko, Ishii Susumu, Kano Masanao, Hayakawa Shōhachi, and Yasumaru Yoshio. Tokyo: Iwanami Shoten, 1994.

Akizuki Toshiyuki. *Nichiro kankei to Saharin tō: Bakumatsu Meiji shonen no ryōdo mondai*. Tokyo: Chikuma Shobō, 1994.

———. *Nihon hokuhen no tanken to chizu no rekishi*. Sapporo: Hokkaidō Daigaku Tosho Kankōkai, 1999.

Arano Yasunori. *Kinsei Nihon to higashi ajia*. Tokyo: Tōkyō Daigaku Shuppankai, 1988.

Asakura Yūko. "Ezo ninshiki no keisei: Toku ni keiki to shite no jōhō o megutte." In *Kita kara no Nihonshi*. Vol. 2. Edited by Hokkaidō-Tōhoku Kenkyūkai. Tokyo: Sanseidō, 1990.

Asao Naohiro. *Sakoku: Nihon no rekishi 17*. Tokyo: Shōgakukan, 1975.

———. *Taikei Nihon no rekishi: Tenka no ittō*. Vol. 8. Tokyo: Shōgakukan, 1993.

Batchelor, John. *The Ainu and Their Folklore*. London: The Religious Tract Society, 1901.

———. *Ainu Life and Lore: Echoes of a Departing Race*. Tokyo: Kyobunkan, 1927.

Batchelor, John, and Miyabe Kingo. "Ainu Economic Plants." *Transactions of the Asiatic Society of Japan* 21 (1893): 197–240.

Batten, Bruce. "Frontiers and Boundaries of Pre-modern Japan." *Journal of Historical Geography* 25, no. 2 (1999): 166–82.

Benedict, Carol. *Bubonic Plague in Nineteenth-Century China*. Stanford: Stanford University Press, 1996.

Berry, Mary Elizabeth. *The Culture of Civil War in Kyoto*. Berkeley: University of California Press, 1994.

———. *Hideyoshi*. Cambridge: Harvard University Press, 1982.

———. "Public Peace and Private Attachment: The Goals and Conduct of Power in Early Modern Japan." *Journal of Japanese Studies* 12, no. 2 (summer 1986): 237–71.

———. "Restoring the Past: The Documents of Hideyoshi's Magistrate in Kyoto." *Harvard Journal of Asiatic Studies* 43, no. 1 (June 1983): 57–95.

Bird, Isabella. *Unbeaten Tracks in Japan*. London: J. Murray, 1880. Reprint, Boston: Beacon Press, 1984.

Bolitho, Harold. "The Han." In *The Cambridge History of Japan*. Vol. 4, *Early Modern Japan*, edited by John Whitney Hall. Cambridge: Cambridge University Press, 1991.

———. *Treasures among Men: The Fudai Daimyo in Tokugawa Japan*. New Haven: Yale University Press, 1974.

Bourdieu, Pierre. *Distinction: A Social Critique of the Judgement of Taste*. Translated by Richard Nice. Cambridge: Harvard University Press, 1984.

Brown, Philip C. *Central Authority and Local Autonomy in the Formation of Early Modern Japan: The Case of Kaga Domain*. Stanford: Stanford University Press, 1993.

Carneiro, Robert. "The Chiefdom: Precursor of the State." In *The Transition to Statehood in the New World*. Edited by G. D. Jones and R. R. Kautz. Cambridge: Cambridge University Press, 1981.

Chiri Mashiho. "Ainu no sake ryō." *Hoppō bunka kenkyū hōkoku* 14 (March 1959): 245–65.

Coaldrake, William H. *Architecture and Authority in Japan*. London: Routledge, 1996.

Cooper, Michael. *Rodrigues the Interpreter: An Early Jesuit in Japan and China*. New York: Weatherhill, 1974.

———, comp. *They Came to Japan: An Anthology of European Reports on Japan, 1543–1640*. Berkeley: University of California Press, 1965.

Critchett, Jan. *A Distant Field of Murder: Western District Frontiers, 1834–1848*. Carlton, Victoria: Melbourne University Press, 1990.

Cronon, William. *Changes in the Land: Indians, Colonists, and the Ecology of New England*. New York: Hill and Wang, 1983.

———. "Turner's First Stand: The Significance of Significance in American History." In *Writing Western History: Essays on Major Western Historians*. Edited by Richard Etulian. Albuquerque: University of New Mexico Press, 1991.

Crosby, Alfred W. *The Columbian Exchange: Biological and Cultural Consequences of 1492*. Westport, Conn.: Greenwood Press, 1972.

———. *Ecological Imperialism: The Biological Expansion of Europe, 900–1900*. Cambridge: Cambridge University Press, 1986.

Deriha Kōji. "Shuryōgu kara mita Hokkaidō Ainu oyobi hokutō ajia shominzoku no kogata mōhijū shuryō katsudō no imi." In *Kita no rekishi-bunka kōryū kenkyū jigyō*. Edited by Hokkaidō Kaitaku Kinenkan. Sapporo: Hokkaidō Kaitaku Kinenkan, 1995.

Diamond, Jared. *The Third Chimpanzee: The Evolution and Future of the Human Animal*. New York: Harper Perennial, 1992.

Duus, Peter. *The Abacus and the Sword: The Japanese Penetration of Korea, 1895–1910*. Berkeley: University of California Press, 1995.

Edmonds, Richard Louis. "Northern Frontiers of Qing China and Tokugawa Japan: A Comparative Study of Frontier Policy." Research paper no. 213, Department of Geography, University of Chicago, 1985.

Emori Susumu. *Ainu no rekishi: Hokkaidō no hitobito (2)*. Tokyo: Sanseidō, 1987.

———. "Ainu no shihai to teikō." In *Sakoku: Kōza Nihon kinseishi*. Edited by Katō Eiichi and Yamada Tadao. Tokyo: Yūhikaku, 1981.

————. "Ezochi o meguru hoppō no kōryū." In *Nihon no kinsei: Jōhō to kōtsū.* Vol. 6. Edited by Maruyama Yasunari. Tokyo: Chūō Kōronsha, 1992.

————. *Hokkaidō kinseishi no kenkyū: Bakuhan taisei to Ezochi.* Sapporo: Hokkaidō Shuppan Kikaku Sentā, 1982.

————. "Jūsan-jūroku seiki no higashi ajia to Ainu minzoku: Gen-Minchō to Saharin-Ainu no kankei o chūshin ni." In *Kita Nihon chūseishi no kenkyū.* Edited by Haga Norihiko. Tokyo: Yoshikawa Kōbunkan, 1990.

Emori Susumu, Kikuchi Toshihiko, and Kuwabara Masato. "Chihōshi kenkyū no genjō: Hokkaidō." Parts 1 and 2. *Nihon rekishi* 561 (February 1995): 34–51; 562 (March 1995): 33–66.

Enomoto Morie. *Hokkaidō no rekishi.* Sapporo: Hokkaidō Shinbunsha, 1981.

Fairbank, John K., and S. Y. Têng. "On the Ch'ing Tributary System." *Harvard Journal of Asiatic Studies* 6 (1941): 135–246.

Farris, William Wayne. *Population, Disease, and Land in Early Japan, 645–900.* Cambridge: Harvard University Press, 1985.

Farris, W. Wayne. "Disease of the Premodern Period in Japan." In *The Cambridge World History of Human Disease.* Edited by Kenneth F. Kiple. Cambridge: Cambridge University Press, 1993.

Foucault, Michel. *The Order of Things: An Archaeology of the Human Sciences.* New York: Vintage Books, 1970.

Friday, Karl F. "Pushing beyond the Pale: The Yamato Conquest of the Emishi and Northern Japan." *Journal of Japanese Studies* 23, no. 1 (winter 1997): 1–24.

————. "The Taming of the Shrewd: The Conquest of the Emishi and Northern Japan." *The Japan Foundation Newsletter* 21, no. 6 (March 1994): 17–21.

Fujii Jōji. "Jūnana seiki no Nihon: Buke no kokka no keisei." In *Iwanami kōza Nihon tsūshi: Kinsei 2.* Vol. 12, bk. 2. Edited by Asao Naohiro, Amino Yoshihiko, Ishii Susumu, Kano Masanao, Hayakawa Shōhachi, and Yasumaru Yoshio. Tokyo: Iwanami Shoten, 1994.

Fujikawa Yū. *Japanese Medicine.* Translated by John Ruhräh. New York: P. B. Hoeber, 1934.

————. *Nihon shippeishi.* Tokyo: Tōyō Bunko, 1969.

Fukuoka Itoko. *Ainu shokubutsushi.* Tokyo: Sōfūkan, 1995.

Fukusawa Yuriko. "Ainu Archaeology as Ethnohistory: Iron Technology among the Saru Ainu of Hokkaidō in the Seventeenth Century." Ph.D. diss., Cambridge University, 1995.

Gaubatz, Piper Rae. *Beyond the Great Wall: Urban Form and Transformation on the Chinese Frontiers.* Stanford: Stanford University Press, 1996.

Giersch, Charles Patterson. "Qing China's Reluctant Subjects: Indigenous Communities and Empire along the Yunnan Frontier." Ph.D. diss., Yale University, 1988.

Glahn, Richard Von. *The Country of Streams and Grottoes: Expansion, Settlement, and the Civilizing of the Sichuan Frontier in Song Times.* Cambridge: Harvard University Press, 1988.

Hall, John Whitney. *Japan: From Prehistory to Modern Times.* New York: Delta, 1970.

———. "Notes on the Ch'ing Copper Trade with Japan." *Harvard Journal of Asiatic Studies* 12 (1949): 444–61.

———. *Tanuma Okitsugu, 1719–1788: Forerunner of Modern Japan.* Cambridge: Harvard University Press, 1955.

Hammel, E. A. "A Glimpse into the Demography of the Ainu." *American Anthropologist* 90, no. 1 (March 1988): 26–41.

Hanley, Susan B. *Everyday Things in Premodern Japan: The Hidden Legacy of Material Culture.* Berkeley: University of California Press, 1997.

Hanley, Susan B., and Yamamura, Kozo. *Economic and Demographic Change in Preindustrial Japan 1600–1868.* Princeton: Princeton University Press, 1977.

Harrison, John A. *Japan's Northern Frontier: A Preliminary Study in Colonization and Expansion with Special Reference to the Relations of Japan and Russia.* Gainesville: University of Florida Press, 1953.

Hatakeyama Saburōta. "Hokkaidō no inu ni tsuite no oboegaki: Senshi jidai kaizuka ken to Ainu ken no hikaku." *Hokkaidōshi kenkyū* 1 (December 1973): 41–68.

Hayashi Yoshishige. "Ainu nōgyō no keiei keitai." *Hoppō bunka kenkyū hōkoku* 17 (March 1962): 39–60.

———. "Ainu no shokuryō shokubutsu saishū." *Hoppō bunka kenkyū* 2 (1967): 157–72.

Hino, Teruaki. "Bird Fauna and Its Distribution in Hokkaido." In *Biodiversity and Ecology in Northernmost Japan.* Edited by Seigo Higashi, Akira Osawa, and Kana Kanagawa. Sapporo: Hokkaido University Press, 1993.

Hirayama Hiroto. *Ainushi o mitsumete: Ainushi kenkyū-Ainushi gaikan.* Sapporo: Hokkaidō Shuppan Kikaku Sentā, 1996.

———. "Chashi bunka to kōeki." In *Ainu no chashi to sono sekai.* Edited by Hokkaidō Chashi Gakkai. Sapporo: Hokkaidō Shuppan Kikaku Sentā, 1994.

Hirose Takahito. "Kunashiri-Menashi no tatakai: Gaisetsu." In *Sanjūnana hon no inau.* Edited by Nemuro Shinpojiumu Jikkō Iinkai. Sapporo: Hokkaidō Shuppan Kikaku Sentā, 1990.

"Hokkaidō." 2 bks. In *Kadokawa Nihon chimei daijiten.* Vol. 1. Edited by Takeuchi Rizō. Tokyo: Kadokawa Shoten, 1978.

Hokkaidō, ed. *Shin Hokkaidōshi nenpyō.* Sapporo: Hokkaidō Shuppan Kikaku Sentā, 1989.

Hokkaidō Chō, ed. *Shinsen Hokkaidōshi.* Vol. 2. Sapporo: Hokkaidō Chō, 1936. Reprint, Osaka: Seibundō, 1991.

Hokkaidō Iryō Shinbunsha, ed. *Hokkaidō no iryōshi.* Sapporo: Seibunsha Insatsujo, 1976.

Honda Katsuichi. *Ainu minzoku*. Tokyo: Asahi Shinbunsha, 1993.

———. *Harukor: An Ainu Woman's Tale*. Translated by Kyoko Selden. Berkeley: University of California Press, 2000.

Horkheimer, Max, and Theodor W. Adorno. *Dialectic of Enlightenment*. Translated by John Cumming. New York: Continuum Publishing, 1972.

Howell, David L. "Ainu Ethnicity and the Boundaries of the Early Modern Japanese State." *Past and Present* 142 (February 1994): 79–80.

———. *Capitalism from Within: Economy, Society, and the State in a Japanese Fishery*. Berkeley: University of California Press, 1995.

———. *Geographies of Japanese Identity: Polity, Status, and Civilization in the Nineteenth Century*. Berkeley: University of California Press, forthcoming.

———. "Kinsei Hokkaidō ni okeru midoru-gurando no kanōsei." In *Basho ukeoisei to Ainu*. Edited by Hokkaidō-Tōhokushi Kenkyūkai. Sapporo: Hokkaidō Shuppan Kikaku Sentā, 1998.

Hucker, Charles O. *A Dictionary of Official Titles in Imperial China*. Stanford: Stanford University Press, 1985.

Ikegami Jirō. "Karafuto no Nayoro monjo no Manshūsho." *Hoppō bunka kenkyū* 3 (1968): 179–96.

Inagaki Reiko. "Ainu minzoku ni taisuru girei shihai: 'uimamu'-'omusha' ni tsuite." In *Kita kara no Nihonshi*. Edited by Hokkaidō-Tōhoku Kenkyūkai. Tokyo: Sanseidō, 1988.

———. "Kinsei Ezochi ni okeru girei shihai no tokushitsu: Uimamu-omusha no hensen o tōshite." In *Minshū seikatsu to shinkō-shisō*. Edited by Minshūshi Kenkyūkai. Tokyo: Yūzankaku, 1985.

Innes, Robert Leroy. "The Door Ajar: Japan's Foreign Trade in the Seventeenth Century." Ph.D. diss., University of Michigan, 1980.

Inukai Tetsuo. "Hokkaidō no shika to sono kōbō." *Hoppō bunka kenkyū hōkoku* 7 (March 1952): 1–22.

———. *Waga dōbutsuki*. Tokyo: Kurashi No Techōsha, 1970.

Irimoto, Takashi. "Ainu Territoriality." *Hoppō bunka kenkyū* 21 (1992): 67–81.

Iwasaki Naoko. "Ainu 'otona' kō." In *Nihon shakai no shiteki kōzō: Kinsei-kindai*. Edited by Asao Naohiro Kyōju Taikan Kinenkai. Tokyo: Shibunkaku, 1995.

———. *Nihon kinsei no Ainu shakai*. Tokyo: Azekura Shobō, 1998.

———. "Zenkindai Ainu no 'takara' to sono shakaiteki kinō." *Shirin* 78, no. 5 (September 1995): 107–28

Jannetta, Ann Bowman. "Disease of the Early Modern Period in Japan." In *The Cambridge World History of Human Disease*. Edited by Kenneth F. Kiple. Cambridge: Cambridge University Press, 1993.

———. *Epidemics and Mortality in Early Modern Japan*. Princeton: Princeton University Press, 1987.

Johnston, William. *The Modern Epidemic: A History of Tuberculosis in Japan*. Cambridge: Harvard University Press, 1995.

Kadosaki Masaaki and Seki Hideshi. "Ezochi ni okeru dōbutsu no bunkengakuteki kenkyū." *Hokkaidō kaitaku kinenkan chōsa hōkoku* 38 (1999): 96–108.

Kadosaki Masaaki and Inukai Tetsuo. *Higuma: Hokkaidō no shizen.* Sapporo: Hokkaidō Shinbunsha, 1993.

Kaiho Mineo. "Akinaiba chigyōsei no mittsu no kinō: Tōitsu seiken-Matsumae han-Ezochi ni taishite." *Hokkaidōshi kenkyū* 19 (August 1979): 1–26.

———. *Bakuhansei kokka to Hokkaidō.* Tokyo: San'ichi Shobō, 1978.

———. "'Chūsei' hoppōshi yori mita 'Ezogachishima ō' no Chōsen kenshi." *Hokkaidōshi kenkyū* 28 (December 1981): 6–17.

———. *Chūsei no Ezochi.* Tokyo: Yoshikawa Kōbunkan, 1987.

———. *Ezo no rekishi: Kita no hitobito to Nihon.* Tokyo: Kōdansha, 1996.

———. "Hoppō kōeki to chūsei Ezo shakai." In *Nihonkai to hokkoku bunka: Umi to rettō bunka.* Vol. 1. Edited by Amino Yoshihiko. Tokyo: Shōgakukan, 1990.

———. *Kinsei Ezochi seiritsushi no kenkyū.* Tokyo: San'ichi Shobō, 1984.

———. "Matsumae han no nidaime: Wakasa-no-kami Morihiro ni tsuite." *Hokkaidō no bunka* 37 (1977): 27–31.

———. *Nihon hoppōshi no ronri.* Tokyo: Yūzankaku, 1974.

———. "Santan kōeki to henmin seido: Shoki roshin kankeishi no shiten yori." In *Kita no rekishi: Bunka kōryū kenkyū jigyō.* Edited by Hokkaidō Kaitaku Kinenkan. Sapporo: Hokkaidō Kaitaku Kinenkan, 1995.

———. "Shakushain no tatakai: Ainu shakaishi ni taisuru bakuhansei kokka seiritsu no igi." In *Kinsei no shihai taisei to shakai kōzō.* Edited by Kitajima Masamoto. Tokyo: Yoshikawa Kōbunkan, 1983.

———. "'Wajinchi' seiritsu no shodankai." *Matsumae han to Matsumae* 12 (July 1979): 1–13.

Kaiho Yōko. *Kindai hoppōshi: Ainu minzoku to josei to.* Tokyo: San'ichi Shobō, 1992.

Kamiya Nobuyuki. "Japanese Control of Ezochi and the Role of Northern Koryŏ." *Acta Asiatica* 67 (1994): 49–68.

Kasaya Kazuhiko. *Kinsei buke shakai no seiji kōzō.* Tokyo: Yoshikawa Kōbunkan, 1993.

———. "Shōgun to daimyō." In *Nihon no kinsei: Shihai no shikumi.* Vol. 3. Edited by Fujii Jōji. Tokyo: Chūō Kōronsha, 1991.

Katō Kyūzō. "Dawn of Russian Ethnology-Researchers and Convicts around Bronislaw Pilsudski." In *European Studies on Ainu Language and Culture.* Edited by Josef Kreiner. München: Alle Rechte Vorbehalten Druck und Bindearbeiten, 1993.

Kawazoe Shoji. "Japan and East Asia." In *The Cambridge History of Japan.* Vol. 3, *Medieval Japan,* edited by Yamamura Kozo. Cambridge: Cambridge University Press, 1990.

Kayano Shigeru. *Ainugo jiten.* Tokyo: Sanseidō, 1996.

———. *Ainu no sato: Nibutani ni ikite.* Sapporo: Hokkaidō Shinbunsha, 1987.

Keene, Donald. *The Japanese Discovery of Europe, 1720–1830*. Reprint, Stanford: Stanford University Press, 1969.

Kelly, William W. "Incendiary Actions: Fires and Firefighting in the Shogun's Capital and the People's City." In *Edo and Paris: Urban Life and the State in the Early Modern Era*. Edited by James L. McClain, John M. Merriman, and Ugawa Kaoru. Ithaca: Cornell University Press, 1994.

Kerr, George H. *Okinawa: The History of an Island People*. Tokyo: Charles E. Tuttle, 1958.

Kikuchi Isao. *Ainu minzoku to Nihonjin: Higashi ajia no naka no Ezochi*. Tokyo: Asahi Sensho 510, 1994.

———. *Bakuhan taisei to Ezochi*. Tokyo: Yūzankaku, 1984.

———. *Hoppōshi no naka no kinsei Nihon*. Tokyo: Azekura Shobō, 1991.

———. "Taka to Matsumae han: Kinsei zenki o chūshin ni." In *Ezochi-Hokkaidō: Rekishi to seikatsu*. Edited by Chihōshi Kenkyū Kyōgikai. Tokyo: Yūzankaku, 1983.

———. "Tsugunai, kishōbun, omemie, hōki chin'atsu to Ainu no seiyaku." In *Miyagi gakuin joshi daigaku kenkyū ronbunshū* 16 (1988): 1–25.

Kikuchi Toshihiko. "Ainu minzoku to hoppō kōeki." In *Hoppōshi no shin shiza: Taigai seisaku to bunka*. Edited by Chihōshi Kenkyū Kyōgikai. Tokyo: Yūzankaku, 1994.

———. "Hokkaidō o meguru hoppō shominzoku no kōryū." In *Kodai no Nihon: Tōhoku- Hokkaidō*. Vol. 9. Edited by Sudō Takashi, Imaizumi Takao, and Tsuboi Kiyotari. Tokyo: Kadokawa Shoten, 1992.

———. *Hokutō ajia kodai bunka no kenkyū*. Sapporo: Hokkaidō Daigaku Tosho Kankōkai, 1995.

Kindaichi Kyōsuke. *Kindaichi Kyōsuke zenshū*. Vol. 12. Tokyo: Sanseidō, 1993.

Kinoshita, Yoshihiro, and Haruo Takemura. *Studies on Disease and the Medical Treatments of Ainu People*. Sapporo: Takeuchi Publishing, 1993.

Klein, Kerwin Lee. *Frontiers of Historical Imagination: Narrating the European Conquest of Native America, 1890–1990*. Berkeley: University of California Press, 1997.

Knaut, Andrew. *The Pueblo Revolt of 1680: Conquest and Resistance in Seventeenth-Century New Mexico*. Norman: University of Oklahoma Press, 1995.

Kondo, Norihisa. "Mammal Fauna and Its Distribution in Hokkaidō." In *Biodiversity and Ecology in Northernmost Japan*. Edited by Seigo Higashi, Akira Osawa, and Kana Kanagawa. Sapporo: Hokkaido University Press, 1993.

Kōno Hiromichi. "Bohyō no keishiki yori mitaru Ainu no shokeitō." *Ezo ōrai* 4 (August 1931): 101–21.

Krasheninnikov, S. P. *The History of Kamchatka*. Translated by James Grieve. Gloucester: R. Raikes, 1764. Reprint, Richmond: Richmond Publishing, 1973.

Kunaishō Shikibushoku. *Hōyo*. Tokyo: Yoshikawa Kōbunkan, 1933.

Kushiro Chōshi Henshū Iinkai, ed. *Kushiro chōshi*. Tokyo: Gyōsei, 1990.

Kuwabara Masato. "Hokkaidō no keiei." *Iwanami kōza Nihon tsūshi* 16 (January 1994): 343–59.

Landor, A. Henry Savage. *Alone with the Hairy Ainu; or, 3,800 Miles on a Pack Saddle in Yezo and a Cruise to the Kurile Islands.* London: John Murray, 1893. Reprint, New York: Johnson Reprint Corporation, 1970.

Lee, Robert H. G. *The Manchu Frontier in Ch'ing History.* Cambridge: Harvard University Press, 1970.

Lensen, George Alexander. *The Russian Push toward Japan: Russo-Japanese Relations, 1697–1875.* Princeton: Princeton University Press, 1959.

LePore, Jill. *The Name of War: King Philip's War and the Origins of American Identity.* New York: Alfred A. Knopf, 1998.

Limerick, Patricia Nelson. *The Legacy of Conquest: The Unbroken Past of the American West.* New York: W. W. Norton, 1987.

———. "Turnerians All: The Dream of a Helpful History in an Intelligible World." *American Historical Review* 100 (1995): 697–716.

———. "What on Earth Is the New Western History?" In *Trails: Toward a New Western History.* Edited by Patricia Nelson Limerick, Charles E. Rankin, and Clyde A. Milner. Lawrence: University Press of Kansas, 1991.

Lock, Margaret M. *East Asian Medicine in Urban Japan: Varieties of Medical Experience.* Berkeley: University of California Press, 1980.

Lopez, Barry. *Arctic Dreams: Imagination and Desire in a Northern Landscape.* New York: Pantheon Books, 1986.

Maehira Fusaaki. "'Sakoku' Nihon no kaigai bōeki." In *Nihon no kinsei: Sekaishi no naka no kinsei.* Vol. 1. Edited by Asao Naohiro. Tokyo: Chūō Kōronsha, 1991.

Mancall, Mark. *China at the Center: Three Hundred Years of Foreign Policy.* New York: The Free Press, 1984.

———. "The Ch'ing Tribute System: An Interpretive Essay." In *The Chinese World Order.* Edited by John K. Fairbank. Cambridge: Harvard University Press, 1968.

Maruyama Yasunari. "Kinsei jōhōka shakai no keisei." In *Nihon no kinsei: Jōhō to kōtsū.* Vol. 6. Edited by Maruyama Yasunari. Tokyo: Chūō Kōronsha, 1992.

———. *Nihon kinsei kōtsūshi no kenkyū.* Tokyo: Yoshikawa Kōbunkan, 1989.

Mass, Jeffrey P., ed. *The Origins of Japan's Medieval World: Courtiers, Clerics, Warriors, and Peasants in the Fourteenth Century.* Stanford: Stanford University Press, 1997.

Matsuki Akitomo. *Hokkaidō no ishi.* Hirosaki: Tsugaru Shobō, 1970.

Matsumae Chō Chōshi Henshūshitsu, ed. *Gaisetsu Matsumae no rekishi.* Tokyo: Gyōsei, 1994.

Matsumae Chōshi Henshūshitsu, ed. *Matsumae chōshi.* Vol. 1. Hakodate: Daiichi Insatsu Shuppanbu, 1974.

McNeill, William H. *Plagues and Peoples*. New York: Anchor Books, 1976.

Merchant, Carolyn. *Ecological Revolutions: Nature, Gender, and Science in New England*. Chapel Hill: University of North Carolina Press, 1989.

———, ed. *Ecology. Key Concepts in Critical Theory*. Atlantic Highlands, N.J.: Humanities Press, 1994.

Miyajima Toshimitsu. *Ainu minzoku to Nihon no rekishi*. Tokyo: San'ichi Shobō, 1996.

Miyoshi Kazumitsu, ed. *Edo-Tōkyō seigyō bukka jiten*. Tokyo: Seiabō, 1960.

Morris-Suzuki, Tessa. "Creating the Frontier: Border, Identity and History in Japan's Far North." *East Asian History* 7 (June 1994): 18–23.

———. "The Frontiers of Japanese Identity." In *Asian Forms of the Nation*. Edited by Stein Tonnesson and Hans Antlov. Surrey: Curzon Press, 1996.

Munro, Neil Gordon. *Ainu Creed and Cult*. Westport, Conn.: Greenwood Press, 1962.

Murayama Shichirō. *Kuriru shotō no bunkengakuteki kenkyū*. Tokyo: San'ichi Shobō, 1987.

Nakai, Kate Wildman. *Shogunal Politics: Arai Hakuseki and the Premises of Tokugawa Rule*. Cambridge: Harvard University Press, 1988.

Nakamura Kazuyuki. "Ezo nishiki to Santan kōeki." *Hokkaidō kōtō gakkō kyōiku kenkyūkai kenkyū kiyō* 24 (March 1987): 45–50.

———. "Santan fuku to Ainu no ibunka." In *Shinpojiumu: Ainu no ifuku bunka*. Edited by Ainu Minzoku Hakubutsukan. Shiraoi: Ainu Minzoku Hakubutsukan, 1994.

Narita Shūichi, ed. *Ezo chizushō*. Tokyo: Sara Shobō, 1989.

Needham, Joseph. *Science in Traditional China*. Cambridge: Harvard University Press, 1981.

Ninomiya Mutsuo. *Kuwata Ryūsai sensei*. Tokyo: Kuwata Ryūsai Sensei Kenkyūkai Jimukyoku, 1998.

Nishimura Saburō. *Bunmei no naka no hakubutsugaku*. Vol. 1. Tokyo: Kinokuniya Shoten, 1999.

Ogihara Shinko. *Hoppō shominzoku no sekaikan*. Tokyo: Sōfūkan, 1996.

Ōi Haruo. "'Shakushain no ran (Kanbun kyūnen Ezo no ran)' no saikentō." Parts 1 and 2. *Hoppō bunka kenkyū* 21 (1992): 1–66; 22 (1995): 1–116.

Okuyama Ryō. *Ainu suibōshi*. Sapporo: Miyama Shobō, 1966.

Ooms, Herman. *Charismatic Bureaucrat: A Political Biography of Matsudaira Sadanobu, 1758–1829*. Chicago: University of Chicago Press, 1975.

———. *Tokugawa Ideology: Early Constructs, 1570–1680*. Princeton: Princeton University Press, 1985.

———. *Tokugawa Village Practice: Class, Status, Power, Law*. Berkeley: University of California Press, 1996.

Ōtsuka Kazuyoshi. *Ainu kaihin to mizube no tami*. Tokyo: Shinjuku Shobō, 1995.

Perrin, Noel. *Giving Up the Gun: Japan's Reversion to the Sword, 1543–1879*. Boston: David R. Godine, 1979.

Philippi, Donald L., ed. *Songs of Gods, Songs of Humans: The Epic Tradition of the Ainu*. San Francisco: North Point Press, 1982.

Piggott, Joan. *The Emergence of Japanese Kingship*. Stanford: Stanford University Press, 1997.

Pilsudski, Bronislaw. *Materials for the Study of the Ainu Language and Folklore*. Cracow: Spolka Wydawnicza Polska, 1912.

Pokert, Manfred. "Epistemological Fashions in Interpreting Disease." *Nihon ishigaku zasshi* 23, no. 1 (1977): 1–18.

Pratt, Edward E. *Japan's Proto-Industrial Elite: The Economic Foundations of the Gōnō*. Cambridge: Harvard University Press, 1999.

Ranger, Terence, and Paul Slack, eds. *Epidemics and Ideas: Essays on the Historical Perception of Pestilence*. Cambridge: Cambridge University Press, 1992.

Ravina, Mark. *Land and Lordship in Early Modern Japan*. Stanford: Stanford University Press, 1999.

———. "State-Building and Political Economy in Early-Modern Japan." *The Journal of Asian Studies* 54, no. 4 (November 1995): 997–1022.

Roberts, Luke S. *Mercantilism in a Japanese Domain: The Merchant Origins of Economic Nationalism in Eighteenth-Century Tosa*. Cambridge: Cambridge University Press, 1998.

Robinson, Kenneth R. "The Jiubian and Ezogashima Embassies to Chōsen, 1478–1482." *Chōsenshi kenkyūkai ronbunshū* 35 (October 1997): 56–86.

Saitō Osamu. "Bringing the Covert Structure of the Past to Light." *Journal of Economic History* 49, no. 4 (1989): 992–99.

———. *Puroto kōgyōka no jidai: Seiō to Nihon no hikakushi*. Tokyo: Hyōronsha, 1985.

Sakai, Robert K. "The Satsuma-Ryūkyū Trade and the Tokugawa Seclusionist Policy." *The Journal of Asian Studies* 23, no. 3 (May 1964): 391–403.

Sakai, Shizu. "A History of Ophthalmology before the Opening of Japan." *Nihon ishigaku zasshi* 23, no. 1 (1977): 19–43.

Sannyo-Aino Toyo'oka. "The Future of Humans and the Creation of a Third Philosophy: An Ainu Viewpoint." Translated by Takeshi Osanai and Richard Siddle. In *Indigenous Minorities and Education: Australian and Japanese Perspectives of Their Indigenous Peoples, the Ainu, Aborigines, and Torres Strait Islanders*. Edited by Noel Loos and Takeshi Osanai. Tokyo: Sanyusha Publishing, 1993.

Sarashina Genzō and Sarashina Kō. *Kotan seibutsuki*. 3 Vols. Tokyo: Hōsei Daigaku Shuppankyoku, 1976.

Sasaki Shirō. *Hoppō kara kita kōekimin: Kinu to kegawa to Santanjin*. Tokyo: Nihon Hōsō Shuppan Kyōkai, 1996.

———. "Shinchō shihai to Amūru kawashimo ryūiki jūmin no esunishiti." In

Minzoku bunka no sekai: Shakai no tōgō to dōtai. Edited by Abe Toshiharu, Itō
  Abito, and Ogihara Shinko. Tokyo: Shōgakukan, 1990.
Sasaki Toshikazu. "Ainu-e ga egaita sekai." In *Ainu bunka ni manabu.* Edited by
  Sapporo Gakuin Daigaku Jinbutsu Gakubu. Sapporo: Hokkaidō Daigaku
  Tosho Kankōkai, 1990.
Satō Tadao. "Ainu no Amam-sake (kokumotsushu) no jittai to sono kigen." In
  Senshū daigaku Bibai nōkō Tanki daigaku nenpō 1 (March 1970): 118–24.
Sekiba Fujihiko. *Ainu ijidan.* Tokyo: Tōzai Shooku Zōhan, 1896.
Serpell, James. *In the Company of Animals: A Study of Human-Animal
  Relationships.* Cambridge: University of Cambridge Press, 1986.
Shepherd, John Robert. *Statecraft and Political Economy on the Taiwan Frontier,
  1600–1800.* Stanford: Stanford University Press, 1993.
Shirayama Tomomasa. *Hokkaidō Ainu jinkōshi.* Sapporo: Hokkaidō Keizaishi
  Kenkyūjo, n.d.
———. *Matsumae Ezochi basho ukeoiseido no kenkyū.* 2 vols. Hakodate: Hokkaidō
  Keizaishi kenkyūjo, 1961.
Shizunai Yakuba, ed. *Shizunai chōshi.* Shizunai: Shizunai Yakuba, 1975.
"The Shoo King." In *The Chinese Classics.* Translated by James Legge. Hong
  Kong: Hong Kong University Press, 1960.
Slezkine, Yuri. *Arctic Mirrors: Russia and the Small Peoples of the North.* Ithaca:
  Cornell University Press, 1994.
Smith, Thomas C. *The Agrarian Origins of Modern Japan.* Stanford: Stanford
  University Press, 1959. Reprint, New York: Atheneum, 1966.
———. *Nakahara: Family Planning and Population in a Japanese Village, 1717–1830.*
  Stanford: Stanford University Press, 1977.
Smits, Gregory. *Visions of Ryukyu: Identity and Ideology in Early-Modern Thought
  and Politics.* Honolulu: University of Hawai'i Press, 1999.
Sone Hiromi. "Prostitution and Public Authority in Early Modern Japan."
  Translated by Akiko Terashima and Anne Walthall. In *Women and Class in
  Japanese History.* Edited by Hitomi Tonomura, Anne Walthall, and Wakita
  Haruko. Ann Arbor: Center for Japanese Studies, The University of
  Michigan, 1999.
Stannard, David. *Before the Horror: The Population of Hawai'i on the Eve of Western
  Contact.* Honolulu: University of Hawai'i Press, 1989.
Stephan, John J. "Ezo under the Tokugawa Bakufu, 1799–1821: An Aspect of
  Japan's Frontier History." Ph.D. diss., University of London, 1969.
———. *The Kuril Islands: Russo-Japanese Frontier in the Pacific.* Oxford: Clarendon
  Press, 1974.
———. *Sakhalin: A History.* Oxford: Clarendon Press, 1971.
Sugimoto Fumiko. "Kuniezu." In *Iwanami kōza Nihon tsūshi: Kinsei 2.* Vol. 12, bk.
  2. Edited by Asao Naohiro, Amino Yoshihiko, Ishii Susumu, Kano Masanao,
  Hayakawa Shōhachi, and Yasumaru Yoshio. Tokyo: Iwanami Shoten, 1994.

———. "Kuniezu sakusei jigyō to kinsei kokka." *Rekishigaku kenkyū* 586 (October 1988): 126–47.

Takagi Shōsaku. *Nihon kinsei kokkashi no kenkyū.* Tokyo: Iwanami Shoten, 1990.

Takahashi Kimiaki. "Ezogachishima ō kara no Chōsen kenshi ni tsuite." *Hokkaidōshi kenkyū* 28 (December 1981): 1–5.

Takahashi Shinkichi. *Ezo tōbai shikō.* Tokyo: Nankōdō, 1937.

Takakura Shin'ichirō. *Ainu seisakushi.* Tokyo: Nihon Hyōronsha, 1942. Reprint, Tokyo: San'ichi Shobō, 1972.

———. "Kinsei ni okeru Karafuto o chūshin to shita Nichiman kōeki." *Hoppō bunka kenkyū hōkoku* 1 (March 1940): 163–94.

———. "Omusha kō." *Minzokugaku kenkyū* 1, no. 3 (July 1935): 83–92.

Takashita Taizō. "Kinsei Ezochi no shippeishi." In *Ezochi no iryō.* Edited by Sapporo Ishigaku Kenkyūkai. Sapporo: Hokkaidō Shuppan Kikaku Sentā, 1988.

Tanaka Takeo with Robert Sakai. "Japan's Relations with Overseas Countries." In *Japan in the Muromachi Age.* Edited by John Whitney Hall and Toyoda Takeshi. Berkeley: University of California Press, 1977.

Tanda Hitoshi. "Ezochi no shippei shōshi: Baidoku." In *Hokkaidō no iryō: Sono ayumi.* Edited by Nihon Ishigaku Kenkyūkai. Sapporo: Hokkaidō Iryō Shinbunsha, 1996.

Tashiro Kazui. "Bakumatsuki nitchō shibōeki to wakan bōeki shōnin: Yunyū yonhinmoku no torihiki o chūshin ni." In *Tokugawa shakai kara no tenbō.* Edited by Hayami Akira, Akimoto Hiroya, Tomobe Ken'ichi, Sugiyama Shinya, and Saitō Osamu. Tokyo: Dōbunkan Shuppan, 1989.

Tawara Hiromi. *Hokkaidō no shizen hogo.* Sapporo: Hokkaidō Daigaku Tosho Kankōkai, 1979.

Toby, Ronald P. "The Birth of the Hairy Barbarian: Ethnic Pejoratives as Cultural Boundary-Marker." Paper prepared for presentation at the Conference on Society and Popular Culture in Medieval and Early Modern Japan, Princeton, N.J., October 25–27, 1995.

———. "Both a Borrower and a Lender Be: From Village Moneylender to Rural Banker in the Tempō Era." *Monumenta Nipponica* 46, no. 4 (winter 1991): 483–512.

———. "Carnival of the Aliens: Korean Embassies in Edo-Period Art and Popular Culture." *Monumenta Nipponica* 41, no. 4 (winter 1988): 415–56.

———. "The 'Indianness' of Iberia and Changing Japanese Iconographies of Other." In *Implicit Understandings: Observing, Reporting, and Reflecting on the Encounter between Europeans and Other Peoples in the Early Modern Era.* Edited by Stuart B. Schwartz. Cambridge: Cambridge University Press, 1994.

———. *State and Diplomacy in Early Modern Japan: Asia in the Development of the Tokugawa Bakufu.* Princeton: Princeton University Press, 1984. Reprint, Stanford: Stanford University Press, 1991.

Totman, Conrad. *Early Modern Japan.* Berkeley: University of California Press, 1993.

———. *The Green Archipelago: Forestry in Pre-industrial Japan.* Berkeley: University of California Press, 1989. Reprint, Athens: Ohio University Press, 1998.

———. *The Lumber Industry in Early Modern Japan.* Honolulu: University of Hawai'i Press, 1995.

Toyohara Shōji. "Chashi to sono kinō." In *Menashi no sekai: Nemuro shinpojiumu 'kita kara no Nihonshi.'* Edited by Hokkaidō-Tōhokushi Kenkyūkai. Sapporo: Hokkaidō Shuppan Kikaku Sentā, 1996.

Tsuda Harumi. "Ainu no yakusō." In *Ezochi no iryō.* Edited by Sapporo Ishigaku Kenkyūkai. Sapporo: Hokkaidō Shuppan Kikaku Sentā, 1988.

Tsukamoto Manabu. *Edo jidai jin to dōbutsu.* Tokyo: Nihon Editā Sukūru Shuppanbu, 1995.

Tsuruta Kei. "Kinsei Nihon no yottsu no 'kuchi.'" In *Ajia no naka no Nihonshi: Gaikō to sensō.* Vol. 2. Edited by Arano Yasunori, Ishii Masatoshi, and Murai Shōsuke. Tokyo: Tōkyō Daigaku Shuppankai, 1992.

Turner, Frederick Jackson. *The Significance of the Frontier in American History.* Edited by Harold P. Simonson. New York: Frederick Ungar, 1963.

Unschuld, Paul U. *Medicine in China: A History of Ideas.* Berkeley: University of California Press, 1985.

Utagawa Hiroshi. *Ainu bunka seiritsushi.* Sapporo: Hokkaidō Shuppan Kikaku Sentā, 1988.

———. *Ainu denshō to chashi.* Sapporo: Hokkaidō Shuppan Kikaku Sentā, 1981.

———. *Hokkaidō no kōkogaku.* Sapporo: Hokkaidō Shuppan Kikaku Sentā, 1995.

Vaporis, Constantine. *Breaking Barriers: Travel and the State in Early Modern Japan.* Cambridge: Harvard University Press, 1994.

Varley, H. Paul. *The Ōnin War: History of its Origins and Background: With a Selective Translation of* The Chronicle of Ōnin. New York: Columbia University Press, 1967.

Vlastos, Stephan. *Peasant Protests and Uprisings in Tokugawa Japan.* Berkeley: University of California Press, 1986.

Vollmer, John E. *Decoding Dragons: Status Garments in Ch'ing Dynasty China.* Eugene: University of Oregon Museum of Art, 1983.

Wakabayashi, Bob Tadashi. *Anti-foreignism and Western Learning in Early-Modern Japan: The New Thesis of 1825.* Cambridge: Harvard University Press, 1991.

Walker, Brett L. "The Early Modern Japanese State and Ainu Vaccinations: Redefining the Body Politic, 1799–1868." *Past and Present* 163 (May 1999): 121–60.

———. "Foreign Contagions, Ainu Medical Culture, and Conquest." In *Ainu: Spirit of a Northern People.* Edited by William W. Fitzhugh and Chisato O. Dubreuil. Washington, D.C.: Arctic Studies Center, National Museum of

Natural History, Smithsonian Institution, in association with the University of Washington Press, 1999.

———. "Reappraising the *Sakoku* Paradigm: The Ezo Trade and the Extension of Tokugawa Political Space into Hokkaidō." *Journal of Asian History* 30, no. 2 (1996): 169–92.

Walthall, Anne. *The Weak Body of a Useless Woman: Matsuo Taseko and the Meiji Restoration.* Chicago: University of Chicago Press, 1998.

Watanabe, Hitoshi. *The Ainu Ecosystem: Environment and Group Structure.* Tokyo: University of Tokyo Press, 1972.

Watts, Sheldon. *Epidemics and History: Disease, Power, and Imperialism.* New Haven: Yale University Press, 1998.

Webb, Herschel. *The Japanese Imperial Institution in the Tokugawa Period.* New York: Columbia University Press, 1968.

White, James W. *Ikki: Social Conflict and Political Protest in Early Modern Japan.* Ithaca: Cornell University Press, 1995.

White, Richard. "Animals and Enterprise." In *The Oxford History of the American West.* Edited by Clyde A. Milner II, Carol A. O'Conner, and Martha A. Sandweiss. New York: Oxford University Press, 1994.

———. "Frederick Jackson Turner." In *Historians of the American Frontier: A Bio-Bibliographical Sourcebook.* Edited by John R. Wunder. Westport, Conn.: Greenwood Press, 1988.

———. *The Middle Ground: Indians, Empires, and Republics in the Great Lakes Region, 1650–1815.* Cambridge: Cambridge University Press, 1991.

———. *The Roots of Dependency: Subsistence, Environment, and Social Change among the Choctaws, Pawnees, and Navajos.* Lincoln: University of Nebraska Press, 1983.

Wigen, Kären. *The Making of a Japanese Periphery, 1750–1920.* Berkeley: University of California Press, 1995.

Wood, Denis. *The Power of Maps.* New York: Guilford Press, 1992.

Yajima Satoshi. "Santan kōekihin Ezo nishiki no meishō to keitai." In *Kita no rekishi: Bunka kōryū kenkyū jigyō.* Edited by Hokkaidō Kaitaku Kinenkan. Sapporo: Hokkaidō Kaitaku Kinenkan, 1995.

Yamada Takako. *Ainu no sekaikan: 'Kotoba' kara yomu shizen to uchū.* Tokyo: Kōdansha, 1994.

Yamagishi Takashi. "Ezochi yakubutsushi." In *Hokkaidō no iryō: Sono ayumi.* Edited by Nihon Ishigaku Kenkyūkai. Sapporo: Hokkaidō Iryō Shinbunsha, 1996.

Yamamoto Hirofumi. *Sakoku to kaikin no jidai.* Tokyo: Azekura Shobō, 1995.

Yamamoto Tadashi. "Ezo nōkō kinshi kō." *Monbetsu shiritsu kyōdo hakubutsukan hōkoku* 5 (1992): 18–33.

————. *Kinsei Ezochi nōsakumotsu nenpyō.* Sapporo: Hokkaidō Daigaku Tosho Kankōkai, 1996.

Yanaga Yoshiko. *Ezo no sakin.* Sapporo: Hokkaidō Shuppan Kikaku Sentā, 1981.

Yang, Lien-sheng. "Historical Notes on the Chinese World Order." In *The Chinese World Order.* Edited by John King Fairbank. Cambridge: Harvard University Press, 1968.

Yiengpruksawan, Mimi Hall. *Hiraizumi: Buddhist Art and Regional Politics in Twelfth-Century Japan.* Cambridge: Harvard University Press, 1998.

————. "The House of Gold: Fujiwara Kiyohira's Konjikidō." *Monumenta Nipponica* 48, no. 1 (spring 1993): 33–52.

Index

Note: *Italicized page numbers refer to figures and tables.*

ozashiki. See audience chamber

payoka kamuy, 232; exorcized from body, 198,
 200; as god of smallpox, 198–200
peasants, 51, 60, 97, 206
Peoples of Foreign Countries (*ikoku jinbutsu*):
 in *Wakan sansai zue,* 39
Peppana, 84
petiwor (patrilineal political alignments), 77
pewtanke (call used by Ainu in emergencies),
 173
pharmaceuticals, 16, 197, 202, 203; and Ainu
 medical culture, 194, 200; bear gallbladder
 as, *198*; cataloging of, 196, 201; as cultural
 capital, 100; Edo shogunate's interest in,
 194, 195–96; and Japanese medical culture,
 195; as standard trade items, 93–94; and
 state-sponsored medicine, 231. *See also*
 medicine
Philippines, 39
Piggott, Joan: on Great Kings and Yamato
 confederacy, 21
Pilsudski, Bronislaw, 256n. 37; and Sakhalin
 Ainu folktales, 111
pipes: and Santan trade, 145
placer mining techniques, 82, 83
Plagues and Peoples, 178, 187
plant gathering, 52, 77; and gender dynamics
 of Ainu subsistence, 87, 161; and pharmaceuticals, 194, 195–97, 201, 202; on
 Sakhalin Island, 128, 147. *See also* agriculture; *eburiko*; grain; *ikema*; kelp; *kuttar*; lily
 grass; millet; rice; *sinkep*; tobacco
poison arrows, 14, 50, *78*, 80; and Urup
 Incident, 163
porcelain, 22; excavated from *casi* sites, 123
post stations, 34; Kakizaki lords granted liberal access to, 104
posts, hawk, 107; and hawk population decline, 108; overseen by *takajō* in Wajinchi,
 105, 106. *See also* hawks
pottery: decreased production of, 93, 109;
 different motifs on, at Okhotsk and Satsumon sites, 25; as evidence of exchange between Japanese and Satsumon cultures,
 22–23. *See also sueki*; *suzuyaki*
preventive therapy, 195
prisoners: as banished to Ezogashima, 26
prostitutes: Ainu men and contact with

Japanese, 188; Ainu women as, 189; as
 bringing syphilis to Wajinchi ports, 188;
 Japanese, at Hakodate, 189; as playing the
 shamisen and singing at Esashi, 188
provincial barriers: and border crossing in
 Japan, 44
provincial maps, 3, 44, 139
pu (elevated storage hut for grain), *24*; and
 Ainu villages, 23
public authority. See *kōgi*
Pusan, 43

Qing dynasty (1644–1911), 130, 136, 142, 143,
 145, 147, 153, 154, 162, 220; Ainu headmen
 as officials of, 150, 152; challenged by Edo
 shogunate on Sakhalin Island, 152, 171;
 compared to Matsumae on foreign affairs,
 207; and trade in animal skins, 145; and
 tributary system, 134–35, 145

rabies: *eburiko* as effective against, 201; and
 Fukushima, *181. See also* disease
Ramai, 53
Rashaukain, 53
Ravina, Mark: on domainal dependency on
 merchant financing, 159; on early-modern
 Japan's political economy, 62
Rebun Island: and smallpox, *181*, 193
red barbarians. *See* Russians
Renkafu: as *sō-otona* from Kamuikotan, 183;
 and smallpox epidemic, 183; *186*
Rezanov, Nikolai: and smallpox at Rebun
 and Rishiri islands, 193
rheumatism, 266n. 14. *See also* disease
Ricci, Matteo, 32
rice, 37, 44, 45, 51, 67, 70, 76, 80, 87, 91, 93,
 97, 100, 126, 144, *199*; and Ainu subsistence, 85, 161; and baled goods trade, 96;
 as gift to Ainu headmen during *omusha*,
 218, 219; and hawk industry, 106; as incentive for trade on Sakhalin Island, 153;
 and Matsumae family's corrupt trading
 practices, 68; Matsumae Norihiro given,
 for war against Shakushain, 64; regulations against importing seeds into Ezochi,
 86; and smallpox, 183; as standard trade
 item, 92. *See also* agriculture; grain; plant
 gathering
Rihachirō, 166

dynasty, 134–36, 152; and Santan trade,
131 (*see also* Santan trade); and
Shakushain's War, 62; and trade-fief
system, 145, 146, 153. *See also* Sakhalin
Island
Sakhalin Island, 2, 4, 11, 13, 15, 25, 26, 123,
128, 129, 130, 143, 145, 146, 148, 153, 155,
156, 158, 164, 172, 187, 192, 193, 202, 203,
205, 207, 220, 223; Aizu troops dispatched
to, 223, 224; Chinese silks acquired on, 138;
distance from Sōya, 132; dogsled hauling
goods on, 149; and eagle feathers trade, 76;
and *eburiko*, 196, 201; and ecological
balance, 131, 144–50; Edo shogunate's direct rule on, 144, 151–53; fisheries on, 139–
44, 150; Japanese facilities on, 144; and
Mongol invasion, 133; mummification of
Ainu headmen on, 24; and *omusha* performance, 223; overhunting on, 146, 147; Qing
posts on, 135; and Russians, 224; and Santan trade, 94, 141, 142 (*see also* Santan
trade); and symbolic economy, 138. *See also*
Sakhalin Ainu
Sakimai: Japanese attacked at, 172
sakoku (closed country), 7, 9, 12, 44, 208, 246n.
83
Sakuemon, 67
salmon, 75, 79, 96, 100, 101, 109, 194; and
Ainu competition, 125; and Ainu industry,
118; and Ainu subsistence, 84–85, 119; and
asircep-nomi, 112, 113; and cultural capital
as gift, 103; and fisheries on Sakhalin
Island, 139, 147; fishing of, 81; and gold
mining, 57, 82–84; and Japanese fishing
practices, 84–85, 76; and Matsumae family's corrupt trading practices, 68; as migratory, 82; and Santan boats, 146; and Satsumon culture, 94; as standard trade item, 94;
and symbolic economy, 100
salt: as standard trade item, 92
Samani, 83
samorkur, 261n. 36. *See also* Santan
Samoyed: and smallpox, 193
samurai. *See* warriors
samurai armor: and Ainu audiences, 215
San: and smallpox epidemic, 184
Sanchiha, 134
Sankichi: and *omusha*, 218
sankin. See attendance

sankin kōtai (alternate attendance), 35
Sansha, 111
Sanshō Hachiman, 201
Santan, 142, 143; and Ainu debt, 151; and
Ainu enslavement, 148–50; and audiences,
151; Biyanko as headman of, 148; and
dogs, 145; linguistic origins of, 261n. 36; as
people of Northeast Asia, 141; and small-
pox, 193. *See also* Nanai; Negidal; Nivkh;
Orochi; Udekhe; Uilta; Ul'chi
santan shimipu. See Chinese silks
Santan trade, 220, 141; and Chinese silks,
141; and colored beads, 141; hunting for,
146; and Edo shogunate, 142, 151–53; and
Matsumae Heikaku, 145–47; and Mogami
Tokunai, 147–50; and Sakakura Genjirō,
141; and smallpox, 187–88, 192–93. *See also*
Chinese silks; colored beads; Sakhalin
Ainu; Sakhalin Island; Santan; Ul'chi
santanjin. See Santan
Sapporo, 181
Saru Ainu, 53; and animals, 79; identity and
territory of, 77, 79
Saru River, 53, 66, 79, 82, 121, 158; and deer
pelt trade, 119
Sarunkur. *See* Saru Ainu
Sarushina *casi*, 124
Sashirui: and *casi*, 125
Satake Yoshinobu, 36
satke (to dry), 262n. 2. *See also* Kamchatka
Peninsula
Satō Genrokurō: on Ainu audiences, 213; and
Edo shogunate's direct rule, 176; and inter-
rogation of Kiitappu fishery manager
Shōjirō, 166–69; and interviews with Ainu
headmen, 169–71; on linguistic origins of
"Ezo," 242n. 11; on linguistic origins of
"Kamchatka," 262n. 2; on Menashi-
Kunashir War, 176; on opening trading
posts, 89; on prohibitions against raising
grain, 86; on Santan trade, 142; and
"secret" Russian trade, 165; on trade-fief
system, 90; on Urup Incident, 162–63
Satō Gonzaemon, 54; landed at Biboku, 66
Satō Kaemon, 82–83
Satō Kamoemon: and surveys on Sakhalin
Island, 139
Satō Masuo, 267n. 16
Satomura Shōha, 40

Yōchiteaino: meeting with Kudō Chōkyū at
  Sōya, 139
Yoichi, 73; Kinkiriu as headman of, 111
Yoichi Ainu: and dependency, 67, 68, 69, 70;
  and Shakushain's War, 49, 63
Yongle emperor: and Nurkan outpost, 133
Yōsa: and smallpox epidemic, *184*
Yoshimura Jōzaemon, 63
Yuan dynasty (1279–1368): and Sakhalin
  Ainu, 132
Yuanshi [Official history of Yuan dynasty],
  133
Yūbari: and Hidaya Kyūbei, 168
Yūbari River, 83
Yūbetsu, 99; and deer pelt trade, 119

Yūfutsu, 66
yuk iramante (autumn deer hunt), 80
yukar. *See* epic poetry
Yuri District, 29
yutarube textiles: and Santan trade, 147

zenbu (lacquered trays and cups): and Ainu
  audiences, 216. *See also* lacquerware;
  ochōshikata; saké
Zhaluha, 134
Zhejiang Province: and Chinese bronze mirrors, 131
zhihui qianshi. *See* assistant commander
zhihui tongzhi. *See* vice commander
zhihuishi. *See* commander

CPSIA information can be obtained
at www.ICGtesting.com
Printed in the USA
BVOW03s2050161116
468116BV00001B/36/P